The Entrepreneurial Discovery Process and Regional Development

There is a broad and long-standing debate on possible solutions to the regional vulnerabilities of globalisation. In 2014, the European Commission began implementing Smart Specialisation Strategy, a place-based strategy of growth, regional transformation and new industrial policy with collective entrepreneurial discovery processes (EDP) at its core. This volume approaches the mystery of entrepreneurial discovery; that is, how relevant knowledge is created, converted and shared in a process of discovery.

These essays bring together scholars from economics, geography, sociology, organisation studies, innovation studies, and complexity theory, offering new approaches to overcome the limitations of place-based development and suggesting improved methods leading to growth.

Åge Mariussen is research manager and senior researcher at the Department of Regional Studies, University of Vaasa, Finland, and Nordland Research Institute, Bodø, Norway.

Seija Virkkala is professor at the Department of Regional Studies, University of Vaasa, Finland.

Håkon Finne is senior research scientist at SINTEF Digital, Trondheim, Norway.

Tone Merethe Aasen is senior research scientist at SINTEF Digital, Trondheim, Norway.

Regions and Cities

Series Editor in Chief
Joan Fitzgerald, *Northeastern University, USA*
Editors
Ron Martin, *University of Cambridge, UK*
Maryann Feldman, *University of North Carolina, USA*
Gernot Grabher, *HafenCity University Hamburg, Germany*
Kieran P. Donaghy, *Cornell University, USA*

In today's globalised, knowledge-driven and networked world, regions and cities have assumed heightened significance as the interconnected nodes of economic, social and cultural production, and as sites of new modes of economic and territorial governance and policy experimentation. This book series brings together incisive and critically engaged international and interdisciplinary research on this resurgence of regions and cities, and should be of interest to geographers, economists, sociologists, political scientists and cultural scholars, as well as to policy-makers involved in regional and urban development.

For more information on the Regional Studies Association visit www.regionalstudies.org

There is a **30% discount** available to RSA members on books in the ***Regions and Cities*** series, and other subject-related Taylor & Francis books and e-books including Routledge titles. To order just e-mail Joanna Swieczkowska, Joanna.Swieczkowska@tandf.co.uk, or phone on +44 (0)20 3377 3369 and declare your RSA membership. You can also visit the series page at www.routledge.com/Regions-and-Cities/book-series/RSA and use the discount code: **RSA0901**

132. China in the Local and Global Economy
History, Geography, Politics and Sustainability
Edited by Steven Brakman, Charles van Marrewijk, Peter J. Morgan and Nimesh Salike

133. The Entrepreneurial Discovery Process and Regional Development
New Knowledge Emergence, Conversion and Exploitation
Edited by Åge Mariussen, Seija Virkkala, Håkon Finne and Tone Merethe Aasen

134. Strategic Approaches to Regional Development
Smart Experimentation in Less-Favoured Regions
Edited by Iryna Kristensen, Alexandre Dubois and Jukka Teräs

For more information about this series, please visit: www.routledge.com/Regions-and-Cities/book-series/RSA

The Entrepreneurial Discovery Process and Regional Development

New Knowledge Emergence, Conversion and Exploitation

Edited by Åge Mariussen, Seija Virkkala, Håkon Finne and Tone Merethe Aasen

Routledge
Taylor & Francis Group
LONDON AND NEW YORK

First published 2019 by Routledge

2 Park Square, Milton Park, Abingdon, Oxfordshire OX14 4RN
52 Vanderbilt Avenue, New York, NY 10017

Routledge is an imprint of the Taylor & Francis Group, an informa business

First issued in paperback 2020

British Library Cataloguing-in-Publication Data
A catalogue record for this book is available from the British Library

Library of Congress Cataloging-in-Publication Data
A catalog record has been requested for this book

ISBN: 978-1-138-57455-7 (hbk)
ISBN: 978-0-367-66313-1 (pbk)

Typeset in Bembo
by Swales & Willis Ltd, Exeter, Devon, UK

Contents

Figures

Tables

Boxes

Contributors

Tone Merethe Aasen is senior research scientist at the Department of Technology Management at SINTEF Digital, Trondheim, Norway. She holds an MSc in engineering physics and a PhD in organizational sociology from the Norwegian University of Science and Technology. Her research interest is in innovation in mature enterprises, including business strategy, innovation management, employee-driven innovation, and collaborative innovation. She is also exploring complexity perspectives as approaches to improved insight in the messy, everyday practices of many people aiming at innovation.

Jiří Blažek is associate professor at the Department of Social Geography and Regional Development, Charles University, Prague, Czech Republic. He does research in regional innovation systems in less developed European countries and investigates the impacts of intersection of companies with global production networks. Jiří is also involved in design of innovation policies at the national and regional level.

Håkon Finne is senior research scientist at the Department of Technology Management at SINTEF Digital, Trondheim, Norway. He holds an MSc in engineering physics and additional social science credits from the Norwegian University of Science and Technology. His research experiences span over a wide range of areas, including fundamental and applied social science research, formative and summative evaluation, and strategic and operative management of complex network organisations. The nature of knowledge and its conversion into innovation is a recurring research interest.

Eli Fyhn Ullern is research scientist at the Department of Technology Management at SINTEF Digital, Trondheim, Norway. She holds an MSc in political science from the Norwegian University of Science and Technology. Her master's thesis focused on innovation processes in the fish farming industry. Her research interest is within the field of innovation management. She currently does research on innovation strategies and sustainability.

Fatime Barbara Hegyi is researcher at the European Commission's Joint Research Center in Seville, working at the Smart Specialisation Platform. Fatime is coordinating the thematic platform on industrial modernisation. She holds a PhD in regional economics. Before joining the European Commission, she worked as a deputy director for the ministry responsible for the implementation of economic development and innovation programmes in Hungary.

Arne Isaksen is professor at the Department of Working Life and Innovation at the University of Agder, Norway. He has a PhD in economic geography from the University of Oslo. His research interest is in theoretical and empirical studies of regional industrial development, focusing on the development of regional clusters, innovation systems, and path development, companies' innovation mode, and policy tools and policy lessons. Isaksen has numerous international publications within these subjects.

Asbjørn Karlsen is professor in geography at the Norwegian University of Science and Technology. His previous research covers topics such as industrial restructuring, regional innovation and cluster formation. More recently, his research focuses on global production networks and sustainable transition. He studies regional, industrial and technology development typically from a historical institutionalist perspective.

Nina Kyllingstad is a PhD student at the Department of Working Life and Innovation at the University of Agder, Norway, and a researcher at the research institute Agderforskning, Norway. Her research interest is in innovation, regional business development, knowledge development, regional innovation systems, and higher education.

Alice Lam is professor of organisation studies at the School of Management, Royal Holloway University of London. She holds a PhD from the London School of Economics. She has researched extensively on how societal institutions influence work organisation, learning and knowledge-creation within firms. More recently she has examined the role of careers as a vehicle for knowledge transfer across organizational and institutional boundaries. Her research has been published in *Human Relations*, *Organisation Studies*, *Journal of Management Studies* and *Research Policy*.

Niklas Lundström is assistant professor of regional studies at the University of Vaasa, Finland. His research has focused on the topics of regional development policies and management in the context of complexity sciences, particularly wicked problems. He developed the concept of wicked game in his dissertation in 2015. He has published in journals such as *Administration and Society*, *Landscape and Urban Planning* and *European Planning Studies*.

Jarle Løvland is an economist and senior researcher at Nordland Research Institute, Group on Entrepreneurship, Industrial and Regional Innovation, Norway. He is engaged in research related to tourism, experience economy and strategic development of tourism destinations. Recently he has been doing research on regional innovation systems development and smart specialisation implementation in peripheral regions of Norway.

Åge Mariussen is research manager of regional studies at the University of Vaasa, Finland, and senior researcher, Nordland Research Institute, Norway.

He has been working as a researcher for almost four decades on questions relating to regional development, regional restructuring, innovation, transnational learning, and smart specialisation.

Kevin Morgan is professor of governance and development in the School of Geography and Planning and the Dean of Engagement for Cardiff University (Wales). He is also Special Advisor to the EU Commissioner for Regional and Urban Policy (Corina Cretu) and member of the mirror group of the Smart Specialisation Platform. His research interests are in innovation and spatial development, food and sustainability, governance and territorial politics, social enterprise and cooperation.

Antti Mäenpää is a doctoral student of regional studies at the University of Vaasa, Finland. His dissertation is focusing on the public organisations' role in smart specialisation processes. Antti was part of the team that developed the Ostrobothnian model for smart specialisation.

Nhien Nguyen is a senior researcher at Nordland Research Institute, Bodø, Norway. She holds a PhD in innovation management and strategy from the Norwegian University of Science and Technology. She is a visiting fellow of Stanford University (SCANCOR program) and MIT Sloan School of Management (MBA program). Nhien is a coordinator of Horizon2020 project, which aims to integrate responsible research and innovation (RRI) into regional development policies, including Smart Specialisation Strategy.

Ruslan Rakhmatullin is a policy researcher working for the European Commission's Smart Specialisation Platform (Joint Research Centre, Seville). Ruslan has also worked for the United Nations Economic Commission for Europe in Geneva, and for the COST Office (European Cooperation in the field of Science and Technology) of the European Science Foundation in Brussels. He has obtained a PhD from the School of Business, Trinity College, University of Dublin.

Jan Ole Rypestøl has recently defended his PhD thesis, with the title *New Regional Industrial Path Development: Entrepreneurs, Knowledge Exchange and Regional Contexts*, at the Department of Working Life and Innovation at the University of Agder, Norway. He is currently working as a researcher at the research institute Agderforskning.

Ann Camilla Schulze-Krogh has recently defended her PhD thesis, focusing on regional policy learning in times of changing context, at the Department of Working Life and Innovation at the University of Agder, Norway. She is currently employed as an adviser at Aust-Agder County Council.

Seija Virkkala is professor of regional studies at the School of Management, University of Vaasa, Finland. Her research interests are regional development and innovation, transnational learning, innovation systems in peripheral regions and smart specialisation. She is a leader of the research program Place-based Society and Regional Development Policies at the University of Vaasa.

Abbreviations

3D	three dimensions
3H	triple helix
4H	quadruple helix
ABB	Asea Brown Boveri
AR	augmented reality
BC	before Christ
BERD	business enterprise expenditure on R&D
CAS	complex adaptive systems
CEE	Central East European countries
CRP	complex responsive processes
DGs	Directorates-General
DG Grow	Directorate-General for Internal market, industry, entrepreneurship and SMEs
DG Regio	Directorate-General for Regional Policy
DG RTD	Directorate-General for Research and Innovation
DMO	destination management organisation
EC	European Commission
ECI	Economic Complexity Index
EDP	entrepreneurial discovery process
ESIF	European Structural and Investment Funds
ESS	the European Spallation Source
EU	European Union
G&M	governance and management
GDP	gross domestic product
GERD	gross expenditure on R&D
GPN	global production network
GPT	general purpose technologies
GVC	global value chain
HS	Harmonized System, an internationally standardised system of names and numbers to classify traded products
ICT	information and communication technology
INKA	Innovatiiviset kaupungit (Innovative cities) programme
IPR	intellectual property rights

ISIC	International Standard Industrial Classification
JRC	Joint Research Centre
KET	key enabling technologies
LDR	less developed region
LEO	Lapin elämystalouden osaamiskeskus (Lapland Centre for Expertise for the Experience Industry)
LNG	liquefied natural gas
NCE	National Centre of Expertise
NTH	Norwegian Institute of Technology
NTNU	Norwegian University of Science and Technology
OECD	Organization for Economic Cooperation and Development
PCI	Product Complexity Index
R&D	research and development
R&D&I	research, development and innovation
R&I	research and innovation
RA	Raufoss Ammunition Factory
RDP	regional development platform
RIS	regional innovation system
RIS3	research and innovation strategies for smart specialisation
RTIM	Raufoss Technology & Industrial Management
RTO	research and technology organisation
S3	Smart Specialisation Strategy
S3P	Smart Specialisation Platform
SDA	Schumpeterian development agency
SECI	socialisation, externalisation, combination and internalisation
SF	structural fund
SFI	Sentre for Forskningsdrevet Innovasjon (Centre for Research-based Innovation)
SMB	small and medium-sized business
SME	small and medium-sized enterprise
SRM	SINTEF Raufoss Manufacturing
SWD	Staff and joint staff Working Documents (European Commission)
TDB	Traceability and Big Data thematic partnership
TotAL	Toten Aluminium Group
UK	United Kingdom
USA	United States of America
VR	virtual reality

Introduction

Smart specialisation: expectations, challenges and solutions

Åge Mariussen and Seija Virkkala

Expectations of smart specialisation

Entrepreneurial discovery processes (EDP) are not something entirely new. As explained in Chapter 1 (Virkkala and Mariussen, 2019), Foray (2015) refers to empirical studies of 'self-discoveries' and economic diversification based on theories within economics. In this book, we also present evidence of EDP and policies similar to and inspiring smart specialisation that pre-date the European Commission's smart specialisation initiative in 2011.

The expectations for the EDP were set against the backdrop of several limitations of earlier innovation policies identified by the European Commission in 2017 (SWD(2017)264), including:

- lack of prioritisation and poor resource allocation;
- weak microeconomic governance, including barriers to the uptake of new ideas – and inflexible governance mechanisms;
- mismatch of EU research strengths and business needs;
- lack of strategic alignment of investment pipelines in industry and research, in both the private and public sector;
- lack of information flows across business sectors, scientific disciplines and EU territories – increasing the degree of information asymmetry;
- lack of inter-regional cooperation between innovation actors across the EU;
- weaknesses in EU value chains – opportunities for demonstration projects and for scaling up of initiatives are missed because of limited economies of scale and scope;
- low leverage effect of EU funding – a failure to attract private investors to realistic and bankable innovation initiatives.

Those limitations have led the European Commission to implement its smart specialisation policies through its cohesion policy. This initiative created a platform where regions could experiment and learn from each other (Mariussen and Virkkala, 2013). A set of core methods and principles was applied to regional planning procedures required as a conditionality access to support from the structural funds. This was disseminated by the smart specialisation platform (S3 platform, http://s3platform.jrc.ec.europa.eu/) as a guide to research and innovation strategies for smart specialisation (RIS3) (Foray et al., 2012) and through an elaborate process of transnational learning and peer reviews. The guide involved certain steps where the regions were asked to use analysis to discover their comparative, place-based strengths and build on them to produce new regional strategies:

Step 1 – Analysis

Step 2 – Governance

Step 3 – Vision

Step 4 – Priorities

Step 5 – Policy mix

Step 6 – Monitoring and evaluation

This initial phase of regional planning led to a second phase, experimental implementation through entrepreneurial discovery processes (Gianelle et al., 2016). The 2012 guide covered a broad range of related theories, with core contributions made by Dominique Foray. The guide put down certain conceptual cornerstones regarding the entrepreneurial discovery process (EDP).

The EDP was based on an identification of the domains of the region and its strong clusters, which, following the principles of analysis of place-based development, could reveal openings in novel directions. This exploration was expected to lead to the discovery and exploitation of new and related domains and business opportunities through collaboration between triple or quadruple helix actors such as university scientists, industrial entrepreneurs, public governance agencies, and citizens/non-governmental organisations (NGOs); see Chapter 1 (Virkkala and Mariussen, 2019).

The 'discovery' in EDP is not an innovation, but an opening of a new area of business opportunities. This area is expected to build on existing knowledge and industrial strengths in the regions (combined with external assets). Based on this dynamic theory of growth, smart specialisation strategies coordinate the search for new business areas. That action is explorative rather than exploitative, which has clear policy implications. Incentives should only be provided to 'new' activities (Morgan, 2017: 51). The strategy aims to seize new opportunity over time and progressively create new options for economic transformation; therefore, regional policy should regularly change the portfolio of prioritised activities (Foray, 2015). In this way, one might say, the EDP is not replacing theories of systems of innovation or clusters but adds another dimension, a strategy of overcoming market failure through exploration which enables the creation of new value chains and clusters. In overcoming market failure, the public sector has an important role.

The strategy starts with an analysis of new opportunities related to existing strengths. The analysis should lead to new forms of governance, new priorities and roadmaps. At the same time, there is a strong element of experimental search and exploration. Nobody has perfect information on new business areas and future possibilities and developments. The idea of the EDP is that awareness and acceptance of new business opportunities emerge in a broad partnership consisting of public and private actors, where the urgency of entrepreneurs is the most important element. That is the reason micro-level dialogues, negotiations and local experimentations are central to smart specialisation. A policy should be seen as a dynamic creation, a joint understanding of what, why and how. It should reflect upon past results, monitor ongoing activities and develop new activities. Successful discoveries of new business opportunities are expected to result in economic growth. In this way, EDP provides a new definition of the entrepreneur. Entrepreneurial discovery is what regional policy-makers and developers should do in alliance with the business world and universities (Foray and Rainoldi, 2013). This is a new set of roles, with a collaborative triple helix set of entrepreneurial actors from economy, science and government.

The EDP has now been tested. What were the strengths and limitations of the understanding of the EDP in 2011, what were the challenges, and how might they be overcome?

Experiences, challenges and a solution

A considerable volume of literature examines the concept of the EDP and its application of smart specialisation strategies across and beyond the European regions. The book *Governing Smart Specialisation* edited by Kyriakou et al. (2017) clarifies the concept of EDP and its policy implications. The book emphasises the role of institutional contexts for the outcome of EDP and focuses on the methods and institutional conditions necessary to generate information supporting the policies. The interaction of public and private entities in the EDP requires behavioural changes by both companies and policy-makers. Companies should become closer to policy-makers and think more strategically and more long term (Grillo, 2017). The policy design should include feedback flows as a necessary element for a sustainable and self-correcting process of developing and choosing priorities, and EDP should be continuous (Gianelle et al., 2016).

The book *The Empirical and Institutional Dimensions of Smart Specialisation* edited by McCann et al. (2017) presents findings of the research project *SmartSpec – Smart specialisation for regional innovation*. The book emphasises that smart specialisation has its roots in many different scientific subjects and disciplines and policy areas, which were once scattered and fragmented, but is now an integrated system and policy model. The book identifies common aspects of smart specialisation, and procedures of particular types of policy interventions in different contexts. Identifying the policy-related features which are similar across regions among those that are different and specific to regions is an important role for policy analysis and policy learning (McCann and actors, institutions and systems with structures. The relation between institutions and actors is crucial. Institutions, according to Giddens, are practices which 'stretch' over long time-space distances in the reproduction of social systems (Giddens, 1984: 28). These 'stretches' of practices are reproduced through micro-level decisions made by actors. These decisions may conform with the institutionalised routines, or they may adjust and change them.

Systems are elements with sustained interdependence, kept in place by institutions. Systems have structures (rules and resources) that impose constraints on actors, but also support their activity. Actors are skilled; they are able to understand situations and norms. Sometimes, these forms of understanding change and actors start to redefine rules and use resources in new ways. These new forms of understanding are skillful approaches which sometimes have the power to change institutions. If they go deep and far enough, these institutional changes can transform structures. This dynamic perspective on structures is called structuration. Structuration is thus understood to *'involve an interplay of meaning, norms and power'* (Giddens, 1977: 161).

Distinguishing between institutions, actors and structures illuminates how micro-level actors operating in different roles can become partially independent of structural constraints. They may change institutions in ways that open a potential for the transformation of structures.

In the geographical tradition, it is common to classify regions in ways that can be seen to favour 'structural determination'. We all know the stories of lock-in, and it is well known that some regions may close in on themselves. They are as stable as clockwork, and they focus on the exploitation of existing knowledge. If they meet unexpected external challenges, say, because the big manufacturer goes bankrupt, their economies might fall apart. Other regions are flexible and resilient. When they are challenged, they adapt, bounce back and survive. But it would be a mistake to accept a distinction made between, on the one hand, dynamic, innovative and explorative regions and, on the other hand, static, regional structures as immutable. Regional actors should undertake both exploration and exploitation.

From the point of departure of structuration theory, we can now start to understand how micro-level actions might create new, institutionalised practices that sometimes have the power to transform structures. These transitions may be enabled by actors capable of knowledge conversion across gaps between helices (policy-makers, entrepreneurs, and scientists) and boundaries between knowledge spaces in different clusters or sectors. Second, this micro-level dynamic involves overlapping, hybrid knowledge spaces. Hybrid knowledge spaces may evolve within different types of networks, systems and ecologies of innovation, and the hybridisation of innovation ecologies may result in entrepreneurial discoveries. These discoveries may be supported by and at the same time support appropriate forms of experimental governance. In this way, we can discover how smart policies and governance strategies may both enable, and at the same time be enabled by, successful exploration and experimentation.

The book suggests that institutional barriers might be overcome through destabilisation (Chapters 7 and 9), knowledge brokering (Chapters 5 and 6), career mobility across knowledge boundaries (Chapter 5), ambidexterity (Chapter 10), citizen involvement (Chapter 4), knowledge spaces (Chapter 8) and also by connecting place-based innovation ecologies and strategies with transnational industrial networks and value chains (Chapter 11).

The book also claims that successful micro-level achievements, in terms of knowledge conversion leading to EDP, are likely to support the development of institutions and organisations which facilitate them and enable the emergence of new clusters. In the concluding chapter, our preliminary answers to the research question are summarised in a discussion of these feedback loops of structuration between governance, innovation ecologies and knowledge. Here, we also outline policy recommendations. The challenges are addressed in this book as shown in Table 0.1.

Table 0.1 Challenges and suggested solutions

Challenge	*Enabling entrepreneurial discovery processes*		
New knowledge-creation	Make entrepreneurial discoveries through new knowledge-creation	Complexity	Chapter 7
		Career mobility	Chapter 5
		Knowledge-brokering	Chapter 6
		Ambidexterity	Chapter 10
		Emergence	Chapter 9
System dynamics	Create hybrid innovation ecologies and European clusters	Connecting place-based and transnational networks	Chapter 11
		Knowledge spaces	Chapter 8
Governance	Grow stronger regional institutions enabling better connectivity between helices	Institutional capacities	Chapter 3
		Taming of wicked problems	Chapter 4
		System entrepreneurship	Chapter 2
		Cluster evolution (fish farming, experience tourism and mechanical)	Chapters 12, 13, 14
		Learning and building institutions	Chapter 15

Source: Own elaboration

References

Foray, D. (2015). *Smart specialisation: Opportunities and challenges for regional innovation policy*. London: Routledge.

Foray, D., Goddard, J., Goenaga Beldarrain, X., Landabaso, M., McCann, P., Morgan, K., Nauwelaers, C. and Ortega-Argilés, R. (2012). *Guide to research and innovation strategies for smart specialisation (RIS 3)*. Occasional report. [Sevilla]: European Commission.

Foray, D. and Rainoldi, A. (2013). *Smart specialisation programmes and implementation*. Luxembourg: European Commission.

Gianelle, C., Kyriakou, D., Cohen, C. and Przeor, M. (eds.) (2016). *Implementing smart specialisation: A handbook*. Brussels: European Commission.

Giddens, A. (1977). *Studies in social and political theory*. London: Hutchinson.

Giddens, A. (1984). *The constitution of society: Outline of the theory of structuration*. Berkeley: University of California Press.

Grillo, F. (2017). Structuring the entrepreneurial discovery process to promote private–public sector engagement. In Kyriakou, D., Martínez, M.P., Periáñez-Forte, I. and Rainoldi, A. (eds.) *Governing smart specialisation*, pp. 62–79. London; New York: Routledge.

Huggins, R. and Prokop, D. (2017). Regional innovation and the network structure of university–industry links. In McCann, P., van Oort, F. and Goddard, J. (eds.) *The empirical and institutional dimensions of smart specialisation*, pp. 57–80. London: Routledge.

Kyriakou, D., Martínez, M.P., Periáñez-Forte, I. and Rainoldi, A. (eds.) (2017). *Governing smart specialisation*. London: Routledge.

Mariussen, Å. and Virkkala, S. (2013). Methodologies and methods of transnational learning. In Mariussen, Å. and Virkkala, S. (eds.) *Learning transnational learning*, pp. 155–195. Abingdon: Routledge.

McCann, P. and Ortega-Argilés, R. (2017). The intellectual and practical bases of the application of RIS3 within EU cohesion policy. In McCann, P., van Oort, F. and Goddard, J. (eds.) *The empirical and institutional dimensions of smart specialisation*, pp. 8–22. London: Routledge.

McCann, P., van Oort, F. and Goddard, J. (eds.) (2017). *The empirical and institutional dimensions of smart specialisation*. London: Routledge.

Morgan, K. (2017). Speaking truth to power: The political dynamics of public sector innovation. In Kyriakou, D., Martínez, M.P., Periáñez-Forte, I. and Rainoldi, A. (eds.) *Governing smart specialisation*, pp. 49–61. London: Routledge.

Radosevic, S., Curaj, A., Gheorghiu, R., Andreescu, L. and Wade, I. (eds.) (2017). *Advances in the theory and practice of smart specialization*. London: Academic Press.

SWD(2017)264 (2017). *Strengthening innovation in Europe's regions: Towards resilient, inclusive and sustainable growth at territorial level*. Commission Staff Working Document. Brussels: Commission of the European Communities.

Vallance, P. (2017). The co-evolution of regional innovation domains and institutional arrangements: Smart specialisation through quadruple helix relations? In McCann, P., Goddard, J. and van Oort, F. (eds.) *The empirical and institutional dimensions of smart specialisation*, pp. 127–144. London: Routledge.

Virkkala, S. and Mariussen, Å. (2019). Self-discovery enabling entrepreneurial discovery processes. In Mariussen, Å., Virkkala, S., Finne, H. and Aasen, T.M. (eds.) *The entrepreneurial discovery process and regional development: New knowledge emergence, conversion and exploitation*. Abingdon: Routledge.

Part I

Entrepreneurial discovery processes and their institutional challenges

1 Self-discovery enabling entrepreneurial discovery processes

Seija Virkkala and Åge Mariussen

1.1 Introduction

The future is unknowable and the global environment turbulent. Nobody is capable of presenting an overall view of how technological and market opportunities will influence regional development. The solution to this dilemma proposed by the EC smart specialisation policy involves governments, companies, universities, and other actors or quadruple helix stakeholders uniting to identify future growth opportunities (Radosevic, 2017b; Foray, 2017). The method governing that search is the *entrepreneurial discovery process* (EDP), which is a collective idea generation mechanism addressing the future of the region in terms of the knowledge economy. The EDP and smart specialisation have the same meaning as practices and approaches to diversify the regional economy. The aim is to expand the regional economy in a direction identified by the relevant quadruple helix stakeholders (i.e. entrepreneurial actors). This is a pressing policy concern, particularly at times of significant restructuring in the world economy, given the relatively slow transition to a more prosperous knowledge economy in parts of Europe.

Regional development is often considered in economic terms as a question of growth, but in this book it is defined more broadly in line with the *Europe 2020* targets for smart sustainable and inclusive growth as also addressing social and ecological policies such as diminishing social inequality, promoting environmental sustainability and championing inclusive government. The broader definition includes implementing smart specialisation strategies (S3). Development is a change of direction, but smart specialisation and EDP particularly emphasise the renewal of the regional economy. S3 is an economic transformation agenda built on each region's strengths. The new business areas or fields of opportunity (domains) which are discovered through the broad partnership are expected to initiate structural changes in different forms: diversification, transition, modernisation, or the radical foundation of industries and/or services (Foray, 2015: 1) – in other words path renewal, path extension or new path creation, in the terminology of economic geography (see Isaksen et al., 2019 – Chapter 2 in this volume).

According to the Smart Specialisation Platform (EC-JRC, 2017):

> The EDP is an inclusive and interactive bottom-up process in which participants from different environments (policy, business, academia, etc.) are discovering and producing information about potential new activities, identifying potential opportunities that emerge through this interaction, while policymakers assess outcomes and ways to facilitate the realisation of this potential. The EDP pursues the integration of entrepreneurial knowledge fragmented and distributed over many sites and organisations, companies, universities, clients and users, specialised suppliers (some of these entities being located outside of the region) through the building of connections and partnerships. The EDP consists of the exploration and opening up of a new domain of opportunities (technological and market), potentially rich in numerous innovations that emerge as feasible and attractive.

The notion of the EDP can be viewed from different perspectives. Rodríguez-Pose and Wilkie (2017) have related the concept of the EDP to an institutional approach by decomposing EDP into three elements (entrepreneurial actors, experimentation and discovery, and the interaction between relevant actors) and exploring the way that institutions interact with these components. They also point to the need to adapt EDP to contextual factors (see also Gianelle et al., 2016). Others, like Morgan (2017b) and Aranguren et al. (2017), explore the human element in smart specialisation governance. Aranguren et al. (2017) examine the concept of smart specialisation with the aid of leadership theories and emphasise the process view on governance.

The notion of *self-discovery* is related to the EDP and emphasises the concept of agency. Hausmann and Rodrik (2003) state that self-discovery means to discover what economic activities can profitably be pursued in a given country, given the existing strengths and specialisations of the national economy. The latent competitive advantage of nations or regions can be discovered in broad partnerships. In terms of regional development policies, self-discovery refers to a region's strengths and unique assets that can form the basis for future business fields.

This book highlights the relations between exploitation and exploration in the context of EDP. Exploitation refers to using existing knowledge to refine existing processes; exploration refers to the discovery and creation of new knowledge. Exploitation crowds out exploration and vice versa (March, 1991). Strong clusters tend to lead to exploitation rather than exploration. Innovation systems oriented towards exploitation may restrict entrepreneurs who try to create new paths. This is where the EDP can contribute by pushing innovation policy and research supporting innovation policy in the direction of more exploration.

This book aims to answer the research question: *How is the transition from exploitation of knowledge to exploration and discoveries possible, and what are the implications for the actors involved, for the transformation of the regional economy, and for knowledge production and creation?*

This chapter examines what the 'self' in self-discovery is; more specifically, it investigates what is required for actors to make the transition from exploitation to discoveries in regional development (Table 1.1). Chapter 9 (Virkkala and Mariussen, 2019) analyses the implication of this transition to exploration for the transformation process of regional economy, and Chapter 5 (Lam, 2019) and Chapter 8 (Virkkala, 2019) focus on the knowledge creation and knowledge space needed for the discovery. The actors, the process, and knowledge are indistinguishable elements despite being addressed separately for the purposes of analysis. In real-life EDPs, these analytical elements interact in the processes of exploration, failures, success and exploitation.

This chapter focuses on self-discovery enabling the EDP. The EDP begins with fragmented knowledge that must be combined, and which, together with additional knowledge resources, is necessary for exploration. The EDP is a move from a state of knowledge and actor fragmentation to a process of self-discovery. Along that road, the fragments of knowledge objects come together into a new, living entity – knowledge as process – that offers a new cognitive understanding of the opportunities available to a region. The start of this journey of self-discovery requires a creation of a collective actor capable of pulling things together and in that way makes sense of the opportunities available to the regional economy in a new way. This point of departure will be discussed in the second section of this chapter, which gives an overview of the process from fragmentation (of knowledge) in the exploitation phase to emergence of a new domain of opportunities for new value creation. In the third section of this chapter, EDP and S3 will be compared with approaches often used in regional development strategies: the cluster approach and the innovation system approach. EDP is an attempt to overcome the shortcomings of policies based on theories of regional innovation system, or RIS. The RIS tradition has been criticised for being too static and not providing relevant policy advice. The RIS literature 'is nearly silent on the conditions that enable growth to accrue in regions where innovation occurs' (Doloreux and Porto Gomez, 2017).

The fourth section of the chapter summarises some critical reflections on the EDP. This chapter presents preconditions that can trigger a change from exploitation to exploration in which the EDP provides a potential solution. The first precondition is to change the static structure to a more complex and dynamic process by moving focus and policy measures from the micro level to the macro level. The second precondition is to recognise the tacit character of knowledge as well as the interaction processes leading to the knowledge spiral, in other words, a continuous EDP. The third precondition is to make the EDP a transnational discovery process. These preconditions can be seen as challenges meriting further examination and will be discussed thoroughly in the later chapters of the book.

Table 1.1 Framing elements of the regional self-discovery process

	Static point of departure	*Road to discovery*	*Theoretical approaches*
	Exploitation Clusters	Exploration RIS3	Regional innovation systems Entrepreneurial discovery processes
Actors	Individual (division of labour)	Collective regional actors	Triple and quadruple helix (Chapters 1, 3, 4) EDP as collective process (Chapter 1) Self as public–private alliance (Chapter 1)
Process	Efficient structures of exploitation	Emergence of new opportunities	Complexity approaches (Chapter 7) Theories of emergence (Chapter 9)
Knowledge	Knowledge as object, specialisation	Knowledge as process, sense-making and conversion	SECI process (Chapters 7, 8) Third spaces (Chapter 5) Knowledge spaces (Chapter 8)

Source: Own elaboration

1.2 The EDP: collective actors searching for new domains

Background of the notion of the EDP

In order to understand the role of collective actors in the EDP, this chapter first introduces the background of the EDP in a stylised way. The concepts of entrepreneurial opportunities and discoveries are used in business and entrepreneurship studies (Shane, 2003) and they originate from Austrian economists such as Hayek (1945; 1978) and Kirzner (1973; 1997).

Entrepreneurs are continually searching for, identifying and evaluating new business opportunities. This process is called entrepreneurial discovery in the business theory literature (Shane, 2003: 3–6). Entrepreneurship requires the existence of opportunities, or situations in which people think that they can recombine resources to generate profits. Entrepreneurship can be characterised as the reaction of certain individuals (entrepreneurs) to the existence of opportunities for profit. However, the exploitation of opportunity is uncertain because it depends on demand, competition and the opportunity to create a value chain. The individual entrepreneur exploits an opportunity and organises and recombines resources in a way that they have not been previously. The opportunities an entrepreneur exploits are created, for instance, by social/demographic change, technological change, and political/regulatory change, as well as by grand challenges like climate change (Shane, 2003).

The Austrian economists saw market equilibrium as a process through which market participants acquire accurate knowledge of potential demand

and supply. The Austrian approach nominates entrepreneurial discovery as the driving force behind the process. Kirzner (1973) pointed out that opportunities are discovered through entrepreneurial alertness, and that better knowledge leads to competition and a new equilibrium. Entrepreneurial processes are seen as carried out by the actions of business entrepreneurs profiting from temporary disequilibrium.

The notion of self-discovery was later used by Rodrik (2004) and Hausmann and Rodrik (2003) on a macro level when they wrote about national economic development. Self-discovery means to discover what economic activities can profitably be pursued in a given country, given the existing strengths and specialisations of the national economy. Self-discovery can benefit the whole economy, not just the firm that originally invested in the discovery, and accordingly, governments should implement economic policies that promote self-discovery.

The concept of smart specialisation was developed in the Knowledge for Growth group as a response to the economic crisis and growth problems in the EU (Foray, 2015). It quickly diffused into mainstream EU regional policy and has been used as an ex-ante condition for Structural Fund (SF) programmes since 2014 (Gianelle et al., 2016; Grillo, 2017). The strengths of the region (the 'self') should be found jointly in public–private alliances. Entrepreneurial discovery is the source of information on the new exploration and transformation activities which should be supported in Research and Innovation Strategies for Smart Specialisation (RIS3). The planners of RIS3 suggested a learning process to discover the business fields in which a region might hope to be competitive.

According to Radosevic (2017b), S3 applied in the EU is one approach to so-called new industrial policies which support diversification and technological upgrading. According to these policy approaches, the constraints of growth and new possible business fields are not known *ex ante*, and the design of the discovery process is important. Instead of an *a priori* defined policy target, search networks should be established to examine technological change and its effects (Radosevic, 2017b: 7). Radosevic (2017b) includes among the new industrial policy approaches Rodrik's notion of self-discovery, diagnostic monitoring (Kuznetsov and Sabel, 2017) based on experimentalist governance, and the product space approach set out by Hausmann and Hidalgo (Hausmann et al., 2011; see Nguyen and Mariussen, 2019 – Chapter 10 in this volume). In addition, approaches such as new structural economics, neo-Schumpeterian and Schumpeterian perspectives emphasising targeting industries that constitute the country's latent comparative advantages can be included among the new industrial policies.

The shift of emphasis from individual to collective entrepreneurship has implications for the process of learning, and these are examined below.

The Austrian approach to microeconomics: the individual entrepreneur and discovery – Hayek and Kirzner

The notion of discovery is central to the Austrian approach. Entrepreneurs drive the market process, and the entrepreneurial role offers a theoretical explanation for its ever-changing nature. Hayek (1945; 1978) emphasised the nature of competition as a discovery procedure. He interpreted the market process as a process of mutual discovery, during which the market participants become better informed of the plans made by other participants. Some plans must prove to have been mistaken; they are seen as errors which tend to be overcome as market experience reveals that they are not viable when some other actions prove themselves profitable. Decision-makers might discover that a plan is not viable when a prior error in their view of the world is revealed, and they can then correct the view. Earlier plans might have overlooked existing profit opportunities, but such opportunities might be reflected in later plans. This example also offers a new insight into the nature of discovery: when people become aware of what they have overlooked previously, their view of the world will change. Discovering previously unknown profit opportunities is different from a successful search based on the deliberate production of information that was known to be missing. Discovery means that surprise comes with the realisation that something that was in fact available had been overlooked. Discoveries occur because human agents are alert (Kirzner, 1973), and the alertness expresses itself in the boldness and imagination. Alertness also means an attitude of responsiveness to available opportunities. The entrepreneurs search for unnoticed features of the environment that could inspire new activity and lead to discoveries.

Kirzner held that entrepreneurial discovery occurs because the price system does not always allocate resources effectively. People's views on the efficient use of resources are based on incomplete information. Their inaccurate decision-making framework can prompt people to make erroneous decisions, which in turn create shortages and surpluses. By responding to these shortages and surpluses, people can obtain resources, recombine them and sell the output in the hope of making a profit. The earlier errors create profit opportunities and tend to stimulate successive entrepreneurial discoveries, when market participants become aware of their errors and make more accurate decisions. Discovery drives pricing, and both output and input quantity and quality, towards values consistent with equilibrium (Kirzner, 1997). Changes in tastes and technology mean that complete equilibrium will never be achieved, even though there is a continuous process pursuing equilibrium.

Kirzner (1973) also stated that opportunities occur when people have differing views on existing information. This view differs from Schumpeter's (1934) perspective that entrepreneurial opportunities are changing and emerging because of the appearance of new information. The changes in technology, regulation, macroeconomic factors, and social trends create new information that entrepreneurs can use to recombine their resources into new forms (Shane, 2003: 34). The creation of new forms of entrepreneurship and new trajectories might require the destruction of existing ones. This is called creative destruction. This idea of creative destruction is also at the core of the transformation of the regional economy through EDP.

Self-discovery and new industrial policy – Rodrik and Hausmann

While Austrian economists presented the view of entrepreneurs driving a discovery process in the market, Rodrik (2004) developed a macro-level concept of self-discovery advocating firms and government explore the future together. Rodrik felt that firms have a knowledge deficit, especially when they are exploring new technologies and emergent markets, where neither costs nor clients are known in advance. Industrial policy should be a process of economic self-discovery (Hausmann and Rodrik, 2003) in which firms and governments learn about underlying costs and opportunities and engage in strategic coordination. Public action should encourage restructuring, diversification and technological dynamism beyond a level market forces would generate.

The idea of strategic cooperation between firms and governments in the EDP is based on Rodrik's (2004) ideas of self-discovery. Rodrik argued in favour of a proactive state and new industrial policy that sets vertical priorities: the state should support experimentation and explore and engage in a process of self-discovery with its industrial partners. The policy needs to allow for experimentation in order to discover what works and what does not in a particular context. Failures must also be noted in order to identify successes (Foray, 2015: 39–49; Rodrik, 2004; 2007). Industrial policy should be an iterative process of economic self-discovery. Evaluation is a central policy task. Policy-makers should design *ex ante* procedures evaluating potentials and priorities as well as ex post procedures identifying success and failure. An exit provision for the supported activities after a certain period of time is central to a policy based on experimentation (Rodrik, 2004). However, it is difficult to assess the stability and sustainability of a specialisation at an early stage (Foray, 2015: 51).

Public sector officials should collate information from the business sector on constraints and possible opportunities. These ideas have much in common with the literature on institutional innovation and social learning (see e.g. Sabel and Zeitlin, 2010). According to Sabel and Zeitlin (2010), learning institutions must be experiment oriented, since discovery requires experimentation on the ways in which restructuring bottlenecks can be released, which necessitates a trial-and-error approach to policy-making (Rodrik, 2014).

The policy design of S3 is inspired by the new industrial policy school established by Rodrik and which has established the design principles of an industrial policy.

The design principles for industrial policy according to Rodrik (2004) and supported by Morgan (2017a) are:

1 Incentives should be provided only to support new activities.
2 There should be clear criteria for success and failure.
3 There must be a built-in sunset clause.
4 Public support must target activities, not sectors.

5 Activities that are subsidised must have potential for providing spillovers.
6 Industrial policy should be driven by competent authorities.
7 Implementing agents should monitor.
8 The agencies carrying out promotion must maintain channels of communication with private sector.
9 Mistakes will occur.
10 Promotion activities need to have the capacity to renew themselves so that the cycle of discovery becomes an ongoing one.

We can now see how Foray designed his collective actor. It was a move from national industrial policy to regional development strategies.

The entrepreneurial discovery process of the collective actor at the regional level – Foray

Foray combined the ideas of entrepreneurial discovery (business studies) and self-discovery (Rodrik, Hausmann) and developed the regional theory in a unique and innovative way based on the notion of the EDP. While entrepreneurial discovery at the firm level equates to the exploration of opportunities, at the regional level it is a question of a process of a collective search for the future desirable business areas for a region. The aim is structural transformation via exploration of new business domains for the regional economy. The starting point of the search is a region's existing strengths, and the idea is to combine entrepreneurial and economic knowledge and discover a region's latent competitive advantage in the process of self-discovery.

The 'self' in EDP is a large set of public and private actors involved in the process of discovering which domains a region should move into so as to best construct its future. By opening and exploring new domains of opportunities, the process of entrepreneurial discovery is a central tool to solve the information problem that the government alone cannot solve. As such, it is characterised by a strong learning dimension (Foray, 2016).

The discovery may be about the potential of general purpose technologies (GPTs) to transform processes in the traditional sector, or it may be the possibility of a diversification path based on the exploitation of potential economies of scope and internal spillovers, or a transition path from a low-productivity area to a higher productivity one (Foray, 2015: 23–24). A new regional capacity may be needed to initiate structural changes such as diversification, transition, modernisation, or the radical foundation of industries and/or services (Foray, 2015: 28–29).

The outcomes of the discovery are the key priorities of a region's smart specialisation strategy, which aims to build the capacity to implement and experiment with the desired domain. It consists of the support agenda for activities and capacities, for instance R&D, which are needed to complement the region's productive assets to create future competitive advantages (Foray, 2015: 5). They can be based on both local assets and extra-regional capabilities. The transformation of the productive structures and capacities requires new resources, new technologies and new competencies, which can be based on regional assets or extra-regional capabilities (Foray, 2015: 1–2). When the resources are concentrated in the selected domains, new activities can be created enabling and facilitating the transformation and renewal of the regional economy. This renewal can form the basis for a unique regional competitive advantage which can be valuable, rare, inimitable and non-substitutable.

Based on the ideas of new industrial policy, Foray (2015; 2016) points to the role of the vertical priorities and vertical policies needed to target activities aimed at exploring and experimenting and also learning what should be undertaken in the future. Foray also describes the EDP as combining these two somewhat conflicting principles: vertical priorities and decentralised entrepreneurial initiatives. Interventions should be based on vertical priorities but support the decentralised decisions of entrepreneurs on R&D, innovation and structural changes.

RIS3 and EDP rely on the theories of experimental learning expounded by Sabel (1993). Experimentation means that mistakes will be made, and failure will be experienced, something sometimes necessary in the discovery process. The aim is not to reduce the risk of error but to minimise its cost. RIS3 processes aim to incorporate trial-and-error mechanisms into their programmes (Morgan, 2017b). The indicators and evaluations are important (McCann and Ortega-Argilés, 2013) and *ex ante* criteria to assess projects or domains and select priorities and to determine exit provisions after a certain period of time are important mechanisms of a continuous process of discovery and are thus drivers of regional economic growth (Foray, 2015: 39; Rodrik, 2004; 2007).

The collective entrepreneurial actor capable of performing self-discovery encounters the problem of knowledge fragmentation, which the individual entrepreneur can choose to disregard by selecting a scope suitable for its own benefit rather than the region's.

Entrepreneurial actors building a collective regional agent

A collective regional agent is a necessary element of the EDP because the entrepreneurial knowledge about opportunities, constraints, and challenges (Foray, 2016) is dispersed and embodied in and possessed by entrepreneurial actors. Single entrepreneurial actors have their own experience, and the entrepreneurial knowledge possessed by any single actor is narrow in scope. This knowledge is valuable, but it should be positioned in relation to entrepreneurial knowledge collected from other sources in the discovery of the new domain (Rodríguez-Pose and Wilkie, 2017; Foray, 2015: 25).

This creates a challenge. Entrepreneurial knowledge involved in EDP is not available in a compact form in one location (or entity), and part of the relevant knowledge might reside outside of the region (Foray, 2015: 34–35). According to the RIS3 guide (Foray et al., 2012) and the handbook of implementation (Gianelle et al., 2016), the challenge can be resolved by forming as broad and inclusive a partnership as possible, involving a wide variety of stakeholders within local societies. Firms are central since they are engaged with the market, they have entrepreneurial knowledge, and they can explore and test new ideas and implement innovations that can trigger the transformation of the regional economy. In addition to firms, the relevant entrepreneurial actors might also be higher education institutes, public research institutes, independent innovators, and other actors able to discover the new domains of R&D and innovation triggering structural change in the regional economy (Foray et al., 2012: 12). All sources of entrepreneurial knowledge are necessary and complementary.

However, many authors have underlined the difficulties in this broad inclusion. McCann and Ortega-Argilés (2013) and Morgan (2017b) have argued that such a shift requires transparency in order to ensure public accountability. Moreover, regional entrepreneurial actors might have rent-seeking and vested interests resulting in lock-in – a situation that can give rise to a wicked game played among the actors (see Mäenpää and Lundström, 2019 – Chapter 4 in this volume). One option to avoid local rent-seeking behaviour and lock-in is to involve non-local actors in the EDP, as well as new players possibly alongside established players. However, those established players with their vested interests should commit to contribute to the development of new specialisations in the region (Boschma, 2017).

EDP is an open and gradually changing process, and a new actor can join during the process. A collective of regional entrepreneurial actors can be seen as a form of regional development network with a specific focus, namely entrepreneurial discovery. The collective regional actor should have a transformative capacity, the ability to reflect the given rules and norms, and also be capable of creating new institutions, which implies it has features typical of an institutional entrepreneur (Sotarauta and Pulkkinen, 2011).

It is important to specify clearly how the collective entrepreneurial actor in a regional process of discovery can come into being, and accordingly the following paragraphs introduce the triple helix.

Triple-helix actors and governance

The triple-helix (3H) model (Leydesdorff and Etzkowitz, 1998; Etzkowitz and Leydesdorff, 2000) is used to describe both dynamic interaction between universities, companies and public institutions and institutional continuity, as these helices consist of historical institutions with selection environments or rules. Universities, as scientific systems, communicate and function in accordance with the code of true/false, companies in accordance with the code of profit/loss, and the public sector in accordance with the code of right/wrong. The concept of 3H has been applied in smart specialisation to form the basis for connectivity within regions. 3H actors (i.e. universities, companies, and public organisations) are expected to be at the forefront of the EDP and they should work along the same lines (Virkkala et al., 2017). Finne and Aasen (2019 – Chapter 6 in this volume) examine the role of universities in the transformation of regional economies and EDP, with particular emphasis on how they can contribute to the conversion and not just transfer of knowledge to entrepreneurial actors.

A connected region is a norm or vision where the three helices work in harmony and mutually reinforce each other (Goddard et al., 2013). They co-evolve and interact through an overlay of recursive networks and organisations, which can be seen as a precondition for innovation. In a disconnected region, there are no boundary spanners, the partnerships are ineffective or non-existent, and there is a lack of understanding of the changes. Entrepreneurs are locked out of regional planning (Goddard et al., 2013) and no EDP can emerge. In other words, 3H connectivity supporting successful implementation of RIS3 should include an option for entrepreneurs to participate in its planning processes. 3H actors should be connected in the search for new growth potential. Better cooperation creates more opportunities for innovative interaction, which can expand the intersection between helices and form a point of departure for additional EDPs (Virkkala et al., 2017).

In the exploitation phase there is a division of specialised labour between different actors and institutions (universities, companies, public agencies, etc.) optimising productivity. But what is productive and necessary in exploitation is fragmented when the focus shifts to exploration. In that case, the public sector acquires a new role.

The role of the public sector in the EDP

The policy design, implementation and evaluation of S3 is challenging and requires the governments involved to have strong competencies. Regional governments are obliged to take the initiative in the process, but they also participate in the discovery process that is based on the interaction between entrepreneurial actors in the broad sense. Although entrepreneurs are the key actors in the discovery, the interactive strategic cooperation should be organised and coordinated by public governments.

Creation of a public–private alliance for discovery is a challenging task for a public organisation. This alliance might be created by design, but it is suggested here that the formation process of this alliance can be compared with the emerging community of practice described by Wenger (1998). We apply the concepts of engagement, alignment, and imagination used in the theory of community of practice when describing the challenges of organising entrepreneurial discovery. The first challenge is *engagement*: the identification and mobilisation of all relevant entrepreneurial actors. Entrepreneurial actors are all stakeholders and individuals who hold knowledge relevant to the discovery process. All relevant stakeholders can be invited, and there should be sufficient variety of voices engaged in building the future opportunities for the region. The government or the facilitator should build connections between the partners. Some of the relationships in the alliance might be strong, but most ties are weak.

The second challenge is to create *alignment* (cohesion) among the diverse entrepreneurial actors, and a trusting atmosphere is essential to generate a common vision. Entrepreneurial actors might have conflicting interests and strategies. They might have vested interests and perhaps no interest at all in regional affairs; they might strive to further their interests; and there is a risk of a lock-in situation. The facilitator should aim to build a common mode of interpretation and common interest in the discovery of new business areas. One possibility is to aim for a dual-reference frame, which is marked by the actors establishing the region as a frame of reference for their thinking and their decisions, alongside an already existing frame of reference. This can be achieved through structured dialogue on the future of the region's economy in which the actors might put the aims and issues not shared by others to one side and think in terms of which aspects are shared by the regional actors. Dualism in the reference frame and the ability to manage that dualism is a key characteristic of the individual leadership required for territorial strategy-making (Aranguren et al., 2017). Dual leadership is especially difficult in less developed regions with low levels of trust (see Blažek and Morgan, 2019 – Chapter 3 in this volume, for an outline design of an inclusive EDP in less developed regions). The community of practice theory focuses on different borders and challenges between the entrepreneurial actors representing different communities of practice. This might hinder the interaction between agents, and translation of the practices will be necessary for knowledge conversion (see Chapter 5 (Lam, 2019)).

Alignment means that the proximities of the entrepreneurial actors change and that new knowledge space will be created. New relations might emerge, and the previously proximate relationships might become more distant; see Chapter 8 (Virkkala, 2019).

Imagination facilitates orientation with the help of analogies and visual representations, symbolic expressions, reflection, scenarios and experimentation. In the context of the EDP, there might be a growing understanding of the opportunities for and limitations to the region's growth which will be discovered through the process (Radosevic, 2017b).

The collectively constructed new opportunities will be captured in the smart specialisation policy. The policy priorities should be identified in an interactive process that generates detailed information about new activities. Afterwards, the regional government assesses the activities' potential and empowers those actors most capable of realising that potential. The government is not neutral in this process but instead selects the relevant vertical priorities. This can be seen as a process of creating disequilibrium instead of equilibrium. Public sector agencies have a central role in implementing RIS3 and selecting projects supporting the early growth of the new business field. They should create incentives to support risky projects exploring a new domain of opportunities in a way that maximises knowledge spillovers from the projects (Foray, 2017).

There can be also shared leadership in the EDP. Government agencies are likely to have the capacity to undertake the leadership role required for process design and to create the optimal conditions to foster the engagement of relevant stakeholders (Aranguren et al., 2017). The appropriate knowledge leadership is more likely to be found in technology centres, universities, leading firms or business clusters. Research and technology organisations (RTOs) (Charles and Ciampi Stancova, 2017) are often able to identify industry needs and technological opportunities, and can collect information on international markets, intermediate in the process and translate the global knowledge for regional firms through their networks. They can play a central role in integrating the relevant entrepreneurial knowledge distributed through entrepreneurial actors. Moreover, they can support the exploration of new opportunities by organising platforms and seminars (Charles and Ciampi Stancova, 2017).

1.3 Smart specialisation in relation to other regional development policy theories

Many of the routines, practices and tools necessary for the implementation of RIS3 have already been discussed in economic geography and related research (Kroll, 2015). The discussion includes concepts such as constructed advantage (Asheim et al., 2011), endogenous approaches (Tödtling, 2011), triple-helix connected regions (Goddard et al., 2013), place-based development (Barca et al., 2012), and the process of discovery and general purpose technologies (Foray et al., 2009). Smart specialisation can therefore be seen as the synthesis of different frameworks and approaches. However, it differs from the earlier theories since it has been formulated as a clear theory- and practice-driven policy by Foray (2015) and others.

The RIS3 is based on the legacy of regional innovation system (RIS) thinking that has been used in regional economic development policy over the past 25 years (Asheim and Gertler, 2005; Cooke et al., 2004). It also draws on the experience gained from previous EU initiatives promoting the development of regional innovation strategies. Doloreux and Porto Gomez (2017) point out that RIS research has explored how regions generate the conditions capable of boosting innovation, and especially how regional dynamics can foster firm-level innovation, but it has not systematically explored the benefits of innovation at the regional level. The RIS literature often assumes that the conditions contributing to innovation will automatically lead to growth, and there is little RIS research on the way local innovation is associated with regional economic growth and the transformation and mutations of RISs. Smart specialisation is one response to the problems of RIS research.

Table 1.2 compares the ideas of cluster theories, innovation system theories and smart specialisation or EDP theories. The focus of the theories differs: cluster theories explain how clusters are emerging and developing; RIS theories explain how innovations are emerging in the interaction of knowledge producers and knowledge users. Isaksen et al. (2019 – Chapter 2) use the RIS approach to distinguish between different regional institutional contexts affecting the EDP. Smart specialisation focuses on exploration and explains how to create new domains for business opportunities. The cluster approach is based on firms in specific sectors and the firms related to them. In that context, the lead firms are the main actors, whereas in both the innovation system approach and smart specialisation, the focus might be on companies, public and private organisations, universities and third sector organisations. However, while RIS theory emphasises the division of labour between knowledge producers and knowledge users, according to the smart specialisation approach, the public–private alliances collectively search for new domains. Government is the main facilitator in both the RIS and smart specialisation approaches, whereas, as mentioned above, cluster theories focus on the role of the lead firms.

Cluster theory tends to rely on knowledge embedded in a relevant, and accordingly restricted, set of sectors. Both RIS and smart specialisation approaches recognise that knowledge is distributed among many actors, any of which can contribute to innovation processes and entrepreneurial discovery. Smart specialisation is related more directly to generating regional growth by recombining existing knowledge and capabilities in a new way to form cross-sectoral domains. This occurs with R&D investments, embeddedness and connectivity through the process of self-discovery. The cluster approach highlights the localisation advantages of a specialised labour market, specialised knowledge circulation and spillovers, and common services. The RIS approach can have urbanisation advantages, but the idea of the EDP is to transform the regional economy. Smart specialisation aims to mobilise the firms and other relevant actors and is characterised by a more bottom–up approach than the cluster and RIS approaches.

Both the role of public sector actors and the objectives of the policies differ between the three approaches. While the cluster policy takes a neutral stance on supplying education and infrastructure, the RIS policy aims to establish better governance of the innovation system and stronger connectivity between the subsystems to generate more innovations, and the smart specialisation policy is non-neutral, prioritising the activities of a new domain with the potential to transform the regional economy. Smart specialisation policy also recognises the possibility of failure and encourages experimentation.

The three approaches also have similarities. They all emphasise place-based development to some extent. Cluster policy and RIS policies are place-based development policies in the sense that the clusters and innovation systems are based on regional networks. However, place-based development is even more essential in smart specialisation; it is an integrated place-based economic transformation agenda that is built on each region's strengths and that focuses policy on key regional priorities. The place-based approach is based on the idea of endogenous development that entails regions identifying, developing and utilising their unique resources. The place-based approach to development dictates that the RIS3s should be tailored to the local context

Table 1.2 Cluster, innovation system, and smart specialisation

	Cluster	*Innovation system*	*Smart specialisation*
Scope	Specific sector and related activities	Regional platforms	Domains for business opportunities
Actors	Firms within certain industry and related fields	Firms, public and private organisations, NGOs	Firms, public and private organisations, NGOs, citizens
Process, activity	Cluster life cycle	Innovation	Self-discovery
Knowledge and innovation	Specialised knowledge, local knowledge spillovers	Regional knowledge spillovers, innovations as social processes	Entrepreneurial knowledge combined with general purpose technologies
Dynamic/driving forces	Localisation advantages	Urbanisation economies, related variety	Entrepreneurial discovery, diversification; transformation of the regional economy New domains; knowledge spillovers; entry of firms; agglomeration
Competitors	Clusters of the same industrial sectors	Other innovation systems attracting knowledge flows; labour force and investments	Other regions of specialised fields attracting knowledge flows; labour force and investments
Governance	Top–down	Top–down	Top–down and bottom–up
Public sector role	Education, training, infrastructure	Innovation system governance; intermediation; education; training; infrastructure	Initiating and managing of the strategy process; financer; cooperation partner
Objective of the policy	Speeding the growth of local clusters and improvement of competitiveness	Stronger connectivity between different subsystems (research and industry)	Discovery of areas of new domains that are difficult to imitate; prioritisation; supporting implementation; experimentation
Most important policy challenge	Renewal of old declining industrial clusters	Creation of structures supporting innovation processes, promoting knowledge flows and learning	Changes in behaviour of firms and public government

Source: Adapted from Rinkinen and Harmaakorpi (2017), Foray (2015), Doloreux and Porto Gomez (2017)

(McCann and Ortega-Argilés, 2013). S3 begins with the region's strengths; clusters thrive on those strengths of the region that are to their benefit.

The three concepts align and interact. An RIS can be established when emerging clusters are promoted by the knowledge generation bodies, and transfer and support organisations are established. RIS can consist of many clusters. RIS theory has informed smart specialisation, and S3 can be seen as a continuation of RIS policies in a new form. The discovery of new business areas may lead to clusters and cluster policies. However, the added value of smart specialisation and EDP compared with cluster and system of innovation policies is a move in the direction of exploration and economic growth, rather than of the facilitation of general frameworks supporting innovation.

1.4 Critical reflections on EDP and smart specialisation

The rapid move from a conceptual idea to mainstream EU policy (Kroll, 2015) has led to criticism of the theories of smart specialisation and EDP as policy models and the implementation of smart specialisation strategies in the EU. Scholars have criticised the theory approach of EDP and smart specialisation especially in terms of the use of regions and regional typologies. Camagni and Capello (2013) point out that space can be more diversified. Less developed regions often have unfavourable research and innovation systems and are typically dealing with organisational thinness, a state of lock-in to declining sectors and outdated technologies, fragmented systems that inhibit networking and knowledge exchange, and a weak capacity to drive transformative change (Healy, 2016; Blažek and Morgan, 2019 – Chapter 3 in this volume). Cooke (2012: 216–220) criticises smart specialisation for its apparent overemphasis on science and technology-led innovation with a focus on high-tech sectors, and Capello and Lenzi (2013) do the same for its focus on imitative innovation. Furthermore, Morgan (2015; 2017b) states that the concept of smart specialisation should take greater account of the role of social innovation and the innovation found within the public sector. The public sector can be a repository of entrepreneurial knowledge and be the main driver in the discovery process. Benner (2017) criticises the S3 for focusing more on macro-level collaboration of stakeholders and collective policy-making than micro-level dynamics leading to smart experimentation. However, micro-level dynamics can be included in a continuous EDP (Foray, 2016), and the loops between different levels (see Chapter 9 by Virkkala and Mariussen (2019) on emergence).

Estensoro and Larrea (2016) argue that political habits, practice, and routines (the policy-making modes) are of substantial importance for the degree of efficacy and efficiency with which RIS3 can be implemented. The smart specialisation approach requires a serious reflection on a region's assets, capabilities and weaknesses. Regional innovation paths depend on deep-rooted territorial elements such as history, culture, and learning processes (see Chapter 3 by Blažek and Morgan (2019)). In addition, RIS3 can be seen as a wicked game played by the different regional, national, and international actors in which some actors define the rules (see Chapter 4 by Mäenpää and Lundström (2019)).

Many scholars have been critical of the implementation of S3. According to Marques and Morgan (2018), S3 is based on many implicit heroic assumptions that might limit its impact, especially in less developed regions with low institutional capacity. It places enormous demands on the stakeholders involved in it, especially the public sector organisations with the key role in the programme design. The state is supposed to be smart enough, but it is often not flexible and ready to adopt experimentation. A triple-helix coalition is assumed to be in place, but in reality, the partners may not be cooperating. Radosevic (2017a) concludes case studies on the implementation of S3 by remarking that the experimental nature of the EDP is repressed by political and administrative requirements. The practices of the European Commission and regions are difficult to adapt to those required by the EDP. Even if the initial selection processes have applied experimentation, implementation is often run as a conventional public funding programme.

The EDP and smart specialisation are arguably unique and creative concepts in that they combine the development of a regional economy with policies, as well as regional priority-setting with the idea of market processes. EDP theory addresses the criticism of RIS since the starting point is regional economic growth and the search for growth areas in which innovations could emerge. In this way EDP theory opens the black box between innovation and growth that RIS fails to.

However, some of the criticism of the EDP is compelling, especially as regards the role of formal and informal institutions and the different contexts of the EDP and its performance. In spite of this criticism we would like to emphasise the advantages of having a common policy approach, because it provides for a common framework for transnational learning (Mariussen and Virkkala, 2013). Some of the policy-related features are similar across regions whereas others are unique to specific regions (McCann and Ortega-Argilés, 2017). The smart specialisation agenda includes advanced knowledge-sharing on regional innovation and development policies in the EU with the help of the S3 platform to enable policy learning (Kroll, 2015). Chapter 11 (Mariussen et al., 2019) documents how the smart specialisation platform aims to help regions and Member States to prioritise and align efforts between public and private stakeholders.

We also suggest some new challenges. The first one is to transform the static structure into a more complex and dynamic process by moving attention from the micro level to the macro level. This process is necessary for the transformation of the regional economy and will be discussed with reference to complexity perspectives in Chapter 7 by Aasen (2019) and in Chapter 9 by Virkkala and Mariussen (2019).

The second challenge is related to the concept of knowledge used in the EDP. Foray (2015) does not discuss sufficiently the role of tacit knowledge and knowledge conversion in entrepreneurial discoveries. Foray asserts that entrepreneurial knowledge is an aggregate of the knowledge possessed by different entrepreneurial actors – however, knowledge is not only aggregate; it should also be processed, combined with other knowledge, and absorbed and assimilated so it may be used as an outcome of the EDP. This knowledge-creation, conversion, and translation process is an interaction process between tacit and codified knowledge, and individuals and organisations. This book seeks to broaden the concept of entrepreneurial knowledge and discovery by placing the EDP in the framework of organisational knowledge-creation theories. All knowledge depends on preconceptions, and the knowledge process can be seen as a process of sense-making. The knowledge process will be discussed further in Chapters 5, 7, and 8 (by Lam; Aasen; Virkkala (2019), respectively), and illustrated in several case chapters.

The third challenge is to combine the strengths of place-based development with emerging European-level thematic partnerships. This means enlarging the field of self-discovery from regional-level entrepreneurial actors to the European level. The entrepreneurial actors of different regions will collaborate in broader transnational and macro-regional strategic frameworks. As the EDP is transforming a regional economy and strengthening the RIS, the newly discovered regional domains can be extended by opening the economy and connecting it to macro-regional and European knowledge networks and systems of innovation. In this way, the regional economy can grow as a part of a larger, stronger and more dynamic innovation system, and also be integrated into the European economy. This challenge is discussed in Chapter 11 by Mariussen et al. (2019).

1.5 Conclusion

The rapid translation into practice of theoretical ideas that are still in development sets challenges for implementation. However, the translation process might also provide an opportunity to develop theory in practice rather than as a linear leap from theory to practice without 'proof of concept' (Nauwelaers et al., 2015: 3).

This chapter has examined self-discovery as a process enabling EDP and the transition between knowledge exploitation and exploration. It examined the requirements of the regional actors involved in the EDP. It revealed the journey of the concepts of self and discovery from one of individual entrepreneurs discovering business opportunities owing to their alertness and incomplete information as proposed by Hayek and Kirzner to one based on the theory of self-discovery by Rodrik in the context of a national economy. Foray (2015) combined the notion of entrepreneurial discovery, the notion of self-discovery from new industrial policy from Rodrik, the ideas of experimentalist governance from Sabel, and the place-based strategies of Barca (2009) in the concept of the EDP. The EDP is a collective search of entrepreneurial actors (i.e. quadruple helix actors) for new future growth opportunities to support the development of regions (Table 1.3). It involves the

Table 1.3 Development of the concepts of 'discovery' and 'self'

	Discovery	*Self*	*Level, context*	*Aim*	*Policy*
Kirzner (1997)	Discovery of previously unknown profit opportunities	Individual entrepreneur	Market economy	Towards market balance with more information	Laissez-faire
Hausmann and Rodrik (2003)	Economic Self-discovery of latent competitive advantage	Firms and government together	National economy, development countries	Restructuring, beyond market forces; iterative process	New industrial policy: diversification; experimentation; non-neutral
Foray (2015)	Self-discovery of latent competitive advantage EDP	Entrepreneurial actors: firms, public, government, universities, civil society	Regions in knowledge economies; place-based development	Transformation of the regional economy	EU cohesion policy; regional innovation policy

Source: Authors' interpretation of Kirzner (1997), Hausmann and Rodrik (2003) and Foray (2015)

discovery of the business fields on which a region should construct its future in the knowledge economy. The EDP means a transition from the exploitation to the exploration of knowledge or to the creation of new knowledge. The EDP is a move from a state of knowledge and division of labour between actors, as in knowledge exploitation progressing towards exploration through a process of self-discovery, a new cognitive understanding of a region's opportunities, and the integration and translation of fragmented knowledge. The EDP can occur spontaneously in a decentralised way without any support. The entrepreneurs have a vision, and the discovery of a new domain and the integration of different types of knowledge can make that vision a reality. Nevertheless, policy support is often necessary, and the EDP is the core method in European cohesion policy. Some of the features of smart specialisation were practised implicitly by regional development policies searching for continuous renewal even before its official launch in 2014 as a cornerstone of EU cohesion policy.

The chapter compared the EDP and smart specialisation as a policy approach with the cluster theories and innovation system approaches. Cluster theories explain cluster life cycles; RIS theories explain how innovation emerges in interaction between actors; and smart specialisation clarifies how to create new business opportunities and transform a regional economy. Cluster policy promotes the development of clusters through education and infrastructure; RIS policy supports the governance of an innovation system with stronger connectivity between actors. S3 focuses on mobilising actors and aims to push the regional economy in the direction of exploration and economic growth. However, S3 and the EDP have been criticised for their too demanding assumptions, for placing too much emphasis on science and technology-led innovations, and for placing too little focus on institutional capacities.

References

Aasen, T.M. (2019). Approaching entrepreneurial discovery and knowledge conversion from a complexity perspective. In Mariussen, Å., Virkkala, S., Finne, H. and Aasen, T.M. (eds) *The entrepreneurial discovery process and regional development: New knowledge emergence, conversion and exploitation*. Abingdon: Routledge.

Aranguren, M.J., Navarro, M. and Wilson, J.R. (2017). From plan to process: Exploring the human element in smart specialisation governance. In McCann, P., Goddard, J. and van Oort, F. (eds) *The empirical and institutional dimensions of smart specialisation*, pp. 165–191. London: Routledge.

Asheim, B.T., Boschma, R. and Cooke, P. (2011). Constructing regional advantage: Platform policies based on related variety and differentiated knowledge bases. *Regional Studies*, 45 (7), pp. 893–904.

Asheim, B.T. and Gertler, M.S. (2005). The geography of innovation: Regional innovation systems. In Fagerberg, J., Mowery, D.C. and Nelson, R.R. (eds) *The Oxford handbook of innovation*, pp. 291–317. Oxford: Oxford University Press.

Barca, F. (2009). *An agenda for a reformed cohesion policy: A place-based approach to meeting European Union challenges and expectations*. Occasional report. Brussels: European Commission.

Barca, F., McCann, P. and Rodríguez-Pose, A. (2012). The case for regional development intervention: Place-based versus place-neutral approaches. *Journal of Regional Science*, 52 (1), pp. 134–152.

Benner, M. (2017). Smart specialisation and cluster emergence: Elements of evolutionary regional policies. In Fornahl, D. and Hassink, R. (eds) *The life cycle of clusters: A policy perspective*, pp. 151–172. Cheltenham: Edward Elgar.

Blažek, J. and Morgan, K. (2019). The institutional worlds of entrepreneurial discovery: Finding a place for less developed regions. In Mariussen, Å., Virkkala, S., Finne, H. and Aasen, T.M. (eds) *The entrepreneurial discovery process and regional development: New knowledge emergence, conversion and exploitation*. Abingdon: Routledge.

Boschma, R. (2017). Regional diversification and smart specialisation policy. In McCann, P., van Oort, F. and Goddard, J. (eds) *The empirical and institutional dimensions of smart specialisation*, pp. 23–38. London: Routledge.

Camagni, R. and Capello, R. (2013). Regional innovation patterns and the EU regional policy reform: Toward smart innovation policies. *Growth and Change*, 44 (2), pp. 355–389.

Capello, R. and Lenzi, C. (2013). Territorial patterns of innovation and economic growth in European regions. *Growth and Change*, 44 (2), pp. 195–227.

Charles, D. and Ciampi Stancova, K. (2017). Entrepreneurial discovery process and research and technology organisations. In Kyriakou, D., Martínez, M.P., Periáñez-Forte, I. and Rainoldi, A. (eds) *Governing smart specialisation*, pp. 80–94. London: Routledge.

Cooke, P. (2012). *Complex adaptive innovation systems: Relatedness and transversality in the evolving region*. Milton Park: Routledge.

Cooke, P., Heidenreich, M. and Braczyk, H.-J. (eds) (2004). *Regional innovation systems: The role of governance in a globalized world*, 2nd ed. London: Routledge.

Doloreux, D. and Porto Gomez, I. (2017). A review of (almost) 20 years of regional innovation systems research. *European Planning Studies*, 25 (3), pp. 371–387.

EC-JRC (2017). *Entrepreneurial discovery process – EDP*. Sevilla: European Commission. Available: http://s3platform.jrc.ec.europa.eu/entrepreneurial-discovery-edp [Accessed 16 June 2018].

Estensoro, M. and Larrea, M. (2016). Overcoming policy making problems in smart specialization strategies: Engaging subregional governments. *European Planning Studies*, 24 (7), pp. 1319–1335.

Etzkowitz, H. and Leydesdorff, L. (2000). The dynamics of innovation: From national systems and 'Mode 2' to a triple helix of university–industry–government relations. *Research Policy*, 29 (2), pp. 109–123.

Finne, H. and Aasen, T.M. (2019). The bond, the bridge and the broker: Knowledge conversion in the university–industry nexus. In Mariussen, Å., Virkkala, S., Finne, H. and Aasen, T.M. (eds) *The entrepreneurial discovery process and regional development: New knowledge emergence, conversion and exploitation*. Abingdon: Routledge.

Foray, D. (2015). *Smart specialisation: Opportunities and challenges for regional innovation policy*. London: Routledge.

Foray, D. (2016). On the policy space of smart specialization strategies. *European Planning Studies*, 24 (8), pp. 1428–1437.

Foray, D. (2017). The economic fundamentals of smart specialization strategies. In Radosevic, S., Curaj, A., Gheorghiu, R., Andreescu, L. and Wade, I. (eds) *Advances in the theory and practice of smart specialization*, pp. 38–50. London: Academic Press.

Foray, D., David, P.A. and Hall, B.H. (2009). Smart specialisation – the concept. *Knowledge Economists Policy Brief*. Brussels: European Commission.

Foray, D., Goddard, J., Goenaga Beldarrain, X., Landabaso, M., McCann, P., Morgan, K., Nauwelaers, C. and Ortega-Argilés, R. (2012). *Guide to research and innovation strategies for smart specialisation (RIS 3)*. Occasional report. [Sevilla]: European Commission.

Gianelle, C., Kyriakou, D., Cohen, C. and Przeor, M. (eds) (2016). *Implementing smart specialisation: A handbook*. Brussels: European Commission.

Goddard, J., Kempton, L. and Vallance, P. (2013). Universities and smart specialisation: Challenges, tensions and opportunities for the innovation strategies of European regions. *Ekonomiaz*, (83), pp. 82–101.

Grillo, F. (2017). Structuring the entrepreneurial discovery process to promote private–public sector engagement. In Kyriakou, D., Martínez, M.P., Periáñez-Forte, I. and Rainoldi, A. (eds) *Governing smart specialisation*, pp. 62–79. London; New York: Routledge.

Hausmann, R., Hidalgo, C.A., Bustos, S., Coscia, M., Chung, S., Jimenez, J., Simoes, A. and Yıldırım, M.A. (2011). *The atlas of economic complexity: Mapping paths to prosperity*. Cambridge, MA: Harvard University, Center for International Development.

Hausmann, R. and Rodrik, D. (2003). Economic development as self-discovery. *Journal of Development Economics*, 72 (2), pp. 603–633.

Hayek, F.A.v. (1945). The use of knowledge in society. *American Economic Review*, 35 (4), pp. 519–530.

Hayek, F.A.v. (1978). Competition as a discovery procedure. In Hayek, F.A.v. (ed.) *New studies in philosophy, politics, economics, and the history of ideas*, pp. 179–190. Chicago: University of Chicago Press.

Healy, A. (2016). Smart specialization in a centralized state: Strengthening the regional contribution in North East Romania. *European Planning Studies*, 24 (8), pp. 1527–1543.

Isaksen, A., Kyllingstad, N., Rypestøl, J.O. and Schulze-Krogh, A.C. (2019). Entrepreneurial discovery processes in different regional contexts: A conceptual discussion. In Mariussen, Å., Virkkala, S., Finne, H. and Aasen, T.M. (eds) *The entrepreneurial discovery process and regional development: New knowledge emergence, conversion and exploitation*. Abingdon: Routledge.

Kirzner, I.M. (1973). *Competition and entrepreneurship*. Chicago; London: University of Chicago Press.

Kirzner, I.M. (1997). Entrepreneurial discovery and the competitive market process: An Austrian approach. *Journal of Economic Literature*, 35 (1), pp. 60–85.

Kroll, H. (2015). Efforts to implement smart specialization in practice—Leading unlike horses to the water. *European Planning Studies*, 23 (10), pp. 2079–2098.

Kuznetsov, Y. and Sabel, C. (2017). Managing self-discovery: Diagnostic monitoring of a portfolio of projects and programs. In Radosevic, S., Curaj, A., Gheorghiu, R., Andreescu, L. and Wade, I. (eds) *Advances in the theory and practice of smart specialization*, pp. 51–72. London: Academic Press.

Lam, A. (2019). Career mobility, hybridity and knowledge combination: A 'third space' perspective. In Mariussen, Å., Virkkala, S., Finne, H. and Aasen, T.M. (eds) *The entrepreneurial discovery process and regional development: New knowledge emergence, conversion and exploitation*. Abingdon: Routledge.

Leydesdorff, L. and Etzkowitz, H. (1998). The Triple Helix as a model for innovation studies. *Science and Public Policy*, 25 (3), pp. 195–203.

March, J.G. (1991). Exploration and exploitation in organizational learning. *Organization Science*, 2 (1), pp. 71–87.

Mariussen, Å., Hegyi, F.B. and Rakhmatullin, R. (2019). Smart specialisation: Interregional learning via thematic partnerships. In Mariussen, Å., Virkkala, S., Finne, H.

and Aasen, T.M. (eds) *The entrepreneurial discovery process and regional development: New knowledge emergence, conversion and exploitation*. Abingdon: Routledge.

Mariussen, Å. and Virkkala, S. (eds) (2013). *Learning transnational learning*. Abingdon: Routledge.

Marques, P. and Morgan, K. (2018). The heroic assumptions of smart specialisation: A sympathetic critique of regional innovation policy. In Isaksen, A., Martin, R. and Trippl, M. (eds) *New avenues for regional innovation systems: Theoretical advances, empirical cases and policy lessons*, pp. 275–293. Cham: Springer International Publishing.

McCann, P. and Ortega-Argilés, R. (2013). Modern regional innovation policy. *Cambridge Journal of Regions, Economy and Society*, 6 (2), pp. 187–216.

McCann, P. and Ortega-Argilés, R. (2017). The intellectual and practical bases of the application of RIS3 within EU cohesion policy. In McCann, P., van Oort, F. and Goddard, J. (eds) *The empirical and institutional dimensions of smart specialisation*, pp. 8–22. London: Routledge.

Morgan, K. (2015). Smart specialisation: Opportunities and challenges for regional innovation policy. *Regional Studies*, 49 (3), pp. 480–482.

Morgan, K. (2017a). Nurturing novelty: Regional innovation policy in the age of smart specialisation. *Environment and Planning C: Politics and Space*, 35 (4), pp. 569–583.

Morgan, K. (2017b). Speaking truth to power: The political dynamics of public sector innovation. In Kyriakou, D., Martínez, M.P., Periáñez-Forte, I. and Rainoldi, A. (eds) *Governing smart specialisation*, pp. 49–61. London: Routledge.

Mäenpää, A. and Lundström, N. (2019). Entrepreneurial discovery processes through a wicked game approach: Civil society engagement as a possibility for exploration. In Mariussen, Å., Virkkala, S., Finne, H. and Aasen, T.M. (eds) *The entrepreneurial discovery process and regional development: New knowledge emergence, conversion and exploitation*. Abingdon: Routledge.

Nauwelaers, C., Magro, E., Aranguren, M.J., Navarro, M., Wilson, J., Trippl, M., Hansen, T., Grillitsch, M., Blažek, J., Morgan, K. and Healy, A. (2015). *Underpinning effective strategy design*. Research Working Paper. [Cardiff]: [Cardiff University].

Nguyen, N. and Mariussen, Å. (2019). Moving beyond related variety: Creating firm-level ambidexterity for economic growth via the entrepreneurial discovery process. In Mariussen, Å., Virkkala, S., Finne, H. and Aasen, T.M. (eds) *The entrepreneurial discovery process and regional development: New knowledge emergence, conversion and exploitation*. Abingdon: Routledge.

Radosevic, S. (2017a). Advancing theory and practice of smart specialisation: Key messages. In Radosevic, S., Curaj, A., Gheorghiu, R., Andreescu, L. and Wade, I. (eds) *Advances in the theory and practice of smart specialization*, pp. 345–355. London: Academic Press.

Radosevic, S. (2017b). Assessing EU smart specialization policy in a comparative perspective. In Radosevic, S., Curaj, A., Gheorghiu, R., Andreescu, L. and Wade, I. (eds) *Advances in the theory and practice of smart specialization*, pp. 1–36. London: Academic Press.

Rinkinen, S. and Harmaakorpi, V. (2017). The business ecosystem concept in innovation policy context: Building a conceptual framework. *Innovation: The European Journal of Social Science Research*, pp. 1–17.

Rodríguez-Pose, A. and Wilkie, C. (2017). Institutions and the entrepreneurial discovery process for smart specialization. In Kyriakou, D., Martínez, M.P., Periáñez-Forte, I. and Rainoldi, A. (eds) *Governing smart specialisation*, pp. 34–48. London: Routledge.

Rodrik, D. (2004). *Industrial policy for the twenty-first century*. Faculty Research Working Papers Series. Cambridge, MA: Harvard University, John F. Kennedy School of Government.
Rodrik, D. (2007). *One economics, many recipes: Globalization, institutions and economic growth*. Princeton: Princeton University Press.
Rodrik, D. (2014). Green industrial policy. *Oxford Review of Economic Policy*, 30 (3), pp. 469–491.
Sabel, C.F. (1993). *Learning by monitoring: The institutions of economic development*. [CLES-CUSL] Working paper 102. Cambridge, MA: MIT.
Sabel, C.F. and Zeitlin, J. (2010). Learning from difference: The new architecture of experimentalist governance in the EU. In Sabel, C.F. and Zeitlin, J. (eds) *Experimentalist governance in the European Union: Towards a new architecture*, pp. 1–28. Oxford: Oxford University Press.
Schumpeter, J.A. (1934). *The theory of economic development: An inquiry into profits, capital, credit, interest, and the business cycle*. Cambridge, MA: Harvard University Press.
Shane, S. (2003). *A general theory of entrepreneurship: The individual–opportunity nexus*. Northampton, MA: Edward Elgar.
Sotarauta, M. and Pulkkinen, R. (2011). Institutional entrepreneurship for knowledge regions: In search of a fresh set of questions for regional innovation studies. *Environment and Planning C: Government and Policy*, 29 (1), pp. 96–112.
Tödtling, F. (2011). Endogenous approaches to local and regional development policy. In Pike, A., Rodríguez-Pose, A. and Tomaney, J. (eds) *Handbook of local and regional development*, pp. 333–343. London: Routledge.
Virkkala, S. (2019). Entrepreneurial discovery processes, knowledge creation and knowledge space. In Mariussen, Å., Virkkala, S., Finne, H. and Aasen, T.M. (eds) *The entrepreneurial discovery process and regional development: New knowledge emergence, conversion and exploitation*. Abingdon: Routledge.
Virkkala, S. and Mariussen, Å. (2019). Emergence of new business areas in regional economies through entrepreneurial discovery processes. In Mariussen, Å., Virkkala, S., Finne, H. and Aasen, T.M. (eds) *The entrepreneurial discovery process and regional development: New knowledge emergence, conversion and exploitation*. Abingdon: Routledge.
Virkkala, S., Mäenpää, A. and Mariussen, Å. (2017). A connectivity model as a potential tool for smart specialization strategies. *European Planning Studies*, 25 (4), pp. 661–679.
Wenger, E. (1998). *Communities of practice: Learning, meaning, and identity*. Cambridge: Cambridge University Press.

2 Entrepreneurial discovery processes in different regional contexts

A conceptual discussion

Arne Isaksen, Nina Kyllingstad, Jan Ole Rypestøl and Ann Camilla Schulze-Krogh

2.1 Introduction

The need for creating more jobs to fight unemployment and social exclusion is evident in nearly all countries and regions in Europe and beyond. The question of how growth and jobs can be created by politics is high on the research agenda. One recent answer to the need of new jobs is the creation of new industrial paths (Martin and Sunley, 2006; Dawley, 2014; Isaksen and Trippl, 2016). The chapter departs from this approach. It contributes, however, to the literature by focusing on how different types of entrepreneurs through entrepreneurial discovery processes can impact on specific path developments in different regional settings.

A regional industrial path contains a set of firms in a region that are related through a value chain, joint input factors or utilisation of similar technologies. Firms' activities are supported by a regional innovation system of knowledge organisations and formal and informal institutions and/or are linked to extra-regional knowledge sources (Binz et al., 2015). An industrial path lasts for some time as these are characterised by the persistence of regional industrial or institutional structures, and by the fact that economic agents continue their behaviour under changing external conditions (Henning et al., 2013: 1352).

New growth paths start, according to Foray (2015: 23–24), by an entrepreneurial discovery made by an individual entrepreneur, a firm, a regional leader and so on. The discovery includes, for example, an innovation or an institutional change. 'Entrepreneurial discovery is the essential phase, the decisive link that allows the system to reorient and renew itself' (Foray, 2014: 495). Entrepreneurial discovery processes also contain the demonstration by an entrepreneur or a firm that, for example, a new production process is possible. Demonstration supports the spillover of the entrepreneurial knowledge to more economic actors, the entry and agglomeration of similar and complementary firms, and as a result some form of industrial and structural changes that can stimulate new growth paths (Foray, 2014). If we extend this line of thinking, a successful entrepreneurial discovery will result in the creation of new knowledge for a region, which can initiate completely new economic activities, modernise existing ones, and further development of the regional innovation system.

Two understandings of the entrepreneurial discovery process (EDP) can be distinguished. These are first *spontaneous* processes that take place without any conscious policy, and, second, organised and managed processes as part of smart specialisation policy initiatives. Foray (2014) presents some historical examples of regional structural changes that illustrate spontaneous entrepreneurial discovery processes. The examples resulted in 'the entry and agglomeration of firms around the new activity' (Foray, 2014: 493) that is 'the formation of regional concentration of co-located activities and resources in related fields' (Foray, 2014: 489). This chapter focuses on spontaneous entrepreneurial discovery processes and regards the achievement of cluster projects approved and financed by Innovation Norway as one result of this process. Knowledge of spontaneous EDPs can provide important information to the organisation and implementation of planned processes as part of regional smart specialisation initiatives.

In addition to firm entrepreneurs, other actors can be included in the entrepreneurial discovery process. A discovery that eventually leads to new activities and system changes can be made, individually and/or collectively, by actors (including entrepreneurs), firms, organisations (such as universities), and agencies (for example regional development agencies). The importance of these actors is assumed to differ between regions. We also expect the entrepreneurial discovery process to occur in different ways and to different extents in various regions. This reflects the fact that 'in general, entrepreneurial discoveries relate to existing structures and local knowledge' (Foray, 2014: 498). Rodríguez-Pose and Wilkie (2015) also argue that formal and informal institutions represent the context within which entrepreneurial discovery and economic activity occur. As 'informal institutions are context and geography specific' (Rodríguez-Pose, 2013: 1040), they vary across regions. A region with 'a sound institutional context seemingly provides the optimal setting for the entrepreneurial discovery process' (Rodríguez-Pose and Wilkie, 2015: 20). When institutions are well functioning, entrepreneurial discovery occurs more or less automatically, i.e. not hampered by institutional constraint (Rodríguez-Pose and Wilkie, 2015). Weak institutional contexts, on the other hand, hardly support entrepreneurial discoveries.

This chapter aims to contribute to the existing literature on entrepreneurial discoveries and regional industrial development in three ways. First, it aims for a better understanding of how different regional contexts affect entrepreneurial discoveries, the entrepreneurial process, and outcomes. Second, the chapter links conceptually regional contexts, entrepreneurial discovery processes, and regional industrial path development. Third, it tries out *one* approach for studying entrepreneurial discoveries by focusing on key actors and regional innovation system changes that initiate cluster building processes. We use the regional innovation system (RIS) concept to characterise different types of regional contexts, while the notion of entrepreneurial discovery process introduces a dynamic element. EDPs need to be institutionalised in different ways through the support of RISs to be able to lead to path changes. EDPs will, however, also trigger changes in RISs, such as the emergence of new firms and possibly new supporting institutions. Thus, the two concepts may complement each other.

The rest of the chapter is organised as follows: section 2.2 discusses and links the three main theoretical building blocks of the chapter: entrepreneurial discovery, regional innovation system, and regional industrial path development. Section 2.3 presents the empirical context and data material for the empirical analysis of three emerging regional cluster projects in Norway. Section 2.4 examines the relevance of the conceptual framework developed in section 2.2 through empirical studies of the entrepreneurial discovery processes underlying the emergence of the three cluster projects. Section 2.5 concludes by discussing general theoretical lessons from the study.

2.2 Theoretical background: regionally differentiated entrepreneurial discovery processes

This section proposes an analytical framework that links regional context, entrepreneurial discovery processes and regional industrial path development. The framework advances the idea that entrepreneurial discovery processes occur differently and tend to result in different outcomes in specific types of regional contexts.

Entrepreneurial discovery processes

Entrepreneurial discoveries are traditionally understood as individual entrepreneurs' actions in competitive markets. The discovery process is then characterised by 'routine-resisting' and risk-taking entrepreneurs who discover and anticipate opportunities for profit that appear in a market (Kirzner, 1997). The first-comers, however, meet competition from other entrepreneurs. The entrepreneurs challenge others in terms of offering the best products in rivalrous processes and are dependent on 'the incentives provided by the possibility of pure entrepreneurial profit' (Kirzner, 1997: 73).

Debates about entrepreneurship and innovation activity in the 1980s and 1990s contributed to a change in the understanding of entrepreneurial discovery processes *from* being driven by individual firm entrepreneurs *to* also including social and economic structures surrounding entrepreneurship and innovation (Lundvall, 1992; 2007; Porter, 1998; Spigel and Harrison, 2017). We draw two lessons from this interpretation of entrepreneurship that are particularly relevant for the conceptual framework in this chapter: first, that a number of contextual factors affect entrepreneurship processes; and, second, that entrepreneurship is also performed by actors other than those individuals who establish new firms or substantially change existing firms. The first understanding corresponds to Spigel's (2013) pointing out that 'entrepreneurship is a social endeavour embedded in multiple cultural and economic contexts' (p. 804), and that 'entrepreneurs largely draw on local resources as they start and grow their firms' (p. 807). We use the well-established concept of regional innovation system to examine the importance of contextual factors for entrepreneurial discoveries, as further developed below.

It follows from the first point that entrepreneurship involves more actors than those who start new firms or initiate innovation activities in existing firms. The entrepreneurial discovery phase and the following process can also include actors that provide complementary assets, develop innovation support structures, are demanding customers and so on (Garud and Karnøe, 2003).

In line with the notion that different types of actors can partake in the entrepreneurial discovery processes, we distinguish analytically between two types of entrepreneurs, i.e. firm-level entrepreneurs and system-level entrepreneurs. Firm-level entrepreneurs are individuals who start new innovative firms or who carry out innovation activities in existing firms. System-level entrepreneurs, on the other hand, are able to change the framework conditions or the 'wider settings' (Edquist, 2005) that affect industrial development within a specific region and industry. System-level entrepreneurs are quite similar to what, among others, Sotarauta and Pulkkinen (2011) denote as institutional entrepreneurs, who are individuals, organisations or groups of actors who 'mobilize resources, competence, and power to create new institutions or to transform existing institutions' (Sotarauta and Pulkkinen, 2011: 98). Institutions, in the meaning of 'taken-for-granted, culturally embedded understandings' (Garud et al., 2007: 958) change slowly and thus tend to support the continuity of industry. Institutional entrepreneurs may be of different types, such as policy-makers, politicians, university leaders and firm leaders. A common characteristic is 'capacity to reflect and act in ways other than those prescribed by taken-for-granted rules' (p. 961). This means that the role of both institutional entrepreneurs and our system-level entrepreneurs, in an entrepreneurial discovery process, is to change how the regional innovation system works.

Regional innovation systems and system-level entrepreneurs

Our outlining of the concept of system-level entrepreneurs departs from the regional innovation system (RIS) approach. An RIS consists of two subsystems underpinned by an institutional infrastructure (Asheim and Isaksen, 2002; Tödtling and Trippl, 2005). The subsystems contain a region's industry (firms, entrepreneurs, clusters) and its knowledge infrastructure of universities, R&D institutes, incubators and so on. The institutional infrastructure includes 'formal regulations, legislation, and economic systems as well as informal societal norms' (Gertler, 2004: 7) that stimulate or hamper knowledge flow and innovation cooperation within and between actors in the subsystems.

Regional innovation systems support innovation and competitiveness of key regional industries. But strong RISs are also 'prone to lock-in and path dependency and largely geared to generate incremental innovations and gradual change' (Boschma et al., 2017: 36). Following this line of thought, strong RISs often hamper entrepreneurship in new areas for a region. We therefore argue that entrepreneurial discovery processes that support new, emerging, and transformed industries need both firm-level entrepreneurs and adaption, and development of regional innovation systems. If an entrepreneurial discovery is to result in new growth paths, the innovation system has to be developed and better adapted to the need of new activities. This also means that EDPs can lead to changes in RISs as RISs respond to new industry needs.

In principle, reconfiguration of RISs to support entrepreneurship and innovation in new, regional industries developed through entrepreneurial discovery processes can be of three main types (Miörner and Trippl, 2017). First, new institutions, organisations and policy instruments can be created (layering); second, existing institutions, organisations and policy instruments can be adapted to fit better emerging industries (adaptation); and third, existing institutions, organisations and policy instruments can be used in new ways (novel application). We interpret system-level entrepreneurs as individuals or organisations who are able to bring about such changes in RISs.[1] In this line of thought, spontaneously emerging growth paths or major path changes are initiated by firm-level entrepreneurs who introduce new activities in a region *at the same time as* the innovation system is further developed or restructured by system-level entrepreneurs.

The literature contends that different types of RISs have different potential for supporting entrepreneurship and innovation in new areas (Isaksen and Trippl, 2016). The potential depends in particular on the learning opportunities stemming from combinations of different types of knowledge, which is supported by cognitive and geographical proximity between actors (Frenken et al., 2007). The chapter distinguishes three types of RISs that are supposed to have different potential for interactive learning, entrepreneurship and innovation. The distinction applies to the number and variety of RIS actors: firms, industries, and knowledge and support organisations present in a region. This decides the number of regional actors with different knowledge that *can* participate in knowledge exchange and entrepreneurial discovery processes.

The three different types of RISs include organisationally thick and diversified RISs, organisationally thick and specialised RISs, and organisationally thin RISs (Isaksen and Trippl, 2016). Organisationally thick and diversified RISs are characterised by the presence of a relatively large number of different firms, a heterogeneous industrial structure and a number of knowledge and supporting organisations that facilitate innovation in different economic and technological fields. This type of RIS is most often found in large core regions such as metropolitan areas and advanced technology regions.

Organisationally thick and specialised RISs host strong clusters in one or a few industries only, and knowledge and support organisations are first of all tailored to their narrow industrial base. These RISs are typical for old industrial areas and industrial districts. Compared with thick and diversified, these RISs are supposed to have poorer conditions for entrepreneurial discoveries and more possibilities for lock-in of existing industrial strongholds (Grabher, 1993). Organisationally thin RISs have only a few knowledge and support organisations and none or weakly developed clusters. Such characteristics are often found in peripheral regions. Because of relatively few local actors and little local knowledge flow, actors with external knowledge links or in-migrants are assumed to be important in entrepreneurial discovery processes in organisationally thin RISs.

Path development

The third building block in the analytical framework includes possible outcomes of the entrepreneurial discovery in the form of different regional industrial paths. Path development theory maintains that future industrial development follows certain pathways anchored in and influenced by history (Arthur, 1989; Martin and Sunley, 2006). This chapter distinguishes three different paths: path extension, path diversification and path creation[2] (Neffke et al., 2011; Isaksen, 2015).

Regional path extension consists of 'incremental product and process innovations in existing industry and along prevailing technological paths' (Isaksen, 2015: 587). Because of the lack of inflow of new, supplementary knowledge, the innovation potential of a regional industry can gradually drop to a level where the industry may stagnate, decline and eventually disappear (Martin, 2010; Tödtling and Trippl, 2013).

Two types of new path developments are pinpointed here: path diversification and path creation. Regional industrial path diversification consists of industries branching into new, but related sectors (Boschma and Frenken, 2011). This industrial mutation process is based on the linking of knowledge and skills in different existing firms and industries, which results in new, economic relevant knowledge. Existing resources and technology enable and restrain the possible outcome of the path diversification, and regions are therefore 'most likely to branch into industries that are technological related to the pre-existing industries in the regions' (Neffke et al., 2011: 237).

The most comprehensive method of regional industrial change is the creation of a new regional industry. New regional paths can develop when firms and industries are transplanted into a new region, or through the commercialisation of knowledge and competence already developed and existing in the region (Tödtling and Trippl, 2013). One should, however, also account for the fact that entrepreneurs and firms can come up with radical new ideas that do not relate to prior knowledge and skills in a region. As discussed above, such ideas still have to meet some kind of support in the existing or updated regional innovation system to initiate a totally new regional industrial path.

Analytical framework

Table 2.1 links the three conceptual building blocks. RISs characterise the regional context into three main types; entrepreneurial discovery processes can trigger changes in RISs through the activities of firm-level and system-level entrepreneurs, and the outcome can be different types of path development that vary between RISs. Empirical studies point to the fact that thick and diversified RISs demonstrate considerable economic dynamism and high rates of firm formations compared with the two other regional types (Feldman and Audretsch, 1999; Duranton and Puga, 2002; Fritsch, 2011). In thick and diversified RISs we therefore expect firm-level entrepreneurs to initiate lots of entrepreneurial discoveries, in the form of creating new firms or innovation activity in existing firms. Regions with thin RISs are far less dynamic (Petrov, 2011). They generally have fewer innovative new firms than thicker RISs (Fritsch, 2011), and we therefore expect system-level entrepreneurs, such as actors in the support system, to be relatively more important in thin, and also in specialised, RISs compared with the thick and diversified ones.

The RIS changes can be of two main types. First, it may involve new or changed organisations, i.e. the establishment of new organisations (such as an incubator) or changes within existing organisations (such as a new study programme) (Miörner and Trippl, 2017). A second type is new or changed relations between the organisations, such as increased knowledge flow and interactive learning between firms and universities (Lundvall, 2007).

Thick and diversified RISs have a variety of knowledge actors and firms. However, a fragmented and complex system may hamper knowledge flow (Tödtling and Trippl, 2005). The strengthening of knowledge links is therefore particularly relevant in thick and diversified RISs. This also applies in thick and specialised and thin RISs, in which knowledge links to extra-regional actors are particularly important (Tödtling and Trippl, 2005). Thin and thick and specialised RISs have by definition few knowledge organisations or organisations within a narrow area of knowledge. Increased regional knowledge exchange then demands new and/or adapted knowledge-creating and diffusion organisations, while such organisations, as said, are more often already in place in thick and diverse regions.

The entrepreneurial discovery process can lead to different regional industrial path development in the three types of regions. Thick and diversified RISs are best suited to support path creation, while the two other types of RIS primarily strengthen path extension (Isaksen and Trippl, 2016). The analytical framework in Table 2.1 guides the empirical investigations of entrepreneurial discovery processes in three evolving cluster projects.

The investigation of the three cluster projects aims to explore the relevance and usefulness of the conceptual framework in Table 2.1 in empirical studies. The objective is not to assess if, for example, entrepreneurial discovery processes are initiated by system-level entrepreneurs in all thin RISs, but rather consider to what extent firm- and system-level entrepreneurs are useful conceptual categories in empirical studies of EDPs. The result of this 'empirical test' can be that the conceptual framework is a useful starting point to study entrepreneurial discovery processes in different regional contexts, or that the framework needs to be revised to a greater or lesser extent in coming, related studies.

Table 2.1 Linking the different types of RIS, entrepreneurial discoveries and regional industrial path development

Type of RIS	*Characteristics of spontaneous entrepreneurial discovery processes*		*Possible regional industrial path development*
	Key entrepreneurs	*RIS changes*	
Thick/diversified	↓ Increasing importance of system-level entrepreneurs	↓ Increasing importance of new and adapted knowledge-creating and diffusion organisations	Path creation and diversification
Thick/specialised			Path extension and diversification
Thin			Path extension

Source: Own elaboration

Based on this line of thought, three types of question for the empirical analyses of the evolving cluster projects emerge from the conceptual framework:

1. Is the distinction between firm- and system-level entrepreneurs useful, and do system-level entrepreneurs tend to be increasingly important for EDPs in thin versus thick RISs?
2. Is the establishment of new knowledge-creating and diffusion organisations vital in distinguishing between entrepreneurial discovery processes in various RISs? Does the establishment of such organisations tend to be increasingly important in thin versus thick RISs?
3. Is it useful to explore possible outcomes of entrepreneurial discovery processes by the approach of different path developments? If so, do path changes tend to be less radical in thin versus thick RISs?

The reasons for choosing the study objects and how the empirical studies have taken place are justified below.

2.3 Context and method

The chapter aims to test and possibly further develop the conceptual framework by use of relevant empirical data. The data should ideally include examples of entrepreneurial discovery processes in the three types of RISs discussed above. Based on former research on the development of regional clusters in Norway, we decided to study the growth of three so-called Arena cluster projects as possible manifestations of entrepreneurial discovery processes.

The Arena cluster initiative, which is part of the Norwegian Innovation Clusters programme run by Innovation Norway,[3] is designed to support the further development of immature clusters or agglomerations of firms that have the potential for increased competitiveness via cluster-building activities.[4] Emerging clusters achieve Arena status through an application to Innovation Norway, where just a few applicants succeed each year. The application requires a substantial local mobilisation of firms, and also often knowledge organisations. Local actors must agree on, commit to and start some common activities such as joint competence-building, marketing or innovation projects. The work by actors to obtain the status as an Arena cluster and the first cluster building was considered as possible materialisations of entrepreneurial discoveries (based on, amongst others, Holmen and Fosse, 2017).

The three selected Arena projects are located in different labour market regions that to some extent coincide with the three types of regional innovation systems described above. Oslo Edtech (education technology) is located in the thick and diversified Oslo region.[5] Oslo is by far the largest labour market region in Norway with just over 650,000 inhabitants. The region is specialised in knowledge-based services with location quotients around 2.4 in information and communication (section J in ISIC Rev. 4) and financial and insurance activities (section K), and about 1.7 in professional, scientific and technical activities, and real estate activities (sections M+N). The cluster organisation has about 40 members, which are mostly small and new firms that are developing new learning programmes (Table 2.2).

While the Oslo region definitely constitutes a thick and diverse RIS, the other two regions, Molde and Hamar, are more difficult to categorise. The traditional manufacturing industry region of Molde with 65,000 inhabitants is located on the west coast of Norway. The region is specialised in manufacturing (section C) with a location quotient of 1.5. Molde is part of Møre and Romsdal County. The county includes three university colleges (of which one has recently become part of the Norwegian University of Science and Technology NTNU in Trondheim), four R&D institutes, and five cluster projects in the Norwegian Innovation Cluster programme. Hamar, with about 91,000 inhabitants, is located in eastern Norway. Hamar has no distinct industrial specialisation beyond agriculture, forestry and fishing (section A) with a location quotient of 1.6. Hamar is part of Hedmark County. This county includes one university college, one research institute and one cluster project, i.e. Arena Heidner analysed in this chapter. Hedmark is thus much thinner than Møre and Romsdal regarding number of knowledge organisations and clusters. Actors in RISs often use extra-regional knowledge for innovation purposes. Firms in Hamar, such as those belonging to the Heidner cluster, can, and actually do, cooperate with knowledge organisations in the Oslo area. Molde is further away from Oslo, but geographically closer to the Norwegian 'technology capital' of Trondheim. All things together, we categorise Molde as part of a thick and specialised RIS and Hamar as part of a comparably thinner RIS.

The Arena cluster project iKuben in Molde includes nearly 40 firms in different sectors that aim to develop competence and activities within industrial internet including big data, sensors and automation (Table 2.2). The member firms are large, traditional manufacturing firms, new firms, the regional university college and a regional R&D institute. The core of Heidner in Hamar is three old, R&D-intensive firms that breed livestock and refine crops, plus three or four spinoffs from these – all with considerable international sales.

Table 2.2 Characteristics of the empirical cases

Cluster name	*Oslo Edtech*	*iKuben*	*Heidner*
Type of RIS	Thick and diversified	Specialised	Thinner
Main type of firms	New, small firms in an emerging industry	Cross-industry manufacturing firms introducing new technology	R&D-based, old agricultural firms and few spinoffs

Source: Own elaboration

The cluster organisation has nearly 40 members that include the value chain within agricultural production from R&D activity to the cooperative-owned manufacturers and market players.

The data material employed in the analyses of the entrepreneurial discovery processes in the clusters is of three types. First, we obtained available information about the clusters and their members from home pages, applications to the Arena cluster programme, newspaper articles and databases with firm figures. Second, and most important in this chapter, interviews were carried out with informants in Oslo Edtech (four), iKuben (four) and Heidner (five). The informants included persons actively involved in initiating the cluster projects and currently leading or participating in the projects. Several of the informants are also firm leaders. The interviews involved discussions about the emergence and running of the cluster projects, key persons involved in initiating the clusters, main activities performed and important changes in the activities of firms and knowledge organisations triggered by the cluster projects.

Third, an internet-based survey to firm members of the cluster organisations has been carried out to achieve additional information of firms' activities. It included questions about basic information about the firms, the firms' innovation activity and learning processes, the firms' use of the cluster organisations, and as regards new firms, questions about the entrepreneurs' education and former careers. Questionnaires were sent to 74 firm members of the three cluster organisations and we received 44 answers. The sample itself demonstrates a large difference between Oslo Edtech, dominated by new firms, and Heidner, with much fewer and older firms, while iKuben occupies a middle position.

2.4 Empirical analyses

Departing from the three cluster projects, we set out to explore who, firm-versus system-level entrepreneurs, initiated the cluster-building processes, before moving on to analysing the RIS changes and potential path development outcomes.

Initiating actors of the entrepreneurial discovery process

The Oslo Edtech cluster was initiated by ICT Norway (an interest organisation) and the leader of the StartupLab at Oslo Science Park. ICT Norway experienced a growing interest in educational technology, but because of the status as an interest organisation, it needed a platform where the 'the goal was to exploit the growing number of companies and their growth potential' (Firm L). In its early start Oslo Edtech saw the digital development within education as an opportunity for paving the way for a new industry in Norway, as '. . .many edtech firms came there [StartupLab], they saw the need to gather these' (Firm B). The vibrant and dynamic industrial structure in Oslo provided the foundation for establishing a business network in 2015 to '. . .support development, commercialisation and export of Norwegian educational technologies' (Oslo Edtech, 2017). Because of their motivation of creating opportunities for a new industry, initiators of Oslo Edtech functioned as system-level entrepreneurs.

The initiator of iKuben may be characterised as both a firm- and system-level entrepreneur. The initiator was the owner and leader of a local family firm that aimed to increase knowledge in a specific field by finding companies with similar challenges. Thus, unlike Oslo Edtech, the initial plan was not to create a cluster project, but rather to increase firm collaboration in the region. The initiator had experienced, through a network project organised by the large research institute SINTEF, how synergies can be created when firms share challenges and experiences with each other. The initiator was also the chairman of the board at Molde Industry Forum.[6] The cluster itself came about by slowly sharing the idea of the advantages of collaboration. In the words of the initiator: 'we continued to spread the idea in meetings with certain firms, who we considered to be firms we had an occupational, professional and close relationship with.' Since then, more and more actors joined the network and a cluster project started in 2012.

When it comes to Heidner, the initiators were leaders at the knowledge park and in established firms. Their main motivation was to revitalise and formalise already existing collaboration, making them system-level entrepreneurs. Prior to Heidner, the biotech milieu had an Arena project in 2003, and the rationale for sparking new life into old structures of collaboration was twofold. First, the region would benefit from a continuation and an extension of biotech knowledge-sourcing activities, and second, a new official cluster organisation would be able to once again apply for funding and other support from the Arena programme. As most of the invited firms shared a long history of formal and informal collaboration, all firms accepted the invitation to participate. Within a few months, the newly born official cluster applied for Arena status, which was granted in 2012.

Our cases demonstrate that the distinction between firm- and system-level entrepreneurs is applicable and relevant to employ in empirical studies, and entrepreneurs can be distinguished from their motivation and action. The distinction may help us substantiate our understanding of how entrepreneurial discovery processes start. System-level entrepreneurs are important initiators in all cases, while start-up entrepreneurs have been essential only in the Oslo Edtech case.

RIS changes

Beyond distinguishing between the initiating actors, the chapter explores whether we could find any changes in the regional innovation system that pertain to the establishment of new knowledge-creating and diffusion organisations or to new relations between organisations. The empirical studies registered RIS changes in all three cases. Most prominent in the Oslo Edtech cluster is the establishment of many new firms in a new industrial sector for the region. The survey shows that new edtech firms in Oslo are often small (with ten employees or fewer) and often have local entrepreneurs that already worked in the Oslo region. The entrepreneurs in general have higher education and various job backgrounds, but several come from the ICT or education sectors.

With regard to other RIS changes, the Oslo Edtech cluster organisation managed to make educational technology a prioritised area for innovation projects for the 2016–2019 period at the Regional Research Fund for the Capital region (Øygarden, 2010). The close proximity to, and collaboration with, the LearningLab of the Norwegian Business School (BI) seems to be an advantage for innovation processes in the firms. The survey also points to the importance of experience-based competence in the firms (ranked as very important for firms' core competence by 87 per cent of the respondents). The survey also points to high importance of ideas and knowledge from customers in innovation processes. The Oslo region is advantaged by proximity to many customers and good possibilities to recruit relevant workers.

iKuben firms have over time strengthened their collaboration with Molde University College. In the beginning of the collaboration in iKuben, one firm expresses that: 'in many ways [the University College] seemed more interesting to work with [. . .] an institute in Canada or someplace else in the world, rather than connecting to the regional business life. We [the cluster organisation] have challenged this a lot, to say the least' (Firm C). The cluster organisation also increased collaboration with other Norwegian clusters and in that process tried to develop their own special competence area in future business modelling (Firm C). The 'future business modelling' priority is supported and facilitated by the Protomore innovation lab, established on behalf of iKuben as an early prototype lab for innovative and emerging business ideas. 'Due to the downturn in the oil and gas sector, the need of restructuring is vast among our firms. At the same time, we face both digitalisation and green shifts. The lab is the most important thing we have at the moment' (Firm F). Since its establishment, the lab has hosted more than 60 workshops with more than 900 participants from the industry.

The iKuben cluster organisation has also contributed to increased collaboration between firms: 'even though we develop and deliver quite different products and services, . . . how we improve and develop our business models is as relevant for us as any other firm in the cluster' (Firm E). The collaboration materialised in ten cross-industry R&D projects during the cluster organisation's first year. One of the ideas behind the iKuben project portfolio was to create a 'bank of challenges' where all firms entered the challenges they thought might be suited for joint projects. Even so, the survey demonstrates that by far the most important knowledge sources in innovation processes are customers, which are most often national and international ones.

Heidner has a history from the 1960s of knowledge-sourcing activities and collaboration between firms' R&D departments, and core companies in

Heidner have developed spinoffs that deliver services to these firms (Firm G). The survey also demonstrates that Heidner firms are comparatively R&D-intensive, both through R&D activities in firms and through collaboration with universities, university colleges and R&D institutes.

The research-intensive firms in Heidner have been a major driving force in the development of research and education in biotechnology at the Hamar campus of the Innland Norway University of Applied Science. A result of the tight collaboration between the university and firms is the launch of a master's programme in industrial biotechnology, in which 'students base their thesis on industry-related challenges (and) will learn not only about applied biotech, but also about commercialisation and other business-related issues' (Firm K). Employees in local biotech firms contribute as supervisors for the master's students, and because many firms hold their own staff of researchers and PhD students, they add to the local academic milieu within the field.

Heidner firms often participate in projects with national and international universities, which have contributed to increase firms' national and international knowledge links. Finally, Heidner firms have increasingly linked their specific expertise to university research milieus at NTNU in Trondheim and the Norwegian University of Life Science close to Oslo. The cluster is also establishing links to a completely different field of gaming technology with a growing number of gaming firms in the Hamar region, and 'their advanced technology is used in several joint projects at the moment' (Firm H).

RIS changes are found in all three cases. These include in particular changes pertaining to the establishment of new knowledge-creating and diffusion organisations, exemplified by the Protomore Lab in iKuben and the industrial biotech master's programme in Heidner. The establishment of such organisations seems more important for iKuben and Heidner than for Oslo Edtech. This is because a relevant knowledge infrastructure, including the BI LearningLab, was already well established in Oslo, while more limited in the other two regions. Therefore, the major RIS change in the Oslo Edtech industry is a number of start-ups and the development of knowledge links between these and existing organisations.

Regional industrial path development

Finally, the empirical analyses deal with possible outcomes of the entrepreneurial discovery process in the three cases. We inquire if it is useful to explore the results of entrepreneurial discoveries as different path developments, and second, if our case study provides evidence to support the theoretically based suggestion that path changes are more radical in thicker RISs than in thinner RISs.

We find it useful to explore the result of entrepreneurial discovery processes as different path developments. This links to an emerging research area in the evolutionary economic geography field and adds a 'qualitative dimension' to the analysis. Rather than just registering a new cluster organisation, we can determine the significance of the entrepreneurial discovery process on the overall regional economy, for example the expansion of existing industry or greater renewal of the industrial structure. Above, we demonstrated that the RIS changes vary in their degree of radicalism between the three cases, as some changes involve more of the same while others include the establishment of new ventures within an industry not already present in the region.

Firms in the Oslo Edtech cluster are developing and introducing a new technology into a growing market. This market-expanding process has escalated into a regional agglomeration of related initiatives, including the creation of a supporting regional industrial infrastructure and policy support. The introduction and growth of the education technology milieu in Oslo indicates a possible start of new path creation in the region.

The cross-industry entrepreneurial discovery process of iKuben illustrates a more customer-driven process of innovation and change. Experiencing increased competition and more demanding customers, local, non-competing firms intensified their cross-industrial collaboration to share experiences and develop new knowledge to achieve improved quality and reduce costs, which mostly supports path extension. However, some of the recent partnership initiatives may result in more industry-renewing innovations and thus pave the way for regional industrial path diversification. The initiatives include collaborations focusing on the use of AR (augmented reality) and VR (virtual reality) technology in new and related areas.

Finally, the entrepreneurial discovery process at Heidner serves as an example of an industry path-extending initiative. The breeding of animals and plants is a time-consuming process evident from a long line of continuing minor adjustments. Building mainly on R&D-generated knowledge combinations, the cluster firms have worked together to make the various Norwegian species of animals and fish more resistant, more climate-friendly, more tailor-made to customers' needs, and to make the breeding process more streamlined and cost-efficient. Some new initiatives have been taken to merge new and unrelated gaming technology, but the practical use of this technology still focuses on the same fundamental question of how to make production more efficient and how to increase the quality of the breeding process.

Overall, the three empirical cases resonate well with the conceptual framework that indicates a possible relationship between regional thickness and diversity and radicalism of path changes.

2.5 Conclusions

This chapter describes in a conceptual way the links between different RISs, entrepreneurial discovery processes and new path development. The relevance of the analytical framework has been discussed through empirical studies of three Norwegian cluster building projects. The empirical discussion is guided by three sets of research questions emerging from the conceptual framework.

Regarding the first question, we find that the distinction between firm- and system-level entrepreneurs is productive in conceptual terms and in empirical studies. The cases demonstrate that system-level entrepreneurs have been vital for initiating the entrepreneurial discovery process in the iKuben and Heidner cases. The Oslo Edtech case has mostly firm-level entrepreneurs found in many start-up companies; however, it has also relied on system-level entrepreneurs to create an organisation that increases firm collaboration and obtains policy support. This may be a small reminder of the role of system-level entrepreneurs in entrepreneurial discoveries and cluster-building processes also in dynamic core regions, where the role of firm-level entrepreneurs as 'change makers' is often highlighted (Feldman et al., 2005).

Regarding the second question, we find that the establishment of new knowledge-creating and diffusion organisations is a distinguishing factor between the cases. New or adapted organisations are found in the Heidner and, in particular, in the iKuben case. This is in line with our conceptual framework. However, we do not claim that the establishment of new knowledge organisations is always less important in thick and diverse RISs. We rather argue that the establishment of new knowledge organisations can be one RIS change to focus on in future studies of entrepreneurial discovery processes in different regions. The RIS change in the Oslo Edtech case is, in particular, a number of new firms, and knowledge links between these and to existing knowledge organisations.

Regarding the final question, we find it useful to analyse potential regional industrial path development resulting from entrepreneurial discoveries because different path developments signify various 'qualitative changes' in the regional economy: the creation of new regional industries or the strengthening of existing ones. The case studies also point to more radical path changes in thick and diverse RISs compared with the other two RIS types, which follows the theoretical arguments.

A general theoretical lesson from the chapter is that many types of entrepreneurs and discoveries can lead to outcomes in terms of, e.g., cluster-building. However, we argue that entrepreneurial discoveries have to become institutionalised in order to result in a substantial industrial outcome. In our cases the entrepreneurial discovery processes are manifested through cluster formations and further development of the knowledge infrastructure. In this way the concepts of entrepreneurial discovery and regional innovation system supplement each other. This is justified by the fact that RIS is a rather static concept that characterises key elements of the innovation capability of regions. EDP is, on the other hand, one approach to studying how new industrial activity emerges, which impacts on and necessitates changes in regional innovation systems.

Notes

1 The concept of social entrepreneurs has some similarities with our definition of system entrepreneurs. Social entrepreneurs act to create and sustain social value; an innovative solution *'to address unmet social needs, so that large scale benefits for society are generated'* (Petrella and Richez-Battesti, 2014:150). System entrepreneurs

also in a sense work for the benefits of society, but in a much more restricted influence area of RISs.

2 The different paths share resemblance with Foray's (2014:498) logics of structural transformation.

3 'The Norwegian Government's most important instrument for innovation and development of Norwegian enterprises and industry' (www.innovasjonnorge.no).

4 For further information, see www.arenaclusters.no/the-arena-programme/.

5 We refer to economic regions as defined by Statistics Norway (Hustoft et al., 1999), established to correspond to NUTS 4; they resemble labour market regions.

6 An independent and non-political interest organization created to coordinate local interests in different industries and professions.

References

Arthur, W.B. (1989). Competing technologies, increasing returns, and lock-in by historical events. *The Economic Journal*, 99 (394), pp. 116–131.

Asheim, B. and Isaksen, A. (2002). Regional innovation systems: The integration of local 'sticky' and global 'ubiquitous' knowledge. *Journal of Technology Transfer*, 27 (1), pp. 77–86.

Binz, C., Truffer, B. and Coenen, L. (2015). Path creation as a process of resource alignment and anchoring: Industry formation for on-site water recycling in Beijing. *Economic Geography*, 92 (2), pp. 172–200.

Boschma, R., Coenen, L., Frenken, K. and Truffer, B. (2017). Towards a theory of regional diversification: Combining insights from evolutionary economic geography and transition studies. *Regional Studies*, 51 (1), pp. 31–45.

Boschma, R. and Frenken, K. (2011). Technological relatedness and regional branching. In Bathelt, H., Feldman, M. and Kogler, D.F. (eds) *Beyond territory: Dynamic geographies of knowledge creation, diffusion and innovation*, pp. 64–81. London: Routledge.

Dawley, S. (2014). Creating new paths? Offshore wind, policy activism, and peripheral regional development. *Economic Geography*, 90 (1), pp. 91–112.

Duranton, G. and Puga, D. (2002). Diversity and specialization in cities: Why, where and when does it matter? In McCann, P. (ed.) *Industrial location economics*, pp. 151–186. Cheltenham: Edward Elgar.

Edquist, C. (2005). Systems of innovation: Perspectives and challenges. In Fagerberg, J., Mowery, D.C. and Nelson, R.R. (eds) *The Oxford handbook of innovation*, pp. 181–208. Oxford: Oxford University Press.

Feldman, M., Francis, J. and Bercovitz, J. (2005). Creating a cluster while building a firm: Entrepreneurs and the formation of industrial clusters. *Regional Studies*, 39 (1), pp. 129–141.

Feldman, M.P. and Audretsch, D.B. (1999). Innovation in cities: Science-based diversity, specialization and localized competition. *European Economic Review*, 43, pp. 409–429.

Foray, D. (2014). From smart specialisation to smart specialisation policy. *European Journal of Innovation Management*, 17 (4), pp. 492–507.

Foray, D. (2015). *Smart specialisation: Opportunities and challenges for regional innovation policy*. London: Routledge.

Frenken, K., Van Oort, F. and Verburg, T. (2007). Related variety, unrelated variety and regional economic growth. *Regional Studies*, 41 (5), pp. 685–697.

Fritsch, M. (2011). The effect of new business formation on regional development: Empirical evidence, interpretation, and avenues for further research. In Fritsch, M. (ed.)

Handbook of research on entrepreneurship and regional development, pp. 58–106. Cheltenham: Edward Elgar.
Garud, R., Hardy, C. and Maguire, S. (2007). Institutional entrepreneurship as embedded agency: An introduction to the special issue. *Organization Studies*, 28 (7), pp. 957–969.
Garud, R. and Karnøe, P. (2003). Bricolage versus breakthrough: Distributed and embedded agency in technology entrepreneurship. *Research Policy*, 32 (2), pp. 277–300.
Gertler, M.S. (2004). *Manufacturing culture: The institutional geography of industrial practice*. Oxford: Oxford University Press.
Grabher, G. (1993). The weakness of strong ties: The lock-in of regional development in the Ruhr area. In Grabher, G. (ed.) *The embedded firm: On the socioeconomics of industrial networks*, pp. 255–277. London: Routledge.
Henning, M., Stam, E. and Wenting, R. (2013). Path dependence research in regional economic development: Cacophony or knowledge accumulation? *Regional Studies*, 47 (8), pp. 1348–1362.
Holmen, A.K.T. and Fosse, J.K. (2017). Regional agency and constitutions of new paths: A study of agency in early formation of new paths on the west coast of Norway. *European Planning Studies*, 25 (3), pp. 498–515.
Hustoft, A.G., Hartvedt, H., Nymoen, E., Stålnacke, M. and Utne, H. (1999). *Standard for økonomiske regioner*. Oslo: Statistics Norway.
Isaksen, A. (2015). Industrial development in thin regions: Trapped in path extension? *Journal of Economic Geography*, 15 (3), pp. 585–600.
Isaksen, A. and Trippl, M. (2016). Path development in different regional innovation systems: A conceptual analysis. In Parilli, M.D., Fitjar, R.D. and Rodríguez-Pose, A. (eds) *Innovation drivers and regional innovation strategies*, pp. 66–84. London: Routledge.
Kirzner, I.M. (1997). Entrepreneurial discovery and the competitive market process: An Austrian approach. *Journal of Economic Literature*, 35 (1), pp. 60–85.
Lundvall, B.-Å. (ed.) (1992). *National systems of innovation: Towards a theory of innovation and interactive learning*. London: Pinter.
Lundvall, B.-Å. (2007). National innovation systems: Analytical concept and development tool. *Industry and Innovation*, 14 (1), pp. 95–119.
Martin, R. (2010). Roepke lecture in economic geography—Rethinking regional path dependence: Beyond lock-in to evolution. *Economic Geography*, 86 (1), pp. 1–27.
Martin, R. and Sunley, P. (2006). Path dependence and regional economic evolution. *Journal of Economic Geography*, 6 (4), pp. 395–437.
Miörner, J. and Trippl, M. (2017). Paving the way for new regional industrial paths: Actors and modes of change in Scania's games industry. *European Planning Studies*, 25 (3), pp. 481–497.
Neffke, F., Henning, M. and Boschma, R. (2011). How do regions diversify over time? Industry relatedness and the development of new growth paths in regions. *Economic Geography*, 87 (3), pp. 237–265.
Oslo Edtech (2017). *About Oslo Edtech Cluster*. Oslo: Oslo Edtech. Available at: http://osloedtech.no/en/om-oss/.
Petrella, F. and Richez-Battesti, N. (2014). Social entrepreneur, social entrepreneurship and social enterprise: Semantics and controversies. *Journal of Innovation Economics & Management*, 2 (4), pp. 143–156.
Petrov, A.N. (2011). Beyond spillovers: Interrogating innovation and creativity in the peripheries. In Bathelt, H., Feldman, M. and Kogler, D.F. (eds) *Beyond territory: Dynamic geographies of knowledge creation, diffusion, and innovation*, pp. 168–190. London: Routledge.
Porter, M.E. (1998). Clusters and the new economics of competition. *Harvard Business Review*, 76 (6), pp. 77–90.

Rodríguez-Pose, A. (2013). Do institutions matter for regional development? *Regional Studies*, 47 (7), pp. 1034–1047.

Rodríguez-Pose, A. and Wilkie, C. (2015). *Institutions and the entrepreneurial discovery process for smart specialization*. Occasional report. Utrecht University, Section of Economic Geography.

Sotarauta, M. and Pulkkinen, R. (2011). Institutional entrepreneurship for knowledge regions: In search of a fresh set of questions for regional innovation studies. *Environment and Planning C: Government and Policy*, 29 (1), pp. 96–112.

Spigel, B. (2013). Bourdieuian approaches to the geography of entrepreneurial cultures. *Entrepreneurship & Regional Development*, 25 (9–10), pp. 804–818.

Spigel, B. and Harrison, R. (2017). Toward a process theory of entrepreneurial ecosystems. *Strategic Entrepreneurship Journal*, 12 (1), pp. 151–168.

Tödtling, F. and Trippl, M. (2005). One size fits all? Towards a differentiated regional innovation policy approach. *Research Policy*, 34 (8), pp. 1203–1219.

Tödtling, F. and Trippl, M. (2013). Transformation of regional innovation systems: From old legacies to new development paths. In Cooke, P. (ed.) *Re-framing regional development: Evolution, innovation, and transition*, pp. 297–317. London: Routledge.

Øygarden, K. (2010). *Fondsregion Hovedstaden – et tyngdepunkt for kunnskaps– og forskningsbasert innovasjon*. Oslo: Norges forskningsråd. Available at: www.forskningsradet.no/servlet/web/prognett-hovedstaden/Om_fondsregion_Hovedstaden/1253953954563.

3 The institutional worlds of entrepreneurial discovery

Finding a place for less developed regions

Jiří Blažek and Kevin Morgan

3.1 Introduction

The fundamental aim of the smart specialisation approach to place-based development has been defined by its proponents as a structural transformation of the European economy towards branches with higher added value and lower unemployment rates (Foray and Rainoldi, 2013). According to these proponents, this should be achieved first of all through a new policy process that involves entrepreneurs and their partners in an orchestrated effort to discover new business opportunities that would focus scarce research and development (R&D) resources on domains of comparative advantage for each country or region. Surprisingly, however, the original concept of smart specialisation seems to underplay the role of institutions (formal, informal as well as organisations), a role that has been considered to be crucial in recent theories of regional development (Gertler, 2010; Morgan, 1997; Rodríguez-Pose, 2013). In particular, the concept of smart specialisation – which is based on a bottom–up entrepreneurial discovery process that involves not only entrepreneurs but also other stakeholders such as researchers and public administrations – pre-supposes a certain maturity of overall institutional framework including participatory behaviour of key stakeholders (not least a well-developed collaboration culture with limited rent-seeking behaviour).

In contrast, in less developed areas, which need targeted help to enhance their research and innovation systems, the challenge of underdeveloped institutional frameworks has been seriously neglected (for examples and exceptions, see Blažek et al., 2013; Charron et al., 2012; Dogaru et al., 2017; Radosevic et al., 2017). This is forcefully illustrated in a recent insightful study by Karo et al. (2017), who elaborated a detailed study of embarking upon RIS3 in Central and Eastern European countries. Those authors argue that during the first RIS3 phase of 'fast' specialisation aiming at satisfying the EU *ex ante* conditionality, the entrepreneurial discovery was interpreted as a process of formal consultation and coordination with stakeholders to legitimise some specialisations, which, because of various sorts of confusions, subsequently proved to be difficult to operationalise into proper policy interventions. Thus, these authors concluded that institutional variety across Europe as well as varying experience and skills of policy-makers and of other stakeholders (entrepreneurs, academics) have been overlooked, thus undermining the applicability of RIS3 concepts in institutionally weak regions (Karo et al., 2017).

Consequently, the question of institutional readiness for this new regional innovation policy era needs to be addressed as a matter of urgency if Europe's poorest countries and regions are to find a place in the world of smart specialisation. This chapter aims to fill the gap in two ways: first, by examining the scope for/barriers to the adoption of the smart specialisation concept in the less developed regions of the European Union, such as those in Central and Eastern European countries or in parts of Southern Europe, where 'institutional bottlenecks' are likely to be most acute (in section 3.2); second, by exploring the policy challenge of how to design a more nuanced and pluralistic entrepreneurial discovery process – the process that is deemed to be the core of smart specialisation strategy (S3) according to the chief architect of the concept (Foray, 2015), and, more generally, looking at how to intervene in institutions to render them more effective. Answers to these questions will be delivered in sections 3.4 and 3.5 based upon a critical scrutiny of institutional challenges and dilemmas elaborated in section 3.3. Therefore, while Karo et al. (2017) provided a detailed examination of the first phase of entrepreneurial discovery process when the domains of specialisation have been selected, our aim is to scrutinise the key challenges as well as the newly emerging experience in the phase when entrepreneurial discovery processes (EDPs) should aim at delivering the crucial benefits, i.e. discovering new business opportunities – see the RIS3 Guide (Foray et al., 2012).

3.2 The role of institutions in regional development

It has been argued that 'the link between institutions and economic development had been fundamentally overlooked by mainstream economic theory in general, and growth theory, in particular', at least until the 1990s (Rodríguez-Pose, 2013: 1035). Consequently, the traditional recipe assumes that economic development will be fostered by investment in infrastructure, education and training, innovation and industrial activities orchestrated at the national level, an approach that effectively sidelines the local institutional context. In contrast, in regional research, concern with institutions and governance and with their relation to economic development has been central to the 'institutional turn' in economic geography in the 1990s. However, thanks to the pioneering work of Douglass North in particular, the role of institutions is gradually being acknowledged in the mainstream economic literature (Acemoglu and Robinson, 2013; North, 2005) – so much so that, in innovation and development debates today, some of the most important questions revolve around the implications of the 'institutional turn', questions such as what do we mean by institutions, what sort of institutions matter for development, and how and to what extent can we reform institutions to render them more effective (Morgan, 2017b; Rodríguez-Pose, 2013)? All these questions have assumed more prominence with the advent of smart specialisation strategies (S3), the largest and most ambitious place-based innovation programme ever launched in the European Union (Foray et al., 2012; Gianelle et al., 2016).

Concerning the definition of institutions, it has to be said that there is no consensus as to what 'institution' actually means in either theory or practice (e.g. Jessop, 2001; Rodríguez-Pose, 2013; Tomaney, 2014). Instead, several conflicting alternative definitions have been formulated, and a thorny problem in all of them is the distinction between institutions and organisations. While some authors regard institutions as organisations that exercise a distinctive influence upon society (for a detailed discussion of varying notions of institutions used by different authors, see Rodríguez-Pose, 2013), other authors see institutions as 'defining the rules and resources of social action, as defining opportunity structures and constraints on behaviour, as shaping the way things are to be done if they are to be done, as path-dependent path-defining complexes of social relations' (Jessop, 2001: 1217). The latter definition of institutions accords closely with that of D.C. North:

> Institutions are humanly devised constraints that structure political, economic and social interaction. They consist of both informal constraints (sanctions, taboos, customs, traditions, and codes of conduct), and formal rules (constitutions, laws, property rights). Throughout history, institutions have been devised by human beings to create order and reduce uncertainty in exchange.
>
> (North, 1991: 97)

In the same vein, Morgan summarised this school of thought by defining institutions as 'recurrent patterns of behaviour – habits, conventions and routines' (Morgan, 1997: 493).

However, bearing in mind the formidable challenges of implementing the concept of smart specialisation in practice, it seems reasonable to deal not only with formal and informal institutions, but with place-based organisational fabrics as well. The relevance of the latter (such as of intermediate institutions like trade associations, chambers, professional associations, etc.) for regional development has been underlined in particular by the theory of regional innovation systems (Cooke et al., 1997; Cooke et al., 2004; Cooke and Morgan, 1998).

The question as to which mix of institutions matters most for regional development is very much an empirical question, but there are strong grounds for thinking that Hirschman was correct to attach such significance to institutions that nurtured the 'art of agreement-reaching' among regional stakeholders, a point to which we return in section 3.6. What seems certain is that formal institutions – such as rule of law – are fundamentally important to economic development. Rodríguez-Pose insists that numerous studies agree that an absence of basic formal institutions has a detrimental effect on economic development (Rodríguez-Pose, 2013: 1038). However, given their ambiguity and intangibility, there is less robust evidence on the merits of informal institutions, even though many authors argue that, by lowering uncertainty and information costs, informal institutions improve conditions for economic activity. For example, North argues that both types of institutions 'provide the incentive structure of an economy' (North, 1991: 97), and this in turn helps to establish a suitable balance between coordination and competition mechanisms among economic actors, thereby facilitating a collective learning process (Cooke and Morgan, 1998).

The question of the quality of regional governance has been addressed on a pan-European scale for the first time thanks to valuable research by Charron et al. (2012). Among other things, this research showed not only the stunning scale of a West–East gradient in the quality of governance as perceived by the local population, but also distinctive patterns of polarisation in the quality of governance among and even within countries with traditional large scale of regional disparities (especially Italy). Not surprisingly, Charron et al. (2012) argue for more vigorous efforts to improve the quality of governance in underperforming regions in order to stimulate economic development. In the same vein, other researchers have made a plea for governance reforms – designed to reduce rent-seeking and combat corruption and so forth – to be seen as *de facto* regional policies because the quality of institutions is deemed to be one of the primary barriers to innovation in the less developed regions of Europe (Di Cataldo and Rodríguez-Pose, 2016).

This plea brings us to what is arguably the most important question of all from a policy standpoint, which is how to intervene in institutions to render them more effective. This is a key question in the context of smart specialisation because the latter makes unprecedented demands on all stakeholders, especially public organisations (Morgan, 2017b). However, before we address this question in section 3.4, we need to appreciate some of the institutional challenges of less developed regions (LDRs), particularly those with a state-socialist heritage (see Blažek and Csank, 2016).

3.3 The institutional dilemma in less developed regions

State-of-the-art regional development theories highlight the significance of informal institutional factors such as trust, responsibility, professionalism, partnership and shared leadership (see e.g. Sotarauta, 2010). This contrasts sharply with underdeveloped institutional frameworks in LDRs, where public institutions are described in some or all of the following ways: excessively bureaucratic, over-politicised, unprofessional, unstable, non-responsive, non-transparent, lacking strategic vision and, above all, short of trust (Blažek et al., 2014). Moreover, within all levels of the public administration in Central East European (CEE) countries there is a deeply embedded 'play it safe' mentality, which severely limits the scope for manoeuvre and flexibility in decision-making (Blažek and Morgan, 2016). Furthermore, public servants in CEE countries are inclined towards a zero-sum mentality in the sense that the interests of the public sector are often construed to be at odds with the interests of private firms and academics, an observation that accords well with the concept of a 'disconnected region' (Foray et al., 2012).

Consequently, regional authorities in these countries frequently lack officers responsible for liaising with local businesses and academics. Consequently, the cooperation among business, researchers and the public sector has to start literally from scratch, underlining the fact that the triple helix model of regional development is a triumph of rhetoric over reality in the vast majority of LDRs (Marques and Morgan, 2018).

There is also an unusually strong tendency among private firms in CEE countries to engage in rent-seeking behaviour and unrestrained individualism (see Blažek and Kuncová (2011) for the cumbersome and problematical process of establishing clusters in the Czech Republic, a process that ultimately had to be parachuted into regions through a national-level initiative). In these regions individualistic behaviour among the key regional development actors (entrepreneurs, knowledge and even intermediary institutions) is common and existing platforms and networks are primarily considered and used as a *de facto* vehicle for lobbying for external support, instead of functioning as endogenous drivers of development as envisaged by the state-of-the-art theories (see Blažek and Kuncová, 2011).

Moreover, in these regions there frequently exists a cleavage of mistrust and misunderstanding between entrepreneurs and academics. This was aptly expressed by one entrepreneur at a smart specialisation meeting facilitated by an intermediate organisation in one of the Czech regions: 'We would cooperate with universities provided the sphere is not vital to our competitiveness' (Blažek and Csank, 2016: 1007). In the case of the Czech Republic there is a widespread dissatisfaction of entrepreneurs with academics as the latter are often uninterested in collaboration with businesses and the system of financing of academic institutions as well as criteria for promotion of academics in their careers is geared to rewarding academic publications, which further exacerbates the business–university gap. Even when academics are willing to engage with businesses, they are often unable to respect the timespan for the joint research effort and they tend not to appreciate the importance of cost-effective solutions in their contractual research. Given this inhospitable institutional context (and disregarding the internal weaknesses of many mid-range universities, see Gál and Ptáček, 2011), it is unlikely that even the leading academics would command sufficient respect among other stakeholders to be considered as leaders or boundary-spanners in line with the smart specialisation concept, still less to be accepted as serious partners within the entrepreneurial discovery process – the key innovation of the S3 approach.

In several CEE member states, this tension between the business and academic spheres has been compounded by misguided supply-side solutions to the lack of innovation, i.e. by the construction of 'cathedrals in the desert' in the form of grandiose R&D facilities which are massively under-utilised by local firms. As a result, some of these facilities are facing serious challenges concerning their sustainability because they require vast amounts of public funding at a time of severe austerity measures, fuelling the antagonism towards academics among entrepreneurs.

In addition to the above-mentioned weaknesses in informal institutions, there are also significant problems in the system of formal institutions. First, the competence over research and innovation (R&I) policy is frequently scattered among several national institutions that in reality operate rather as competitors jealously guarding their silo competence, which stymies the development of truly systemic measures that would enhance the overall coherence of the R&I system. In contrast, regional authorities in many of these countries lack not only legally endowed competence in the sphere of R&I policy and practice, but also command truly limited know-how. This represents significant barriers for more proactive bottom–up approaches towards place-based innovation and development. Another problem in the formal institutional framework is the unstable and inadequate system of financing of R&I activity; this concerns not only the one-sided stress on rewarding easily measurable results such as the number of scientific articles without sufficient recognition of other forms of outputs of R&I institutions, but there are even cases when the newly adopted criteria are applied retroactively. Yet another example of imperfect formal institutions is a woefully inadequate system of protection of intellectual property rights (IPRs).

While there is a general dissatisfaction with bureaucratic load across many countries, this is especially true for post-state-socialist countries. Excessive bureaucratic load in these countries can be attributed at least to two specific factors. First, there was the sheer scale of the legislative changes required to change the principles upon which these societies and economies functioned under the command economy. Even though it is now more than 25 years since the system of state-socialism collapsed in these countries, the process of transforming former legislative frameworks is still not fully accomplished. Second, in some of these countries there is a tendency to try to solve problems through an overly detailed specification of what behaviour is considered legal and what is not. Therefore, some basic pieces of legislation – such as business law or public tendering rules – are being amended several times a year in some of these countries.

In addition to weaknesses in both formal and informal institutions, there are specific features of the economic structure of LDRs that impinge directly upon the character of their R&I systems. Three of these specific features are well known: (1) the generally weak endogenous sector of small and medium-sized enterprises (SMEs) and, consequently, (2) the branch-plant character of these economies; and (3) local firms are often locked in to the lowest tiers of global production networks/global value chains (GPNs/GVCs). Taken together, these factors imply limited innovation demand (Blažek et al., 2014).

In CEE countries there is one more fundamental factor that needs to be taken into account when designing the S3 plan. The theoretical basis for S3 accords a lot of significance to the concept of related variety – which asserts that mutual learning among companies in the region is enhanced when their production is technologically related (Boschma, 2013; Frenken et al., 2007). While this concept proved to be powerful in explaining the economic development of regions with advanced R&I systems, where their competitiveness is often based on knowledge that is mutually related (Boschma et al., 2009), the economies of LDRs are by definition less knowledge-intensive and, even more importantly, frequently technologically unrelated. This sort of 'unrelatedness' is especially typical in regions with a post-state-socialist heritage as their economies have been for decades moulded by a command economy philosophy. Under the command economy, location decisions were frequently based on overestimating the role of 'hard' factors such as natural resources while underestimating the significance of 'soft' factors such as local traditions, because quantity was extolled over quality under state socialism.

Moreover, when these command economies were opened up to foreign competition after the collapse of state socialism in the late 1980s, their economic structure was transformed fundamentally once more, this time upon a low-cost basis. Therefore, a vast number of foreign direct investments were motivated by reaping low-cost advantages in CEE countries, once again disregarding assets of a 'softer' nature – such as local tradition or know-how. In consequence, the economic structure in many of these regions became disconnected from local traditions, which resulted in the development of a relatively broad spectrum of companies in unrelated industrial branches often requiring different skills. Significantly, the primary activity of these companies is frequently focused on production of low value-added components produced for export. Consequently, the 'common denominator' among companies in these regions is unusually small and significantly hinders the potential for applying the concept of related variety as envisaged by the RIS3 Guide (Foray et al., 2012).

In addition, the continuing tradition of locating basic research in academies of sciences built according to the Soviet model on the one hand, and privatisation of the former institutions of applied research, which frequently resulted in their closure, created a vast gap between businesses and research. As a result, economic specialisation of these regions – even if discernible – is barely reflected in existing R&D institutions. Therefore, all these factors limit the potential for applying the concept of related variety in these regions, and, consequently, these factors have to be considered carefully within the process of designing and implementing S3 projects.

To sum up, less developed regions in CEE countries are facing not only the challenge stemming from internal weakness of all pillars of triple/quadruple helix (i.e. low innovation capability of local business, underperformance and non-transparency of public administration, weak production of internationally recognised outputs of academic institutions, underdeveloped and, in the best cases, the emerging fabric of civic society organisations), but, even more seriously, also deep cleavages among these pillars. Importantly, these cleavages exist not only because of the low quality of informal as well as formal institutions, but also because of structural weaknesses of these regional economies, such as low innovation demand given by a weak endogenous SMEs sector (see Table 3.1).

Table 3.1 Key weaknesses in less developed regions

	Deficiencies of a 'broad' innovation system (the overall institutional framework and specifics of economic structure)	*Deficiencies of a 'narrow' innovation system (public and private R&D sector)*
Formal institutions	Unclear or fragmented competence over R&D&I policy at the national level Lack of legal competence of regional authorities in the sphere of business support and R&D as well as limited know-how over innovation policies One-sided and unstable model of financing and evaluation of R&I institutions Improper or unstable legislative framework High red-tape societies	Academic institutions frequently lack the internal rules for cooperation with business sector Insufficient quality of education system, education system is weakly aligned with the needs of business
Informal institutions	Low-trust societies Non-professionalism, instability or even unpredictability in decision-making of public sector Individualism, missing leadership Weak entrepreneurial culture among university graduates Disregard for strategies	Deficiencies in the collaborative culture (e.g. 'Berlin wall' between academic and business spheres – different values, expectations, time horizons or rent-seeking behaviour among companies, etc.) Cooperation with businesses is considered by some academics as a betrayal of academic values
Organisational fabric	Lack of strategic vision within public administration High fluctuation of staff within public administration Missing or weak intermediate organisations	Low ability of universities to commercialise research findings
Economic base	Local firms are often locked in within the lowest tiers of GPN/GVC Branch-plant economy syndrome Low knowledge intensity and unrelatedness	Significant mismatch between research focus of R&D institutions and the needs of the economy

Source: Own elaboration

These limitations are compounded by a weakness of intermediate organisations (such as regional development agencies, innovation centres, chambers of commerce, etc.) that are frequently struggling just with their own survival, which severely curtails their capability to enhance the R&I system in their regions.

The countries and regions that we have schematically portrayed in this section can be described as 'low-trust, high red-tape societies'. Therefore, the distance between the 'ideal' situation and the everyday practice is – at least in the case of some of these regions – of such a scale that it could create a passive or even hostile attitude towards 'imported' concepts such as S3. Even though positive reactions towards S3 do exist in this type of region, this unfavourable institutional context has to be acknowledged if the concepts of smart specialisation and of entrepreneurial discovery process are to become more than mere concepts.

3.4 Policy implications for S3 and EDP in less developed regions

The combination of weak institutional architectures and highly dependent economic structures means that a much more nuanced and pluralistic approach to S3 is needed in the CEE countries and regions. While the S3 concept portrays the entrepreneurial discovery process as the key mechanism for the identification and exploitation of new business opportunities, such an approach is much more problematical in LDRs because – as we have seen – it presumes a high quality of formal and informal institutions such as trust, collaborative culture, reciprocity and leadership as well as a large common denominator within regional economies. Launching the entrepreneurial discovery process along the lines drafted by the EC Guide to RIS3 (Foray et al., 2012) is therefore likely to fail unless the guidelines are modified to take account of the institutional specificity of the LDR context.

For all these reasons we argue that the entrepreneurial discovery process should begin not with an effort to discover new business opportunities, but rather with a much more basic process of building mutual understanding among entrepreneurs and between entrepreneurs and other regional stakeholders, focusing on the key local bottlenecks to innovation and development. Building mutual understanding is an important phase because, in the case of some regions, entrepreneurs might meet with the regional authority and educational institutions for the very first time. Moreover, this initial phase would need to be relatively inclusive as the participation would not be restrained by a targeted focus on a particular industrial branch. In our experience, the quality of informal institutions could be enhanced significantly through such interactive trust-building exercises. Such broadly conceived policy platforms furnish a basis upon which more thematically/sectoral-focused platforms aiming at an interactive process of knowledge development among stakeholders can emerge in the near future. Thus, to summarise, we can say that the entrepreneurial discovery process as envisaged by the RIS3 Guide (Foray et al., 2012) is predicated on an institutional architecture that is assumed to pre-date the process, when in actual fact it has to be fashioned from scratch in many less developed countries and regions.

From a conceptual point of view, therefore, two adjustments to the S3 approach need to be made. First, a special form of 'horizontal priorities' should be introduced into the list of key priorities. Second, as we argue below, the 'vertical priorities' should be distinguished from the 'domains of possible economic specialisation', as envisaged by Foray et al. (2012).

Let us turn first to the horizontal priorities. While the RIS3 Guide conceptualises horizontal priorities primarily as 'the diffusion and/or application of Key Enabling Technologies' and only subsequently as 'aspects related to social innovation, or the financing of the growth of newly established companies' (Foray et al., 2012: 51), we argue for a different definition of these priorities for the sake of the LDRs.

In the case of LDRs, horizontal priorities should be conceptualised as cross-cutting priorities that aim to strengthen the overall institutional environment and innovation system (at either national or regional level or both). Thus, the role of horizontal priorities would be to address the main shortcomings in the formal and informal institutional framework with respect to both narrow and broad innovation systems (see Table 3.1 for examples). It is reasonable to suppose that the evolutionary trajectory of these regions will remain unchanged if these cross-cutting issues are not adequately addressed. Reaching agreement on the key bottlenecks to development in the region and finding agreed solutions are no mean feats, as these would represent huge advances in the context of less developed countries and regions – as Albert Hirschman discerned with such prescience when he spoke of the developmental importance of the 'art of agreement-reaching' and the 'cooperative component of entrepreneurship', intangible assets that he believed were less readily transferable than industrial knowledge and technology (Hirschman, 1958: 19). Nurturing the 'art of agreement-reaching' would be the best way to stimulate the active involvement of entrepreneurs in regions where the latter are frustrated by the underperformance of public sector institutions and where strategic documents fail to resonate because they suffer from a chronic lack of practical relevance. However, to deliver such an ambitious strategy, much more attention will need to be paid to the composition and the calibre of the stakeholders involved in these early phases of the entrepreneurial discovery process, an issue we address in section 3.5.

Concerning the priorities of economic specialisation, it should be emphasised that there is a fundamental difference between the relatively broad 'vertical' priorities which have been often selected in LDRs to meet the S3 *ex ante* conditionality and the new domains of economic specialisation canvassed in the official S3 literature (see e.g. Foray et al., 2011; Foray et al., 2012; McCann and Ortega-Argilés, 2011). While the 'vertical' priorities were in principle selected by national authorities on the basis of quantitative analysis of various statistical data on the level of relatively broad sectors (for example, one of the Czech vertical priorities is defined as 'production of transport means' encompassing not only the automotive industry, but also the aircraft industry as well as industries supplying these two industries), and then submitted for consultation to businesses, the genuine entrepreneurial discovery process should in principle consist of a much more granular level of the economy. Consequently, even though in most countries and regions vertical priorities have already been selected, this should be considered rather as a point of departure for a much more focused and more granular entrepreneurial discovery process than as a final result. In consequence, in less developed regions, 'vertical' priorities and 'domains of prospective economic specialisation' should be distinguished carefully and not used interchangeably. Therefore, the main argument here is that the challenging process of searching for new domains of specialisation with a high value-added character cannot start from scratch. On the contrary, before such an advanced level of sophistication is reached, the effort should focus on the identification of systemic shortcomings and their overcoming via horizontal priorities. Significantly, this approach would also help to create a certain level of mutual awareness and of trust among stakeholders, thus enhancing the quality of informal institutions.

3.5 Designing policy platforms and (feasible) entrepreneurial discovery processes in less developed regions

From the above analysis it follows that we need to develop a more nuanced and less prescriptive approach to the entrepreneurial discovery process. Among other things, this would involve a very careful selection of stakeholders to ensure it was a truly participatory process – a novelty for many less developed countries and regions.

To facilitate the understanding of policy platforms (or working groups) that might be feasible vehicles for the entrepreneurial discovery process – understood as broad platforms and not exclusively composed of entrepreneurs – the first task is to find a suitable name. For example, these platforms might be called 'Innovation Platforms', which would clearly convey their mission to all relevant stakeholders and therefore open the space for interested academics as well. In order to facilitate mutual understanding among entrepreneurs, academics, educational institutions and public administration, and especially to ensure 'ownership' of the identified problems, it is imperative that the membership of Innovation Platforms include representatives of these spheres as well. Moreover, given the immaturity of the 'cooperative component of entrepreneurship' in such regions, it seems likely that it will fall to the public administration (perhaps with some external support from consultants) to initiate the formation and management of these platforms, at least in the early phases of the process when the critically important 'rules of the game' need to be established (see Aranguren et al. (2016) for an illustration of this process in the Basque Country). This approach would provide valuable feedback to representatives of public administration and of educational institutions from the perspective of local entrepreneurs and would exert considerable pressure upon them to deliver what is needed and to overcome the notorious mismatch between producer-driven services and business user needs. Thus, there are strong arguments to involve not only entrepreneurs and researchers, but representatives of public administration and education institutions as well. It should be underlined that we are explicitly using the term 'educational institutions' instead of 'higher education institutions' because – according to our experience – among the most pressing problems hindering business activities in LDRs is the lack of a qualified labour force, particularly with respect to secondary-level education (i.e. qualified workers), along with an interactive and collective process of inter-organisational learning among key actors in emergent knowledge-based activities.

Consequently, the following steps need to be considered. First, the effort of stakeholders should focus upon the identification of key bottlenecks for business and innovation activities (i.e. identification of horizontal priorities), agreeing the method for their elimination and assigning the responsibility for accomplishing this task. Importantly, this phase should not only result in the creation of a common perception of key cross-cutting challenges in the R&I system, but also enhance the mutual knowledge and understanding among stakeholders, i.e. informal institutions. Crucially, given the generally poor pace of implementation of innovation strategies in these regions, public administration representatives should guarantee to entrepreneurs and academics that their contributions will be taken seriously. Therefore, public officials have to prove that progress is being made in addressing and redressing the bottlenecks that have been collectively identified, not least because this is the only sure way to prove that the public administration is a credible interlocutor.

Second, as one of the key principles of S3 plans should be a thorough examination of comparative advantages of individual regions and full acknowledgement of the fact that 'one size does not fit all' (McCann and Ortega-Argilés, 2011; Tödtling and Trippl, 2005), a search for the comparative advantages of the region should be undertaken. Identification of comparative advantages should build up the quality of informal institutions further and would also create a basis for the third step.

Third, a locally authentic entrepreneurial discovery process should be launched to identify new market opportunities offering high value-added products and services. Within this phase, the branching of relatively broadly conceived innovation platforms into more granular ones might be considered. Importantly, a suitable mix of instruments should be contemplated and implemented to make maximum use of comparative advantages and of discovered market niches. Despite all above reservations concerning the institutional framework and economic structure of regions in CEE, some of these regions have made huge efforts to put EDP into practice. Examples of these embryonic activities in launching EDP are provided in Table 3.2, distilling the key experience with emerging EDPs in the Czech region of South Moravia, which is widely considered as an innovation leader in the Czech Republic. The South Moravia region, originally dominated by textile and heavy-machinery industries, which proved to be largely uncompetitive after the economic liberalisation in the early 1990s, subsequently suffered high unemployment. Nevertheless, the economic base underwent a fundamental restructuring orchestrated predominantly by foreign investors. The bottom–up effort of regional stakeholders has been enabled by the re-establishment of regional self-government only in 2000 and was sparked a year later by a closure of a major foreign-owned company, leaving 2,700 unemployed (Blažek and Csank, 2016). Currently, the economic structure of the region is dominated by electro-technical, precise-machinery and ICT industries. The economic base consists not only of subsidiaries of large foreign-owned companies (such as Honeywell, FEI, ABB), but also of a relatively strong endogenous sector. Regional companies benefit from local universities in numerous ways, such as labour force training, industrial PhDs and via various collaborative projects including jointly performed R&D. Research teams in the region form a sufficiently diverse, yet well-connected, sphere of knowledge. This creates important stimuli for the knowledge development process among key stakeholders in the region. For example, South Moravia excels in electron microscopy and in the production of medical instruments. A particular asset of the regional innovation system in South Moravia represents a well-functioning partnership encompassing all five universities, regional government, city of Brno administration as well as key private stakeholders supported by a network of intermediaries such as the South Moravian Innovation Centre and the South Moravian Centre for International Mobility (Blažek and Csank, 2016).

Finally, and fully in line with the RIS3 Guide, this sequence of steps should be embedded within an adequate monitoring and evaluation system, which is rarely delivered properly even though it is nominally mandatory. Therefore, at the moments when particular solutions are being agreed within the innovation platforms, suitable milestones or targets need to be identified so that local actors can be held accountable (Barca, 2009).

In countries that opted for a regional approach towards S3 design and implementation, or a combination of regional and national RIS3 strategies, this policy process should be supported by a robust multi-level governance system because less developed countries and regions should not be expected to shoulder the entire burden of development on their own. For example, a multi-level governance system might take the form of the National Coordination Board for S3, in which the membership could *inter alia* consist of representative(s) of regional innovation platforms. In this way the voice from the regional level would gain a hearing at the national level among representatives of relevant national authorities – this would be a major step forward in highly centralised countries such as Romania (Healy, 2016).

If such a process is to succeed under immature institutional conditions, the question of S3 leadership comes to the fore. In recognition of the fact that public administration suffers from many weaknesses, and where the regional level

Table 3.2 The variety of approaches to discovering new business opportunities via the EDP: the case of South Moravia

Instrument	*Rationale*	*Design*	*Key bottlenecks*	*Main benefits and impacts*
'Idea Labs'	The rationale is to mobilise external expertise to search for prospective pathways of innovation effort in companies	Key experts with relevant knowledge domain from the public research institutions are selected and engaged in detailed discussion with researchers from a single company with large innovation potential	Very demanding preparation of such events Firms do not want to do research with external experts Many firms are lacking ambition, while capable and ambitious firms are lacking time Disconnection with funding schemes – Czech regions do not have any funds for support of R&D activities while the state is 'far away'	So far limited, two pilot research projects prepared as a result of discovering two promising arenas of future research
'120 seconds for innovation'	Speed-dating events to develop new contacts, either among companies or between companies and public R&D institutes	Each stakeholder has one minute to explain what they can offer and one minute to explain what they are searching for Subsequently an informal space is provided for potential partners Two to three such events are being organised annually, with 60 participants on average	Limited pool of relevant actors in the region Preference of regional actors to engage especially with limited number of flagship companies nested in the region	Dozens of new contacts developed, which in several cases already resulted in subsequent joint collaborative projects

(continued)

Table 3.2 (continued)

Instrument	*Rationale*	*Design*	*Key bottlenecks*	*Main benefits and impacts*
'Starcube'	International accelerator for technology start-ups	Selected start-ups (about 10 per year) receive a bundle of services such as high-quality mentoring, access to networking activities, financial support, free co-working space, enhanced marketing visibility and preferential access to external financial resources (venture capital, business angels)	High competition among accelerators in Europe providing basically the same services Limited number of relatively developed technology-oriented projects Small size of the Czech market and limited number of technology partners in the region	Some supported start-ups underwent phenomenal growth (e.g. air ticket company Kiwi using novel software 5 years later has already employed more than 1,100 employees)

Source: interviews with managers responsible for these instruments has no legal competence over businesses, it seems desirable to use a pragmatic approach towards the management of the S3 process. Consequently, while the public administration has the formal authority to set up innovation platforms and provide the necessary organisational support for the process, it might be reasonable to allow a representative of the business sector to lead the process as soon as the 'rules of the game' have been established and as soon as a credible personality has been identified. Finding a credible personality – who enjoys the respect of the key stakeholders – is another challenge that should not be underestimated, particularly in LDRs where clientelism and rent-seeking loom large (Morgan, 2017a).

3.6 Conclusions and future research challenges

The aim of this chapter was to examine the barriers to the adoption of the smart specialisation concept in less developed regions and to explore the policy challenge of how to design a more nuanced and pluralistic entrepreneurial discovery process in such challenging settings.

The main argument of this chapter can be succinctly summarised as follows: the entrepreneurial discovery process that lies at the heart of the S3 exercise is predicated on a highly developed architecture of formal and informal institutions and these attributes are seldom found in less developed countries and regions. Consequently, we have argued that the entrepreneurial discovery process needs to be understood in a much more nuanced and pluralistic manner if it is to have any economic resonance and political traction in such less developed spatial contexts. What this means in policy terms is that *horizontal* priorities should be given parity of esteem with the *vertical* priorities that command so much attention in S3 guidelines. In the less developed context, horizontal priorities should be conceived as cross-cutting priorities focused on the elimination of key bottlenecks within the emerging innovation systems of these regions (i.e. low level of mutual knowledge and of mutual understanding among key stakeholders, inadequate educational system, improper legal framework, etc.). Unless these much-neglected horizontal priorities are addressed, it is hard to imagine how any 'smart choices' can be made with respect to any aspect of the S3 process.

Given the broadly conceived vertical priorities that have been selected in many less developed countries and regions, these priorities should be carefully distinguished from the 'domains of prospective specialisation' that are deemed to offer high value-added opportunities in newly discovered market niches (Foray et al., 2012). The 'vertical' priorities were in principle selected by responsible national authorities on the basis of predominantly quantitative analysis of various statistical data often at the level of broad sectors. In contrast, the genuine entrepreneurial discovery process should in principle deal with a much more granular level of the economy. Therefore, vertical priorities that have already been selected within the S3 process should be considered as a point of departure for a more focused entrepreneurial discovery process rather than as a final result.

In practical terms, we argued that the following steps could help to fashion a more authentic entrepreneurial discovery process in less developed regions: (1) identify the key bottlenecks for business and innovation activity (i.e. identification of horizontal priorities) and agree the method for their elimination by assigning responsibility for accomplishing these tasks; (2) search for the comparative advantages of the region; (3) launch the entrepreneurial discovery process so as to identify new market opportunities offering high value-added products and services.

Importantly, we concur with the argument of Isaksen et al. (2019) (Chapter 2 in this volume): to reap the benefits of the entrepreneurial discovery process, the EDP should not only be properly institutionalised, but also supported by adaption and development of particular regional innovation systems via creation or adaptation of institutions, organisations and policy instruments (for more, see Isaksen et al., 2019).

Finally, three points for a possible future research agenda can be suggested. First, while it has been widely acknowledged that different types of imperfect regional innovation systems exist (see Tödtling and Trippl, 2005), little effort has been devoted to designing novel specific instruments and their particular mixes to address these special challenges. Consequently, while the concept 'one size does not fit all' has been widely accepted in the sphere of design of regional and innovation strategies, the development of particular instruments addressing the specific needs of less developed regions cries out for attention. However, given the need to respect context specificity, we must also acknowledge that the same policy instruments can have radically divergent outcomes in different spatial settings, which means that we need to attend to the regional milieu as well as the policy mix because regional innovation policy repertoires exhibit a strong path-dependent character (Morgan, 2017a).

Second, within regional research and innovation studies an important gap exists concerning our understanding of the role of various types of institutions in fostering growth and development; indeed, even the methodology for a suitable form of institutional analysis seems to be lacking. Consequently, a much deeper understanding of the role of both formal and informal institutions is needed as well as a finer appreciation of the *politics* of regional development because it cannot be assumed that regional elites are as committed to innovation (and change) as they are to control (and continuity).

Lastly, whatever its shortcomings, one of the great merits of the smart specialisation concept is that it recognises that innovation is fundamentally a collective social endeavour rather than the product of heroic individual entrepreneurs. As in any collective endeavour, one of the greatest challenges is to acquire the 'art of agreement-reaching' because the 'shortage of the cooperative component of entrepreneurship in many underdeveloped countries is the more unfortunate as . . . the need for this component is particularly pronounced' (Hirschman, 1958: 19). Although Hirschman was writing of less developed countries, exactly the same point can be applied to less developed regions faced with the collective action challenge of smart specialisation. In this chapter we have argued that the 'art of agreement-reaching' is one of the informal institutional assets that needs to be developed as a horizontal priority as a prelude to the vertical priorities that loom so large in the institutional world of smart specialisation. A future research agenda would do well to address the scope for/barriers to collective action in less developed regions.

References

Acemoglu, D. and Robinson, J. (2013). *Why nations fail: The origins of power, prosperity and poverty*. London: Profile Books.

Aranguren, M.J., Morgan, K. and Wilson, J. (2016). *Implementing RIS3: The case of the Basque Country*. San Sebastian: Orkestra.

Barca, F. (2009). *An agenda for a reformed cohesion policy: A place-based approach to meeting European Union challenges and expectations*. Occasional report. Brussels: European Commission.

Blažek, J. and Csank, P. (2016). Can emerging regional innovation strategies in less developed European regions bridge the main gaps in the innovation process? *Environment and Planning C: Politics and Space*, 34 (6), pp. 1095–1114.

Blažek, J., Healy, A., Wilson, J., Magro, E., Trippl, M., Grillitsch, M., Hansen, T., Goddard, J. and Vallance, P. (2014). *Smart specialisation for regional innovation: Regions with less developed research and innovation systems*. Reflection paper for Work Package 3, FP7 Project, Smart Specialisation for Regional Innovation. Occasional report.

Blažek, J. and Kuncová, I. (2011). Klastry – módní pojem nebo skutečný zdroj konkurenceschopnosti? *Ekonomický časopis*, 59 (3), pp. 224–241.

Blažek, J. and Morgan, K. (2016). *Launching entrepreneurial discovery process in regions with less developed research and innovation systems*. SMARTSPEC Policy Brief. Cardiff: Cardiff University.

Blažek, J., Žížalová, P., Rumpel, P., Skokan, K. and Chládek, P. (2013). Emerging regional innovation strategies in Central Europe: Institutions and regional leadership in generating strategic outcomes. *European Urban and Regional Studies*, 20 (2), pp. 275–294.

Boschma, R. (2013). *Related variety and smart specialisation*. Keynote lecture at the kick-off conference of SMARTSPEC project. Presented at *Smartspec kickoff*, 2013-11-06. Brussels.

Boschma, R., Eriksson, R. and Lindgren, U. (2009). How does labour mobility affect the performance of plants? The importance of relatedness and geographical proximity. *Journal of Economic Geography*, 9 (2), pp. 169–190.

Charron, N., Lapuente, V. and Dijkstra, L. (2012). *Regional governance matters: A study on regional variation in quality of government within the EU*. Regional Policy Working Papers. Brussels: European Commission.

Cooke, P., Gomez Uranga, M. and Etxebarria, G. (1997). Regional innovation systems: Institutional and organisational dimensions. *Research Policy*, 26 (4), pp. 475–491.

Cooke, P., Heidenreich, M. and Braczyk, H.-J. (eds) (2004). *Regional innovation systems: The role of governance in a globalized world*, 2nd ed. London: Routledge.

Cooke, P. and Morgan, K. (1998). *The associational economy: Firms, regions and innovation*. Oxford: Oxford University Press.

Di Cataldo, M. and Rodríguez-Pose, A. (2016). *What drives employment growth and social inclusion in EU regions?* London: Centre for Economic Policy Research.

Dogaru, T., van Oort, F. and Cortinovis, N. (2017). Smart specialisation and local economic development in Eastern Europe. In McCann, P., Goddard, J. and van Oort, F.

(eds) *The empirical and institutional dimensions of smart specialisation*, pp. 145–164. Abingdon: Routledge.

Foray, D. (2015). *Smart specialisation: Opportunities and challenges for regional innovation policy*. London: Routledge.

Foray, D., David, P. and Hall, B.H. (2011). *Smart specialization: From academic idea to political instrument, the surprising career of a concept and the difficulties involved in its implementation*. MTEI Working Paper. Lausanne: EPFL.

Foray, D., Goddard, J., Goenaga Beldarrain, X., Landabaso, M., McCann, P., Morgan, K., Nauwelaers, C. and Ortega-Argilés, R. (2012). *Guide to research and innovation strategies for smart specialisation (RIS 3)*. Occasional report. [Sevilla]: European Commission.

Foray, D. and Rainoldi, A. (2013). *Smart specialisation programmes and implementation*. Luxembourg: European Commission.

Frenken, K., Van Oort, F. and Verburg, T. (2007). Related variety, unrelated variety and regional economic growth. *Regional Studies*, 41 (5), pp. 685–697.

Gál, Z. and Ptáček, P. (2011). The role of mid-range universities in knowledge transfer in non-metropolitan regions in Central Eastern Europe. *European Planning Studies*, 19 (9), pp. 1669–1690.

Gertler, M.S. (2010). Rules of the game: The place of institutions in regional economic change. *Regional Studies*, 44 (1), pp. 1–15.

Gianelle, C., Kyriakou, D., Cohen, C. and Przeor, M. (eds) (2016). *Implementing smart specialisation: A handbook*. Brussels: European Commission.

Healy, A. (2016). Smart specialization in a centralized state: Strengthening the regional contribution in North East Romania. *European Planning Studies*, 24 (8), pp. 1527–1543.

Hirschman, A.O. (1958). *The strategy of economic development*. New Haven, CT: Yale University Press.

Isaksen, A., Kyllingstad, N., Rypestøl, J.O. and Schulze-Krogh, A.C. (2019). Entrepreneurial discovery processes in different regional contexts: A conceptual discussion. In Mariussen, Å., Virkkala, S., Finne, H. and Aasen, T.M. (eds) *The entrepreneurial discovery process and regional development: New knowledge emergence, conversion and exploitation*. Abingdon: Routledge.

Jessop, B. (2001). Institutional re(turns) and the strategic – relational approach. *Environment and Planning A: Economy and Space*, 33 (7), pp. 1213–1235.

Karo, E., Kattel, R. and Cepilovs, A. (2017). Can smart specialization and entrepreneurial discovery be organized by the government? Lessons from Central and Eastern Europe. In Radosevic, S., Curaj, A., Gheorghiu, R., Andreescu, L. and Wade, I. (eds) *Advances in the theory and practice of smart specialization*, pp. 269–292. London: Academic Press.

Marques, P. and Morgan, K. (2018). The heroic assumptions of smart specialisation: A sympathetic critique of regional innovation policy. In Isaksen, A., Martin, R. and Trippl, M. (eds) *New avenues for regional innovation systems: Theoretical advances, empirical cases and policy lessons*, pp. 275–293. Cham: Springer International Publishing.

McCann, P. and Ortega-Argilés, R. (2011). *Smart specialisation, regional growth and applications to EU cohesion policy*. Economic Geography Working Paper. Groningen: Faculty of Spatial Sciences, University of Groningen.

Morgan, K. (1997). The learning region: Institutions, innovation and regional renewal. *Regional Studies*, 31 (5), pp. 491–503.

Morgan, K. (2017a). Nurturing novelty: Regional innovation policy in the age of smart specialisation. *Environment and Planning C: Politics and Space*, 35 (4), pp. 569–583.

Morgan, K. (2017b). Speaking truth to power: The political dynamics of public sector innovation. In Kyriakou, D., Martínez, M.P., Periáñez-Forte, I. and Rainoldi, A. (eds) *Governing smart specialisation*, pp. 49–61. London: Routledge.

North, D.C. (1991). Institutions. *Journal of Economic Perspectives*, 5 (1), pp. 97–112.

North, D.C. (2005). *Understanding the process of economic change*. Princeton, NJ: Princeton University Press.

Radosevic, S., Curaj, A., Gheorghiu, R., Andreescu, L. and Wade, I. (eds) (2017). *Advances in the theory and practice of smart specialization*. London: Academic Press.

Rodríguez-Pose, A. (2013). Do institutions matter for regional development? *Regional Studies*, 47 (7), pp. 1034–1047.

Sotarauta, M. (2010). Regional development and regional networks: The role of regional development officers in Finland. *European Urban and Regional Studies*, 17 (4), pp. 387–400.

Tomaney, J. (2014). Region and place I: Institutions. *Progress in Human Geography*, 38 (1), pp. 131–140.

Tödtling, F. and Trippl, M. (2005). One size fits all? Towards a differentiated regional innovation policy approach. *Research Policy*, 34 (8), pp. 1203–1219.

4 Entrepreneurial discovery processes through a wicked game approach

Civil society engagement as a possibility for exploration

Antti Mäenpää and Niklas Lundström

4.1 Introduction

The entrepreneurial discovery process (EDP) is one of the central concepts in S3 because it is the main instrument facilitating evidence-based regional specialisation. The combination of local expertise and market knowledge is a mix that is hard for any region to resist. EDP is primarily designed to create something new out of existing capabilities or resources (Mariussen and Virkkala, 2019, the introduction to this volume). Current cases of EDP, however, seem to indicate something more evidence based and perhaps fewer new ideas (Kroll, 2016; Perianez Forte et al., 2016; Teräs and Mäenpää, 2016) – a situation that could eventually lead to regional path dependency. One indication of such path dependency may be the fact that the concept of domain has not been expressly mentioned by many regions (Mäenpää and Teräs, 2018), even though the domain concept is meant to highlight the novel thinking in the region and is officially stated to be an outcome of successful EDP.

As Mäenpää and Teräs (2018) observe on the subject of domains, the exploration is often based on analysis of the existing capabilities and previous knowledge. After choosing the domains, the process seems to stop. Results from Kroll (2016: 4) show that EDP continues 'strongly and comprehensively' in only a little over 20 per cent of the 179 cases analysed. Why is this happening and what should be done to encourage actors to maintain the cooperation that forms the core of whole EDP? One example of good practice is presented by Rodrik (2004), who suggests that there are ten issues that must be addressed in policy design (see also Chapter 1 in this volume, Virkkala and Mariussen, 2019). Of those ten principles, only one (incentives) addresses the collaboration between actors directly. This chapter argues that the failure to make EDP an ongoing process may be because the EDP does not explore all the options offered by a complex world. A failure in exploration may thus lead to lock-in on existing strong sectors, which may lead to long-term challenges.

One explanation may stem from previous research about the role of wickedness in regional development policies. Wicked problems are problems that defy a clear solution and are subject to constant change (Rittel and Webber,

1973). Their changing status means it is impossible to find an objective solution to these kinds of problems in which subjectivity always plays a crucial role. The previous research has concluded that regional development practices, such as S3 or EDP, are themselves wicked *games* – a viewpoint that emphasises the active role of the stakeholders in the problem formulation and any attempts to find resolutions (Lundström, 2015, 2016; Lundström and Mäenpää, 2017; Lundström et al., 2016). This viewpoint of a wicked game also highlights the actors' roles in EDP. The concept of the wicked game makes it possible to study EDP in practice and offers insights into how EDP works in a wicked environment, where there are no easy processes to advance regional development. Only by accepting the complexity of regional innovation can one focus on finding the optimal procedures and solutions.

Previous literature argues that one possible way to discover new solutions is to elicit citizens' views. The utilisation of the fourth helix (i.e., civil society) has been debated at great length; some studies (e.g. Marinelli and Perianez Forte, 2017) indicate that the use of citizens in strategy formulation has been useful, but others come to the opposite conclusion (Kroll, 2016; Vallance, 2017). The question is why in some cases civil society involvement enhances EDP while sometimes it does not.

Usually the fourth helix or civil society refers to more organised, or categorised citizen involvement (Carayannis and Campbell, 2012), but the authors have included individual citizens in the same concept. This is based on suggestions that individual citizens could be a good addition to EDP as they may provide new insights on regional innovation and help to challenge the thinking behind its implementation (Aranguren et al., 2017; Benner, 2014; Lundström and Mäenpää, 2017).

The key research questions of this chapter address the complexity surrounding EDP and especially how to utilise civil society in a meaningful manner, and they also examine where new ideas appear. To answer these questions, we focus on the following:

- How does the wicked game approach describe EDP exploration?
- How might such exploration be enhanced through civil society engagement?

This chapter continues by demonstrating how EDP can be seen as a wicked problem. This also provides a starting point for the discussion of the wicked game concept and how it affects EDP. We also discuss the somewhat paradoxical idea that the inclusion of more actors could enhance emergence, or generation of ideas, while bearing in mind that involving more actors has not worked in all S3 cases – something that demands an explanation. After this discussion, the chapter focuses on turning the complexity aspect into a positive driver for new ideas and suggests that different actors could support that. Finally, in the conclusion section, we answer the research questions presented above.

The chapter is based on literature analysis and aims to explore the relevance of the concepts of the wicked problem and wicked game in the interpretation of the EDP. This means that EDP is conceptualised using the notions of wicked problems and the wicked game to build a new kind of understanding of EDP. This kind of investigation is needed because the current practices do not seem to comprehend the EDP itself as a complex process, which may result in good ideas being omitted.

4.2 Wicked problems and the wicked game

Rittel and Webber (1973) originally introduced wicked problems and the term has been used to describe wicked policy issues, although it was also a critique aimed at the planning theory of that time. The original study emphasised that the crisis facing planning was not about the planners' lack of knowledge or intelligence, but about the very nature of the problems they tried to address. The main idea of Rittel and Webber was to divide problems into two different categories: tame and wicked.

First of all, tame problems have an objective solution and once that solution is found, the problem ceases and does not reappear; an example offered by Rittel and Webber (1973) was that of a chess player trying to achieve a checkmate in five moves. In this example, the objective is clear and there is no question of whether the problem has been solved. That is because the game is governed by rules known by each player. In addition, according to Mason and Mitroff (1981), tame problems can be separated and reduced. This means that the problem can be removed from its context and broken down into pieces, which can in turn be solved individually. In addition, Lundström and Raisio (2013) underline that in societal problems the tame aspect is found in the repeatability and lucidity of the process. Once a solution is found, similar problems can be solved in the same way. Of course, this is not the case with most societal problems. Rittel and Webber (1973) described tame problems as relatively easy, but wicked problems as far more stubborn. Tame problems might be complicated, but are not complex per se. From the complexity point of view, being complex and being complicated are not synonymous. When we use the terms complex and complexity they refer to the worldview of complexity, especially complexity thinking (Richardson and Cilliers, 2001) unless otherwise stated; see also Chapter 7 in this volume (Aasen, 2019) for clarifying variations in complexity thinking.

Wicked problems cannot be solved for good, and even the definition of the problem is ambiguous. Some examples are healthcare or environmental issues, as they are never solved (Levin et al., 2012; Vartiainen, 2005). It is impossible to deliver a definitive solution because the stakeholders have contending views and beliefs. Of course, the backgrounds of stakeholders and their value systems play a crucial role as well. For some the proposed solution is the only option, while others cannot even live with that proposal. The environment or the outside also change the problem and impose new limitations on the process.

Rittel and Webber (1973) originally stated that every wicked problem is a symptom of another wicked problem – something identified as at the core of wicked problems (McCall and Burge, 2016). When one problem is temporarily resolved, it then transforms into a different problem. This property has been portrayed as resembling the Hydra of Greek mythology; when one head was chopped off, the monster would regrow a couple more (Mason and Mitroff, 1981). It also resonates with the complexity point of view and especially the concept of emergence as random change and something that emerges from nothing when looking from the perspective of the whole (Goldstein, 1999; Lundström and Mäenpää, 2017; see also Aasen, 2019).

In addition to the original list of the properties of wicked problems (see Box 4.1), researchers have compiled a number of lists of their characteristics (cf. Conklin, 2005; Danken et al., 2016; Norton, 2005, 2012). Danken et al. (2016) conducted a literature review on the core properties of wicked problems. According to their analysis, the present understanding of wicked problems can be summarised in three interrelated properties. First, wicked problems do not have a clear solution. Property one forms the basis of the second property, which leads us on to the role and properties of the stakeholders, who have diverging values and interests. Third, wicked problems are not fully understood, and therefore the definition of the implications and the nature of the problem differ, too.

Box 4.1 The properties of wicked problems summarised

1. No definite solution
2. No stopping rule
3. Solutions are not true/false, but good/bad
4. No immediate or ultimate test of a solution
5. Every solution has consequences; every solution is a one-shot operation
6. Do not have an exhaustive set of potential solutions
7. Are essentially unique
8. Are a symptom of another wicked problem
9. The causes can be explained in numerous ways
10. The planner has no right to be wrong

Source: Based on Rittel and Webber (1973)

The worldview of complexity, especially complexity thinking (Richardson and Cilliers, 2001), and wicked problems share similar presumptions (e.g. Zellner and Campbell, 2015). Wicked problems are seen to influence and are influenced by complex systems. The boundary between wicked and complex is somewhat vague. To begin with, wicked problems and complex adaptive systems (CAS) have similar characteristics (Waddock et al., 2015). They must both be treated holistically, both involve emergence and co-evolutive patterns and both are unpredictable. They both acknowledge that relationships are non-linear, emphasise the significance of initial conditions and interpret the systems as open (Peters, 2017). However, wicked problems are not just complex problems. Wicked problems are regarded as '. . . intractable masses of complexity, so conflict-prone and/or knotty that they defy definition and solution' (Alford and Head, 2017: 399), while merely complex problems are problems where the definition is agreed upon but the consensus on how to solve it is missing (Roberts, 2000). Interestingly, Peters (2017: 385) sees the recognition of wicked problems as a precursor to the complexity sciences in the social sciences (see also Zellner and Campbell, 2015). The notion of wicked problems can be seen as a way to practicalise complexity (Raisio, 2010).

If wicked problems are truly problems that cannot be solved, what approaches can be applied to them? No one owns the wicked problem, and every stakeholder owns only a part of the truth, while no one is in total control (Lundström and Mäenpää, 2017; Roberts, 2000). The importance of collaboration is emphasised in the literature about wicked problems. Danken et al. (2016: 25) identified that scholars underline the importance of cross-boundary collaboration and public leadership and management when seeking to live with wicked problems. In the segment of cross-boundary collaboration, stakeholder deliberation and dialogue are seen as a fruitful way to address wickedness. In Roberts' (2000: 13) words, we need to get 'the whole system in the room' and the citizens' perspective should be included (Lundström et al., 2016). Stakeholder participation also enables the emergence of shared knowledge (Conklin, 2005). In addition, when it comes to management, policy-makers need to know how to separate tame problems from wicked problems (Danken et al., 2016). If a wicked problem is treated as a tame one, the outcomes will not be desirable (Lundström, 2016; Lundström and Mäenpää, 2017). It is about tackling the right problem with the broad participation of stakeholders. One could argue that communication and interaction are at the heart of the process (Zellner and Campbell, 2015). The worldview of complexity shares this same presupposition. Therefore, they both see the process as one of continuous exploration and discovery because the problem formulation and problem resolution are unknown.

It is suggested that this kind of interaction, where no one is in charge, where the stakeholders might share the concern over addressing the same problem (not always), but where their remedies may be totally different, should be interpreted as a wicked game (Lundström, 2015; Lundström and Mäenpää, 2017; Lundström et al., 2016). The concept of a wicked game is a quest to emphasise the role of the actors or players instead of only theorising about the quality of the problems. The wicked game perspective incorporates both tame and wicked aspects similar to Rittel and Webber's original dichotomy of wicked problems.

A tame game can be seen as the opposite of a wicked game. In a tame game, the problems are not seen as wicked, and even if they are, they are treated as if they were tame. This kind of gaming has certain outcomes. First, if the problems are treated as tame, the answers are engineered solutions and therefore mechanistic. This approach can also lead to categorising problems into similar types, which means that the problems are treated in a similar way in many regions. The tame game also has a stopping point; the problem disappears when the problem is solved, and the next issue can be addressed. The tame game is the framework in which the taming of wicked problems takes place (Conklin, 2005; Daviter, 2017; Roberts, 2000). The results will be sub-optimal if the players do not address the reality sufficiently, that is, if they get involved in playing a tame game instead of a wicked game (Lundström and Mäenpää, 2017). Daviter (2017: 578–579) describes that treating wicked problem as tame '. . . allows public authorities to limit participation and debate, assign administrative responsibility, reduce the need for cross-sector coordination, take swift action, draw on the available expertise, and apply pre-existing policy instruments and evaluative criteria'. All of this is understandable if the resources limit the process, but it does not sound very innovative. It is argued later in this chapter that the presence of a tame game can be seen in past experiences of EDP.

The development of a region can be a wicked problem (Lundström, 2015; Lundström and Mäenpää, 2017) because the definition of development *per se* is ambiguous, let alone when the context is as wide as a region, which includes so many different players, organisational levels, ambitions, goals, etc. The wicked game (Lundström, 2015; Lundström and Mäenpää, 2017; Lundström et al., 2016) is a framework in which the region is developed in the presence of wicked problems. The wicked game includes players from different horizontal and vertical regions or arenas as outlined by van Bueren et al. (2003). Although the aim of the game is to develop the region, the aims and interests of the various players sometimes clash. Actors may also have different ambitions or perceptions of the goals, so some try to be a negotiator and some pursue only their vested interest. It is clear that not all of the players are interested in acting for the benefit of the region. However, it is also possible that different actors have mutual goals, and that the cooperation may be very efficient as the collaborators all focus on developing the aspects that they know well or can influence. In such cases, the wicked game may also include coalitions of different kinds of players. The key point is that the players' involvement changes constantly and that the importance or role of a certain player might change during the game, and some players may be totally dismissed; in addition, some players influence the game more than others do. These characteristics have also been noted in the context of S3 (Lundström and Mäenpää, 2017; Mieszkowski and Kardas, 2015).

Generally, wickedness has a negative connotation, but that is not the case with a wicked game. On the contrary, the very idea of a wicked game must be interpreted as the positive side of wickedness and as something to be embraced and perhaps to benefit from (Raisio, 2010) and not merely something that must be tolerated (Norton, 2012). The wickedness cannot be eliminated or resolved for good; therefore those affected by it must change their perception of it. One way to do so is to study how innovation could prosper in a complex environment and perhaps even benefit from it.

4.3 EDP exploration in the wicked environment

Regional development as a whole has been recognised as a wicked problem (Lundström, 2015; Lundström and Mäenpää, 2017) and this suggests that EDP itself falls into the same category. As Aranguren et al. (2017: 170) state: 'A region is a complex system and in a complex system the knowledge necessary to overcome challenges and take advantage of opportunities is distributed, and not only among other territorial actors, but at a global level.' The idea of a wicked game is thus encapsulated in the thought that EDP is a continuing process (Marinelli and Perianez Forte, 2017; Perianez Forte et al., 2016), as final solutions cannot be found for regional innovation or development. This adds to the idea that EDP might be seen as a wicked game. It is also the reason why EDP cannot stop when the domains are found; exploration must continue if new ideas and solutions are to be found.

The typical players involved in smart specialisation are actors from the research and development sector and representatives of civil society, but also include research leaders, education institutions, inventors, non-governmental organisations (NGOs), societal associations, researchers, suppliers, manufacturers, service providers, entrepreneurs and consumers (Mieszkowski and Kardas, 2015). But this is of course only the official side of the game. According to Lundström and Mäenpää (2017), the players involved with S3 can be divided into three different major player groups: the public sector, companies, and universities. Each group has a different role and diverse aims in the wicked game. To summarise, the university's role in the wicked game of smart specialisation is to be a research partner, and the public sector tries to be a mediator, negotiator, or enabler of RIS3. Companies bring market knowledge to the game and seek partnerships and opportunities for future profit. The role of different actors has been discussed recently (Kroll, 2016; Marinelli and Perianez Forte, 2017) and some studies (Kroll, 2016: 7–8; Lundström and Mäenpää, 2017) indicate that regional governments are perhaps the major actors aiming for the original goals of S3, whereas the other actors are acting more or less according to their own interests.

One could argue that overall EDP exploration consists of three distinct phases. Existing knowledge of the region (usually gathered by regional governments and sometimes involving research commissioned from universities) forms the basis. After that there is some sort of participation of public organisations, firms and universities (known as triple helix, or 3H) with the addition of civil society (known as quadruple helix, or 4H) and the established knowledge is either verified or adjusted to meet the views of the regional actors.

The last phase is the formulation of the ideas or concepts to promote regional strength (Mäenpää and Teräs, 2018) (see Figure 4.1).

This presentation of the phases of an EDP may seem simplistic, as the RIS3 process can involve numerous iterations and rounds of dialogue between various actors. There are, however, indications that several regions have utilised a quite similar style when deciding upon their regional specialisation (Aranguren et al., 2017: 172; Mäenpää and Teräs, 2018), and this process-like approach (where regional innovation is analysed and then 'solved') may be an indication of tame practices to develop regional innovation. Ideally, EDP should be an ongoing process (Perianez Forte et al., 2016) but evidence suggests that EDP has slowed down after the RIS3 implementation (Kroll, 2016: 4), which supports the view of a tame process appearing in problem-solving.

A particularly interesting phase of EDP exploration is that in the middle, as the different stakeholders can then have their say on issues around innovation. Discussions in the triple/quadruple helix (3H/4H) setting are often mentioned in the official RIS3 documents as they explain the decisions being made and what should be done in the future to enhance the chosen specialisation aspects or goals. Several cases seem to verify this pattern where 4H is utilised, but not necessarily throughout the whole process (Teräs and Mäenpää, 2016; Vallance, 2017).

The overall outcome of EDP can be affected by the configuration and participation of different types of stakeholders (Benner, 2014; Lundström and Mäenpää, 2017) and even by the actual individuals involved (Aranguren et al., 2017). The role of stakeholders and individuals is particularly highlighted in the preparation process as local public actors might adjust the outcomes of EDP when they compose the RIS3 document and set its goals. This phase is interesting because it shows that within EDP exploration there is still room for regional politics. EDP is usually understood as 3H or 4H cooperation, but it

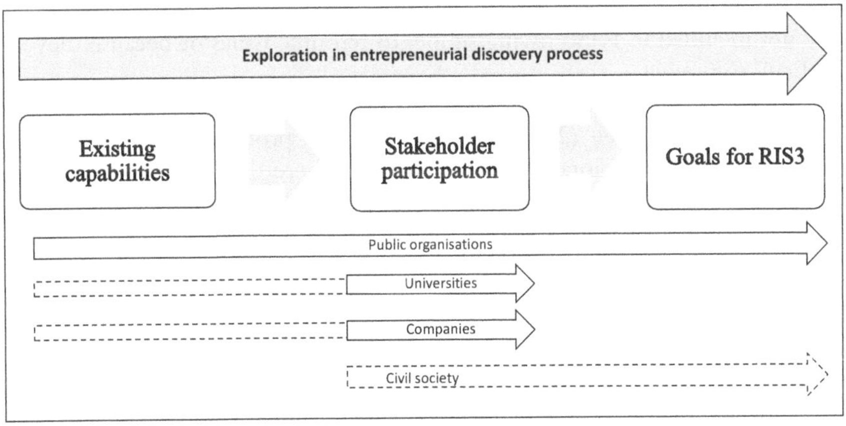

Figure 4.1 The distinctive phases of exploration in the EDP and usual stakeholder participation in a linear model

is important to see that it includes phases with varying degrees of cooperation. Some research indicates that the RIS3 process may even involve a 'mix and rotation of leadership' during specific phases of its formulation and implementation (Aranguren et al., 2017: 172). Indeed, different stakeholders hold different positions and may therefore have greater or lesser influence during the strategy process (e.g., universities might lead a regional analysis, while companies might lead EDP). However, only regional governments can influence and react to the whole process. This is understandable of course, as public actors are usually the only regional stakeholders who know which resources are available, which obviously can affect their decisions on the chosen domains and on their implementation, which then transforms into regional innovation. This reality suggests, however, that rotation of leadership is perhaps a little artificial as regional government has control of the process.

In addition to the internal game played within a region, a wicked game is also played between regions (Lundström and Mäenpää, 2017). This is also integral to the idea of S3, because the regions compete with each other if they are working on similar types of products or services, regardless of whether the regions are in Europe or even in the USA. Consequently, the different regional levels interact, which brings the wickedness to the fore. The interconnectedness is also due to players from various fields participating in the wicked game and the environment causing mixed messages to be brought into the game. After all, the environment plays a crucial role in the game.

The environment here means exogenous properties, in other words, what takes place outside a certain region that affects that region and its actors. Such properties would embrace the trends and flows in the global economy, the political climate, and actual climate issues, innovations, and public will. These issues often have an unexpected influence on regional innovation and may exert different effects on individual actors. They also can change unpredictably, are often emergent, and the results may be chaotic (see Raisio and Lundström, 2017; Zellner and Campbell, 2015). Very often these environmental effects are not included in RIS3 owing simply to resource issues or because they are difficult to predict.

A wicked game does not stop even if some temporary resolution is found. Zellner and Campbell (2015: 464) describe the problem-solving process as 'one of on-going exploration and discovery, where the system is understood by trying to define and explain it through explicit representation, simulation, and evaluation and reflection from a variety of perspectives and with a variety of tools'. Therefore, the EDP should not stop at any point. According to the literature, many of the experiences of EDP indicate that the game played is often tame, as the processes have slowed down after the initial implementation rounds (Kroll, 2016; Mäenpää and Teräs, 2018). The regional consensus does not seem to generate very new ideas and, therefore, there is a need to deepen and perhaps to reinvigorate the EDP in order to fully utilise regional capabilities and to evaluate whether they are having a sufficient impact on innovation.

In addition to the above findings, Benner (2014) emphasises the importance of even single actors, such as employees, directors, students, and professors, as innovators. The objective of the game is the same for all players in theory – to identify the domains of specialisation – but when considering the wide spectrum of possible participants, clearly interests and agendas can collide. This might be one of the reasons for tame answers and the tame game: the need to keep the participants satisfied, and the belief that the problems can be solved. Nevertheless, a coping strategy involving a broad collaboration is not unproblematic (Roberts, 2000), especially if the participants are not satisfied with the results. The question of collaboration is a wicked one; when only experts and recognised players play the game, the results are somewhat tame or predictable, but when more players are introduced, the risk of conflict and regional disparity rises. The problem of the role of single actor is already built into EDP. The people who are summoned to the table are the ones who get to have their say (Lundström and Mäenpää, 2017). The public sector representatives have an important role in considering who they call to attend and, ultimately, they also formulate the RIS3 and thus decide what specialisation benefits the region. A single political actor may have huge impact on the overall process.

Interestingly, Foray (2015: 29) has mentioned the possibility for 'radical foundation', which can be understood as specialisation without necessarily having a direct existing knowledge base. This sort of inclusion might benefit regional innovation and especially EDP. Radical foundation also paves the way for the introduction of new stakeholders, as it is not based purely on existing knowledge and therefore does not require prior expertise on regional matters. The authors find this to be innovative as it allows for true citizen participation and therefore opens the innovation discussion to the whole of the region not merely 3H actors and experts. This inclusion of radical elements may truly influence or enhance regional innovation discussion.

4.4 Enhanced EDP exploration through civil society inclusion

As mentioned above, current EDP exploration practices may be based on a more tame view of regional development, even though EDP operates in a wicked environment and is in itself a complex entity. One way to bypass the mechanistic process and to elicit new ideas is to accept that there are no certain truths and ready-made tools for the task. In practical terms that means that every idea counts, so to have the best chance to obtain optimal results, one has to understand and utilise the whole system (Roberts, 2000: 13). This adds to the challenges of EDP, as a process based on such an understanding of the whole system must include citizens and end users of innovations alongside the usual 3H stakeholders.

This inclusion of citizens has been mentioned in the original strategy guidebook, where the fourth helix is mentioned (Foray et al., 2012) and thus it has been endorsed right from the beginning of the S3 process. Despite this, however, the fourth helix has been undermined in RIS3 implementation, as a recent study by Marinelli and Perianez Forte (2017: 8) states: 'EDP largely emerges as 3-ple helix business.' There are also several other studies emphasising that despite good intentions, 4H collaboration has not been very comprehensive, even when the focus has been on living labs (Vallance, 2017), or even involved EDP steering group participation (Aranguren et al., 2017). Indeed, even when civil society has been involved in the process, there are indications that it is engaged more often in a monitoring role, whereas companies and universities are approached to formulate and assess proposals (Marinelli and Perianez Forte, 2017: 10). Essentially this means that the fourth helix is engaged after the decisions have been made. This sort of engagement is rather limiting, and we would suggest there should be citizen participation at the beginning of the EDP to improve insight and ideas.

It is understandable that citizen activation can be a challenge in EDP, as citizens are not perhaps that keen on discussing innovation (Lundström and Mäenpää, 2017). This may be due to a lack of expertise or interest in regional development. People are usually keener to address issues that concern them on a practical level, and matters of regional innovation activities are perhaps not among those. Another issue lies in the disparity of the fourth helix. It is far easier to target companies or universities as their leaders/experts are known. The fourth helix consists of various types of citizens and some know more than others. And all are difficult to contact.

Civil society inclusion has been studied in an S3 setting by Aranguren et al. (2017), who investigated 4H utilisation in Navarre and the Basque Country. Although the base premises for both Spanish regions were quite similar, the results indicated that 4H inclusion was perhaps more profound in Navarre, but the results were perhaps more concrete in the Basque Country, as dialogue was established between the actors. The authors of the study indicate several reasons for their results, including notions on the regional institutions. For example, the Basque Country had a more collaboration-heavy culture and lots of locally-owned companies, which made collaboration easier, even without full 4H participation. Navarre, on the other hand, utilised 4H in its EDP process and even included civil society representatives (e.g. politicians and labour representatives) in the steering group. However, because of larger companies and a more political EDP process, there was relatively little evidence of consensus on the directions the region should take.

Another study of a pair of 4H cases examines health-based domains in Tampere (Finland) and Northern Ireland (United Kingdom) (Vallance, 2017). Both regions had based their domains on an existing knowledge base, although they had different specifications (health technology in Northern Ireland and ICT in Tampere). Although he considered both cases to be good examples of domain construction, Vallance (2017: 140) states that: ' . . . emerging innovation systems have yet to take the form of a quadruple (rather than triple) helix arrangement in which societal users are centrally integrated. This is despite both regions exhibiting aspirations to move in this direction.' Vallance explains that civil society participation in actual innovation-related matters is quite minimal as they are mostly used to gather data in a living lab fashion.

The participation of civil society is important despite the issues involved because the citizens' view complements the ideas and thoughts of the regional experts. Citizens are able to view the innovation environment that surrounds the region, as they do not necessarily know about all of the megatrends or latest research. This environment includes some relatively fixed characteristics (location, history, etc.) but is also subject to change, as new trends (products, ideas, companies, etc.) come and go. Citizens' views are therefore valuable, as they may represent the 'local buzz' of the region (Bathelt et al., 2004: 13) and thus offer insights into what sort of activities are supported by the local citizens. Knowledge of the environment adds more elements that are spontaneous because it is impossible to know when new ideas arise and how they affect the region or its citizens. By adding the fourth helix into the mix, the region can receive information from the ground level and this may even include hints about future sunrise industries (Lundström and Mäenpää, 2017). Citizens can also pitch new ideas and challenge existing ones, which further enhances the thinking process and may lead to new ideas concerning RIS3 implementation (Cavalli et al., 2016: 130).

When should citizens be involved? The authors suggest that because of the nature of S3, the regional governments who are officially responsible for the formulation of RIS3 should lead the overall process. However, this does not mean that a living lab model (Vallance, 2017) should always be utilised, where citizens simply provide data for analysis. Citizens should be engaged in all the different phases of EDP exploration, and especially during the collation of existing capabilities, as wider participation generates more ideas, which ensures that the chosen specialisation is truly relevant to the local residents. This is especially important in regionally based solutions, as local citizens may have deeper insight into the region itself than some experts (who might live in a different region altogether). According to Hajer (2005: 461), planning should not be based on 'facts-as-information but on facts-as-experience'. It has already been suggested that civil society actors may spot future sunrise industries (Lundström and Mäenpää, 2017) and that in itself should be a reason for the more extensive inclusion of members of civil society (see Figure 4.2).

One could also argue that spontaneous ideas (or the radical foundation suggested by Foray, 2015) might come more naturally from regular citizens, who see the possibilities because they do not know of all the limitations. Experts can then consider these ideas and evaluate if they are feasible to implement. This process would help with the verification of the EDP as well because the experts would have to explain why suggestions do or do not work for the region. The importance of citizens' external knowledge can also be viewed through the literature of innovation. For example, Strambach and Klement (2012: 1844), who apply the notion of combinatorial knowledge to describe the combination of different bases and scales of knowledge, also seem to acknowledge the benefits of micro-level inclusion and point towards the options individual actors can provide by operating 'between networks of firms and organizations'. The study does not specifically mention civil society, but the principle is applicable.

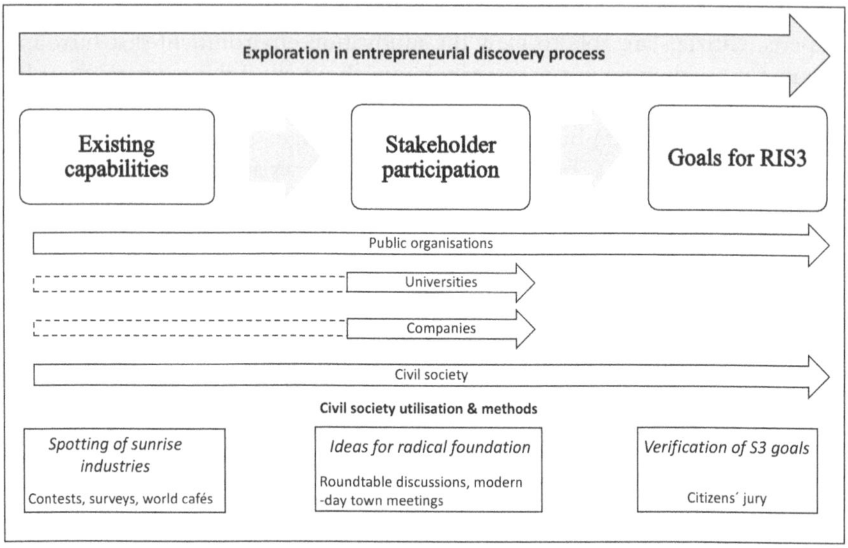

Figure 4.2 Suggested civil society inclusion methods with possible benefits for the EDP exploration process

Methods of deliberative democracy, such as citizens' juries (Crosby and Nethercut, 2005) are one possible specific tool to harvest citizens' views (Lundström et al., 2016). In short, operating citizens' juries means that the citizens' perspective is acknowledged alongside that of the usual experts or the recognised players. Possibilities for innovation stem from the pure unpredictability of wicked problems; if the problem (such as regional innovation) is undergoing constant change, the resolutions must be dynamic as well. Of course, there are many more possible methods besides the citizens' jury, for example, world cafés, modern-day town meetings, planning cells, consensus conferences, twenty-first-century town meetings, to name but a few (cf. Lukensmeyer and Brigham, 2002; Fung, 2003; Wilson, 2009). The number of possible methods helping to foster public deliberation has continued to grow in the twenty-first century, as new technologies, methods and applications have been developed.

It is important to understand that different kinds of methods may be used to elicit different sorts of ideas and forms of verification from civil society. For example, world cafés are useful mechanisms to gather good ideas and hear, for example, about sunrise industry suggestions or even radical ideas. This happens naturally as the respondents are not necessarily aware of the regional economy or only understand some parts of it well. Their suggestions are then based on their subjective views and experience and are therefore unique. Radical foundations for innovation can also be sought by utilising semi-formal modern-day town meetings where there is some sort of event for discussion (cf. Fung, 2003; Lukensmeyer and Brigham, 2002). Citizens' juries, in contrast, are more structured, and regional experts give the respondents additional background information before they have discussions and try to reach conclusions (Lundström, 2016). This sort of method would be ideal for the later stages, where the strategy is verified. This sort of verification would also help in the introduction of the strategy, as civil society members are well equipped to spread the word and the strategy could thus slowly alter the whole image of a region.

The citizens' view is also a tool for making the EDP a more bottom–up approach. This idea of cross-boundary collaboration is the most recommended approach in the literature on wicked problems (Danken et al., 2016) and has also been advocated in the context of S3 (Lundström and Mäenpää, 2017).

4.5 Conclusion

The main aim of this chapter was to look at EDP and 4H collaboration especially via the wicked game approach. In addition, the chapter focused on how EDP might be enhanced through engagement with civil society. The chapter's main findings can be presented as three suggestions regarding civil society engagement:

1 Focus on civil society members in addition to the experts
2 Civil society engagement requires proper methods
3 Development projects are one way to bring people together

The idea of including more members of civil society than are currently involved stems from a wicked game viewpoint, which illustrates how the EDP could function in a more actor-based framework. Accordingly, it is clear that some of the chosen methods, such as 4H application, might be a very useful addition to the EDP, as the inclusion of a spread of civil society has been seen as one way to enhance the search for solutions to wicked problems. The authors nevertheless agree that contributions in S3 should come from all possible sources and not just from civil society actors (Cavalli et al., 2016: 135). However, members of civil society may offer new ideas and solutions, without the constraints arising from relying on a too narrow expertise of the regional experts. At the very least, the ideas originating from civil society could be given due consideration and help develop the thinking in the region, as the experts will need to explain their decisions on feasibility. By utilising the right methods during the right phases, civil society can be a good additional asset in the strategy formulation process.

Examination of former 4H collaboration in the S3 setting revealed that there have been cases when EDP has benefitted from 4H collaboration, and some when it has not. The potential reasons for that are intriguing. Closer EDP analysis distinguished three major phases in the EDP during the exploration phase and this allowed for closer examination of the possible civil society

Goldstein, J. (1999). Emergence as a construct: History and issues. *Emergence*, 1 (1), pp. 49–72.

Hajer, M.A. (2005). Rebuilding Ground Zero: The politics of performance. *Planning Theory & Practice*, 6 (4), pp. 445–464.

Kroll, H. (2016). *Policy brief on smart specialisation*. Occasional report. Karlsruhe: Fraunhofer ISI.

Kuznetsov, Y. and Sabel, C. (2011). New open economy industrial policy: Making choices without picking winners. *Prem Notes*. Washington, DC: World Bank.

Levin, K., Cashore, B., Bernstein, S. and Auld, G. (2012). Overcoming the tragedy of super wicked problems: Constraining our future selves to ameliorate global climate change. *Policy Sciences*, 45 (2), pp. 123–152.

Lukensmeyer, C.J. and Brigham, S. (2002). Taking democracy to scale: Creating a town hall meeting for the twenty-first century. *National Civic Review*, 91 (4), pp. 351–366.

Lundström, N. (2015). *Aluekehittämisen pirullinen peli [Wicked game of regional development]*. Vaasa: Vaasan yliopisto.

Lundström, N. (2016). Exploring the theoretical foundations of a wicked game. Presented at *Building bridges: Cities and regions in a transnational world*, 2016-04-03. Graz: Regional Studies Association.

Lundström, N. and Mäenpää, A. (2017). Wicked game of smart specialization: A player's handbook. *European Planning Studies*, 25 (8), pp. 1357–1374.

Lundström, N. and Raisio, H. (2013). Kansalaisraadit aluekehittämisen pirullisissa peleissä: deliberaation mahdollisuuksista muuttaa näkemyksiä alueen kehittämisestä [Citizens' juries in the wicked games of regional development: About the possibilities of deliberation changing views on the development of a region]. *Hallinnon Tutkimus*, 32 (3), pp. 179–196.

Lundström, N., Raisio, H., Vartiainen, P. and Lindell, J. (2016). Wicked games changing the storyline of urban planning. *Landscape and Urban Planning*, 154, pp. 20–28.

Marinelli, E. and Perianez Forte, I. (2017). *Smart specialisation at work: The entrepreneurial discovery as a continuous process*. Luxembourg: Publications Office of the European Union.

Mariussen, Å. and Virkkala, S. (2019). Introduction. In Mariussen, Å., Virkkala, S., Finne, H. and Aasen, T.M. (eds) *The entrepreneurial discovery process and regional development: New knowledge emergence, conversion and exploitation*. Abingdon: Routledge.

Mason, R.O. and Mitroff, I.I. (1981). *Challenging strategic planning assumptions: Theory, cases, and techniques*. New York: John Wiley & Sons.

McCall, R. and Burge, J. (2016). Untangling wicked problems. *Artificial Intelligence for Engineering Design, Analysis and Manufacturing*, 30 (2), pp. 200–210.

Mieszkowski, K. and Kardas, M. (2015). Facilitating an entrepreneurial discovery process for smart specialization: The case of Poland. *Journal of the Knowledge Economy*, 6 (2), pp. 357–384.

Mäenpää, A. and Teräs, J. (2018). In search of domains in smart specialisation: Case study of three Nordic regions. *European Journal of Spatial Development*, 68, pp. 1–20.

Norton, B.G. (2005). *Sustainability: A philosophy of adaptive ecosystem management*. Chicago: University of Chicago Press.

Norton, B.G. (2012). The ways of wickedness: Analyzing messiness with messy tools. *Journal of Agricultural and Environmental Ethics*, 25 (4), pp. 447–465.

Perianez Forte, I., Marinelli, E. and Foray, D. (2016). The entrepreneurial discovery process (EDP) cycle from priority selection to strategy implementation. In Gianelle, C.,

Kyriakou, D., Cohen, C. and Przeor, M. (eds) *Implementing smart specialisation: A handbook*, pp. 14–35. Brussels: European Commission.

Peters, B.G. (2017). What is so wicked about wicked problems? A conceptual analysis and a research program. *Policy and Society*, 36 (3), pp. 385–396.

Raisio, H. (2010). *Embracing the wickedness of health care: Essays on reforms, wicked problems and public deliberation*. Vaasa: Vaasan yliopisto.

Raisio, H. and Lundström, N. (2017). Managing chaos: Lessons from movies on chaos theory. *Administration & Society*, 49 (2), pp. 296–315.

Richardson, K. and Cilliers, P. (2001). Special editors' introduction: What is complexity science? A view from different directions. *Emergence*, 3 (1), pp. 5–23.

Rittel, H.W.J. and Webber, M.M. (1973). Dilemmas in a general theory of planning. *Policy Sciences*, 4 (2), pp. 155–169.

Roberts, N. (2000). Wicked problems and network approaches to resolution. *International Public Management Review*, 1 (1), pp. 1–19.

Rodrik, D. (2004). *Industrial policy for the twenty-first century*. Faculty Research Working Papers Series. Cambridge, MA: Harvard University, John F. Kennedy School of Government.

Strambach, S. and Klement, B. (2012). Cumulative and combinatorial micro-dynamics of knowledge: The role of space and place in knowledge integration. *European Planning Studies*, 20 (11), pp. 1843–1866.

Teräs, J. and Mäenpää, A. (2016). Smart specialisation implementation processes in the north: Lessons learned from two Finnish regions. *European Structural and Investment Funds Journal*, 4 (2), pp. 75–86.

Vallance, P. (2017). The co-evolution of regional innovation domains and institutional arrangements: Smart specialisation through quadruple helix relations? In McCann, P., Goddard, J. and van Oort, F. (eds) *The empirical and institutional dimensions of smart specialisation*, pp. 127–144. London: Routledge.

van Bueren, E.M., Klijn, E.H. and Koppenjan, J.F.M. (2003). Dealing with wicked problems in networks: Analyzing an environmental debate from a network perspective. *Journal of Public Administration Research and Theory*, 13 (2), pp. 193–212.

Vartiainen, P. (2005). Wicked health care issues: An analysis of Finnish and Swedish health care reforms. In Savage, G.T., Chilingerian, J.A., Powell, M. and Xiao, Q. (eds) *International health care management*, pp. 159–182. Bingley: Emerald Group Publishing.

Virkkala, S. and Mariussen, Å. (2019). Self-discovery enabling entrepreneurial discovery processes. In Mariussen, Å., Virkkala, S., Finne, H. and Aasen, T.M. (eds) *The entrepreneurial discovery process and regional development: New knowledge emergence, conversion and exploitation*. Abingdon: Routledge.

Waddock, S., Meszoely, G.M., Waddel, S. and Dentoni, D. (2015). The complexity of wicked problems in large scale change. *Journal of Organizational Change Management*, 28 (6), pp. 993–1012.

Wilson, P.A. (2009). Deliberative planning for disaster recovery: Remembering New Orleans. *Journal of Public Deliberation*, 5 (1), pp. 1–23.

Zellner, M. and Campbell, S.D. (2015). Planning for deep-rooted problems: What can we learn from aligning complex systems and wicked problems? *Planning Theory & Practice*, 16 (4), pp. 457–478.

Part II

Collaborative micro-level arrangements creating new knowledge

5 Career mobility, hybridity and knowledge combination

A 'third space' perspective

Alice Lam

5.1 Introduction

Career mobility across organisational and social space has been widely seen as a key mechanism that facilitates creative knowledge combination (Saxenian, 1996; Lam, 2007). Extant research has focused on social networks forged through the mobility of people as conduits through which knowledge flows from one domain to another (Kleinbaum, 2012; Almeida and Kogut, 1999; Raider and Burt, 1996). Much of the literature has tended to treat career mobility primarily as physical movement of people between contexts, and views individuals as vehicles for the transmission of knowledge across intertwined networks. This chapter argues that the network knowledge flow perspective does not capture in full the micro-dynamics of creative knowledge combination associated with the movement of people. It neglects the socio-cognitive aspect of mobility and the agency of career actors in breaking down barriers between knowledge domains to achieve creative outcomes. Mobility involves not only movement in physical space but also the capacity to move across socio-cognitive space. Career theorists recognise the importance of psychological mobility accompanying physical mobility (Sullivan and Arthur, 2006). Knowledge is necessarily situated and does not flow easily across domain boundaries because of differences in perspectives and lack of common understandings and interests (Bechky, 2003; Carlile, 2004). Creative knowledge combination involves integrating divergent perspectives and knowledge that originates from previously separate domains to achieve novelty (Amabile, 1983; Koestler, 1964). It requires the active engagement of actors in overcoming interpretive barriers and reconciling differences in knowledge practices between domains.

This chapter contributes to our understanding of how career mobility influences creative knowledge combination by highlighting the active role of career actors in knowledge-brokering as they move from one work domain to another. It treats career mobility as a boundary-crossing process involving work-role transitions. It examines how movement in space and time triggers a dynamic interplay between actors and contexts, and it brings about changes in the cognitive frames of individuals and their propensity to connect knowledge across contexts. Work-role transition is not a unidirectional move from one work role to another but involves learning, adaptation and reorientation at the intersection of two previously separate work domains (Nicholson, 1984; Ibarra, 1999). The unsettled state during the transition can cause tension, conflict and ambivalence (Ibarra and Barbulescu, 2010). However, it is also a time of heightened reflectiveness and gives career actors ample opportunity and freedom for reorientation and experimentation by mixing and blending resources from the two previously separate domains. Work-role transitions, especially among professional knowledge workers, commonly involve a hybridisation process of role-taking and role-making (Ibarra, 1999; Pratt et al., 2006). Knowledge provides a critical resource for adaptation because it is part of individuals' cognitive interpretive structures and a key dimension for professional group membership identification (Barley, 1989; Gao and Riley, 2009). Individuals may acquire the perspectives and knowledge associated with the new roles and contexts, and they may also draw on the cognitive frames and knowledge resources acquired from previous work roles in adapting to the new contexts (Beyer and Hannah, 2002). As a result, knowledge originated from one domain can be reinterpreted and rearticulated from the viewpoint of another, and prior knowledge can be reconstituted for use in new contexts.

This chapter argues that career mobility across professional role boundaries or institutional sectors can nurture hybrids as knowledge brokers who engage actively in knowledge translation and transformation across domain boundaries. It employs Homi Bhabha's (1994) concept of the 'third space of hybridity' to denote the agency space where career actors construct hybrid role identities and undertake knowledge-brokering. The spatial metaphor of 'third space' was first introduced by Bhabha to describe the phenomenon that occurs when different cultural systems come into contact. For Bhabha, hybridity is the 'third space' where actors translate difference and negotiate affinity between cultural discourses for dynamic exchange and inclusion. It is a site of articulation, contestation and transformation between two cultural systems. The concept has been used in a variety of contexts to refer to sites and processes of hybridisation that lead to creative combination of ideas and resources that originate from different domains (Moje et al., 2004). It highlights the agentic and creative potential of actors situated at the intersection of social domains, and the newness that emerges from dialogical encounters between heterogeneous social groups. In contrast to the structural network perspective, which treats career actors as conduits for knowledge flows, the third space perspective emphasises a generative process underpinned by the active engagement of career actors. The evidence presented in the chapter is based on the authors' empirical research on the knowledge-creation activities of two groups of hybrids, 'scientist-entrepreneurs' and 'artist-academics' whose careers and work experiences straddle the academic and practitioner communities (Lam, 2007, 2010, 2011a, 2011b, 2017). The analysis focuses on how these individuals negotiate and reconcile the knowledge differences between the two domains and the third space that emerges to connect them. It provides concrete illustrations of how career boundary-crossing and common work experience can nurture hybrids who actively construct third spaces wherein knowledge-brokering occurs.

The analysis presented in this chapter makes a distinctive contribution by broadening the conceptualisation of career mobility to examine its social psychological aspect in work-role transitions and highlights the agency role of career actors in constructing third spaces of hybridity wherein knowledge-brokering occurs. Career mobility is a boundary-crossing process that creates intersecting spaces between social domains. The 'third space' perspective enriches our understanding of such intersecting spaces as sites and resources for creative knowledge combination. The rest of the chapter is structured as follows. The next section discusses the main concepts and framework, followed by the two illustrative examples of hybrids, the scientist-entrepreneurs and artist-academics, who develop cognitive-behavioural orientations to broker knowledge between the academic and practitioner fields as a result of their boundary-crossing work experiences. The chapter concludes by discussing the theoretical and practical implications.

5.2 Concepts and framework

Career mobility and knowledge combination: missing actor agency

Research on career mobility as a mechanism that facilitates creative knowledge combination has largely been dominated by a structural network perspective and focuses on the formation of social networks that enable knowledge to flow from one domain to another. Some authors, notably in economic geography, use the concept of 'unintended knowledge spillovers' to explain how knowledge travels alongside the mobility of people (Almeida and Kogut, 1999; Song et al., 2003). However, the concept of knowledge spillovers is ambiguous and how knowledge is actually transferred between individuals and firms remains a black box. Others emphasise the blurring of boundaries between firms resulting from employee mobility and the formation of dense professional networks that serve as conduits for the diffusion of tacit knowledge (Saxenian, 1996; Godart et al., 2013). Implicit in this strand of work is the assumption that knowledge combination is a product of interlinked social networks. In other words, it is not the individuals who combine and generate knowledge but the networks flowing through them. Individuals are regarded as 'passive vessels through which information and knowledge flow unimpeded and unchanged' (Phelps et al., 2012). Scholars who examine the influence of career mobility on individual-level creativity also draw heavily on the structural network tradition by showing how boundary-spanning ties accumulated through careers give individuals access to diverse, non-redundant knowledge and thus enhance their potential for creative idea-generation (Perry-Smith, 2006; Sosa, 2011). However, access to diverse knowledge is only a first step to creative knowledge combination. It does not guarantee that individuals are able and willing to exploit the creativity potential of their positional advantage (Dokko et al., 2014). Theories of creativity highlight the combination of opposites and previously unrelated knowledge as a vital process in the generation of new knowledge (Amabile, 1983; Koestler, 1964). What is conspicuously missing in much of the literature is the role of career actors in undertaking the complex task of integrating knowledge across domain boundaries to achieve creative results. Moreover, the process through which this occurs and why career actors are motivated to do so remain obscure.

Knowledge is a situated accomplishment and embedded in social practice (Bechky, 2003; Orlikowski, 2002). For knowledge originating from different social domains to be integrated and combined for new use, actors must overcome what Carlile (2004) describes as three progressively complex knowledge boundaries: syntactic (language), semantic (interpretation) and pragmatic (political). Syntactic boundaries refer to knowledge differences created by divergence in symbols, labels and languages. Here the problem of knowledge transfer and combination amounts to being able to match difference across boundaries by using a common syntax or ways of representing knowledge to each other. Semantic boundaries refer to differences in accepted interpretations and meanings amongst actors. At semantic boundaries, knowledge cannot simply be transferred but needs to be translated through perspective-taking so that actors are able to recognise and accommodate differences in interpretations. The creation of shared space for dialogical encounters is necessary for crossing semantic boundaries (Tsoukas, 2009). Pragmatic or political boundaries refer to the differences in interests and assumptions about what constitutes valuable and legitimate knowledge in particular contexts. Knowledge is invested in practice and so is 'at stake' for those actors who have developed it (Carlile, 2002). Knowledge that is developed in one domain may have negative consequences in another. Overcoming pragmatic knowledge boundaries requires actors to transform their own knowledge and reconcile differences in knowledge practices between domains.

The network knowledge flow perspective treats these knowledge boundaries as unproblematic and overlooks the agency role of career actors in overcoming them. In contrast, the analytical framework developed in this chapter highlights their active role in knowledge-brokering. The concept of knowledge-brokering refers to the processes and activities whereby individuals use their in-between vantage position to translate, transform and combine knowledge across domain boundaries (Hargadon, 2002; Meyer, 2010). It is a critical aspect of the creative process in which individuals integrate divergent resources and perspectives to generate something new (Lingo and O'Mahony, 2010; Obstfeld, 2005). Unlike the flow of information or material goods where the role of brokers is the bridging of structural holes, brokers in complex knowledge activities must actively induce cooperation and connect knowledge from dissimilar others. In other words, they need to have the cognitive ability to overcome the interpretive barriers that arise from the habitualised beliefs and practices of any one domain (DiMaggio, 1997). They also need to be sufficiently motivated to overcome the 'action problem' posed by the inherent difficulties in integrating knowledge embedded in different social domains (Obstfeld, 2005).

In these regards, Wenger's (1998: 109) definition of knowledge-brokering captures well the cognitive-relational challenges:

> brokering . . . involves processes of translation, coordination and alignment between perspectives. It requires enough legitimacy to influence the development of practice, mobilise attention, and address conflicting interests. It also requires the ability to link practices by facilitating transactions between them, and to cause learning by introducing into a practice elements of another.

It suggests that constructing identities of multi-membership across communities is an essential condition that facilitates knowledge-brokering. It also directs attention towards the intimate connection between work (doing), identity (being) and knowledge (knowing).

This chapter postulates that work-role transitions in career boundary-crossing influence the cognitive-behavioural orientations of career actors to engage in knowledge-brokering. The notion of the 'third space' denotes the zone of movement between established work domains. There, career actors break out of domain-specific constraints and negotiate knowledge boundaries, exploiting its liberatory potential for knowledge combination. In other words, it is the agency space where role identity hybridisation and knowledge-brokering occur.

The three facets of careers: work, identity and knowledge

The study conceptualises careers in terms of their three inter-related facets: work, identity and knowledge. A career can be thought of as a sequence of work roles that an individual experiences over time. While work experiences constitute the primary mechanism through which careers occur, the content and quality of a career reside in the knowledge and perspectives that are acquired or changed as a result of work experiences. Viewing careers as repositories of knowledge, Bird (1994) directs our attention to the effects of career moves and job changes on an individual's opportunity to create and use knowledge in different ways across contexts. Nonaka and Takeuchi's (1995) theory of knowledge-creation also stresses the critical role of work experiences across contexts in facilitating knowledge-creation.

Work also provides an important context for identity-formation and self-expression. Knowledge is central to identity because it is part of the cognitive structure of the self and is a key dimension used for group membership identification. Identification induces individuals to acquire the knowledge, interpretive schemas and social codes of the group. In occupational socialisation, the acquisition of specific perspectives and vocabularies is pivotal for identity-formation and legitimating one's position in the occupational group (Barley, 1989). People construct their professional identities by adopting the appropriate role behaviours, partaking in the community's language games (Boland and Tenkasi, 1995) and representing their knowledge in particular ways (Boland et al., 2001). The types of knowledge valued and modes of knowledge-creation and articulation are intimately bound up with one's professional identity. Work, identity and knowledge therefore are intimately linked.

Boundary-crossing careers, hybridity and the 'third space'

The term 'boundary-crossing careers' denotes careers and work experiences straddling professional/occupational role boundaries that involve relatively radical role transitions. It highlights the importance of focusing on boundaries themselves, viewing career mobility as a boundary-crossing process, encompassing not only physical movement but also psychological transition between work roles. Career theorists describe the transition as a status passage or occupational socialisation that invokes significant changes in individuals' identities, cognitive frames and role behaviours (Barley, 1989). Work-role transition requires considerable effort on the part of individuals to learn, negotiate and adapt to the new roles and new work contexts. Nicholson (1984) considers a person's adjustment to role transitions as a kind of personal development in which change is absorbed by a person altering their self-identity, cognitive frames, skills and knowledge, or as role development when the person changes the role requirements so that they better match their ability, knowledge and identity. There can be different modes of adjustment depending on job conditions, but it is not uncommon for changes in both the person and role requirements to occur, which Nicholson refers to as 'exploration'. Ibarra's (1999) work on how professionals adapt to new roles also highlights negotiated adaptation by which they strive to improve the fit between themselves and their new work environment. It shows that individuals use selective learning to construct new customised hybrid identities and seek to transfer to their new roles some of the skills, knowledge and behaviour they had previously acquired. An important insight from the literature is that work-role transitions in career boundary-crossing usually entail role-identity hybridisation. This is especially common among professional and creative knowledge workers, who often seek to preserve aspects of their former identities when adapting to new roles. These individuals usually enjoy high work autonomy and are engaged in high-novelty jobs which permit the exercise of prior knowledge, skills and established habits in new roles (Nicholson, 1984).

Hybridisation reflects the need to accomplish work-role transitions at the boundaries between two domains. It is a means of opening up a 'third space' where individuals can be loosened, momentarily or even perpetually, from the constraints of the established domains for reorientation, redefinition and experimentation. Bhabha (1994) conceived of third spaces and hybridity as being characteristics of encounters between actors from two different social systems. It is the loci where identities and worldviews are negotiated, and the assumed or imposed hierarchy between them are questioned, with the outcome being hybrid identity and perspectives. Bhabha's third space concept directs attention to actors' agency during the moments or processes of transition, and their capacity to challenge the established power structures by constructing alternative positions and worldviews to the dominantly legitimated (Chulach and Gagnon, 2016). It also highlights the 'newness' – new ways of thinking and new practices – that emerges from the encounter in the third space. The concept is therefore particularly useful for illuminating the agentic and knowledge-creation potential of career actors engaged in such space during work-role transitions. It allows us to zoom in to explore the process and outcomes of hybridisation, and the actions undertaken by career actors in constructing and sustaining third spaces.

In this study, the third space denotes an agency space where career actors mobilise the resources originating from the two associated work domains to construct hybrid role identities and overcome knowledge boundaries in work-role transitions. Agency can manifest itself in the form of cognitive work at the individual (intra-personal) level and in the form of relational work at the collective (inter-personal) level. Cognitive work refers to self-reflectiveness and the capacity of the human mind to go beyond domain-specific constraints (Bandura, 2001). Work-role transitions in career boundary-crossing expose individuals to novel and discrepant situations. This may trigger the development of reflective capacity, enabling individuals to break out of their old cognitive frames and see things from the perspectives of others. Louis and Sutton (1991) use the phrase 'cognitive gear switching' to describe the capacity of actors to operate in more than one cognitive mode, switching between different modes of thinking. The third space is the locus where cognitive gear-switching is made possible, and individuals engage in perspective-taking to translate and reinterpret their own knowledge and that of others. Cognitive work enables individuals to overcome syntactic and semantic knowledge boundaries.

Relational work refers to the actions undertaken by career actors to negotiate connectivity between the knowledge and people of the two associated work domains. The authenticity and validity of one's identity and knowledge often come under serious challenge in radical work-role transitions (Ibarra and Barbulescu, 2010). People may experience tension and identity threat when their knowledge or ways of knowing are devalued or not seen as transferrable or relevant in new roles. This is because the basis for what constitutes legitimate and valuable knowledge varies considerably across contexts, creating the potential for conflict. Carlile (2002) refers to this as a pragmatic or political knowledge boundary. The desire to maintain self-continuity while gaining legitimacy across contexts may prompt career actors to reconcile the differences and negotiate alternative ways of defining legitimate knowledge. Relational work is necessary for overcoming pragmatic knowledge boundaries.

In short, this chapter posits that boundary-crossing careers can nurture hybrids as knowledge brokers who actively construct third spaces in work-role transitions and undertake cognitive-relational work to overcome knowledge boundaries. Hybrids operating in the third space can be effective knowledge brokers because they develop the cognitive ability and motivational orientation to connect the knowledge and people of the two domains with which they identify. The section that follows looks at two illustrative examples of hybrids who broker knowledge between the academic and practitioner communities: the 'scientist-entrepreneurs' who connect Mode 1 and Mode 2 knowledge and the 'artist-academics' who integrate analytical and experiential knowledge.

5.3 Hybrids as knowledge brokers in the 'third space' between academic and practitioner communities

Academics and practitioners are often seen as belonging to two distinct communities characterised by divergent goals and values, epistemological assumptions and modes of knowledge-creation (Caplan, 1979; Rynes et al., 2001). This polarised view overlooks the mobility of people between the two communities and the formation of an overlapping zone where many individuals work across the boundaries. In the scientific and technological fields, 'scientist-entrepreneurs' who combine scientific research with business ventures have been known for some time (Jain et al., 2009; Lam, 2007, 2011b; Louis et al., 1989). In the creative and artistic disciplines, boundary-crossing careers and hybrid mix of people between the two communities are particularly common. This is due, in part, to the practice-led or practice-based nature of research whereby many artist-academics work with or as practitioners to contextualise and shape their research (Niedderer and Reilly, 2010). Moreover, professional artists have historically always played a crucial role on university campuses as 'visitors' or regular faculty members owing to the widespread practice of learning-by-doing (Adler, 1976). Knowledge-creation in the creative disciplines is closely intertwined with shifting work roles and relationships as artist-academics move between the academic and practitioner worlds in a reiterative manner (Crossick, 2006).

The two examples of hybrids – 'scientist-entrepreneurs' and 'artist-academics' – examined here are based on the author's empirical research conducted over several years in the UK (see Lam, 2007, 2010, 2011a, 2011b, 2017). These cases are chosen for illustration in this chapter because they are particularly revealing of the agentic effort of individuals in reconciling and overcoming the complex knowledge boundaries between two distinct communities in career boundary-crossing. For the scientist-entrepreneurs, constructing hybridity and working at the interface of science and business requires them to reconcile the conflicting goals and norms between 'open science' in academia and 'proprietary science' in business. They also need to find a way of connecting Mode 1 disciplinary knowledge with Mode 2 industrial problem-solving (Lam, 2007; Gibbons et al., 1994). For the artist-academics, their dual work roles require them to overcome the stark contrast between 'academic' and 'artistic' knowledge-production. The type of knowledge valued, and its process of creation and articulation, differs significantly between academia and professional arts. Academic knowledge is analytical and abstract and is usually articulated and transmitted in texts based on highly specialised language. In contrast, artistic knowledge has strong experiential and symbolic dimensions (Ewenstein and Whyte, 2007), and is commonly expressed in non-textual forms (e.g. artefacts, performances and exhibitions). Artist-academics must reconcile the potential tensions and find ways to connect the two disparate sets of knowledge practices if they are to succeed in their dual careers.

The summary evidence presented below focuses on the ways in which the two groups of hybrid actors construct third spaces between the academic and practitioner worlds and their cognitive-relational work in brokering knowledge.

'Scientist-entrepreneurs' as 'strategic' knowledge brokers in the 'bridging' space: connecting Mode 1 and Mode 2 knowledge

Following Ben-David (1971) and Louis et al. (1989), the term 'scientist-entrepreneurs' is used here to denote those academic scientists who make connections to business firms in their research, and who combine academic goals with knowledge application by building organisational ties between academic research groups and firms. It includes those who engage directly in commercial activities such as formation of spinoff companies. The majority of the scientist-entrepreneurs looked at in the author's study had developed long-term relationships with key industrial partners throughout their careers and were the focal points of firms' links to the universities. They constitute a kind of 'extended human resource' for the firms (Lam, 2007, 2011a). Their career mobility can be described as 'linked' mobility which involves working at bench level with industrial scientists without changing their employment affiliation (Zucker et al., 2002). Some had previously worked as industrial scientists before joining academia and sought to maintain their network ties and reputation in both science and business.

Although their main employment affiliation is academia, these scientist-entrepreneurs are active participants in the industrial world. They are aware of the industrial contexts of their scientific work and play an active role in bridging the interface between science and business. At the cognitive level, the scientist-entrepreneurs are adept at resolving normative tensions and avoiding conflicts of interest by means of cognitive reframing. At the collective level, they play a pivotal role in setting up hybrid organisational arrangements for connecting Mode 1 and Mode 2 knowledge production. They are 'strategic' knowledge brokers who actively negotiate boundaries and reconcile differences in cognitive frames, research goals and interests between science and business. The third space of hybridity is the site where they bridge the cognitive-relational distance between the two domains characterised by divergent norms and knowledge production systems.

Dual cognitive mode and knowledge application

For the scientist-entrepreneurs, deep engagement with industry and knowledge transfer constitute part of their established work routines and hybrid role identities. For example, one in computer science described 'entrepreneurial engagement' as part of 'the repertoire, base skills' that he should retain as a professional scientist. Another pointed out in the interview that knowledge transfer in his case was his 'academic self' talking to his 'industrial self': 'It all happens together . . . that's the heart of how it works, no barriers right. You can do the same thing at once.' This 'talking to himself perspective' reflects the fusion of two different role identities into a hybrid, two-faced one.

These individuals develop a 'dual cognitive mode' in their research, focusing both on scientific advances and applications of their knowledge. They are what Etzkowitz (1998) refers to as 'knowledgeable participants' in industry. Many are cognisant of the value of combining Mode 1 fundamental research with Mode 2 industrial problem-solving, and they saw the multidisciplinary nature of industrial problems as a source of intellectual challenge and creativity. For example, a professor of chemistry, who had worked in industrial R&D in the past, said:

> if you inter-twine your academic thread with fundamental curiosity with your industrial thread of tackling important problems to solve then, I think, then you come up with the best combination of research to do . . . So there are engineering problems, there are chemistry problems and always there are fundamental chemistry problems to be solved and you have to come up with creative, ingenious solutions.

Unlike the traditional academics, the scientist-entrepreneurs did not appear to experience cognitive dissonance or role identity tension when they embarked on commercial ventures. At the socio-cognitive level, they used 'mediating beliefs' (Pratt and Foreman, 2000: 33) to reconcile the normative tension associated with their simultaneous participation in science and business. For many, knowledge application and commercialisation amounted to an extension of their scientific role following long years of fundamental research. They perceived such endeavours as largely legitimate and would use 'old' academic frames to interpret the meaning of commercial engagement. Patenting and company formation, for example, were not seen as vehicles for profit-making but as mechanisms that enabled them to have control over knowledge exploitation and thus to protect the integrity of science. At the more practical level, they were meticulous in maintaining clarity and social order across the academic–business boundary in their daily work. They would ensure that their commercial ventures were kept separate from their publicly funded research in the academic laboratories to avoid conflicts of interest. As one professor/company founder said:

> I had to be careful not to get into a conflicted state, so I kept the topics distinct and I kept the equipment distinct, I duplicated things if necessary. I had a yellow line down the middle of the lab, you couldn't see it, but nothing crossed it. (professor, biochemistry)

The scientist-entrepreneurs are 'strategic' in the way they incorporate commercial practices into their repertoire of behaviour without sacrificing their academic identity. They construct their hybridity by actively reconstituting the meanings of commercialisation so as to resolve the cognitive dissonance emanating from the conflicting logics of science and business. This amounts to what El-Sawad et al. (2004) refer to as a 'double think' strategy for alleviating any psychological discomfort generated from holding contradictory norms.

Hybrid organisations for boundary negotiation and knowledge co-creation

At the organisational level, the scientist-entrepreneurs are instrumental in developing hybrid organisational arrangements such as joint projects and collaborative research groups/centres between their universities and industrial partners. These hybrid arrangements constitute 'third spaces' that facilitate two-way flow of people across permeable and fluid boundaries. They allow the collaborating partners to organise projects and mix research teams flexibly outside the established disciplinary boundaries and organisational structures. They create what Galison (1997) describes as 'trading zones' in which the different knowledge-creation goals and interests between scientists and firms are subject to negotiation. These connecting third spaces make it possible for the industrial partners to contextualise the research carried out in academia and to connect Mode 1 knowledge-production with Mode 2 industrial problem-solving. They enable firms to embed themselves within the wider scientific networks, including the scientist-entrepreneurs' local laboratory networks of researchers and doctoral students.

My study shows that the scientist-entrepreneurs are the key players in creating and sustaining these hybrid organisational arrangements (Lam, 2007, 2010, 2011a). They are strongly motivated to do so because the hybrid structures provide an institutional framework for negotiation and for supporting their boundary-crossing work roles. The hybrid organisations allow them to engage in flexible industrial projects while remaining well integrated into the academic scientific community. By enacting their brokering role, the scientist-entrepreneurs seek to promote and incorporate their hybrid modes of operation into the established academic structure. For example, one scientist-entrepreneur in biosciences actively championed and developed what he described as an ideal 'organisational structure' to 'allow companies to do their research within the university lab'. Others challenged the academic norm of communism that gives priority to publication over patents and used the freedom of the third space to promote the legitimacy of patenting as an alternative source of scientific credit. One, who headed a hybrid research centre, stated in the interview that 'every postdoc and every professor should know what a patent is' because patents are an economic resource that must be exploited:

> it's important as part of assessing the impact of someone's research you know, if it's good enough to do a thriving patent . . . it means you've been concentrating hard enough, they're asking you important questions. So when I'm thinking about a research project, I'm definitely always thinking about the intellectual property.

The brokering role at the interface of science and business also enables the scientist-entrepreneurs to create a web of dependence relations so as to enhance their credibility and influence across domain boundaries. Although entrepreneurial science has gained increased acceptance in academia in the past two decades, many traditional academics remain sceptical and adopt an ambivalent attitude towards it. Scientist-entrepreneurs could be seen by some as having crossed over to the 'dark side' and their commercial activities may arouse suspicion. The knowledge-brokering role enables them to leverage resources from academia and industrial partners and to engage in visible connecting activities valued by both groups. They are 'strategic' knowledge brokers who create structures to sustain their own hybridity as well as to facilitate knowledge co-creation between their academic colleagues and industrial partners.

'Artist-academics' as 'embedded' knowledge brokers in the 'overlapping' space: integrating analytic and experiential knowledge

In the creative disciplines such as drama, music, media arts and design, there are many instances of individuals combining dual academic and practitioner roles on an ongoing basis. These artist-academics experience frequent and recurrent micro role transitions in their day-to-day work. Their repeated alternation between academic and practitioner roles and their physical and psychological proximity made the transition relatively automatic. They displayed psychological mobility and cognitive flexibility and were able to slip easily from one role identity to another according to situational demands. Role-boundary flexibility and permeability enable these individuals to integrate the two identities to create a two-faced one. This is what Pratt and Foreman (2000) refer to as 'Janusian integration', whereby individuals seek to exploit the synergistic benefits between them. Many interviewed by the author saw the two roles as equal and complementary, and stressed the career and cognitive benefits of having two different but interconnected work roles. For example, one described how his work in performing arts and academic research 'come together in an organic and interesting way'. Another spoke about the intellectual benefit of switching between the two roles, describing the experience as being like taking 'holidays' from the established mode of thinking and working. For the artist-academics, role identity hybridisation occurs naturally in everyday work as they integrate their work in academia and creative arts. They appear to be in a permanent state of role transition – what Nicholson (1984) describes as exploration. These people blur the boundaries between the two knowledge domains and operate at the 'overlapping' zones.

The artist-academics can be considered as insiders to both the art and academic worlds. The third space of hybridity is the 'overlap' between the two domains where they internalise the cognitive and relational distance between them. They are able to draw, internally, on the cognitive frames of their academic and practitioner selves in knowledge-creation, and externally, they use multiple forms of knowledge-representation to engage with members of both communities. Knowledge-translation and integration occur naturally and constitute an integral part of their routine knowledge-creation and dissemination activities: they are 'embedded' knowledge brokers.

Cognitive switching and knowledge-integration

The artist-academics operating in the overlapping space are able to operate in more than one cognitive mode and display cognitive-switching and Janusian thinking capacities (Louis and Sutton, 1991; Rothenberg, 1976). They often adopt the perspectives of both an academic and a creative artist and move smoothly between analytical and experiential mental structures in their work. For example, the aforementioned drama professor who worked also as a theatre director, described how he enjoyed the 'pleasures of forming rigorous thoughts and arguments . . . and enlightenment and understanding' in academic research. At the same time, he stressed the need to use an 'aesthetic judgement' rather than a scientific 'cognitive' approach when working among his fellow performing colleagues. To these individuals, combining the different types of knowledge and ways of knowing is entirely consistent with their hybrid role identities. In the interviews, they stressed the 'complementarity' and 'equal importance' of both 'theory' and 'practice', and the need to find 'meeting points' or 'common grounds'.

The artist-academics' ability to adopt the perspectives of two different others (or selves) facilitates knowledge-brokering because it opens up possibilities for self-distanciation and critical reflection. Knowledge is necessarily situated and thus being an insider is critical for perspective-taking. However, people's ability to translate and transform knowledge across contexts also requires moments of separation and autonomy (Ackermann, 1996). Artist-academics are capable of momentarily stepping out of the social worlds to which they belong to take on the role of 'different others' and revisit their own experience as if it were not theirs. This enables them to re-articulate the experience to themselves from the perspective of others, and thus making it more tangible and sharable. New knowledge can be created as a result of these individuals' academic selves engaged in 'productive dialogues' with their practitioner selves. A productive dialogue is a joint activity between two speech partners which provides an opportunity for mutual influence and developing shared meaning and new understanding (Tsoukas, 2009).

Multiple forms of knowledge representation and knowledge co-creation

Knowledge-brokering also forms an integral part of the artist-academics' engagement with members of both communities in knowledge-creation. The equal status of the two role identities within their hybrid self-conceptions enables the artist-academics to be devoid of prejudice in their encounters with members of both groups. Beech et al. (2010) argue that knowledge co-creation through dialogic encounters is only possible when partners meet as equals in shared space with no assumed knowledge hierarchy. The artist-academics interviewed by the author are skilled at forging dialogical relationships with both academic and non-academic partners. Their frequent encounters with both groups and the ability to use both academic and artistic communication tools facilitate knowledge co-creation. One professor, who worked also as a co-curator in arts development agencies, saw himself as 'a respondent and a channel for some things of knowing' and not simply 'a repository of knowledge'. In the interview, he vividly described how knowledge is generated through dialogue with others and iteration between non-textual collaborative activities and academic writing. The use of a mix of relational artistic activities (e.g. events and dialogues), in addition to conventional academic writing, facilitates effective engagement with members of both communities.

Working across the boundaries of the two communities enables the artist-academics to acquire the languages, interpretive conventions and knowledge-representation practices of both. They are 'bi-lingual' and capable of using the communication tools of one community to articulate the knowledge and experience derived from another, and of representing their knowledge in multiple forms. They often reframe the same materials in different ways, for example, converting academic textual knowledge into an artistic talk, producing a 'practitioner' edition of a book or a DVD. Clark and Karmiloff-Smith (1993) use the term 'representational redescription' to refer to this mental process for representational change whereby the human mind enriches itself by re-representing the knowledge that it has stored in different formats. The ability to do so facilitates knowledge-translation and co-creation across community boundaries.

The artist-academics' simultaneous engagement in academic research and creative arts, and recurrent work-role transitions, generate an 'overlapping space' where hybridity is constructed and expressed in everyday work. At the overlap, domain differences are displaced, and career actors develop dual cognitive modes and adopt a Janusian approach to knowledge-creation. Their capacity for representational re-description of knowledge and generative dialogical encounters with members of both communities enables them continuously to translate and integrate knowledge across domain boundaries. Knowledge-brokering is a continuous and situated activity that forms an integral part of their routine knowledge-creation and dissemination activities.

5.4 Discussion and conclusion

Mobility across traditional career and professional role boundaries is widely seen as an important mechanism that facilitates knowledge combination. However, our understanding of the process through which this occurs has been limited by the dominance of a structural knowledge flow perspective that overlooks the agency role of career actors. This study highlights their role as knowledge brokers who actively negotiate differences and combine knowledge across domain boundaries. The third space perspective directs attention to the in-between connecting space in career boundary-crossing where career actors construct hybrid role identities and undertake brokering to overcome knowledge boundaries. The two categories of hybrid career actors looked at in this chapter, who work at the interface between the academic and practitioner communities, illustrate well the agentic effort of career actors in exploiting the combinative capability of their hybridity in the third space. Both categories of hybrids have developed the cognitive ability and motivational orientation to broker knowledge. However, the type of knowledge-brokering and the topology of the third space generated differ between the two groups. It reflects the cognitive-relational distance between the two associated work domains, and the psychological ease in making role transitions and overcoming knowledge boundaries.

The scientist-entrepreneurs, who cross the boundaries of science and business governed by divergent norms and goals of knowledge production, experience more radical role transitions. They make conscious efforts to bridge the cognitive-relational distance between the two discrete work domains by using mediating beliefs and creating supporting organisational structures where they can be free from the constraints of the established systems. The 'bridging space' is where they negotiate knowledge differences and conflicting interests, making it possible to connect Mode 1 scientific knowledge production with Mode 2 knowledge application. The knowledge-brokering activities that scientist-entrepreneurs undertake are deliberative and strategic – they sustain hybridity both at the individual and organisational levels. The artist-academics, whose careers span arts and academia concurrently, experience greater psychological and cognitive ease in everyday micro-role transitions. Although the modes of knowledge-creation and articulation differ between the two domains, academics and artists share many common motivations and goals in knowledge-creation of which the uppermost is the generation of newness or novelty. Psychological proximity of the two roles enables artist-academics to draw simultaneously on the cognitive frames of both and adopt a Janusian approach to knowledge-creation. They are 'natural' hybrids situated at the 'overlapping space' between the two domains. To these people, the divide between different types of knowledge (theory vs. practice) and ways of knowing (thinking vs. doing) ceases to have meaning. They engage in ongoing knowledge-translation and integration by representing knowledge in multiple forms and dialogical encounters with members of both groups. Knowledge-brokering is an incremental process embedded in routine knowledge-creation and dissemination that sustains their hybridity in the overlapping space.

By showing the variation between the two categories of hybrids in eroding and dismantling knowledge boundaries, the analysis sheds new light on the multiform nature of knowledge-brokering. Knowledge-brokering can take the form of cognitive work at the individual level and of relational work at the collective level. The two aspects are closely related because negotiating relations and connectivity are heavily dependent on the actor's ability to empathise with and understand the perspectives of the connecting parties (Bandelj, 2012).

Furthermore, brokering can be dispositional and embedded in everyday work as in the case of the artist-academics, or deliberative as exemplified by the strategic brokering activities of the scientist-entrepreneurs. A common instigator, though, is the hybrids actors' career-driven and identity-based motivations. Knowledge-brokering is instrumental in sustaining their hybridity in the third space and multi-group membership negotiation across domain boundaries.

This chapter contributes to our understanding of career boundary-crossing as a mechanism that facilitates combination of knowledge in two ways. First, by stressing the agency of career actors as knowledge brokers, the study gives insights into the motivational process that energises knowledge combination. Much of the existing literature has tended to de-emphasise the importance of individual agency in favour of structural explanations of the influence of career mobility on knowledge combination in terms of patterns of relationships that give actors access to diverse knowledge. However, combining diverse knowledge for creative generativity does not automatically occur as a result of structural connectivity; it requires the action of skilled and motivated actors who are receptive to the available diverse knowledge and who perceive the benefits of integrating knowledge and perspectives that differ from their own (Dokko et al., 2014). The question of why career actors are willing to spend the time and effort required to overcome complex knowledge boundaries begs an answer. The analysis presented in this chapter suggests that they acquire the cognitive resources and have identity-based motivations to connect the knowledge that originates from the two work domains with which they identify.

Second, this chapter employs the spatial metaphor of a third space to denote the agency space where role identity hybridisation and the cognitive-relational work of knowledge-brokering occur. It advances our understanding of how mobility generates its own space beyond the fixity of place and time that serves as a site and a resource for knowledge combination. The often-mentioned idea that new knowledge can be generated at the boundaries between existing domains does not tell us much about what goes on at the boundaries or how they are made productive. The notion of the third space regards boundaries as places where divergent perspectives interact to produce hybridity. The third space can be generative and productive because it is a movement space where knowledge originating from different domains can be transposed and reconstituted across domain boundaries. It is also a navigational space that tolerates ambiguity and gives individuals the freedom to think beyond a set of binaries associated with established knowledge systems.

All professional groups have a degree of closure, and this creates barriers to knowledge exchange and combination. The academic–practitioner knowledge divide is not unique, and so the analysis presented in this chapter and the practical insight gained have wider relevance. Hybridity, both at the individual and institutional levels, is increasingly seen as important for promoting creativity and innovation across growing segments of the contemporary knowledge economy (Klein, 1996). Entrepreneurial scientists and creative artists can be seen as forerunners of this trend. What this study has shown is that career boundary-crossing and common work experience can erode professional role boundaries and nurture hybrids capable of blending different types of knowledge and ways of knowing for generative knowledge combination.

References

Ackermann, E. (1996). Perspective-taking and object construction: Two keys to learning. In Kafai, Y.B. and Resnick, M. (eds) *Constructionism in practice: Designing, thinking, and learning in a digital world*, pp. 25–37. Mahwah, NJ: Lawrence Erlbaum Associates.

Adler, J. (1976). Academic artists. *Society*, 14 (1), pp. 46–50.

Almeida, P. and Kogut, B. (1999). Localization of knowledge and the mobility of engineers in regional networks. *Management Science*, 45, pp. 905–917.

Amabile, T.M. (1983). *The social psychology of creativity*. New York: Springer-Verlag.

Bandelj, N. (2012). Relational work and economic sociology. *Politics & Society*, 40 (2), pp. 175–201.

Bandura, A. (2001). Social cognitive theory: An agentic perspective. *Annual Review of Psychology*, 52 (1), pp. 1–26.

Barley, S.R. (1989). Careers, identities, and institutions: The legacy of the Chicago School of Sociology. In Arthur, M.B., Hall, D.T. and Lawrence, B.S. (eds) *Handbook of career theory*, pp. 41–65. Cambridge: Cambridge University Press.

Bechky, B.A. (2003). Sharing meaning across occupational communities: The transformation of understanding on a production floor. *Organization Science*, 14 (3), pp. 312–330.

Beech, N., MacIntosh, R. and MacLean, D. (2010). Dialogues between academics and practitioners: The role of generative dialogic encounters. *Organization Studies*, 31 (9–10), pp. 1341–1367.

Ben-David, J. (1971). *Scientist's role in society*. Englewood Cliffs, NJ: Prentice Hall.

Beyer, J.M. and Hannah, D.R. (2002). Building on the past: Enacting established personal identities in a new work setting. *Organization Science*, 13 (6), pp. 636–652.

Bhabha, H.K. (1994). *The location of culture*. London: Routledge.

Bird, A. (1994). Careers as repositories of knowledge: A new perspective on boundaryless careers. *Journal of Organizational Behavior*, 15 (4), pp. 325–344.

Boland, R.J., Singh, J., Salipante, P., Aram, J.D., Fay, S.Y. and Kanawattanachai, P. (2001). Knowledge representations and knowledge transfer. *Academy of Management Journal*, 44 (2), pp. 393–417.

Boland, R.J. and Tenkasi, R.V. (1995). Perspective making and perspective taking in communities of knowing. *Organization Science*, 6 (4), pp. 350–372.

Caplan, N. (1979). The two-communities theory and knowledge utilization. *American Behavioral Scientist*, 22 (3), pp. 459–470.

Carlile, P.R. (2002). A pragmatic view of knowledge and boundaries: Boundary objects in new product development. *Organization Science*, 13 (4), pp. 442–455.

Carlile, P.R. (2004). Transferring, translating, and transforming: An integrative framework for managing knowledge across boundaries. *Organization Science*, 15 (5), pp. 555–568.

Chulach, T. and Gagnon, M. (2016). Working in a 'third space': A closer look at the hybridity, identity and agency of nurse practitioners. *Nursing Inquiry*, 23 (1), pp. 52–63.

Clark, A. and Karmiloff-Smith, A. (1993). The cognizer's innards: A psychological and philosophical perspective on the development of thought. *Mind & Language*, 8 (4), pp. 487–519.

Crossick, G. (2006). *Knowledge transfer without widgets: The challenge of the creative economy*. London: Goldsmiths' College, University of London.

DiMaggio, P.J. (1997). Culture and cognition. *Annual Review of Sociology*, 23, pp. 263–287.

Dokko, G., Kane, A.A. and Tortoriello, M. (2014). One of us or one of my friends: How social identity and tie strength shape the creative generativity of boundary-spanning ties. *Organization Studies*, 35 (5), pp. 703–726.

El-Sawad, A., Arnold, J. and Cohen, L. (2004). 'Doublethink': The prevalence and function of contradiction in accounts of organizational life. *Human Relations*, 57 (9), pp. 1179–1203.

Etzkowitz, H. (1998). The norms of entrepreneurial science: Cognitive effects of the new university-industry linkages. *Research Policy*, 27 (8), pp. 823–833.

Ewenstein, B. and Whyte, J. (2007). Beyond words: Aesthetic knowledge and knowing in organizations. *Organization Studies*, 28 (5), pp. 689–708.

Galison, P. (1997). *Image and logic: A material culture of microphysics*. Chicago, London: University of Chicago Press.

Gao, Y. and Riley, M. (2009). Knowledge and identity: A review. *International Journal of Management Reviews*, 12 (3), pp. 317–334.

Gibbons, M., Limoges, C., Notwotny, H., Schwartzman, S., Scott, P. and Trow, M. (1994). *The new production of knowledge*. London: Sage.

Godart, F.C., Shipilov, A.V. and Claes, K. (2013). Making the most of the revolving door: The impact of outward personnel mobility networks on organizational creativity. *Organization Science*, 25 (2), pp. 377–400.

Hargadon, A.B. (2002). Brokering knowledge: Linking learning and innovation. *Research in Organizational Behavior*, 24, pp. 41–86.

Ibarra, H. (1999). Provisional selves: Experimenting with image and identity in professional adaptation. *Administrative Science Quarterly*, 44, pp. 764–791.

Ibarra, H. and Barbulescu, R. (2010). Identity as narrative: Prevalence, effectiveness, and consequences of narrative identity work in macro work role transitions. *Academy of Management Review*, 35 (1), pp. 135–154.

Jain, S., George, G. and Maltarich, M. (2009). Academics or entrepreneurs? Investigating role identity modification of university scientists involved in commercialization activity. *Research Policy*, 38 (6), pp. 922–935.

Klein, J.. (1996). *Crossing boundaries: Knowledge, disciplinarities, and interdisciplinarities*. Charlottesville, London: University of Virginia Press.

Kleinbaum, A.M. (2012). Organizational misfits and the origins of brokerage in intra-firm networks. *Administrative Science Quarterly*, 57 (3), pp. 407–452.

Koestler, A. (1964). *The act of creation*. London: Arkana.

Lam, A. (2007). Knowledge networks and careers: Academic scientists in industry-university links. *Journal of Management Studies*, 44 (6), pp. 993–1016.

Lam, A. (2010). From 'ivory tower traditionalists' to 'entrepreneurial scientists'? Academic scientists in fuzzy university-industry boundaries. *Social Studies of Science*, 40 (2), pp. 307–340.

Lam, A. (2011a). University-industry collaboration: Careers and knowledge governance in hybrid organisational space. *International Journal of Strategic Business Alliances*, 2 (1–2), pp. 135–145.

Lam, A. (2011b). What motivates academic scientists to engage in research commercialization: 'Gold', 'ribbon' or 'puzzle'? *Research Policy*, 40 (10), pp. 1354–1368.

Lam, A. (2017). Boundary-crossing careers and the 'third space of hybridity': Career actors as knowledge brokers between creative arts and academia. *Environment and Planning A*, pp. 0308518X17746406.

Lingo, E.L. and O'Mahony, S. (2010). Nexus work: Brokerage on creative projects. *Administrative Science Quarterly*, 55 (1), pp. 47–81.

Louis, K., Blumenthal, D., Gluck, M. and Stoto, M. (1989). Entrepreneurs in academe: An exploration of behaviors among life scientists. *Administrative Science Quarterly*, 34 (4), pp. 596–606.

Louis, M.R. and Sutton, R.I. (1991). Switching cognitive gears: From habits of mind to active thinking. *Human Relations*, 44 (1), pp. 55–76.

Meyer, M. (2010). The rise of the knowledge broker. *Science Communication*, 32 (1), pp. 118–127.

Moje, E.B., Ciechanowski, K.M., Kramer, K., Ellis, L., Carrillo, R. and Collazo, T. (2004). Working toward third space in content area literacy: An examination of everyday funds of knowledge and discourse. *Reading Research Quarterly*, 39 (1), pp. 38–70.

Nicholson, N. (1984). A theory of work role transitions. *Administrative Science Quarterly*, 29, pp. 172–191.

Niedderer, K. and Reilly, L. (2010). Research practice in art and design: Experiential knowledge and organised inquiry. *Journal of Research Practice*, 6 (2), pp. 1–11.

Nonaka, I. and Takeuchi, H. (1995). *The knowledge-creating company: How Japanese companies create the dynamics of innovation*. New York: Oxford University Press.

Obstfeld, D. (2005). Social networks, the tertius iungens orientation, and involvement in innovation. *Administrative Science Quarterly*, 50 (1), pp. 100–130.

Orlikowski, W.J. (2002). Knowing in practice: Enacting a collective capability in distributed organizing. *Organization Science*, 13 (3), pp. 249–273.

Perry-Smith, J.E. (2006). Social yet creative: The role of social relationships in facilitating individual creativity. *Academy of Management Journal*, 49 (1), pp. 85–101.

Phelps, C., Heidl, R. and Wadhwa, A. (2012). Knowledge, networks, and knowledge networks: A review and research agenda. *Journal of Management*, 38 (4), pp. 1115–1166.

Pratt, M.G. and Foreman, P.O. (2000). Classifying managerial responses to multiple organizational identities. *Academy of Management Review*, 25 (1), pp. 18–42.

Pratt, M.G., Rockmann, K.W. and Kaufmann, J.B. (2006). Constructing professional identity: The role of work identity learning cycles in the customization of identity among medical residents. *Academy of Management Journal*, 49 (2), pp. 235–262.

Raider, H.J. and Burt, R.S. (1996). Boundaryless careers and social capital. In Arthur, M.B. and Rousseau, D.M. (eds) *The boundaryless career: A new employment principle for a new organizational era*, pp. 187–200. Oxford: Oxford University Press.

Rothenberg, A. (1976). Janusian thinking and creativity. *Psychoanalytic Study of Society*, 7, pp. 1–30.

Rynes, S.L., Bartunek, J.M. and Daft, R.L. (2001). Across the great divide: Knowledge creation and transfer between practitioners and academics. *Academy of Management Journal*, 44 (2), pp. 340–355.

Saxenian, A. (1996). Beyond boundaries: Open labor markets and learning in Silicon Valley. In Arthur, M.B. and Rousseau, D.M. (eds) *The boundaryless career: A new employment principle for a new organizational era*, pp. 23–39. Oxford: Oxford University Press.

Song, J., Almeida, P. and Wu, G. (2003). Learning-by-hiring: When is mobility more likely to facilitate interfirm knowledge transfer? *Management Science*, 49 (4), pp. 351–365.

Sosa, M.E. (2011). Where do creative interactions come from? The role of tie content and social networks. *Organization Science*, 22 (1), pp. 1–21.

Sullivan, S.E. and Arthur, M.B. (2006). The evolution of the boundaryless career concept: Examining physical and psychological mobility. *Journal of Vocational Behavior*, 69 (1), pp. 19–29.

Tsoukas, H. (2009). A dialogical approach to the creation of new knowledge in organizations. *Organization Science*, 20 (6), pp. 941–957.

Wenger, E. (1998). *Communities of practice: Learning, meaning, and identity*. Cambridge: Cambridge University Press.

Zucker, L., Darby, M. and Torero, M. (2002). Labor mobility from academe to commerce. *Journal of Labor Economics*, 20 (3), pp. 629–660.

6 The bond, the bridge and the broker

Knowledge conversion in the university–industry nexus

Håkon Finne and Tone Merethe Aasen

6.1 Introduction

The idea of building the new development strategies for EU regions around smart specialisation, with a significant role for universities, came out of a research project investigating why the substantial EU funding of R&D over several decades had not improved the competitiveness of European industry as much as wanted. The Knowledge for Growth project, with Dominique Foray in a leading role, identified the main problem to be that the R&D investments had been dispersed too widely (EUR 24047, 2009). Each region (or country, in some cases) would be better off specialising their R&D capacities, differentiated from other regions, and entrepreneurial discovery processes could 'reveal what a country or region does best in terms of science and technology' (Foray et al., 2009: 25). Develop these, and prosperity will follow.

Since then, smart specialisation has become a broader concept with greater emphasis on other place-based strengths than just science and technology. Most notably this includes industrial strengths that embody competencies and regional institutional support that can be used to successfully expand into related activities. Specialised research aligned with these strengths would still be essential, of course; the RIS in the RIS3 acronym stands for research and innovation strategies and not for regional innovation systems or strategies.

But what if part of the problem lies not in the lack of specialisation but in the way universities and their knowledge interact (or not) with industry? And as a corollary, would this improve (or worsen) with a greater division of science between regions?

In section 6.2 we illuminate these questions by positing structural explanations of knowledge transfer as the handling of an object against a deeper understanding of the essential role of knowledge conversion as a socio-cognitive process. In section 6.4 we narrate a selection of 70 years of events and solutions to the science–industry nexus from one university considered to be successful in this respect. The design of this inquiry is outlined in section 6.3. In section 6.5 we distil some of the findings from section 6.4 into the conceptual apparatus developed in section 6.2, and in section 6.6 we take a cautious look at what universities in other settings might learn from this exercise about developing their role in smart specialisation.

6.2 University knowledge matters, but how?

Opening the road to the ivory towers

Until fairly recently, economic policy did not consider universities and their knowledge production of any significant value. Schumpeter (1934 [1912]) posited that economic growth was driven by innovation, which in turn was the new combination of elements of knowledge – but without any reference to universities, at the time being mostly considered ivory towers harbouring irrelevant activity (Shapin, 2012). The job of exploring new combinations and converting knowledge to innovation and subsequent profit, Schumpeter left entirely to entrepreneurs. Kirzner (1997) later fruitfully developed the role of these individual entrepreneurial discoveries in economic theory, but only with scant reference to innovation as such, and even less attention to the sources of knowledge. Knowledge is knowledge, but not all knowledge is relevant to economic progress.

The post-World War II sentiment in the Western world was to step up scientific research, but the policy was to rely on the social contract of science spillovers (Bush, 1945): fund university research, and scientists will follow a moral obligation to turn their discoveries into social and economic benefits. The waterfall of scientific knowledge into practical consequences was not questioned; scientists in white coats followed their products all the way to consumers in popular imagery.

Changing higher education from the purpose of educating a small elite into furnishing a much larger meritocracy also gave baby boomers unprecedented access over the following decades to the culture of knowledge production and verification called research. There were many forces at work that broadened the road to the ivory towers.

Knowledge markets that don't work – or is it a systems weakness?

During the 1980s and 1990s, researchers amassed solid evidence that technical change matters for economic development (Dosi et al., 1988). They also developed the notions of *systems of innovation* or *innovation systems* (Lundvall, 1992; Nelson, 1993) – institutionalised science–industry linkages – and showed that knowledge from universities gave significant contributions to industrial innovation and hence to growth. These were systems that could be improved by public intervention, and the bottlenecks in knowledge transfer could be considered institutional coordination problems rather than related to the usefulness or applicability of university-based knowledge per se. Open the roads to the ivory towers and the division of labour will take care of the conversion of knowledge – although some researchers increasingly pointed to interactive rather than linear linkages in the systems as a point of possible concern, since interaction is much more difficult to coordinate than the linear handover of fixed entities of knowledge (Lundvall, 1988).

The OECD picked up on these ideas and concluded that private investment in research and innovation was socially suboptimal because of market failures. This understanding was probably important in an organisation whose staple recipe for growth policy was to deregulate markets, but whether or not it is a good analysis, it is a very sticky one. Now they could recommend increased public funding of university research as a measure for growth. They also suggested measures to actually establish university–industry linkages as knowledge markets. First, they defined knowledge as an intellectual property and a tradable good, owned by its creator, and knowledge transfer as a transfer of intellectual property (OECD, 2003). Second, they recommended legal regulations for intellectual property rights (IPR) to incentivise the interest of universities to take an active part in providing knowledge for and through these markets. In other words, let the forces of supply and demand control the direction of research in the universities and of innovation in industry, and the actors on both sides of the market relation will take care of the actual transformation of new (technological) knowledge into industrial innovation processes.

IPR regulation was indeed one of the major aspects of the American successes first communicated under the *triple helix* heading (Leydesdorff and Etzkowitz, 1996; Etzkowitz, 2008). Promoting an entrepreneurial spirit among staff and students was another one – not just to direct their research in a 'useful' direction but to actually change careers and establish spinoff companies, becoming entrepreneurs themselves (Schulte, 2004). However, the major contribution of research under the triple helix label has been to show the different and lasting institutional orientations (in values, goals, culture, etc.) of the three specialised spheres – which of course was acknowledged in advance – and then how government participation in its many forms can improve their interaction and the outcome for growth, or not – which was the new insight. Despite the institutional inertia involved, there is also a complex dynamic that underlies the attempts at changing their behaviour at the borders or more deeply (Leydesdorff, 2003; Leydesdorff and Meyer, 2006) – hence the metaphor of the three intertwining helices; government is part of the system and can be as unpredictably changed as the other parties by playing its roles. Expect to see individuals pursuing careers in all three helices, unstable boundaries, overlapping and competitive behaviour rather than division of labour, and specialised intermediaries crowding out those that took the first coordination steps at the outset. But in the process, perhaps new competences in knowledge transfer and conversion develop.

Despite the implementation of appropriate IPR regulations and phenomenal increases in government funding of university research in Europe over the last few decades, the volume of knowledge transfer in markets is much lower than hoped for. Universities are increasingly exposed to market forces and to some extent act as any other businesses, but even though many of the leading universities are learning to handle market mechanisms (Wissema, 2009), knowledge transfer in the OECD sense seems not to keep up. Hence when the European Commission appointed an expert group to develop national indicators for knowledge transfer, the outcome was a composite indicator where

holes requires sufficient knowledge and trust on both sides for the bridge to be accepted as a source of mutual benefit and become more than just a weak link. This opens up for brokers, whose role it is to establish and maintain these bridges that, when activated, give an opportunity to benefit for both the connected parties and the broker (brokers do it better). Network innovation studies confirm the value of using external networks for innovation purposes, provided someone can function as a broker.

Obstfeld (2005) has then observed that although Burt (2005) has identified the value of creating linkages, brokers can also choose to build the links directly between the two parties and not remain in between with a monopoly on the information flows. This of course assumes that the communities on both sides develop capacities to understand each other.

Clearly, there are differences between marginalised local communities getting on by means of reciprocity and businesses profiting from exploiting their existing knowledge by tightening the production links towards their suppliers. Nevertheless, the importance of the underlying social mechanisms for keeping activities afloat seems to be very similar. Even Kuhn (1977) concluded that what kept a scientific paradigm together was the social structure of the community that maintained the paradigm's cognitive practices. Paradigms die with their practitioners, only after competing paradigms have won the battle of recruitment of new members.

We question the strict division between bonds as exclusive ties and bridges as inclusive. It was instrumental in developing the theory in the first place, but we also find room for bonds or strong ties that act as effective bridges for connecting the practices of two otherwise separate communities, neither as mere conduits for information or resources sanctioned by a trusted broker, nor as a *de facto* integration of the two communities. There is no denying that with the increasing total volume of knowledge at work in society, many work roles become increasingly specialised. However, certainly in a pluralistic society, many people do, and find acceptance for, playing several roles, thus effectively becoming members of multiple communities. The scope for handling cognitive incongruences may be wider than found in the original studies of social capital; so also the range of available options for changing positions or employment should the incongruence become too tough to handle. Even the traditionally strongest socially bonded unit, the family, is much more open-ended now. Handling all these relations is not always easy but it is increasingly done.

Furthermore, the dynamic aspect is missing from these theoretical considerations. The concrete social structures change continuously, and even if the underlying processes tend to recreate the same structural patterns over time, weak links can turn into strong ones and vice versa, networks merge and dissipate. What interests us the most is singular bridges that are complemented over time by parallel linkages that integrate communities to some extent, at least enough to create a common space where they can develop a hybrid knowledge base.

How does this help us understand why relations between universities and industry are developing much more slowly than anticipated?

Academics and industrialists not only work under different institutional logics, they clearly pursue different practices and thus embrace different bodies of knowledge – even though some of them may have overlapping knowledge bases from attending the same programs of higher education. Even within a single firm or a single university the division of labour results in multiple communities of practice where the contents of applicable knowledge and the norms for what tacitly is acknowledged as being good and relevant knowledge and even counts as knowledge at all, may vary between them (Wenger, 1998). The same goes for universities, except that their communities of research practice usually span international networks between specialists as much as, or even more than, colleagues down the same corridor.

Coordination between communities of practice in a production flow or other forms of productive collaboration usually requires continuous adaption as practices change on one or the other side. These efforts can fruitfully be understood as shared reflection over *boundary objects* regulating the workflow between them (Star and Griesemer, 1989). If the cognitive distance between academics and industrialists is too long for an effective collaboration, which is frequently the case unless the firm has its own R&D capabilities, or the academics have industrial experience themselves, the establishment of boundary objects and the time and resources to develop practices and associated knowledge bases around them can be a good strategy. Carlile (2004) has identified such boundary work to encompass syntactic, semantic and pragmatic issues, corresponding to transfer, translation, and transformation, respectively, of the knowledge in question. Our concept of conversion could refer to any and all of these levels. Lam (2010) has traced the conditions for being able to straddle the knowledge boundaries as an individual bridge through dual scientist-entrepreneur personal careers. These conditions include the possibilities to develop a third, hybrid knowledge space that overlaps science and business but becomes sufficiently different from either of them to award it a separate existence (Lam, 2011).

Intertwined in all these relations are, at all times, the question of trust. To say that trust underpins strong links, bonds, bridges, and the acceptance of the intervention of brokers, is too simple, as much of the trust is developed as a consequence of the interactions and not only as a matter of prerequisite for them. However, referral from someone trusted helps the relation to get going, not because you trust their conclusion but because you trust they have used the same criteria as you would. The importance of trust in the acceptance of knowledge claims can hardly be overestimated (Belenky et al., 1986). One's trust in particular institutions can confer on their members, although with caution; institutional distrust definitely does.

6.3 Case design

We will investigate alternative and complementary ways of achieving transfer and conversion of knowledge from universities to industry by means of a single university case as it developed over a period of nearly 70 years, deploying new mechanisms over time. A single case design should be understood as this and no statistical generalisation to other universities is implied. Its value beyond itself clearly depends on explaining its success (or failure) in context and the relevance for universities in other contexts.

The case we are using to illustrate this development is our shared alma mater, the Norwegian Institute of Technology (NTH), to which we have had personal links since the 1970s, and its spinoff research institute SINTEF, where we both have been gainfully employed for a number of years. NTH was established in Trondheim in 1910. It remained the only provider of chartered engineering training (MSc) in Norway until 2002. At that time, NTH had already merged with other faculties to become a comprehensive university, currently named the Norwegian University of Science and Technology (NTNU). It has always held the position as the academic institution in Norway with the best working relations with industry, whether measured by industrial opinion polls, by commissioned impact studies (Damvad, 2017), or by independent academic studies (Tijssen et al., 2009). It should therefore serve well as a case to study precisely that. The establishment of SINTEF (an acronym for the Foundation for Industrial and Technical Research at NTH) in 1950 is part of the story and not just a contextual issue; we will return to that below. In the following, the term institute refers to the research institute (SINTEF) and not to the teaching institute (NTH), which we call the university, also before it formally acquired university status.

The data for this case study come from internal documents from the two organisations, observations and interviews over several years, and from published material.

6.4 The related university

Academic–industrial bonds that combined into a bridge

NTH was based on a pre-existing mining seminar and a technical educational institution and expanded its range of disciplines up to World War II. Teaching of practical engineering skills prevailed, built on a German educational model, where requirements for professors as well as students included lengthy periods of work in a relevant industry. The curriculum emphasised construction skills rather than analytical abilities. Students probably spent far more time at the drawing board than in the laboratory. They were socialised into a culture of calculation, obviously, and of self-confidence in solving problems, to prepare them for technical as well as management roles (Brandt and Nordal, 2010).

After the war, NTH was still strongly linked with local and national industry, with a practically oriented teaching ethos that appeared to be all set for the post-war reconstruction effort. Even as late as 1972, a professorial candidate with superbly excellent academic qualifications was requested to work for one year at a shipyard before commencing his teaching duties (Moe, 1999). He declined to comply but was still given the job and went on to become a significant research and research policy actor, perhaps marking a cultural turning point for the university.

However, the post-war Western belief in science and even scientific research as an integral component of rebuilding society was spreading from the USA through the Marshall Plan (also called the European Recovery Program) and other channels and now imbued national policy. In 1949, the newly established research council for science and technology proposed to establish a new institute for applied engineering research under its auspices. It would be located in the country's capital, because of the extent of existing research activities at the science departments of the University of Oslo. Its purpose would be to provide new and better scientific solutions to industrial problems and opportunities. The idea predated the war but at that time it had not caught any real interest, neither politically nor at the universities. This time the reception was quite different, and the proposal gained momentum. NTH was taken off guard and displayed surprise, not entirely of the positive kind.

It was not that the professors in Trondheim wanted the new research institute for themselves. In fact, most of the Trondheim professors were hardly interested in research at all, oriented as they were towards the practical needs of the industries they were serving with their engineering teaching. There were some variations in this attitude, obviously, with chemistry and later the emerging fields of electronics and control engineering more inclined towards experimental and theoretical work, but these fields hardly had any industrial base at the time. True, the organisation had some 15 professors with doctorates, half of them in chemistry, and professors were nominally required to perform research, but their cultural inclination was elsewhere. Even today, older staff reminisce that they are much more inclined towards using their scientific knowledge to provide high-quality solutions for industry than to write theoretical and experimental papers for scientific journals that are only read – if at all – by other academics.

Rather, the professors of 1949 considered the proposed research institute a threat to their university. They were afraid a research institute in Oslo would drain the labour market for suitable candidates for teacher positions in Trondheim and eventually also attract good students to science studies in Oslo rather than engineering studies in Trondheim, with equal prospects of employment in industry. Oslo being the capital of Norway and the larger city could offer better job prospects and better access to just about anything, despite Trondheim being considered the preferred location for students, as it is still today.

Entrepreneurially oriented as the NTH professors were, they came up with a countermove. They proposed to establish research facilities at their own university in order to be able to attract the right personnel in competition with the new research institute that they expected would be set up with state funding in Oslo anyway, regardless of what happened in Trondheim. Who knows, maybe some current professors even might become interested in research? Actually, a few already were, as they saw this as an opportunity for the future. But there was a problem: whereas NTH operated on fixed government budgets for teaching and administration, government would not guarantee stable funding for research activities there. The ministry and the research council were not uninterested, but funding would have to be ad hoc, determined on a yearly basis by national experts. As a state institution, NTH was not capable of handling such a risky prospect.

The solution came with a proposal to establish a private, not-for-profit foundation with a formal financial independence of NTH but with a strategic linkage to the university, in the form of having professors in charge of the research activities at the foundation. The personal–professional bonds that professors had to individual firms were joined together to provide an institutional bridge between the university and industry.

To discover, elaborate and then settle for this business model can be considered an entrepreneurial discovery in its own right. Universities are not considered economic actors, neither in current legal provisions regulating their government funding, nor – and particularly not – in theories of how they interact (or not) with 'proper' economic actors in industry. Still, obviously they depend on revenue streams and other resources. Our case university, populated as it was with entrepreneurial professors, in 1950 discovered how they could secure both their recruitment base and additional future funding, while maintaining the integrity of their university. The golden egg was the establishment of an external research institute with which they kept the strategic control at the level of individual professors. Plus, they focused on industrial and technical rather than on technical and scientific research, as would be the focus of the government-owned institute in Oslo.

Perhaps they could even recruit some of the better students to work in research awaiting tenure-track positions at the university. Many did not exactly think of research as the best way to serve industry, since they were already providing them with the best candidates. Additionally, many professors also had a consultancy relationship with firms, providing services based on scientific and practical knowledge for the direct benefit of the firms. However, an added benefit – for these professors – of the new institute, once in place, could be that since they would be able to control its activities, it could also provide them with more personnel to solve the problems of industry while at the same time maintain their personal revenue streams to compensate for the lower salary level at NTH than in industry. We should emphasise that we have little data on the scope of this consultancy and we don't know how important it was for the selection of the business model that was actually chosen. Not all professors opted to channel their activities through the institute.

A bridge to bond on

Today, the idea of organising research as projects – with goals, timed deliverables, budgets, and so on – is ubiquitous and alternatives are hardly ever considered. Even personal scholarships frequently appear as part of a larger project. Records of the early activities in SINTEF show, however, that the idea of a project, let alone a commissioned project, was not how activities were organised or accounted nor sold or invoiced. Grants and donations, including government assignments, loosely linked to areas of research, dominated at first. Nevertheless, the portfolio of activities paid for by industrial clients grew rapidly. It appeared that at least certain segments of industry were ahead of many professors in terms of their readiness for research. By 1960 the staff at the research institute had grown steadily to 100, which by comparison was nearly 20 per cent of the contemporary staff at the university. Some individuals had their primary employment in one of the organisations and a part-time job in the other one. Even up to a few years ago, when SINTEF had grown to more than 2,000 employees, the two organisations boasted that they had 500 people with dual appointments, attesting to the close links between the university with its teaching and increasingly fundamental science research on the one hand and the institute with its applied industrial and technical research on the other.

Over the next several decades a large number of research institutes in practically all disciplines were established throughout the country. At one time over 100 organisations were registered as research institutes – quite a large number for a small country. The two business models of 1950 dominated. National institutes tended to be owned by a research council or by a ministry, whereas their competitors were established more or less on the SINTEF model as private, not-for-profit foundations with links – although of varying degree – to a university or a university college. However, our impression is that the driving force in many of these cases was the opportunity to create jobs serving a growing market for empirical studies, particularly aimed at public agencies and ministries, rather than to liaise professors better with industry or other segments of the private sector.

Returning to SINTEF, it was generally agreed all the way up through the 1960s that those departments where professors had a strong formal and informal influence on the research activities were the most successful. This actually worked several ways. Professors were able to provide the latest scientific insights into projects for industry, their direct contact with industry resulted in improving the relevance of their own research activities, and they managed to use the flexibility of their research institute to provide investments and new technologies for new research and teaching directions more rapidly than they possibly could have done using the formal channels of their university.

The computing centre established in 1962 is a case in point for the latter effect, where SINTEF provided both the infrastructure, the personnel, and the services to university needs for teachers and students alike on a scale not seen before at any other university in the country. Nearly 1,000 students learned how to program the first computer over the next year, on top of their already full workload.

But by and large, the personal linkages to industry that professors could establish, maintain and develop through SINTEF, supported, redirected and multiplied by staff employed at the research institute, were considered the essential success criterion.

SINTEF grew rapidly, responding to industrial needs as well as funding opportunities from the research council. Not all new departments had as strong a connection to university professors as did the first ones. As already noted, not all professors were equally keen on research, and some chose to maintain their industrial relations to themselves. SINTEF did, however, become popular with engineering students for their first job. This was partly because of the growing attractiveness of working in research – and at a somewhat higher salary than the corresponding position at the university – but mostly, we believe, because engineers with a SINTEF job on their CV were very attractive candidates to jobs in many large or advanced industrial firms. Three years working in SINTEF on the latest technology in projects with an applied industrial angle was a boon. Firms have always complained that it takes them three years of in-house training to turn graduates into productive and self-propelled engineers. Not only engineering educations are subjected to this type of criticism, clearly; it is rather commonplace to complain that university education is too 'theoretical' – meaning not sufficiently practical – and sometimes even outdated. If engineers could be recruited from other firms that had taken the burden of making proper engineers within a relevant domain, that would be better. And even one step better still if that training was related to a key technology that could help the firm get a competitive edge. In fact, many of the engineers in question had been working on research projects where their future employer was one of the major stakeholders. Thus, their SINTEF job had even been an introduction to the actual use of the technology and the corporate culture. When firms employed them, they could benefit maximally from the knowledge conveyed by the professors and further converted to practical implementation in the firms.

But these young engineers did not only bring the new technology and state-of-the-art knowledge with them to their new employers and implemented it there. They also brought an ethos of research that made them understand perfectly well what could – and could not – be achieved in commissioned research projects. The could-not factor was often important; reticence sometimes prevailed, particularly among impatient firms that only wanted the practical results and not the sometimes painstaking path towards them. However, by and large they brought with them a friendly if not actively positive relationship to the world of research in general and to the researchers and the professors in particular.

A significant product of research work at the institute, then, was an increasing number of people with bonds to both industry and university, and they could go either way or stay in the institute.

The practice of channelling promising students from the university into applied research in the institute and from there over to industry after a few years increased in numbers as SINTEF kept growing. It was probably one of the more cost-effective mechanisms of knowledge transfer from universities to industry ever in operation. It helped build the absorptive capacity of firms as a by-product of the relation with the professors at the university.

Many firms have worked well together with professors to provide summer jobs and master's thesis assignments in order to pre-screen potential job candidates before they even completed their studies. However, to be able to do this in conjunction with a high-level project of practical consequence was clearly one step up.

Cost-effective or not, the costs and the benefits do not necessarily accrue to the same actors. Towards the mid-1980s, personnel turnover became close to 15 per cent, and several other developments also led to SINTEF focusing more on itself as an independent actor with a responsibility of its own, and to some degree less on its traditional role in knowledge transfer. For one, government now started to insist on turning untraded dependencies between the university and the institute into traded ones with market prices on all mutual use of people, equipment, space, and other resources. Public–private synergy was not necessarily a positively laden word in the increasingly neo-classical foundation for running the public sector. One effect was a change in SINTEF's recruitment criteria, recruiting for a research career rather than for a stepping stone to an industrial career. The stepping stone pathway is still there but it is much less frequently used. When one of the present authors delivered his first independent research report (on the organisation of computer-aided design) in 1981, one of the involved research managers responded, 'interesting research design, do you want a permanent job with us?' and the other one responded, 'interesting practical implications, which firm do you want a job with?' Today, when someone quits after three years, the emphasis is on hoping they will come back as clients, but better still as researchers.

The client role should not be underestimated, as we have indicated before. As industry's need for a more rapid access to new knowledge from universities was growing, and the growth rate of new knowledge was itself on the rise, the recruitment of spot-on engineers would not be enough to keep up. Hardly any firms could increase their engineering staff every three years. So, the ones they did recruit could be used to improve their capabilities to commission further research and implement the results, and not only to implement and improve the technical solutions that gave them a job in the first place.

Brokers for the many

Two other changes in the environment at about the same time (late 1980s) were aimed at securing a stronger user orientation (or usefulness to industry) of funding from the research council. One was the reorganisation of the institutes organised under the research council into free-standing institutions, more like the original model of SINTEF. Stronger market exposure and less reliance on government funding and strategy were the key issues for this phase of the restructuring of the research sector that took many years. What was implemented more rapidly was the decision to channel much more of the funding from the research council through firms, which would be the owners and benefiters of the activities in the institutes, for which they would also have to contribute (financially or in kind); this would secure industry relevance. This further emphasised the project, in particular the user-owned project, as a dominant organisational form for the activities. Firms that had built an absorptive capacity for relating to research institutes managed to benefit more clearly from this arrangement. Many firms that are large consumers of public R&D support have managed to use these resources for great benefit. Small firms that could not muster projects on their own, however, would still depend on activities that were developed for the benefit of many. These did not fit so well in the scheme any more, even though their need to upgrade through new knowledge was growing rather than declining. Some institutions had existed to guide their selection and implementation of new technology but several of these would require updates on a widening array of technologies themselves if they were to be able to assist firms in their target group. Many of these firms did not even have a chartered engineer on their staff, let alone one with personal connections to a university or a research institute. How could their needs be addressed under the new circumstances?

A small number of experienced and well-connected researchers and research managers at the institute came together in the late 1980s and proposed an activity of technology diffusion support to small firms. They clearly saw the need to continue being a bridge to the high number of small firms that did not have the capacities of large firms to take charge of projects with researchers involved. Waiting for new knowledge to eventually pass down to commercial technology providers would simply put these firms at a disadvantage.

They explored several organisational forms, service packages, business models, and funding sources before they landed on a combination that stayed more or less constant over the next 30 years. It consisted of the following. A number of knowledge brokers (originally called technology attachés) would each serve small and medium-sized firms in a region – mostly industrial firms, although this scope was later expanded. They would proactively visit the firms and discuss with the manager and/or board director the strategy of the firm and their potential needs for knowledge support from researchers. If they agreed on something, they would match the firm with a suitable researcher. Originally these would come from SINTEF; later from all research institutes and universities, including foreign ones. If and when the firm and the researcher agreed on a project description, and the broker found it to be sound, the broker could allocate non-competitive and easily accessible funding to the project within a limited amount. This funding would come from public sources, and the funding of the brokerage service also ended up being public; neither firms nor researchers would accept a matchmaking fee. Also, significantly, the brokers could not generate projects for themselves; their loyalty would be with the firms and their needs.

The policy rationale for assigning public funding to the scheme was partly to open the roads to the ivory tower (provide new technology, later also knowledge from other areas of research locked in within the communities of research), partly to give the firms a first taste of using research, hoping to change their R&D behaviour for their own good, and partly (but less emphasised) to train researchers to relate better to the needs of small firms.

Originally generously funded directly by the Ministry of Regional Development, for the benefit of small firms in the periphery, the programme rapidly became very popular because of the combination of a broker who understood the challenges of the firms, who most of the time found relevant expertise, and who could provide 'non-bureaucratic' funding. The model also became popular with other research institutes and the five largest ones banded together and shared the public funding and their networks to the expertise, brokering across organisational and regional boundaries. Over the first 20 years, where the programme funding was also channelled through the research council as an 'experimental approach' for recruiting more firms to R&D, several thousand firms had been serviced. Over the last ten years, regional funding has supplemented the arrangement in many regions, the service provision has become more popular and consultants have basically crowded out the brokers from the research institutions, and brokers are no longer allowed to guarantee project funding, with a 'bureaucratic' procedure in place (but still with a high acceptance rate). Many consultants in these positions discover that it is much harder than they thought to get sufficient access to both firms and researchers; their skill sets and trust relations go in other directions (Finne and Thorsen, 2017).

Future challenges

We could add more. All current master's students at the university have to take a practical course in multidisciplinary cooperation, which would add to their repertoire of approaches to knowledge conversion. The university is famed for its entrepreneurship school, where students, not limited to technology and engineering, are trained to commercialise ideas of others and then typically go to work in regular firms for some years to learn the business before they launch their own ideas for growth. They are also experimenting with a number of ways to contribute to commercialisation of research and to connect students and faculty with firms, realising that there are many other ways of achieving this than the classical approaches. Some fail and some succeed. For example, positioning an online portal between firms and students/faculty has been difficult, most likely because so many firms do not know what to request or what to look for; they need the trusted broker to get going. And the university knows they may even meet competition from non-university actors in the burgeoning differentiation of species (organisational solutions) that are appearing under the broad heading of an innovation ecology. We will leave all those for another occasion.

Research institutes and other intermediary organisations, including brokerage services, abound today across large parts of Europe. NTNU was not necessarily the first one to implement all of these, but they were certainly early movers, and solutions in each of the three phases described were responses to industrial needs and opportunities given by contemporary status of available resources. The important impacts of these have been the entrepreneurial discoveries and the concrete innovations that they have either given rise to or participated in over a period of 70 years. In this chapter, we are more concerned with the continued development of the university as a participant in those entrepreneurial discoveries involved in strategies of smart specialisation. Both the establishment of the research institute and the provision of the brokerage service came out of entrepreneurial discovery processes initiated by either the university or its spinoff institute for their own sake. In both cases, the solutions were widely copied across the country (and abroad) and gave rise to similar establishments and offerings close to home for nearly every organisation in all sectors. Now, several drivers for change in the roles of universities are strong and increasing; the need for better involvement with industry is only one of them. With the other changes in a university, also the triple helix dynamic will change.

Wissema (2009) has described several current (mega)trends to which universities need to respond on their way to becoming third-generation universities, as an alternative to the Humboldt ideal and the openings in knowledge production provided through Mode 2 (context-sensitive) or even Mode 3 (context-driven) research (Gibbons et al., 1994; Carayannis and Campbell, 2009). Those trends that seem to impinge the most on the role of universities in smart specialisation include the rising cost of cutting-edge research, globalisation of research relations (and just about anything else), the need for transdisciplinary research, emergence of highly specialised research institutes, and increased pressure to contribute to commercialisation. Place-based strategies seem to concur with most of these trends, except that smart specialisation seems to assume that the region's universities already have come quite a way along these lines.

To this we would add that the current digitalisation is a strong enabler of delocalised presence, bridging and even bonding, i.e. increased connectivity in the world of research, worldwide outreach to students (although so far language dependent) and better conditions for linking up with interesting firms in any part of the world; and that practically any organisation needs to relate to this digitalisation turn simply in order to survive. The threats and opportunities given by the possibilities of participating in a global buzz while the need is for pipelines to the local industry (cf. Bathelt et al., 2004, for the original opposite formulation) represent an uncertainty for smart specialisation; it could work both ways.

6.5 Discussion

In establishing in 1950 a private not-for-profit foundation to perform applied research for the industry that the engineering education was serving, entrepreneurial professors at the university in the periphery had discovered a successful defensive countermove towards the establishment of a competing government-operated institute in the country's capital. It also turned out to create a successful revenue stream for research activities of the future, in the first phase for activities in the hands of a few professors and in later phases also for a wider set of activities adjusted to the needs of industry, less dependent on professorial participation but not entirely without it. In the first phase, professors were able to use the institute as an arena for bonding with significant industrial firms. Because of the important role these professors played in their department – with a great influence over teaching, student allocation for summer jobs, industrial project assignments, and later industrial employment – and also the dependence of junior teaching staff on their professors at that time, we could characterise these relations as bonding rather than bridging in some respects. Even though the two communities (industry and university) were distinctly separate, we hesitate to talk about a mere bridging because of the close connections instigated by one of the parties rather than an external broker. But the professors remained professors. Institutionally, though, it is clear that the multitude of individual bonds together constituted a bridge between university and industry.

In the second phase, we witnessed young engineers becoming researchers and then deviating from that career path to become captains of industry, partly carrying and implementing the knowledge they had helped generate through research and partly helping establish bridgeheads towards the university and the institute by means of their understanding of the social and economic logic of research. The institute had served as a bridge between industry and university in the first place but even more so in the second phase, and mostly because of the broad range of knowledges that travelled across it all the time. Not only that, but the institute provided a third space between the two worlds as laid out by Lam (2019), by providing young researchers an experimental space in which to internalise the ethos of both the technological rationality of the university and the economic rationality of the firm and finding solutions that balance these. The bridge was a fine place for young researchers to bond either way and for a long time they were as important an export from the institute as the technology they were travelling along with. Plus, they became not only captains of industry but also the embodiment of industry's absorptive capacity.

In the third phase, we witnessed a group of practically oriented researchers with wide industrial networks reacting to the new rules of the game for acquiring research council funding: the user-driven project. Their reaction was not to go for more researcher-driven projects, as was a major reaction by the university and the strategic management of the institute. Rather, their concern was with all the small firms that would not be capable of taking charge of research projects on their own. So, they set up a service of technology attachés, later renamed competence brokers, to assist small firms in developing (small) projects in order to tap the substantive expertise of researchers in universities, university colleges and research institutes. Taking the role of the altruistic broker as permitted and assumed by the business model, they used their own bonding capabilities to establish new bridges and bonds directly between firms and researchers.

6.6 Conclusions

The two research questions for this chapter related to specialisation in research or knowledge relations and conversion processes as being the issue for increasing the industrial impact of university research. What is quite clear in our case study is that the professors, researchers and brokers we have studied in this chapter all combined an intimate knowledge of subject matter and context of use on both sides of the bonds and bridges they went into, knowledge and relations they started acquiring simultaneously once they were introduced to a firm and its challenges and technology, and that the institutional bridge that the university established as a defensive business measure in 1950 has served well as a space for developing these exact knowledge-conversion skills and their concomitant trust relations. This at least looks like a requisite condition for success in our case study, even as industry has built its absorptive capacity by taking over many of the bridge travellers.

Closer relations between a relatively narrow range of highly specialised researchers and industrial firms as assumed by smart specialisation in the strict sense may work well as long as the relationship-building starts early; otherwise the cognitive distance may become too long to easily bridge. And, remember, we have not said much about the limits to bridging, either. Without relations to the context of future use the new expertise may end up in the ivory tower again.

Even though this was a single case study, there are probably some lessons to be learned for others.

One lesson is that universities may be capable of responding to threats or opportunities in the environment. What external pressures will have priority, however, will depend on the circumstances. Pressures to cater for the third mission may result in institutional layering (that is, requiring separate staff and additional funding); this is partially what happened in our case in 1950, but the clue was to make sure it was well integrated with the professorial duties and interests. Other research also suggests that the recruitment policy of university departments may be more important than incentive structures for changing the orientation of a department toward industry (Finne and Hetland, 2005).

Another lesson is that the mechanism of building relations and absorptive capacity at the same time, as done with the young researchers in the second period of our case, can be cost-effective but too costly for the university or an institute unless properly funded. Remember, the incentive for young people to select this two-step career choice was most likely that it was an attractive item on the CV, so a measure designed to do this must make sure the second career step is intended from the outset.

A third lesson is that brokers can be really effective for firms with very little absorptive capacity, provided the basic trust relations are in place or can be developed. Today's regulations for public support to private actors tends to tear apart effective brokerage packages. This can be overcome, but measures against opportunistic rent-seeking must be in place, based on local risk assessments.

A fourth and final lesson, which does not come directly out of these experiences, is that the movement towards more differentiated innovation ecologies is an invitation to experimentation. New solutions may be preferable to old ones that were optimal under other conditions. In a setting where triple or quadruple helix partnerships set up proper structures for governance and diagnostic monitoring (Kuznetsov and Sabel, 2017), these need not apply to the substantive matter of the entrepreneurial discoveries but could also be applied to the testing of new forms of collaboration for knowledge conversion. However, it is important to have a good understanding of the timescale required to properly test new approaches.

References

Bathelt, H., Malmberg, A. and Maskell, P. (2004). Clusters and knowledge: Local buzz, global pipelines and the process of knowledge creation. *Progress in Human Geography*, 28 (1), pp. 31–56.

Belenky, M.F., Clinchy, B.M., Goldberger, N.R. and Tarule, J.M. (1986). *Women's ways of knowing: The development of self, voice, and mind*. New York: Basic Books.

Brandt, T. and Nordal, O. (2010). *Turbulens og tankekraft. Historien om NTNU*. Oslo: Pax.

Briggs, X.d.S. (1998). Brown kids in white suburbs: Housing mobility and the many faces of social capital. *Housing Policy Debate*, 9 (1), pp. 177–221.

Burt, R.S. (1992). *Structural holes: The social structure of competition*. Cambridge, MA: Harvard University Press.

Burt, R.S. (2005). *Brokerage and closure: An introduction to social capital*. Oxford: Oxford University Press.

Bush, V. (1945). *Science the endless frontier*. Washington, DC: United States Government Printing Office.

Carayannis, E.G. and Campbell, D.F.J. (2009). 'Mode 3' and 'Quadruple Helix': Toward a 21st century fractal innovation ecosystem. *International Journal of Technology Management*, 46 (3/4), pp. 201–234.

Carlile, P.R. (2004). Transferring, translating, and transforming: An integrative framework for managing knowledge across boundaries. *Organization Science*, 15 (5), pp. 555–568.

Cohen, W.M. and Levinthal, D.A. (1990). Absorptive capacity: A new perspective on learning and innovation. *Administrative Science Quarterly*, 35 (1), pp. 128–152.

Damvad (2017). *Economic impact of research collaborations with NTNU*. Copenhagen: Damvad Analytics.

Dosi, G., Freeman, C., Nelson, R., Silverberg, G. and Soete, L. (eds) (1988). *Technical change and economic theory*. London: Pinter Publishers.

Etzkowitz, H. (2008). *The triple helix: University-industry-government innovation in action*. New York: Routledge.

EUR 24047 (ed.) (2009). *Knowledge for growth: Prospects for science, technology and innovation*. Brussels: European Commission.

Finne, H., Day, A., Piccaluga, A., Spithoven, A., Walter, P. and Wellen, D. (2011). *A composite indicator for knowledge transfer*. Report from the European Commission's expert group on knowledge transfer indicators. [Trondheim/Brussels]: [European Commission].

Finne, H. and Hetland, P. (2005). Meritteringssystemer i FoU-sektoren i forhold til nærings- og innovasjonsrettet FoU-virksomhet. *Arbeidsnotat*. Oslo: NIFU STEP.

Finne, H. and Thorsen, H.W. (2017). *– Må det være så vanskelig? Sluttevaluering av forsøk med kompetansemegling i VRI Trøndelag*. Trondheim: SINTEF Teknologi og samfunn.

Foray, D., David, P.A. and Hall, B.H. (2009). Smart specialisation: The concept. In EUR 24047 (ed.) *Knowledge for growth: Prospects for science, technology and innovation*, pp. 25–30. Brussels: European Commission.

Gibbons, M., Limoges, C., Notwotny, H., Schwartzman, S., Scott, P. and Trow, M. (1994). *The new production of knowledge*. London: Sage.

Granovetter, M.S. (1973). The strength of weak ties. *American Journal of Sociology*, 78 (6), pp. 1360–1380.
Jensen, M.B., Johnson, B., Lorenz, E. and Lundvall, B.Å. (2007). Forms of knowledge and modes of innovation. *Research Policy*, 36 (5), pp. 680–693.
Kirzner, I.M. (1997). Entrepreneurial discovery and the competitive market process: An Austrian approach. *Journal of Economic Literature*, 35 (1), pp. 60–85.
Kuhn, T.S. (1977). *The essential tension: Selected studies in scientific tradition and change*. Chicago: University of Chicago Press.
Kuznetsov, Y. and Sabel, C. (2017). Managing self-discovery: Diagnostic monitoring of a portfolio of projects and programs. In Radosevic, S., Curaj, A., Gheorghiu, R., Andreescu, L. and Wade, I. (eds) *Advances in the theory and practice of smart specialization*, pp. 51–72. London: Academic Press.
Lam, A. (2010). From 'ivory tower traditionalists' to 'entrepreneurial scientists'? Academic scientists in fuzzy university-industry boundaries. *Social Studies of Science*, 40 (2), pp. 307–340.
Lam, A. (2011). University-industry collaboration: Careers and knowledge governance in hybrid organisational space. *International Journal of Strategic Business Alliances*, 2 (1–2), pp. 135–145.
Lam, A. (2019). Career mobility, hybridity and knowledge combination: A 'third space' perspective. In Mariussen, Å., Virkkala, S., Finne, H. and Aasen, T.M. (eds) *The entrepreneurial discovery process and regional development: New knowledge emergence, conversion and exploitation*. Abingdon: Routledge.
Latour, B. (1987). *Science in action: How to follow scientists and engineers through society*. Milton Keynes: Open University Press.
Leydesdorff, L. (2003). The mutual information of university-industry-government relations: An indicator of the triple helix dynamics. *Scientometrics*, 58 (2), pp. 445–467.
Leydesdorff, L. and Etzkowitz, H. (1996). Emergence of a triple helix of university-industry-government relations. *Science and Public Policy*, 23, pp. 279–286.
Leydesdorff, L. and Meyer, M. (2006). Triple Helix indicators of knowledge-based innovation systems: Introduction to the special issue. *Research Policy*, 35 (10), pp. 1441–1449.
Lundvall, B.-Å. (1988). Innovation as an interactive process – from user-producer interaction to national systems of innovation. In Dosi, G., Freeman, C., Nelson, R.R., Silverberg, G. and Soete, L. (eds) *Technology and economic theory*. London: Pinter Publishers.
Lundvall, B.-Å. (ed.) (1992). *National systems of innovation: Towards a theory of innovation and interactive learning*. London: Pinter.
Moe, J. (1999). *På tidens skanser*. Trondheim: Tapir.
Nelson, R.R. (ed.) (1993). *National innovation systems: A comparative analysis*. New York, Oxford: Oxford University Press.
Nonaka, I. and Takeuchi, H. (1995). *The knowledge-creating company: How Japanese companies create the dynamics of innovation*. New York: Oxford University Press.
Obstfeld, D. (2005). Social networks, the tertius iungens orientation, and involvement in innovation. *Administrative Science Quarterly*, 50 (1), pp. 100–130.
OECD (ed.) (2003). *Turning science into business: Patenting and licensing at public research organisations*. Paris: OECD.
Polanyi, M. (1983). *The tacit dimension*. New York: Doubleday.
Putnam, R. D. (2000). *Bowling alone: The collapse and revival of American community*. New York: Simon & Schuster.

Schulte, P. (2004). The entrepreneurial university: A strategy for institutional development. *Higher Education in Europe*, 29 (2), pp. 187–191.

Schumpeter, J.A. (1934). *The theory of economic development: An inquiry into profits, capital, credit, interest, and the business cycle*. Cambridge, MA: Harvard University Press.

Shapin, S. (2012). The Ivory Tower: The history of a figure of speech and its cultural uses. *British Journal for the History of Science*, 45 (1), pp. 1–27.

Star, S.L. and Griesemer, J.R. (1989). Institutional ecology, 'translations' and boundary objects: Amateurs and professionals in Berkeley's Museum of Vertebrate Zoology, 1907–39. *Social Studies of Science*, 19 (3), pp. 387–420.

Tijssen, R.J.W., van Leeuwen, T.N. and van Wijk, E. (2009). Benchmarking university-industry research cooperation worldwide: Performance measurements and indicators based on co-authorship data for the world's largest universities. *Research Evaluation*, 18 (1), pp. 13–24.

Wenger, E. (1998). *Communities of practice: Learning, meaning, and identity*. Cambridge: Cambridge University Press.

Wissema, J.G. (2009). *Towards the third generation university: Managing the university in transition*. Cheltenham: Edward Elgar.

Zahra, S.A. and George, G. (2002). Absorptive capacity: A review, reconceptualization, and extension. *Academy of Management Review*, 27 (2), pp. 185–203.

7 Approaching entrepreneurial discovery and knowledge conversion from a complexity perspective

Tone Merethe Aasen

7.1 Introduction

The complex responsive processes perspective draws on analogues from the natural complexity sciences as well as from Mead (1934) and Elias (1939) to explain human action and interaction. From this perspective entrepreneurial discovery and knowledge conversion can be seen as phenomena inherent in all human interaction and should therefore be interpreted neither as designable courses of action nor as events evolving by chance, but rather as emergent phenomena – paradoxically generalised and particularised in the experiences of everyday localised interaction.

The approach adopted in this chapter implies taking a radical process perspective of human development, based on a fundamental idea that social life is always under construction by the intentional actions of interdependent humans. Complex processes involving a large number of actors should therefore be explored and explained in terms of communicative interaction (Fonseca, 2002; Griffin, 2002). Inherent in this is the view that there should be a change of perspective on regional processes from perceptions of 'wholes' to notions of joint human interaction. This means that increased attention should be on the detail of local interaction between people striving to construct meaning out of new and ongoing themes, for the region, their organisation, their responsibilities, and for them.

7.2 Complexity perspectives

In acknowledgement of the complex and collective nature of human interaction, researchers increasingly question the approach of isolating (human) phenomena disembodied from space and time, and to ascribe to them an objective, universal validity (e. g. Chia, 2002; Dopson, 2005; Elias, 1978; Fløysand and Jakobsen, 2011; Stacey et al., 2000; Tidd, 2001; Tsoukas and Chia, 2002; Tsoukas and Hatch, 2001). Consequently, attention is moved towards the quality of relations, emergence, instability, and unpredictability (e. g. Byrne and Callaghan, 2014; Weick, 2000). This engagement in the dynamics of organised life is recognisable in systems dynamic thinking, process traditions, and incidentally also in postmodern perspectives on organisations. In addition, such ideas find resonance with contemporary theories of complexity (Chia, 2003). In this section, complexity science is briefly reviewed, before the particular perspective of complex responsive processes (CRP) is brought into focus.

Complexity science is not one science but covers several strands and modes of thoughts originated from natural sciences like mathematics, physics and biology. In different ways, they all show how particular kinds of dynamics arise when interaction is attributed characteristics of non-linearity, diversity and connectivity, which both enable and constrain interaction between entities (Fonseca, 2002). A complex system is defined to be a 'whole' made up of many entities (parts) that interact in complex ways according to some local rule(s) or force(s) (Caldart and Ricart, 2004; Simon, 1996). Incidentally, it is more than 50 years since Thompson (1967) pointed out the existence of similar characteristics in complex organisations, and claimed that such organisations were composed of interdependent parts, amounting to a 'whole' that was also interdependent with a larger environment.

The non-linear relation between cause and effect of complex systems implies that variation in strength or intensity of some condition or action will lead to variation in outcome (Stacey, 2007). Mathematically, this means that when exposed to infinitesimal differences in initial condition, two entities with similar initial states can end up following radically divergent paths over time. In cybernetic terms, a non-linear system can be seen as a system that operates according to both negative and positive feedback. This implicates the possibility of non-equilibrium and unexpected system behaviour, which is seen to be a defining characteristic of dynamic systems. The positive/negative feedback properties lead to the paradoxical state of instable stability, or stable instability. Interpreted in organisational terms, non-linearity means that repetition and change should be seen as co-existing processes that are equally essential for novelty to emerge and evolve (Leana and Barry, 2000).

Three key complexity strands – *mathematical chaos, dissipative structures* and *complex adaptive systems* – have been developed as approaches to the mathematical modelling of the emergent, evolving and essentially unpredictable characteristics of complex, non-linear systems. The theories of mathematical chaos and dissipative structures provide models that in essence are an extension of system dynamics (Stacey, 2007). These theories are based on ideas of non-linearity, feedback loops, unpredictability, and distance in time and space between cause and effect, but their focus is on a macro level. While chaos theory is built on assumptions of average entities constituting parts of average interaction, dissipative structure models make allowance for micro-events, or variety, which leads to self-organising activity and to the emergent order of a 'whole'.

The complex adaptive systems (CAS) theory was developed to explain the complex behaviour of large populations of autonomous adaptive interacting agents (Gell-Mann, 1994; Holland, 1998; Kauffman, 1993; Langton, 1996). Data simulation models have demonstrated that local, self-organising behaviour may evolve in the absence of overall plans or common rules and yield emergent patterns of interaction common to the whole system, perceived as 'order'.

They have further shown that the prevailing patterns of interaction influence, and have the potential to change, the individual agents. At the same time, the agents influence, and have the potential to change, the patterns. This research suggests that the dynamics of self-organising networks is determined by the number and the strength of the connections between participating agents, but even more importantly, by the differences between agents.

The strands of complexity thinking that are built on ideas of non-average behaviour and interacting, interdependent agents use the concept of 'paradox' to explain the presence together, at the same time, of self-contradictory, essentially conflicting ideas, none of which can be eliminated (Stacey, 2007). This is a core conception, implying that there is no option involving choice between opposing tensions, or of defining them into distinct and separable classes. The interpretation of paradox in heterogeneous complexity thinking deviates from the more common use of the word, which is to describe conflicting demands, opposing perspectives or seemingly illogical or irrational connections (Lewis, 2000). The move from systemic to heterogeneous complexity thinking therefore is a move towards a view that paradox cannot be resolved, only endlessly transformed.

A CAS perspective on organisations and innovation

Like the other two strands, the CAS theory is a theory about systems, but attention is on the micro level of the individual, interacting agents. In recent years, a growing group of authors has been exploring the properties of CAS theory in order to develop new theories about innovation embracing change as an emergent self-organising process rather than as orderly, controllable steps (e.g. Byrne and Callaghan, 2014; Price, 2004; Roundy et al., 2016; Van de Ven et al., 2000). In their pioneering research on the management of innovation, Van de Ven and his colleagues adopted a CAS perspective to explain the progress of innovation processes (Poole and Van de Ven, 2004; Poole et al., 2000; Van de Ven et al., 1999; Van de Ven et al., 2000). By this they were the first to demonstrate that innovation processes display non-linear and self-organising characteristics. The CAS approach has also led to alternative explanations of innovation networks and systems (e.g. Brown and Eisenhardt, 1997; Frenken, 2000, 2006a, 2006b; Hirooka, 2006; Van Buuren and Edelenbos, 2006), and of regional innovation (Cooke, 2012).

Self-organisation

One of the most important ideas of complexity thinking is that change and novelty emerge in self-organising processes that cannot be predicted or decided. The complexity-based understanding of self-organisation is fundamentally different from the ideas of systems thinking, where the concept of self-organisation is perceived to be dynamic processes contributing to the creation of a holistic system (Stacey, 2007). Some complexity scientists see self-organisation as a fundamental principle of the universe, where the consumption of energy is needed to create and sustain order (Kelly and Allison, 1999). Such energy consumption is believed to take place under conditions referred to as bounded instability, or the edge of chaos. This has also been described as forces pulling organisations in two directions at the same time, towards 'fossilisation' and disorganisation (Boisot, 1999).

One of the ideas that has evolved as part of the CAS perspective is that bounded systems (companies, regions) compete for survival through self-organisation and adaptation. Some authors suggest that a system's comparative fitness can be represented as a point within a multidimensional fitness landscape (Caldart and Ricart, 2004; Cooke, 2012; Kelly and Allison, 1999; Marion, 1999). The complexity of the 'landscape' is determined by the degree of interaction and interdependence between the attributes of its constituting parts, implying that the landscape itself is produced in the interactions (Allen, 1994). The metaphor of fitness landscape can be tracked back to biological theory (Wright, 1932), but was suggested by Kauffman (1993) as a means to explain the relationship between biologists' idea of selection and complexity scientists' idea of self-organisation. His idea was that order does not emerge because of evolutionary processes of variation, selection and retention, because complex systems inherently are more resistant to environmental changes than envisioned in systems thinking. The 'ordering element' is seen to be self-organisation.

Nobel laureate Ilya Prigogine (1997) was particularly engaged with the phenomenon of self-organisation as a source to understand and explain irreversibility, and by that, time. His work confirmed what CAS scientists had found, which is that differences between agents, referred to as micro-diversity or 'disorder', are prerequisite to the unpredictable self-organising emergence of order from disorder in nature. The importance of micro-diversity has been further elaborated by Allen (1998a, 1998b). He showed that when the assumption of average components and events was abandoned, phenomena displayed the capacity to evolve completely new structures. This suggests that micro-diversity, or non-average behaviour, is the prerequisite source to continued movement, and to the emergence of novelty. This has led to the view that self-organisation in human terms would mean heterogeneous individuals participating in local interaction (Stacey, 2001). Interest is directed towards the patterning processes of local communicative interaction, whence the phenomenon of self-organisation is emerging. Self-organisation is then the co-evolving repetitive and transformative patterning of communicative themes created when humans interact with each other (Johannessen and Aasen, 2007).

7.3 Complexity science in the social world

Complexity science was developed for the particular purpose of capturing the complexity of the interconnected actions of agents in a system and the apparent unpredictable outcome of their interaction. Stacey (2001) opportunely points out that since these perspectives do not take into account human ability to learn and evolve, they are unsuitable for explaining human relationships, although they may contribute with some insight into dynamic processes.

The characteristics of complex systems contradict the idea that predictors of and prescriptions for long-term innovative success can be worked out (Stacey, 2005). Nevertheless, most researchers seem to understand complexity theories in terms of systems thinking, meaning that the adoption of a CAS perspective involves little else than adoption of a complex thinking vocabulary. Accordingly, the search for generalised tools and techniques continues, rephrased into complexity terms (Eoyang, 2004; Surie and Hazy, 2006; Webb et al., 2006). One of the major problems with this is that the fundamental differences between the physical and the social worlds are not taken into account (Johannessen and Aasen, 2007). Mathematical calculations and computer simulations will never be able to capture the full range of human experience, and they will always fall short in the description of emotional responses, power relations and identity formation – phenomena which are often sustained by unconscious group processes (Stacey, 2003). Such processes serve the function of including persons, ideas and behaviours adhering to established patterns of action (Dalal, 1998; Elias and Scotson, 1965) and excluding persons who represent patterns of action that are new or different, and therefore carry in them the seed to innovation.

Some authors, for example Tsoukas (2005), Van de Ven and Poole (2005) and Stacey (2007), explore approaches to change and innovation involving a mix of processual thinking and natural-science-based complexity perspectives (Aasen, 2009). According to Burnes (2005), Stacey (1991) was, however, the first author to link natural-science-based complexity thinking with ideas of emergent organisational change as an alternative to systemic ways of thinking about process in human action. Stacey has adopted a radical process perspective of human development, which means that social life is seen as being always under construction by the intentional actions of interdependent humans (Aasen, 2009). Stacey's concern is with what people are actually doing in their 'ordinary, everyday activities of leading, managing or organising', resulting in the simultaneous emergence of local everyday interaction and widespread patterns of actions common to many people: the 'organisation' or 'the society' (Stacey, 2007: 243).

Complex responsive processes

The idea that analyses of processes and effects can be made on different levels is widely accepted. This makes the use of concepts such as 'organisation' and 'region' as synonyms for the arenas of action of human professional life, or even as the outcome of human action, a natural thing to do. A few authors, among them Mead (1934), argue, however, that there is no split between the individual and the social. The individual and the social are not seen to be different levels of a system but are regarded as two aspects of the same process. Incidentally, the same perspective as claimed by Mead (1934) can be recognised in Elias's process sociology (1978, 1991). This view forms part of the basis of the *complex responsive processes* (CRP) perspective, a perspective in which all human relating is seen as fundamentally communicative, paradoxically involving the forming of the social by individuals, who at the same time are formed in social interaction (Stacey, 2001, 2007; Stacey et al., 2000). The CRP perspective is founded in sociological theory and at the same time drawing on analogues from complexity studies. Thus, it is a more coherent and valid theory of organised human life than those directly translating computer simulation results into an understanding of social action (Johannessen and Aasen, 2007).

According to Stacey and Griffin (2005a), the complex responsive processes perspective is based on a few generalised, idealised propositions, of which the most important is that human interdependence is a fundamental reality of human experience. Human relating is power relating, held to be self organising, and leading to the emergence of patterns of thought–talk–action that are the temporary organisation of experience. Humans are further seen to have the capacity for spontaneity and reflection, including the capacity to take the attitude of others. This makes them able to evaluate alternatives, to consciously choose their actions, and implicitly make people accountable for their choices.

The causal framework applied in the CRP perspective is that of transformative teleology, derived from the German philosopher Hegel as interpreted by Mead (Stacey, 2001). The future is seen as being under perpetual construction as concurrent continuity and potential transformation, created in responsive processes of relating between individuals.

'Complex' refers to the particular dynamic that is patterned by human relationship and characterised by the co-existence of certainty and uncertainty, predictability and unpredictability, known and unknowable, stability and change. Such complex dynamics are seen as an inherent and natural part of human interaction. In correspondence with the CAS perspective, self-organisation is conceptualised as the interaction of individuals based on their own local organising principles. Self-organisation is therefore understood as the co-evolving repetitive and transformative patterning of communicative themes created when heterogeneous individuals participate in local interaction (Stacey, 2001). However, in social processes, participation is not seen as a premise for self-organisation, but rather 'participation is self-organisation' (Griffin, 2002: 125). This indicates that interest in organisational processes should be directed towards the patterning processes of local communicative interaction from where the phenomenon of self-organisation is emerging.

In line with the above, organised life is seen as patterns of joint action between individuals, iterated as the present (Stacey and Griffin, 2005b). An implication of this is that it is impossible for individuals to take an objective, external position to exert influence on a system (organisation, region), because interaction is not understood to create any system existing as a separate entity or level. What is caused by interaction is seen to be nothing but further interaction, meaning that the basic unit of analysis is the social act (Mead, 1934). The complex responsive processes perspective therefore holds no notion of a Kantian universal, or 'whole', acting as a causal power on interaction, because interaction is seen to be its own cause. Stacey and Griffin (2005a: 21) assert that this perspective should rather be seen as 'an evolutionary theory of values and ideologies arising in social processes of self-formation and ongoing conflictual negotiation'. Interaction, which is experience, will lead to the emergence of different ideologies, further evolving into imaginary, idealised and generalised ideas, temporarily seen to be 'truth'. In their functionalisation, 'truths' may be confirmed and reinforced, or negated and transformed.

Such truths, or generalised ideas, can be idealised into 'cult values' by a group or groups of individuals as the 'right' way to do things, independent of time and space (Mead, 1923). Griffin (2002: 116) explains cult values to be the 'collective idealisations that divert attention from the detail of interaction in the living present'. Organisational mission and vision statements, and desired capabilities like 'innovation', are commonly articulated and specified in the form of cult values. This encourages the idea that a particular process can be intentionally designed, and its outcome chosen. What we do by this, is to attribute meaning to patterns of action as if they were a substance or a thing, rather than emerging processes of communicative interaction. By reducing processes to states in this way, the particularisation processes in which meaning is created, repeated and potentially transformed, are ignored. Idealisations need therefore to be distinguished from the specific actions taken by individuals in their local settings. The view that the evolving patterns of communication, including figurations of power and ideological ideas, are 'not universal but contingent on the specific interaction of specific people, negotiating the particularisations of their generalisations/idealisations with each other at specific times in specific situations' is particularly emphasised by Stacey and Griffin (2005b: 22).

Emergence

One of the core keywords in both the natural and social sciences is 'emergence'. Like so many concepts, this one has also been attributed various meanings, depending on perspective. For example, the complexity-based view that emergent order arises from self-organisational processes involving the interaction between intentions, contrasts the assumption of cybernetic systems thinking, which is that new order can be imposed on to a system from 'outside' (Goldstein, 2000). Another interpretation is based on the ideas of emergence as random change. It is something that 'just happens', and as such it is the opposite of intention (Stacey, 2007). An example of this, incidentally taken not from science, but from strategy research, is Mintzberg (1987: 69), who describes emergent strategies as 'strategies without clear intentions, actions simply converging into patterns'. In consequence, within a spectrum of strategies, Mintzberg places deliberate strategies at one extreme point, and emergent strategies at the other. Another example is Kirzner (1997: 72), who situates discovery somewhere between the idea of deliberately produced information described in search theory and that of 'windfall gain generated by pure chance'. In Kirzner's interpretation, 'discovery' is neither something someone can do, nor a random phenomenon.

One of the main problems connected with the concept of emergence has to do with causality. From the perspective of rational 'if, then' causality, particular individuals can choose the direction and outcome of development. Emergence – seen as chance development – is therefore ruled out. If some people, e.g. managers, can decide a future and manipulate organisational qualities to support the materialisation of that future, development is about the unfolding of events which are enfolded in the system beforehand, meaning that causality is formative. In an evolutionary perspective, ideas about rational and formative causalities are, however, rejected for the benefit of adaptionist causality (Fonseca, 2002), which explains the emergence of novelty as natural selection on chance variation at the level of entities ('survival of the fittest'). Both the formative and the adaptionist causalities seem to imply that humans must comply with developmental processes on which they have no influence. The three alternative ways to think about causality, whether they involve the idea of specific humans being in total control of processes, or without the means of influence at all, seem to exclude the possibility of spontaneous emergence of unplanned ideas and events and the intentional following-up on such ideas (Aasen, 2009). In systemic perspectives, the concept of 'emergence' is therefore more or less irrelevant. The dual causality of rational planning and formative implementation leaves no room for surprise, and the formative and adaptionist views do not take into account human intention and free will.

As an example, Deacon (2007) discusses three (vertical) levels of emergent phenomena, which all appear to involve adaptionist causality. The first-order emergence is connected to the higher-order properties of an aggregate (such as water). Second-order emergence is related to autopoiesis, meaning that a system can reproduce. Finally, third-order emergence focuses on emergence as an evolutionary process, potentially leading to radical change of the nature of a system.

Based on Deacon's models of emergence, Martin and Sunley (2012) seek to develop new insight in the economic landscape and its evolution. For them, a key problem is the ambiguity attached to the concept of emergence, which they interpret as an umbrella term 'for a related but diverse set of processes' (Martin and Sunley, 2012: 350). They maintain that emergence in economic evolution is driven largely by relationships, making Deacon's notion of 'third-order emergence' topical as a possible framework for analysing potential connections between economic action and economic actors. As Cooke (2012) points out, 'emergence' as discussed by Martin and Sunley appears to be spontaneous, self-organising effects that come into being without any intervention in a system.

Byrne and Callaghan (2014) give an account of several approaches to 'emergence'. They hold on to the notion of system and system components, but question the explanations offered by natural-science-based complexity thinkers, because 'there is more to emergence than the product of interaction of objects or even agents. . .' (Byrne and Callaghan, 2014: 23). In complexity theories based on radical process perspectives, emergence does indeed take on a very different meaning. The causality is transformative because new patterns are seen to emerge in paradoxical processes of stability and change, where the evolvement of patterns over time is unknowable and unpredictable (Stacey, 2001).

A focus in understanding social phenomena from a complexity perspective is the study of the simultaneous emergence of local everyday interaction and widespread patterns of actions common to many people. This point was of main concern to Elias (1939), who aimed at explaining the becoming of social order and civilisation through history without someone having made long-term plans for the evolution. In terms of Elias, 'emergence' is the emergence of pattern in the interplay between human intentions, and not a product of chance. Emergence leads to population-wide patterns that continually evolve and change in local interaction. Elias (1939) links the interplay of intentions with the development of identity and power relations. His reasoning leads to the idea that when people articulate some global pattern, or attempt to design or change it, they are doing nothing more than making a gesture, although this can be a very powerful gesture. The crucial point is that the emerging pattern can be found only in the local responses to this gesture (Stacey, 2005), and that what is emerging is novel patterns of themes which no one individual could have decided, and which may involve the recognition of novelty.

Self-organisation and emergence can thus be understood as the co-evolving repetitive and transformative patterning of communicative themes created when humans interact. People can and do generalise existing and emerging patterns of themes (Stacey, 2005). To be able to act, it is, however, necessary for people to particularise and functionalise the patterns into specific situations, and this inevitably involves some kind of conflict related to interpretation and the formation of meaning. The non-linearity of human interaction means that differences in particularisation, even small ones, have the potential to amplify into new general patterns completely different from the preceding, and in this way, patterns of themes evolve, and even transform.

7.4 Entrepreneurial discovery and knowledge conversion as acts of participation

As accounted for in the introductory chapter of this book (Mariussen and Virkkala, 2019), Foray (2015) explains smart specialisation dynamics as the combination of several types of processes, including entrepreneurial discovery, knowledge spillover, and entry and agglomeration of firms into economic activity. In other words, smart specialisation dynamics is about the emergence, acceptance and diffusion of new themes that will result in value-creation. Accordingly, a lot of research effort is now on the question of how processes of entrepreneurial discovery and the conversion of knowledge form the basis for new industries, or for the redirection of established industry.

Adopting a complex responsive processes perspective implies a general shift of focus from notions of overall systems towards individual characteristics, like emotion, intention, spontaneity, and reflection, and to the dynamics of human interaction as a source for conservation, disruption and change. While this emphasises aspects of human communicative interaction to be of more generalised validity, the emerging, evolving patterns of such communication are not seen to be universal, but contingent on time, place, situation, and the persons involved. This implies that change cannot be understood as the deliberate transfer from one 'entrepreneurial state' to a new one, but emerges from the perpetual construction of new possible futures by interdependent humans engaged in communicative interaction. In some aspects, this appears to be in line with Foray's (2015) ideas of entrepreneurial discovery, which are the broad search for opportunities through new combinations of knowledge by many people representing diverse functions and positions.

The notion of entrepreneurial discovery used by Foray (2015) is in line with Schumpeter (1934), who claims that opportunities are discovered, in the form of new (surprising) combinations of existing resources (competencies, products, markets, processes). Another explanation is offered by Kirzner (1997), who connects opportunity to the recognition of some kind of 'fault' or 'imperfection', which can be addressed through the invention of new resources. Combining the two perspectives, Alvarez and Barney (2007) conceptualise 'opportunity formation' as a combination of discovery and creation processes. Whether discovered or created, new ideas will usually be accepted as business opportunities only after being evaluated in light of existing knowledge about customers, markets, competitors, technological alternatives, industry structures, firm and regional knowledge base, etc. The acknowledgement of a business opportunity is referred to by Foray as 'entry', constituting 'the confirmation that others see this discovery as meaningful' (2015: 28).

Seen from a CRP perspective, the key word in this is 'meaning'. New meaning is perpetually created, recreated and potentially transformed in the ongoing interaction between people in each living situation. Knowledge and meaning are seen as two dimensions of the same process, emerging within the conflicting, enabling constraints of power relations, and thus, they are closely related to identity. This means that changes bringing about the need for new types or combinations of knowledge have a potential impact on individuals' perception of identity, including established relations of power and perceptions of 'us' and 'them'. Knowledge can thus be seen as thematic patterns that organise people's experience of being together (Stacey, 2001). Such themes are continuously reproduced in the form of beliefs, habits and variations on them. As people interact, various phenomena will emerge, independent of any conception of regional or organisational boundaries. Furthermore, by the responding processes they create, the reality of both themselves and their environment is transformed in unpredictable ways. Accordingly, the quality of relations becomes decisive for the local capacity for change and innovation, i.e. for the creation of emergent new meaning. 'Learning' is also part of the same process, hardly distinguishable from the knowledge processes. In other words, knowledge and learning are understood to be social acts, emerging as new meaning 'whether people are conscious about it or not' (Stacey, 2001: 189; Aasen, 2009). This leads to the assertion that knowledge assets alter when relational patterns are disrupted (Aasen, 2009; Stacey, 2001).

Fonseca (2002) indicates that 'the new meaning may be embodied in some new "thing" that is apparently detached from the messy process of its creation'. In his view, the diffuse, 'illogical' and uncertain processes of communicative interaction in which new meaning may emerge, are masked by people's inclination to ascribe in hindsight what happens to someone's intentional choice. One of the issues Fonseca brings up is how apparently structured development processes relate to the 'messy' emergent processes of innovation (Fonseca, 2002). In a similar line of reasoning as Foray (2015), he suggests that the structured, 'visible' phases are preceded by a long period of conversations and ambiguous actions, or, in the terminology of Foray, 'entrepreneurial discovery'. The entrepreneurial discovery phase involves speculation, imagination and fantasy on the part of numerous people in various roles, inspired among other things by regional knowledge resources, local characteristics and current trends. Gradually, recognisable patterns of 'discoveries' may emerge as the consequence of recurring themes and negotiations of the meaning of such themes. If accepted by sufficiently many, or supported by somebody who has the power to authorise the use of resources, openly or covertly, the recurrent themes, perceived as opportunities, may be attempted to be realised through experiments and development activities.

In Fonseca's (2002) terms, official development projects are initiated based on knowledge (meaning) which is already stabilised, at least within a community of interest. The development activities may result in new tools, technology or work process descriptions, but they are also the source of further conversation, which may be redundant in nature, referred to as 'spillover', having the potential of leading to new ideas and further innovation. He points out that to be able to come up with, and reflect on, new themes, people need the freedom to fantasise and exchange ideas without the constraints, for example, of strict meeting agendas and fixed expectations. He is also occupied with the idea that redundant diversity will be experienced in conversations as misunderstanding. By 'misunderstanding' he seems to mean the lack of joint meaning, leading to a continual shift and evolvement of the patterning processes of new themes because of the current introduction of new themes and ideas into the emerging patterns. Such continued disturbance may prevent premature or unwanted stabilisation of patterns of themes. I perceive this interpretation of 'misunderstanding' to support the view that innovation emerges from prolonged conversational processes characterised by conflict, ambiguity and persuasion, involving negotiation activities caused by diverse interpretations of the ongoing, evolving themes. As previously discussed (Aasen and Johannessen, 2009), the tolerance for such misunderstanding in organisations is generally limited.

Perceiving entrepreneurial discovery as learning processes means that new ideas are formed as existing and new knowledge is shared, developed and changed in various ways. A similar line of thought can be found with Nonaka and Takeuchi (1995). According to them, learning can be framed as the result of destabilisation of an accepted 'truth', and the movement towards new ways of understanding current problems and their possible solutions. In their model, tacit and explicit knowledge are mutually complementary forms of qualifications, and 'learning' means completing a full circle of their SECI model (socialisation, externalisation, combination, internalisation) (Nonaka and Toyama, 2003), moving from old 'know-how' to new 'know-how'. A core idea of this perspective is that to be of use in a particular setting, explicit knowledge must undergo a conversion. The concept of 'knowledge conversion' refers to two elements (Nonaka, 1994; Nonaka and von Krogh, 2009). One element is individual knowledge, which can be brought together with the knowledge of others so that the knowledge 'expands'. The other element is the alternating nature of knowledge, internalised as tacit experiences, or articulated as explicit themes. New explicit and tacit knowledge is created as knowledge is shared. Knowledge conversion can be understood as a key concept, core to entrepreneurial discovery as well as to the subsequent events leading to the perceived existence of an opportunity for profit on the part of many people (Shane, 2003), and further actions on the perceived opportunity.

Nonaka and Takeuchi (1995) see knowledge as contextual and partial, and as such an unstable phenomenon. In processual terms, 'tacit knowledge' could be referred to as (non-articulated) experience, while 'explicit knowledge' could be seen as (temporary) stabilisations of ideas (or understanding) entering into conversations as generalised patterns of themes. Such themes will be repeated yet are subject to change or even transformation in the processes of repetition. Generalised, stabilised themes should be understood as themes that are reiterated over time. Stabilised themes will influence the emergence of new themes, the way new themes are perceived, and the way they are interpreted in specific situations – which in this case is referred to as 'knowledge conversion'.

Another important idea is that such knowledge conversion is situated in more or less staged 'Bas', or places, and will result in new kinds of contextualised knowledge, forming a basis for innovation (Nonaka and Konno, 1998). The interpretation of knowledge into a particular context is seen to be the most important step of the SECI circle. For Nonaka and Takeuchi (1995), the 'medium' of interpretation is tacit knowledge. Lam (2000) is in line with this view, but she also opportunely points out that tacit knowledge will be formed and used according to the broader context. In other words, the outcome of knowledge conversion processes is dependent on the process participants.

It must be emphasised that from a complex responsive processes perspective, interaction is seen as always being local. This means that at any point in time, individuals interact with only a small fraction of the total population of an organisation or of a society. Thus, local interaction can be explained as the particularising of population-wide general experience, where the general can only be found in the experience of the particular, and has no existence outside of it (Stacey, 2007). To render possible the coordinated action between many people, local interaction must produce 'emergent, coherent, meaningful patterns of interaction both locally and population-wide at the same time' (Stacey, 2007: 434). These processes are interpretive processes of human interaction involving reflection, emotion and imagination. Conflict is an inherent part of such processes, and so is the possibility of transformation and novelty.

Elias (1978) refers to such local interaction as *interplay of intentions*. His choice of words reflects the view that people do plan and do have intentions, but at the same time, they will always have to negotiate their actions with other people pursuing other intentions. Communicative interaction should therefore be seen as a political process, in which people mutually enable and constrain each other in their social actions. Because all relationships have these characteristics, they are power relations (Elias, 1998). When interdependent people interact in such 'figurations of power', conflicts between differing actions, plans and purposes are bound to arise. This entails the recognition of the unlikeliness that one person's plan or intention should become prevalent as the long-term reality of all. Sotarauta (2016) pursues the same idea when pointing out the fallacy of assuming that individual actors can change organisations alone. In the myriad local interactions between people, unpredictable and widespread coherence is rather envisioned to emerge without (or in spite of) any programme, plan or blueprint for that widespread pattern itself (Stacey and Griffin, 2005c).

7.5 Final reflections

A view of entrepreneurial discovery and knowledge conversion as emerging patterns of action consciously and unconsciously influenced by many people through their ongoing participation in work-related social interaction indicates that such processes may lead to outcomes that were neither planned nor wanted. Furthermore, the perceived difference between 'the new' and 'the existing' should also be attributed importance as an aspect generating a spectrum of responses, including resistance and recognition. Such responses reflect temporary individual–collective perceptions of meaning, knowledge, identity and the power relations in which the responding persons are part, and may substantially influence the course of the ongoing innovation initiatives.

A focus of attention in understanding inter-human phenomena from a complexity perspective is the study of 'I' and 'we' identities, emerging and re-emerging in local interaction where global patterns always are expressed and implied (Johannessen and Aasen, 2007). The sense of identity (meaning, direction, structure, flow and continuity) is experienced by each individual as they are structuring the generalised patterns of action in each living moment. The generalised patterns are experienced as global themes played out as the experience of local interaction or local themes of communication. An example is when public policy-makers meet to talk about what measures to take to stimulate innovation in their region. The theme of 'innovation' is clearly a global theme, a theme that many other policy-makers are talking about all over the world at the same time. Simultaneously, in any particular local meeting, meaning will arise as to what this might mean for their region and for them. These discussions will be influenced by the participants' relationships and the quality of their relating, where power is always experienced. In what way do they understand their individual contribution to the discussion, their role and their influence? How is their understanding of what is going on between them expressed and made available for discussion? How do they see their own ability to keep on working with emerging themes? How do they understand what it means to go on working with these themes in interaction with others, attending to different interests?

The ways in which all of these questions are dealt with contribute to wider patterns of interaction between many people, which in turn are the generalised/globalised patterns. Seen from a complexity perspective, the widespread generalised patterns and the local particularised interactions are emerging at the same time. These different aspects of patterning, the global and the local, cannot be separated from each other. Any pattern is acted out locally. No human being can avoid being in local interaction: and when doing this, individuals are expressing both their particularities and global themes at the same time; and as they are expressing this, they are contributing to the emergence of both local meaning and further generalisation of themes and actions. They are globalising as they are particularising and vice versa – simultaneously as the same process.

References

Aasen, T.M.B. (2009). A complexity perspective on innovation processes for subsea technology development. *International Journal of Learning and Change*, 3 (3), pp. 294–307.

Aasen, T.M.B. and Johannessen, S. (2009). Managing innovation as communicative processes: A case of subsea technology R&D. *International Journal of Business Science and Applied Management*, 4 (3), pp. 22–33.

Allen, P.M. (1994). Coherence, chaos and evolution in the social context. *Futures*, 26 (6), pp. 583–597.

Allen, P.M. (1998a). Evolving complexity in social science. In Altman, G. and Koch, W.A. (eds) *Systems: New paradigms for human sciences*, pp. 3–38. New York: Walter de Gruyter.

Allen, P.M. (1998b). Modelling complex economic evolution. In Schweitzer, F. and Silverberg, G. (eds) *Selbstorganisation*. Berlin: Dunker and Humbolt.

Alvarez, S.A. and Barney, J.B. (2007). Discovery and creation: Alternative theories of entrepreneurial action. *Strategic Entrepreneurship Journal*, 1 (1-2), pp. 11–26.

Boisot, M.H. (1999). *Knowledge assets: Securing competitive advantage in the information economy*. New York: Oxford University Press.

Brown, S.L. and Eisenhardt, K.M. (1997). The art of continuous change: Linking complexity theory and time-paced evolution in relentlessly shifting organizations. *Administrative Science Quarterly*, 42 (1), pp. 1–34.

Burnes, B. (2005). Complexity theories and organizational change. *International Journal of Management Reviews*, 7 (2), pp. 73–90.

Byrne, D. and Callaghan, G. (2014). *Complexity theory and the social sciences: The state of the art*. Abingdon: Routledge.

Caldart, A.A. and Ricart, J.E. (2004). Corporate strategy revisited: A view from complexity theory. *European Management Review*, 1 (1), pp. 96–104.

Chia, R. (2002). Essai: Time, duration and simultaneity: Rethinking process and change in organizational analysis. *Organization Studies*, 23 (6), pp. 863–868.

Chia, R. (2003). Organization theory as postmodern science. In Tsoukas, H. and Knudsen, C. (eds) *The Oxford handbook of organizational theory*. Oxford: Oxford University Press.

Cooke, P. (2012). Knowledge economy spillovers, proximity, and specialization. In Asheim, B.T. and Parrilli, M.D. (eds) *Interactive learning for innovation*. London: Palgrave Macmillan.

Dalal, F. (1998). *Taking the group seriously: Towards a post-Foulkesian group analytic theory*. London: Jessica Kingsley Publishers.

Deacon, T. (2007). Three levels of emergent phenomena. In Murphy, N.C. and Stoeger, W.R. (eds) *Evolution and emergence: Systems, organisms, persons*, pp. 88–110. Oxford: Oxford University Press.

Dopson, S. (2005). The diffusion of medical innovations: Can figurational sociology contribute? *Organization Studies*, 26 (8), pp. 1125–1144.

Elias, N. (1939). *The civilizing process*. Oxford: Blackwell.

Elias, N. (1978). *What is sociology?* New York: Columbia University Press.

Elias, N. (1991). *The society of individuals*. Oxford: Blackwell Publishing.

Elias, N. (1998). *On civilization, power, and knowledge*. Chicago: University of Chicago Press.

Elias, N. and Scotson, J.L. (1965). *The established and the outsiders*. London: Sage.

Eoyang, G. (2004). The practitioner's landscape. *Emergence: Complexity and Organization*, 6 (1–2), pp.

Fløysand, A. and Jakobsen, S.-E. (2011). The complexity of innovation: A relational turn. *Progress in Human Geography*, 35 (3), pp. 328–344.

Fonseca, J. (2002). *Complexity and innovation in organizations*. London: Routledge.

Foray, D. (2015). *Smart specialisation: Opportunities and challenges for regional innovation policy*. London: Routledge.

Frenken, K. (2000). A complexity approach to innovation networks: The case of the aircraft industry (1909–1997). *Research Policy*, 29 (2), pp. 257–272.

Frenken, K. (2006a). *Innovation, evolution and complexity theory*. Northampton, MA: Edward Elgar.

Frenken, K. (2006b). Technological innovation and complexity theory. *Economics of Innovation and New Technology*, 15 (2), pp. 137–155.

Gell-Mann, M. (1994). Complex adaptive systems. In Midgley, G. (ed.) *Systems thinking*. Thousand Oaks, CA: Sage.

Goldstein, J. (2000). Emergence: A construct amid a thicket of conceptual snares. *Emergence*, 2 (1), pp. 5–22.

Griffin, D. (2002). *The emergence of leadership: Linking self-organization and ethics*. London: Routledge.

Hirooka, M. (2006). Complexity in discrete innovation systems. *Emergence: Complexity and Organization*, 8 (2), pp. 20–34.

Holland, J.H. (1998). *Emergence: From chaos to order*. New York: Oxford University Press.

Johannessen, S. and Aasen, T.M.B. (2007). Exploring innovation processes from a complexity perspective. Part I: theoretical and methodological approach. *International Journal of Learning and Change*, 2 (4), pp. 420–433.

Kauffman, S.A. (1993). *The origins of order: Self-organization and selection in evolution*. New York: Oxford University Press.

Kelly, S. and Allison, M.A. (1999). *The complexity advantage: How the science of complexity can help your business achieve peak performance*. New York: McGraw-Hill.

Kirzner, I.M. (1997). Entrepreneurial discovery and the competitive market process: An Austrian approach. *Journal of Economic Literature*, 35 (1), pp. 60–85.

Lam, A. (2000). Tacit knowledge, organizational learning and societal institutions: An integrated framework. *Organization Studies*, 21 (3), pp. 487–513.

Langton, C.G. (1996). Artificial life. In Boden, M.A. (ed.) *The philosophy of artificial life*. New York: Oxford University Press.

Leana, C.R. and Barry, B. (2000). Stability and change as simultaneous experiences in organizational life. *Academy of Management Review*, 25 (4), pp. 753–759.

Lewis, M.W. (2000). Exploring paradox: Toward a more comprehensive guide. *Academy of Management Review*, 25 (4), pp. 760–776.

Marion, R. (1999). *The edge of organization: Chaos and complexity theories of formal social systems*. Thousand Oaks, CA: Sage.

Mariussen, Å. and Virkkala, S. (2019). Introduction. In Mariussen, Å., Virkkala, S., Finne, H. and Aasen, T.M. (eds) *The entrepreneurial discovery process and regional development: New knowledge emergence, conversion and exploitation*. Abingdon: Routledge.

Martin, R. and Sunley, P. (2012). Forms of emergence and the evolution of economic landscapes. *Journal of Economic Behavior & Organization*, 82 (2–3), pp. 338–351.

Mead, G.H. (1923). Scientific method and the moral sciences. *International Journal of Ethics*, 33 (3), pp. 229–247.

Mead, G.H. (1934). *Mind, self and society*. Chicago: Chicago University Press.

Mintzberg, H. (1987). The strategy concept I: Five Ps for strategy. *California Management Review*, 30 (1), pp. 11–24.

Nonaka, I. (1994). A dynamic theory of organizational knowledge creation. *Organization Science*, 5 (1), pp. 14–37.

Nonaka, I. and Konno, N. (1998). The concept of 'Ba': Building a foundation for knowledge creation. *California Management Review*, 40 (3), pp. 40–54.

Nonaka, I. and Takeuchi, H. (1995). *The knowledge-creating company: How Japanese companies create the dynamics of innovation*. New York: Oxford University Press.

Nonaka, I. and Toyama, R. (2003). The knowledge-creating theory revisited: Knowledge creation as a synthesizing process. *Knowledge Management Research & Practice*, 1 (1), pp. 2–10.

Nonaka, I. and von Krogh, G. (2009). Tacit knowledge and knowledge conversion: Controversy and advancement in organizational knowledge creation theory. *Organization Science*, 20 (3), pp. 635–652.

Poole, M.S. and Van de Ven, A.H. (eds) (2004). *Handbook of organizational change and innovation*. New York: Oxford University Press.

Poole, M.S., Van de Ven, A.H., Dooley, K. and Holmes, M.E. (2000). *Organizational change and innovation processes: Theory and methods for research*. New York: Oxford University Press.

Price, I. (2004). Complexity, complicatedness and complexity: A new science behind organizational intervention? *Emergence: Complexity and Organization*, 6 (1–2), pp.

Prigogine, I. (1997). *The end of certainty: Time, chaos and the new laws of nature*. New York: The Free Press.

Roundy, P., Bradshaw, M. and Brockman, B. (2016). Venturing towards the edge of chaos: A complex adaptive systems approach to entrepreneurial ecosystems. In USASBE (ed.) *Entrepreneurship everywhere*. Boca Raton, FL: United States Association for Small Business and Entrepreneurship.

Schumpeter, J.A. (1934). *The theory of economic development: An inquiry into profits, capital, credit, interest, and the business cycle*. Cambridge, MA: Harvard University Press.

Shane, S. (2003). *A general theory of entrepreneurship: The individual–opportunity nexus*. Northampton, MA: Edward Elgar.

Simon, H.A. (1996). *The sciences of the artificial*, 3rd ed. Cambridge, MA: MIT Press.

Sotarauta, M. (2016). Place leadership, governance and power. *Administration*, 64 (3–4), pp. 45–58.

Stacey, R.D. (1991). *The chaos frontier: Creative strategic control for business*. Oxford: Butterworth Heinemann.

Stacey, R.D. (2001). *Complex responsive processes in organizations: Learning and knowledge creation*. London: Routledge.

Stacey, R.D. (2003). *Complexity and group processes: A radically social understanding of individuals*. Hove: Brunner-Routledge.

Stacey, R.D. (2005). Introduction: Emergence and organizations. In Stacey, R.D. (ed.) *Experiencing emergence in organizations: Local interaction and the emergence of global patterns*, pp. 1–16. Abingdon: Routledge.

Stacey, R.D. (2007). *Strategic management and organisational dynamics: The challenge of complexity to ways of thinking about organisations*, 5th ed. Essex: Prentice Hall.

Stacey, R.D. and Griffin, D. (2005a). Experience and method: A complex responsive processes perspective on research in organizations. In Stacey, R.D. and Griffin, D. (eds) *A complexity perspective on researching organizations: Taking experience seriously*, pp. 13–38. Abingdon: Routledge.

Stacey, R.D. and Griffin, D. (2005b). Introduction: Leading in a complex world. In Griffin, D. and Stacey, R.D. (eds) *Complexity and the experience of leading organizations*, pp. 1–16. Abingdon: Routledge.

Stacey, R.D. and Griffin, D. (2005c). Introduction: Researching organizations from a complexity perspective. In Stacey, R.D. and Griffin, D. (eds) *A complexity perspective on researching organizations: Taking experience seriously*, pp. 1–12. Abingdon: Routledge.

Stacey, R.D., Griffin, D. and Shaw, P. (2000). *Complexity and management: Fad or radical challenge to systems thinking?* London: Routledge.

Surie, G. and Hazy, J. (2006). Generative leadership: Nurturing innovation in complex systems. *Emergence: Complexity and Organization*, 8 (4), pp. 13–26.

Thompson, J.D. (1967). *Organizations in action: Social science bases of administrative theory*. New York: McGraw-Hill.

Tidd, J. (2001). Innovation management in context: Environment, organization and performance. *International Journal of Management Reviews*, 3 (3), pp. 169–183.

Tsoukas, H. (2005). *Complex knowledge: Studies in organizational epistemology*. Oxford: Oxford University Press.

Tsoukas, H. and Chia, R. (2002). On organizational becoming: Rethinking organizational change. *Organization Science*, 13 (5), pp. 567–582.

Tsoukas, H. and Hatch, M.J. (2001). Complex thinking, complex practice: The case for a narrative approach to organizational complexity. *Human Relations*, 54 (8), pp. 979–1013.

Van Buuren, A. and Edelenbos, J. (2006). Innovation in the Dutch polder: Communities of practice and the challenge of coevolution. *Emergence: Complexity and Organization*, 8 (1), pp. 41–48.

Van de Ven, A.H., Angle, H.L. and Poole, M.S. (eds) (2000). *Research on the management of innovation: The Minnesota studies*, 2nd ed. New York: Oxford University Press.

Van de Ven, A.H., Polley, D.E., Garud, R. and Venkataraman, S. (1999). *The innovation journey*. New York and Oxford: Oxford University Press.

Van de Ven, A.H. and Poole, M.S. (2005). Alternative approaches for studying organizational change. *Organization Studies*, 26 (9), pp. 1377–1404.

Webb, C., Lettice, F. and Lemon, M. (2006). Facilitating learning and innovation in organizations using complexity science principles. *Emergence: Complexity and Organization*, 8 (1), pp. 30–41.

Weick, K.E. (2000). Emergent change as a universal in organizations. In Beer, M. and Nohria, N. (eds) *Breaking the code of change*. Boston: Harvard Business School Press.

Wright, S. (1932). The roles of mutation, inbreeding, crossbreeding and selection in evolution. In Jones, D.F. (ed.) *Proceedings of the VI International Congress of Genetics*, pp. 356–366. Menasha, WI: Brooklyn Botanic Garden.

8 Entrepreneurial discovery processes, knowledge creation and knowledge space

Seija Virkkala

8.1 Introduction

The focus of this book is the transition from exploitation to exploration in an entrepreneurial discovery process (EDP) and the preconditions and implications of that change for entrepreneurial actors, the regional economy and knowledge creation. Whereas Chapter 1 (Virkkala and Mariussen, 2019b) focuses on agency or the 'self' in self-discovery and Chapter 9 (Virkkala and Mariussen, 2019a) on the changes to a regional economy through emergence and through transnational networks, this chapter describes EDP as a process of knowledge creation. Entrepreneurial knowledge is a driver of the discovery process (Foray, 2015: 24) both in the phase of searching for new business fields (domains) and in the implementation phase of the smart specialisation strategies (S3). In the discovery process, regional stakeholders should combine various types of knowledge: knowledge of local capabilities and assets of the region; relevant scientific and technological knowledge; knowledge of the competitive market; and knowledge of the organisations and firms providing the required knowledge. In addition, visionary knowledge of the region's future specialisation within the knowledge economy is required. According to Foray (2016), the knowledge needed for discovery is dispersed, fragmented and hidden.

This chapter argues that when knowledge is generated, the space for knowledge will also be created. The search for new regional business fields can be seen as a knowledge-creation process as well as a process of the creation of knowledge space. In this process, the proximities and distances between the stakeholders, or entrepreneurial actors, are changing and a new balance between proximities and distances will be created. This argument is based on the reasoning of Nonaka and Takeuchi (1995) that learning is knowledge creation and its context is *ba*,[1] which is the place where knowledge is created. This chapter aims to contribute to the emerging literature on EDP from the points of view of knowledge creation and knowledge space. The current study distinguishes the space for knowledge from the bounded administrative territory. In the context of regional development policies like S3, regional economies are understood as territorially bounded areas, which must be renewed and transformed due for instance to the challenges of globalisation, digitalisation, ageing and climate change. The knowledge space as the context for knowledge creation is more abstract and flexible. The current chapter examines a research question: *how are the knowledge-creation process and the construction of the knowledge space connected in the context of the EDP?* This research question will be approached with the help of a framework based on theories of organisational learning and communities as well as geographical theories on space. Knowledge creation in the EDP can be organised in different ways, but the interaction between entrepreneurial actors and the spaces for this interaction are crucial.

When viewing the discovery process as a knowledge-creation process, it is important to recognise the role of tacit knowledge. The latent competitive advantage of the region involves tacit knowledge that is difficult for formal bodies to discover. It is necessary to introduce theories of knowledge creation with tacit knowledge at their core. The next section presents some of these approaches including the SECI model and knowledge in action or communities in practice, and the chapter then applies these approaches in its explanation of the EDP. The third section approaches the notion of knowledge space with the help of concepts of relational space and dimensions of proximity. The fourth section builds a framework based on the combination of previously presented knowledge-creation approaches and notions of knowledge spaces. The framework describes the EDP as an evolutionary process of sense-making consisting of searching, interacting, interpretation visioning and experimentation with varying features of a knowledge space.

In the fifth section, two examples of knowledge creation and knowledge space are presented: focus group meetings as a part of a connectivity analysis and also the regional development platform method. Both methods connect entrepreneurial actors from different communities of practice like a specific industry, universities and public government. The connectivity analysis identifies gaps in the innovation system and measures them in terms of the difference between the experience and expectations of a relationship. These gaps are the issues to be discussed and bridged in the focus group meetings (Virkkala et al., 2017). The platform seeks to align several actors to boost future regional economic development (Harmaakorpi, 2006). The final section summarises and discusses the framework developed in the chapter.

8.2 Approaches to the knowledge-creation process in the EDP

Knowledge is interpreted as justified true belief (Nonaka and Takeuchi, 1995). Academic knowledge, for example, is justified in relation to the epistemic culture. The truth, understood as shared beliefs, results from processes where people justify and substantiate their beliefs within an organisation (Mariussen, 2013). The dialogue on new opportunities in public–private alliances in the EDP is an explanatory process in the field of regional culture. Knowledge created through the EDP is then substantiated through practices and experiments, and by way of future regional development.

To illuminate the EDP as a knowledge-generation process it is necessary to examine different approaches to the knowledge process. The EDP as collective knowledge creation can be explained with the help of organisational knowledge-creation theories (organisational learning). There are many approaches in organisational studies but the most famous is the SECI model by Nonaka and Takeuchi (1995).

The SECI model

The SECI model[2] by Nonaka and Takeuchi (1995) describes how organisations create knowledge. It draws a distinction between explicit (codified) and tacit knowledge. Explicit knowledge is expressed in codified form such as texts, whereas tacit knowledge is deeply rooted in individuals' actions and experience, and the latter contains an important cognitive dimension helping individuals to perceive and define their world. For tacit knowledge to be communicated and shared it has to be converted into words that everyone can understand. When this conversion takes place – from tacit to explicit, and back again into tacit – organisational knowledge is created (Nonaka and Takeuchi, 1995). The interaction of these two types of knowledge triggers a knowledge-conversion process, that is, the SECI process. The four stages of the SECI process form a spiral of knowledge creation, one that unites the creators (individual, group and organisation) with knowledge (tacit and explicit). The knowledge spiral becomes larger in scale as it moves up the ontological levels. When tacit and explicit knowledge interact, the result is an innovation (Nonaka and Takeuchi, 1995; Nonaka et al., 2001). Knowledge creation is a continuous process of interaction between tacit and explicit knowledge.

The knowledge possessed by individuals must be shared and amplified through interaction with others, and *ba* is a space where such interaction takes place. Therefore, the knowledge-creating process is also a process of creating *ba*, and a new boundary of interaction (Nonaka et al., 2000). Nonaka and Toyama (2003) consider *ba* to be a time and space which is shared in order to encourage the emerging relationships among individuals and groups, leading to the creation of knowledge.

The SECI model has been criticised for overemphasising the thing-like nature of tacit knowledge. Tsoukas (2003) argues that tacit and explicit knowledge are two sides of the same coin as even the most explicit kind of knowledge rests on tacit knowledge. Tacit knowing is a necessary component of all knowledge and it is inscribed into the artefacts of codified knowledge (Amin and Cohendet, 2004). In addition, tacit knowing is unintended knowing in action and as such exists only in relation to the focused aspect and cannot be separated from that to be examined independently (Vissers and Dankbaar, 2013). Tacitness is a matter of degree, and in between explicit skills which can easily be communicated and tacit skills which are deeply engrained and not even accessible to the knowledge holders themselves, there is a group of skills that have not yet been articulated, but that could be if people were asked to do so, and there is also a group of tacit skills that can be accessed through pictures and symbols rather than through language (Virkkala and Mariussen, 2013).

Knowing as action and communities of practice

The approach of knowledge in practice emphasises that what is known is not a thing or a static property; instead it should be seen as the ability to act. Knowing is our action. Knowledge does not exist independently of social actors and practical contexts. Knowledge should instead be conceived of as embodied and contextually situated in time and space. Knowledge only becomes meaningful in relation to a distinct social practice (Lave and Wenger, 1991). Knowing constitutes action in itself and in purposeful intervention. The practice view, that is, the embeddedness of knowledge in practice, stresses the collective nature of knowing. The dichotomy between tacit knowing and codified knowledge does not make any sense from this theoretical perspective. Knowing is an ongoing social activity, constituted in everyday practice (Orlikowski, 2002). Practical understanding refers to knowing how to carry out a specific activity, what it makes sense to do, and being able to put into practice competently (Lave and Wenger, 1991). Knowledge cannot be transferred but it has to be translated when used under different local and historical conditions (see Chapter 5, (Lam, 2019)). While quanta of knowledge can be exchanged between actors, the essence of distinct practice has to be translated across cultural boundaries (Ibert, 2007).

The knowledge-creation process is difficult because knowledge is embodied in actors and in their practices. Combining knowledge requires common frameworks and understandings. Entrepreneurial actors in the EDP often represent different communities of practice, implying that knowledge is embodied in them and their practices. The community is an active entity of knowing (Lave and Wenger, 1991). From this perspective, the borders of knowledge practices are important and the creation of the knowledge space representing many communities of practice should focus on the borders and how to transcend the boundaries of practices. In order to create knowledge for discovery, entrepreneurial actors should interact. Such interaction can range from participation in focus groups and workshops to broader community meetings and surveys. It is also possible that during the EDP, a regional community of practice will emerge when a collective agency forms to pursue a discovery process (see Chapter 1 (Virkkala and Mariussen, 2019b)).

Knowledge as object and knowledge as an activity in the EDP

Vissers and Dankbaar (2013) and Amin and Cohendet (2004) distinguish two different knowledge approaches: knowledge as an asset or object and knowledge as action, that is, social and embodied practice (knowing). Existing research places more emphasis on the view that knowledge is conceived as an activity and process. The notion of knowledge as action implies a constructionist approach according to which knowledge is conceived as a practice created in interaction, and knowledge is inseparable from the person holding that knowledge (Amin and Cohendet, 2004).

It is possible to analyse the EDP by way of two different approaches to the knowledge process: knowledge as an object, based on the content perspective, and knowledge as action based on the relational perspective emphasising the agents and their relations like the theory of communities of practice (Wenger, 1998). Although the SECI model has been criticised for treating knowledge in the manner of a thing, it does have the character of the community of practice and can be seen as linking the two contrasting approaches. It is suggested in the current work that both the SECI model and the knowledge as action or knowing approach can be applied in interpreting the EDP as a process of knowledge generation.

Entrepreneurial actors search out the elements of a new business field and in that search process their tacit knowledge will be translated according to the knowledge-as-action perspective. This implies changing proximities between the actors. This collective knowledge will become a new relational knowledge which will be one cornerstone of the new business area. However, the tacit knowledge of entrepreneurial actors is also converted to explicit knowledge and combined with the knowledge of local capabilities and general purpose technology (GPT) so that the result will be the knowledge of the new business field. In the EDP, knowledge as an object is transformed into knowledge as a (discovery) process and finally into a knowledge spiral which is a continuous EDP (see Table 8.1).

Table 8.1 Two perspectives on knowledge creation

	Knowledge-as-object	*Knowledge-as-action*	*The EDP as a knowledge-conversion process*
Perspective	Content perspective	Relational perspective: knowing agents and the knowledge context	From content to relational and collective knowledge
Form of knowledge	Knowledge as an asset, resource	Knowing, knowledge activity	From asset to new business area (domain)
Method	Follow knowledge	Follow the knowledge agent: relations between agents, what knowledge agents do	Interaction between entrepreneurial actors is crucial
Policy	Input to knowledge stock	Creation and support conditions that foster interaction	Fora for knowledge sharing

Sources: based on the ideas of Ibert (2007), Bathelt and Glückler (2011) and Vissers and Dankbaar (2013)

8.3 Knowledge spaces and proximities

Knowledge processes depend on the spatial contexts, or spaces of knowledge creation. Space and time come together in knowledge creation (Hautala and Jauhiainen, 2014). In order to approach knowledge spaces constructed by the entrepreneurial actors for the discovery, the chapter presents two approaches to space used in geography: relational space, which is in line with networking and the relational economy (Bathelt and Glückler, 2011), as well as places as 'becoming', which is in line with the process thinking and constructivist approaches (Pred, 1984).

Recent geographical literature addresses the cooperation of actors and focuses on relations and networking. The relations and networks between actors or entities can build a space, known as *relational space*. Relational spaces emerge alongside territorially bounded regions, but they cannot be characterised as discrete geographical units (Cresswell, 2013). They are 'spaces of flows' according to Castells (1998). Relations can move across scales from the local to the global (Massey, 2005). According to the relational approach, objects and their relations create the space. Relational space happens at the same time as the things that are supposed to occur in space. There is no prior existing thing called space, but there are objects and their relations creating the space (Cresswell, 2013; Massey, 2005).

In order to create new knowledge and knowledge space, enough proximity is required to connect actors and to enable interactive learning and innovation. Boschma (2005) suggests five dimensions of proximity: geographical, social, institutional, organisational and cognitive proximity. Geographical proximity promotes unique local competencies, skills and new knowledge, which can diffuse spontaneously through personal contacts via the 'local buzz' (Bathelt et al., 2004). However, geographical proximity alone is not enough to foster knowledge creation, but it can facilitate other forms of proximity and the sharing of tacit knowledge. Social proximity refers to personal relationships between actors; institutional proximity to joint formal and informal rules; organisational proximity to the membership of the same organisational entity; and cognitive proximity to the distance between the knowledge base of actors. To support knowledge creation, there should be optimal cognitive proximity between actors. Social proximity is likely to be more localised than cognitive proximity.

The notion of *ba* as an arena of knowledge creation by Nonaka and Konno (1998) can be seen as relational space. *Ba* is created through interaction between individuals and with their environment. *Ba* is not necessarily a physical space, but rather a context that harbours meaning. It can be physical (office), virtual (email, teleconference), mental (shared experiences, ideas, ideals) or any combination of these. It can be space and time that is shared within a project team, a space for informal dialogue, for sharing experiences with customers, for interdivisional cooperation, or a space shared by virtual companies (Nonaka et al., 2001: 18–19). In the EDP context, *ba* is a space of self-discovery. It can for instance be epitomised in focus group meetings and workshops, in which entrepreneurial actors collectively search for new business fields.

The knowledge space is a dynamic category that is *becoming* rather than *being*. The notions of 'becoming' and 'being' in the regional context originate with Pred (1984), who looked upon regions as historically contingent and dynamic categories, which instead of *being* are constantly *becoming*. Regions are in a constant state of construction by the agents. Pred applied the ideas of structuration theory to the notion of place. The regions will always be in the process of transformation, and the state of 'becoming' implies a constant balancing of structure and agency. These ideas have been applied in the social construction of the regions via human action and relations between the actors. Regions are social constructs; actors produce and give meaning to them in more or less bounded material and symbolic worlds (Paasi, 2002). Since relations between actors and networks are continuously changing, relational space is in constant process of *becoming*.

In the context of EDP, knowledge space can have two meanings: first, it is the space in which different knowledge is integrated, and the relations between entrepreneurial actors will be changed as a result of alignment between the entrepreneurial actors (see Chapter 1 by Virkkala and Mariussen (2019b)). In this knowledge space, activities and R&D measures will be identified which are likely to bring success to a region given its existing capabilities and also the new opportunities for commercially viable lines of business. According to the second interpretation, knowledge space is the result of the discovery of the new business area (=domain) which is the basis for regional S3 (Foray, 2015). The notion of domain can be seen as encapsulating a relational space emerging as a result of changing proximities between the actors. The domain is in the process of 'becoming' when the entrepreneurial actors and other actors implement the regional strategies through experiments. However, the EDP is a continuous exploration since the business opportunities are changing because of the turbulent global environment (Table 8.2).

Knowledge space in the EDP context can be discussed by applying the notions of object space, communicative space and cognitive space (Hautala and Jauhiainen, 2014). Knowledge creation is an interactive process between entrepreneurial actors. An object space is the material environment of an individual, and in the context of the EDP might refer to the facts of the region, such as its demographic and economic structure. A communicative space is formed as a result of interaction: when people, ideas, information and rituals interact with the communicative space (Amin and Cohendet, 2004). That communicative space refers to networks, epistemic cultures and communities of practice (Wenger, 1998). In this space, people interact and discuss issues through various communication channels. Cognitive space treats knowledge as taking the form of interconnected concepts, theories and ideas: it is what one can analyse, understand and discuss when interpreting interaction. Knowledge is interpreted and substantiated. It comprises mental models of individuals and shared mental models of groups. In a cognitive space, one becomes cognitively closer or more distant.

8.4 EDP as a process of sense-making: evolution of knowledge creation

The knowledge-conversion process resulting in the discovery of a future specialisation in a region should be embedded in existing local capabilities. The knowledge of entrepreneurial actors should be combined with general purpose technology (GPT) like ICT, nanotechnology or biotechnology aligned with a region's vision.[3] The EDP will benefit the existing activities in which the region already specialises (Boschma, 2017). However, many activities cannot be meaningfully combined. Combinations are more likely to emerge from technologies or industries with similar knowledge bases (Frenken et al., 2007; Boschma, 2017). New specialisations emerge from the combination of local capabilities across sectors or technologies, and the result might be novel combinations for the region. The EDP allows room for unexpected connections between unrelated local activities, in that it builds on local activities that have not been connected to date (Boschma, 2017).

The discovery processes should start with a situation in which the actors – for instance in a cluster – utilise and refine the existing regional knowledge base. The relations between the actors are fixed, and this situation is seen as exploitation, which might exhaust the regional knowledge base. New knowledge is needed, and it can be detected by combining existing knowledge or translating the knowledge of entrepreneurial actors, and that outcome demands a new type of knowledge space. It might be a hybrid space in which the agents share and translate their knowledge. The aim is to combine existing knowledge and capabilities in new and perhaps more complex ways. This exploration phase might mean that the proximity between the actors changes, and the result might be more proximate relations between distant actors. This is a largely cognitive dimension of proximity. Knowledge space moves from a fixed structure of exploitation to the new knowledge space in the exploration (see Table 8.2). This new knowledge is an outcome of discovery: it is a new domain that can be exploited to generate new growth in the region. Knowledge space and the exploitation–exploration–exploitation phases of EDP are interrelated.

Next, this study explicates the design of the phases of the discovery process from the perspective of creating knowledge and knowledge space.

At the beginning of the process of discovery, the facilitator should identify and engage with critical entrepreneurial actors who hold knowledge on a region's resources, its strengths, weaknesses and potential. They should have the capacity to engage in exploration and contribute to the EDP. The entrepreneurial actors explore new technological domains and interact with the market. During the discovery, the interaction between the actors and interpretation of knowledge are key. Knowledge gathered, combined and converted during the search process requires interpretation so as to be substantiated and become meaningful. The frame for interpretation is the vision of a region's place in the future knowledge economy. However, interaction and interpretation occur simultaneously in the search process, even if these activities are treated separately in the analysis.

Table 8.2 Knowledge space and time, from exploitation to exploration

	Knowledge dynamics	*Knowledge space*	*EDP phase*
Exploitation	Cumulative based on existing knowledge	Proximity, fixed relations	Beginning of discovery process
Exploration	Combinatory knowledge dynamics	Substitution, new proximity relations Hybrid space	Search for new knowledge discovery
Exploitation	Cumulative knowledge dynamics	New knowledge space: new balance between proximity and distance of agents	Result of discovery: new domain (business areas): innovation and growth of the business area

Source: Own elaboration

Interacting and searching in the communicative space

Entrepreneurial actors often belong to different communities of practice, but in order to create new knowledge, the knowledge of different practices must be translated. Knowledge sharing often occurs spontaneously between actors, but to facilitate the deliberate search for the transformation of a regional economy, places should be organised to facilitate interaction among actors. There might be borders between different communities and cognitive distance between entrepreneurial actors, but collaboration and structured dialogue is one way of overcoming such cognitive distances. The interaction can occur in different workshops and focus group meetings but also through communication channels in the social media. This space can be seen as a communication space. Interaction can be described as the socialisation phase of the SECI model when the entrepreneurial actors share the same objective of finding new business fields for the regional economy.

Interpretation in the cognitive space

The members of a community of practice might have a similar mental model that helps them to interpret knowledge; for example, the mental models of electrical engineers might diverge from those of marketing specialists or of experts in regional development. The knowledge shared in interaction will be interpreted through mental models of the entrepreneurial actors in the cognitive space. Ideas, concepts, statements, and thoughts arising from interaction are organised into mental models as dynamic and incomplete representations of the world. The mental models of various actors can converge in the cognitive space. The interpretation process occurs both at the individual and group levels. These knowledge bases change and broaden because people learn and correct false combinations through interaction (Weick, 2001). The mental models can be only partly explained, or made explicit, but much of this knowing remains tacit (Nonaka and Takeuchi, 1995; Hautala and Jauhiainen, 2014). Interpretation transforms information into meaningful and applicable knowledge. In the case of the EDP, the mental models connect a vision of the regional development, the local capabilities and potential GPT. Interpretation of knowledge is sense-making and it corresponds to the externalisation phase of the SECI model.

Visioning and new domain

A new domain is the future specialisation of the region which has been found through the processes of searching, interacting and interpreting the knowledge of entrepreneurial actors and combining this new knowledge with a general purpose technology (GPT) like ICT, and with other extra-regional knowledge. It can be seen as the combination phase in the SECI model when the knowledge created by explicated tacit knowledge is combined with the existing codified knowledge. It is based on the shared understanding of the future of the regional economy. The combination of different knowledge affects the proximities between agents. The new domain is also a new knowledge space, in which there is a new balance between proximities and distances between the entrepreneurial actors. Creating spaces creates borders to communities of practices. Discovering a new domain might mean that some actors are more important and more central to the new knowledge space and some others more remote from it.

Experimentation and implementation

A new domain informs the whole regional economy of possible new business opportunities. One region can have many new domains, for instance one domain renewing the old industries and another domain creating a new business field based on knowledge spinoffs from universities. The results of discovery will be captured in the smart specialisation strategy encapsulating different priorities. The government should support the activities and projects that appear promising in terms of future innovations and potential for the transformation of the existing structures and that offer economies of scale. A policy should also support the emergence of a micro-system of innovation so that the regional economy might be transformed (Foray, 2016). The implementation and experimentation can be compared with the internalisation phase of the SECI process, when the actors begin to act according to the tangible new knowledge. However, implementation requires reflective learning by trial and error as well as a policy environment supporting experimentation. The continuous evaluation of the experiment is crucial, and the new domain as knowledge space is a relational space which is *becoming*.

8.5 Examples from Finland of knowledge spaces in the EDP

The smart specialisation approach has similarities with programme-based regional development which started in Finland in 1994. The regional development work was based on bottom–up processes relying on a broad partnership of regional actors but also on coordination by the state, for instance through the budgets of regional state offices (Virkkala, 2002). The strength of the Finnish system is its good connections between triple helix actors and high levels of investment in private and public RDI compared with some other EU countries (Reid and Maroulis, 2017). The weakness of the economy is a too centralised network structure based on a narrowly defined export base. The need for diversification with the help of smart specialisation was obvious after the crisis in ICT and the forestry industry at the time of launching the S3 (Mariussen et al., 2014). Finland has no national S3, although some national-level policies have similarities with S3 principles (Reid and Maroulis, 2017; Rinkinen, 2015). The S3 process was conducted at regional level by regional councils. Some regions embedded S3 in their regional development plans while others prepared a separate S3 document (Nissinen, 2017), an example being the regional council of Lapland (Teräs and Mäenpää, 2016) to support the smart transformation of the economy. Many regions developed new planning methods and approaches to S3. This chapter describes two methods developed as action research by Finnish researchers and used in the framework for entrepreneurial discovery: a connectivity tool and a regional development platform. Both are based on ideas on the promotion of interactive collective learning among stakeholders.

Connectivity tool: knowledge space and discovery through gap analysis

The aim of the connectivity model developed by Virkkala et al. (2017) is to create a knowledge space for discovery to generate social and cognitive proximities among stakeholders. This model consists of a survey that maps the structures of the networks that make up relations between various stakeholders, including gaps measured as tensions between expectations and experiences. The model is based on the idea that the driver of change in a relationship between two actors is the tension between expectations, which may be confirmed and strengthened, or frustrated. The gap between the values of expectations and experiences is used as an input in a structured dialogue in focus groups in which companies, universities, and public administration (or entrepreneurial actors) participate. Discussions on such gaps can improve the connectivity between stakeholders, and they can open the door to the discovery of emergent connections (weak relations that may be strengthened) and structural holes (lack of relations), which may reveal an opportunity for EDPs in the region as entrepreneurial actors resolve the issues hindering cooperation on various aspects of innovation. Gap analysis helps stakeholders to identify problems and set the parameters of the dialogues set up to resolve them. They can be used in constructing a shared vision and pooling scattered resources, but also in detecting the need for policy interventions, for example the alignment of educational, research and innovation policies in line with the regional strategy. Such usage adds experimental learning and gradual improvements to S3.

The model can be seen as one tool to assist EDP and collective knowledge creation. The SECI model by Nonaka and Takeuchi (1995) can be used as an analytical framework for understanding how mutual expectations or connectivity can be created. According to the SECI model, organisational and spatial proximity enables the creation of four stages of knowledge conversion. Below the relation between these stages and the connectivity model is explained (see Table 8.3).

In the stage of *socialisation*, tacit knowledge is created and shared between individuals mainly through face-to-face communication in a specific place (*ba*). This open communication relies upon a certain level of mutual trust and openness, in short, *social proximity*. Through *externalisation*, tacit knowledge is articulated in the form of metaphors and diagrams so it might be understood by others: this is knowledge conversion. In the connectivity model, a researcher is asking about the tacit knowledge of the relationship; here, the expectations and experiences will be codified, and their distance will represent the gap index. This creates *cognitive proximity*, a shared and codified analysis of the situation in the relation, the achievements and challenges.

During the *combination* stage, explicit knowledge is then connected with existing knowledge through sorting, adding, systemising and categorising. Here, a shared theory or model of the problem at hand is developed, and new organisational solutions are suggested. In a connectivity model, this phase corresponds to a focus group meeting with the relevant stakeholders, who look for the explanation of the gap. Sometimes causal explanations are needed and sometimes more theoretical ones; this fosters discussion of the challenges discovered through the gap analysis. The aim of such discussion is to reach a consensus on the reasons for the relevant gap, as well as on possible policy interventions. A focus group meeting is *ba*, that is, time and space, which is shared in order to encourage the emerging relationships among individuals and groups, leading to the creation of knowledge. In the fourth stage, explicit knowledge is internalised and converted into practice, when individuals apply the new knowledge. *Internalisation* is closely related to learning by doing and processes of institutional transformation, as the relations change and new practices are developed. In the connectivity model, public actors should make decisions and prepare policy interventions. The implementation of the policy bridging the gaps needs to be internalised by the actors. The tacit knowledge accumulated at the individual level is in turn shared with others through socialisation, setting off a new spiral of knowledge creation.

The connectivity model aims to create knowledge improving the connectivity in the actor network and this knowledge corresponds to the organisational knowledge of the SECI process. The intention is to build a learning organisation incorporating the key regional stakeholders, and then use the

SECI framework to organise the knowledge-creation processes and to build higher levels of connectivity. In the focus group meetings, the reasons for the distance between partners are discussed, mental models are shared and strategies for knowledge bases are agreed upon.

In Ostrobothnia, the connectivity tool has been used among stakeholders of the main export cluster since 2014. The regional council has organised focus group meetings based on the findings of gap analysis every second year. Those focus group meetings have been structured dialogues on possible reasons for the biggest gaps. For instance, the companies in the energy sector reported that they do not get enough support from their local universities. There were also large differences in the expectations and experiences of companies and their regional

Table 8.3 Phases of the SECI model and of the connectivity model

SECI model	*Explanation of the phases*	*Connectivity model*	*Proximities and spaces in connectivity model*
Socialisation	Sharing tacit knowledge	Expectation and experience in relations (as tacit knowledge)	Social proximity
Externalisation	Articulation of tacit knowledge: metaphors, diagrams, models, prototypes, explicating tacit knowledge	Codifying the gaps between expectations and experiences (e.g. on a 1–10 scale)	A codified analysis of the relation, gap index Cognitive proximity
Combination	Connecting newly created explicit knowledge with existing knowledge	Focus group meeting Explanation of the gaps through structured dialogue Preparation of policy interventions	Knowledge space (*ba*) encouraging emergent relationships Organisational proximity
Internalisation	Internalising new explicit knowledge and organisational solutions in practice by individuals	Policy interventions influence actors and their relations	Improved proximity between actors
Socialisation	Sharing new knowledge with others Setting off a new spiral of knowledge creation	New relations and improved proximity influence	Better connectivity in the network

Source: Own elaboration

subcontractors and the high expectations of the quality of production were mentioned. The gaps were analysed by origin and consequences, and policy interventions were planned by the regional council (Virkkala et al., 2014, 2017).

Regional development platform (RDP): a space for discovering future clusters

The concept of a platform is one used in many contexts, like that of the S3 platform guiding the regions or research platforms supporting interdisciplinary research. The concept of a platform can also refer to an innovation platform, a space to facilitate co-creation, which enables various actors to participate in innovation processes (Kautonen et al., 2017). In this chapter, the concept is used to explain how knowledge creation might be broadened based on existing clusters. It is important to bring together different but complementary pieces of knowledge, as well as the different technological domains which should be cross-fertilised. Knowledge creation through cross-fertilisation can happen on platforms, which can then be considered knowledge spaces.

The regional development platform (RDP) method was developed by Harmaakorpi (2006) and colleagues and tested in the Lahti region of Finland. The method describes the business potential in the region by offering promising combinations of industries, areas of expertise and future megatrends. The RDP method is a way of creating new paths from existing resource configurations. It describes the potential to form future regional clusters from the existing resource base. The actors of an RDP are the firms, technology centres, expertise centres, research centres, educational institutions, etc., that define a development platform, and the process engages the actors in the discussion. The RDP consists of different phases, such as the analysis of the features of regional industries and their areas of expertise, expert panels and the assessment of future scenarios, the definition of potential development platforms, conceptualising the regional system, the search for the core processes of the regional innovation system and the definition of the management system (Harmaakorpi, 2006). Areas of expertise are formed by skills, capabilities and competencies assessed to be important independent of industry. It is a question of GPTs but also of other skills and competencies such as design.

Experts have a broad overview of the business life in the region, and they can verify the validity of the views of participants, and possibly update them in terms of agreed megatrends (Cooke, 2007). Megatrends should be reflected in the resource base of the regional innovation system in order to create new paths conferring regional competitive advantage. This phase should be effectuated as a result of interaction between the main actors of a region using futures research methods, such as the Delphi method. The process might increase the regional visionary capability of the participants (Harmaakorpi and Uotila, 2006). The potential development platforms in the region will be defined based on promising combinations of industries and areas of expertise. When the platforms have been identified, the core processes should be defined. Those core processes will aim to exploit the potential within the development platforms and enhance a region's dynamic capabilities. The core processes can also include some phenomena or future megatrends with the potential to bring business opportunities for the companies in the region. The knowledge-creation and management approach used in the RDP method is based on the SECI and *ba* models, and the model created includes the learning spiral with tacit/explicit knowledge conversions and examples of *ba* where the knowledge conversion takes place. The collective regional search process is also the EDP.

The regional development strategy work in the Lahti region is based on the RDP method and core process thinking (Harmaakorpi, 2006; Melkas and Uotila, 2013). Expert panellists from different fields evaluated the current situation of the industries, as well as the areas of expertise and the conditions they would offer for regional development. The panels were given four tables, each with two dimensions: grading each industry and area of expertise from 1–10 according to the various criteria, for instance the growth potential, innovativeness, and regional adequacy of educational opportunities. The different areas of expertise were also assessed. Expertise in this study was defined as expertise independent of the various industries, which is thus necessary for many industries. One of the new clusters which was founded as a cross-fertilisation of existing areas of expertise and industries and defined as a platform was the Cleantech cluster that specialises in waste management and recycling, and water and soil management (Melkas and Uotila, 2013).

Table 8.4 compares the two tools for discovery developed for the EDP in Finland. Both use the SECI model as a framework to obtain tacit knowledge either from gaps in regional innovation networks (connectivity analysis) or from hidden resource configurations evaluated by expert panels. While the RDP method emphasises variety creation, the connectivity model aims to improve connectivity between entrepreneurial actors and influence the proximities between them by bridging the existing gaps in the innovation system. Such gaps should be viewed as full of expectations, and as containing the seeds of something new, a possible new domain.

Both focus group meetings and RDPs can be interpreted as knowledge spaces aiming to connect different entrepreneurial actors, and which can be constructed by the agents in the discovery process. These agents are drawn from different helices (business, academia, or government) or communities of practice like the cluster or industry, and it is a challenge for a regional developer to dismantle the borders of communities of practice. To foster connectivity, some degree of cognitive proximity is needed so that people can learn from each other and collaborate successfully, and other dimensions of proximity such as the social, institutional, and organisational forms may facilitate that (Virkkala et al., 2017).

8.6 Discussion and conclusions

The current chapter approaches the mystery of discovery by examining the EDP as a knowledge-creation process. It has posed a question regarding the connection between the creation of knowledge and the knowledge space in

Table 8.4 Comparison of the RDP method and the connectivity model

	Regional development platform (RDP) method (Lahti region)	*Connectivity model (Region of Ostrobothnia)*
Aim and EDP role	New growth trajectories combining existing industrial knowledge Cross-sectoral variety creation Discovery strategy	Identification and bridging relevant gaps and structural holes in innovation system Discovery strategy
Main concept	Related variety Megatrends	Gaps between experience and expectation in relations in innovation system
Actors	External experts, main stakeholders	Main stakeholders, can be within the cluster
Proximities between actors	Combining proximity and distance	Creation of social and temporary organisational proximity
Problems	Connecting different economic activities and actors	Too cluster-oriented From gaps to discovery
Time horizon	Future-oriented, megatrends	Present: gaps between expectations and experiences
Epistemic object	Future scenarios and technologies	Gaps are expectations to be fulfilled
Knowledge space (Ba)	RDP seminars with stakeholders, expert seminars	Focus group meetings among stakeholders

Source: Own elaboration

the context of the EDP. The chapter contributes to the emerging literature on smart specialisation, first by recognising the crucial role of tacit knowledge in discovery, which was possible owing to employing the SECI model describing how the tacit knowledge of individuals is converted so as to be shared with others, and with the aid of ideas around communities of practice, according to which knowledge is embedded in the action and knowledge sharing must be translated.

The second contribution of the chapter is to add the concept of knowledge space in conceptualising the EDP as a knowledge process. The knowledge space will be created simultaneously with knowledge. This argument is based on the reasoning of Nonaka and Takeuchi (1995) that learning is knowledge creation and its context is *ba*, which is the place where knowledge is created. The chapter developed the concept of knowledge space with the help of the notion of relational space explaining that space is constructed by the actors and the relationships between them. Knowledge space is a place in which knowledge from different sources and scales is combined, converted and translated. The concept of knowledge space is an abstract notion that has various features in the different phases of the EDP. The knowledge space emerges as relational space when the relations between entrepreneurial actors are changing.

Knowledge sharing might occur spontaneously between the actors, but in the deliberate search for ways to transform a regional economy, places for interaction of actors and interpretation of knowledge as well as searching and visioning should be organised. Knowledge space can be an organised RDP, a focus group meeting or a meeting place of local actors.

The current chapter developed a framework of EDP as knowledge-creation process based on the SECI model, communities of practice and the notion of relational space, in which:

- Tacit knowledge is embodied in the practice of entrepreneurial actors, often drawn from different communities of practice.
- Entrepreneurial actors should be mobilised and connected in a knowledge space where they can interact and translate knowledge.
- Entrepreneurial actors reflect the knowledge communicated by others in a cognitive space in which interpretation is important. Individual and collective mental models are important to the interpretation of knowledge. Discovery is a process of applying sense and meaning to the knowledge.
- The new knowledge created and shared by the entrepreneurial actors can be combined with existing knowledge, such as the knowledge of general purpose technologies.
- The discovered new domain can be seen as a knowledge space. During implementation, new activities and firms will be launched using the knowledge created during discovery.
- Since the EDP is a continuous process, the knowledge space is also changing; it is a relational space that is in the process of *becoming* (see Figure 8.1).

The chapter presented and compared two approaches developed by Finnish researchers for the design of knowledge space in the context of the EDP: the first being the focus group meeting organised around the gaps in the knowledge or the expectations of the stakeholders, as used in the region of Ostrobothnia; the second being the RDP method built around future expertise, as used in the Lahti region. Both methods use designed knowledge spaces that can be designed as tangible places of interaction, and which can result in a new knowledge space constructed by the actors involved. This new knowledge space can be at the core of the new domain.

The framework does have its issues: first, the discovery as a knowledge-creation process depends on the regional institutional context of the emerging domain. Many authors (Morgan, 2017; Rodríguez-Pose and Wilkie, 2017) emphasise the role of sound institutions in enabling the EDP. The design of knowledge space has no meaning if the entrepreneurial actors are not motivated to share their knowledge. However, even in the less-developed

Domain consists of the knowledge of the search process and how it should be implemented and subject to experiment.
Combination of new knowledge refers to knowledge created in interaction by entrepreneurial actors with existing knowledge such as GPTs.
Entrepreneurial actors create knowledge spaces across borders between communities of practice through *interaction* (both of the virtual form and in meeting places) and *interpretation*, leading to discoveries. These spaces can be designed.
Communities of practice refer to the context of specialised forms of knowledge.
Humans use their embodied knowledge in practice. Embodied knowledge may be both tacit and codified.

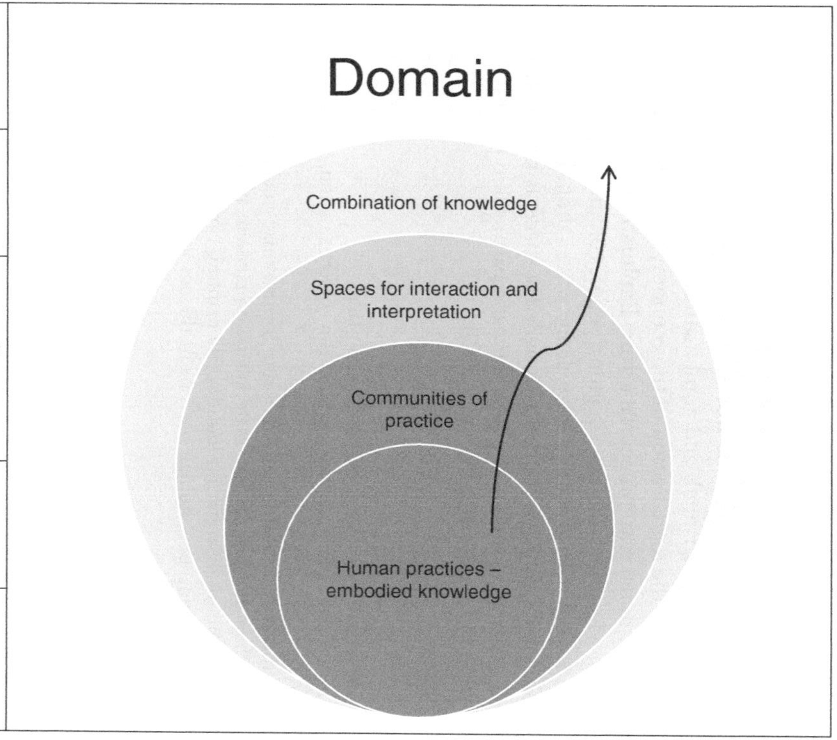

Figure 8.1 EDP as a process of creating knowledge and knowledge space

Source: Own elaboration

regions with weak connectivity between the entrepreneurial actors and an environment that discourages cooperation and experimentation, it is possible to improve connectivity through structured discussions (see Chapter 3 by Blažek and Morgan (2019)).

The second issue arises from the inward-looking perspective of the framework. The sources and channels and combinations of knowledge are affected by globalisation and the digitalisation of the economy. It might not be enough to engage only regional entrepreneurial actors. Exploration requires combinatorial knowledge dynamics and extra-regional sources of knowledge (Sotarauta, 2017). To respond to this challenge, knowledge spaces should stretch to wider regions. One possibility is to construct knowledge space as transregional and transnational soft spaces, such as the new thematic partnership initiative by the EU; see Chapter 11 by Mariussen et al. (2019).

Notes

1 The Japanese word *ba* translates into English as place.
2 SECI is an acronym of the words socialisation, externalisation, combination and internalisation.
3 ICT can be used for instance in modernising tourism; nanotechnology in the forest industry when developing new materials to supplement plastics; biotechnology is important in the modern fishing industry. 3D printing can be used in the medical industry for producing new human parts or in the automotive industry to produce components, for instance.

References

Amin, A. and Cohendet, P. (2004). *Architectures of knowledge: Firms, capabilities, and communities*. Oxford: Oxford University Press.

Bathelt, H. and Glückler, J. (2011). *The relational economy: Geographies of knowing and learning*. Oxford: Oxford University Press.

Bathelt, H., Malmberg, A. and Maskell, P. (2004). Clusters and knowledge: Local buzz, global pipelines and the process of knowledge creation. *Progress in Human Geography*, 28 (1), pp. 31–56.

Blažek, J. and Morgan, K. (2019). The institutional worlds of entrepreneurial discovery: Finding a place for less developed regions. In Mariussen, Å., Virkkala, S., Finne, H. and Aasen, T.M. (eds) *The entrepreneurial discovery process and regional development: New knowledge emergence, conversion and exploitation*. Abingdon: Routledge.

Boschma, R. (2005). Proximity and innovation: A critical assessment. *Regional Studies*, 39 (1), pp. 61–74.

Boschma, R. (2017). Regional diversification and smart specialisation policy. In McCann, P., van Oort, F. and Goddard, J. (eds) *The empirical and institutional dimensions of smart specialisation*, pp. 23–38. London: Routledge.

Castells, M. (1998). *The rise of the network society*. Oxford: Wiley-Blackwell.

Cooke, P. (2007). To construct regional advantage from innovation systems first build policy platforms. *European Planning Studies*, 15 (2), pp. 179–194.

Cresswell, T. (2013). *Geographical thought: A critical introduction*. Chichester: Wiley-Blackwell.

Foray, D. (2015). *Smart specialisation: Opportunities and challenges for regional innovation policy*. London: Routledge.

Foray, D. (2016). On the policy space of smart specialization strategies. *European Planning Studies*, 24 (8), pp. 1428–1437.

Frenken, K., Van Oort, F. and Verburg, T. (2007). Related variety, unrelated variety and regional economic growth. *Regional Studies*, 41 (5), pp. 685–697.

Harmaakorpi, V. (2006). Regional development platform method (RDPM) as a tool for regional innovation policy. *European Planning Studies*, 14 (8), pp. 1085–1104.

Harmaakorpi, V. and Uotila, T. (2006). Building regional visionary capability: Futures research in resource based regional development. *Technological Forecasting and Social Change*, 73 (7), pp. 778–792.

Hautala, J. and Jauhiainen, J.S. (2014). Spatio-temporal processes of knowledge creation. *Research Policy*, 43 (4), pp. 655–668.

Ibert, O. (2007). Towards a geography of knowledge creation: The ambivalences between 'knowledge as an object' and 'knowing in practice'. *Regional Studies*, 41 (1), pp. 103–114.

Kautonen, M., Pugh, R. and Raunio, M. (2017). Transformation of regional innovation policies: From 'traditional' to 'next generation' models of incubation. *European Planning Studies*, 25 (4), pp. 620–637.

Lam, A. (2019). Career mobility, hybridity and knowledge combination: A 'third space' perspective. In Mariussen, Å., Virkkala, S., Finne, H. and Aasen, T.M. (eds) *The entrepreneurial discovery process and regional development: New knowledge emergence, conversion and exploitation*. Abingdon: Routledge.

Lave, J. and Wenger, E. (1991). *Situated learning: Legitimate peripheral participation*. Cambridge: Cambridge University Press.

Mariussen, Å. (2013). Sociological preliminaries: The societal context of transnational learning. In Mariussen, Å. and Virkkala, S. (eds) *Learning transnational learning*, pp. 13–50. Abingdon: Routledge.

Mariussen, Å., Hegyi, F.B. and Rakhmatullin, R. (2019). Smart specialisation: Interregional learning via thematic partnerships. In Mariussen, Å., Virkkala, S., Finne, H. and Aasen, T.M. (eds) *The entrepreneurial discovery process and regional development: New knowledge emergence, conversion and exploitation*. Abingdon: Routledge.

Mariussen, Å., Johnson, J. and Virkkala, S. (2014). Towards a smart specialisation strategy in Ostrobothnia and Finland. In Virkkala, S., Mäenpää, A. and Mariussen (eds) *The Ostrobothnian model of smart specialisation*, pp. 133–145. Vaasa: University of Vaasa.

Massey, D. (2005). *For space*. Los Angeles: Sage.

Melkas, H. and Uotila, T. (2013). Foresight and innovation: Emergence and resilience of the cleantech cluster at Lahti, Finland. In Cooke, P. (ed.) *Re-framing regional development*, pp. 203–233. London: Routledge.

Morgan, K. (2017). Speaking truth to power: The political dynamics of public sector innovation. In Kyriakou, D., Martínez, M.P., Periáñez-Forte, I. and Rainoldi, A. (eds) *Governing smart specialisation*, pp. 49–61. London: Routledge.

Nissinen, M. (2017). Smart specialisation entering the Finnish territory. In Kyriakou, D., Martínez, M.P., Periáñez-Forte, I. and Rainoldi, A. (eds) *Governing smart specialisation*, pp. 179–200. London: Routledge.

Nonaka, I. and Konno, N. (1998). The concept of 'Ba': Building a foundation for knowledge creation. *California Management Review*, 40 (3), pp. 40–54.

Nonaka, I., Konno, N. and Toyama, R. (2001). Emergence of 'Ba': A conceptual framework for the continuous and self-transcending process of knowledge creation. In Nonaka, I. and Nishiguchi, T. (eds) *Knowledge emergence: Social, technical and evolutionary dimensions of knowledge creation*, pp. 13–29. Oxford: Oxford University Press.

Nonaka, I. and Takeuchi, H. (1995). *The knowledge-creating company: How Japanese companies create the dynamics of innovation*. New York: Oxford University Press.

Nonaka, I. and Toyama, R. (2003). The knowledge-creating theory revisited: Knowledge creation as a synthesizing process. *Knowledge Management Research and Practice*, 1 (1), pp. 2–10.

Nonaka, I., Toyama, R. and Konno, N. (2000). SECI, ba and leadership: A unified model of dynamic knowledge creation. *Long Range Planning*, 33 (1), pp. 5–34.

Orlikowski, W.J. (2002). Knowing in practice: Enacting a collective capability in distributed organizing. *Organization Science*, 13 (3), pp. 249–273.

Paasi, A. (2002). Place and region: Regional worlds and words. *Progress in Human Geography*, 26 (6), pp. 802–811.

Pred, A. (1984). Place as historically contingent process: Structuration and the time-geography of becoming places. *Annals of the Association of American Geographers*, 74 (2), pp. 279–297.

Reid, A. and Maroulis, N. (2017). From strategy to implementation: The real challenge for smart specialization policy. In Radosevic, S., Curaj, A., Gheorghiu, R., Andreescu, L. and Wade, I. (eds) *Advances in the theory and practice of smart specialization*, pp. 294–319. London: Academic Press.

Rinkinen, S. (2015). Smart regional innovation policies – from cluster approaches to place-based policies. *International Journal of Innovation and Regional Development*, 6 (2), pp. 204–218.

Rodríguez-Pose, A. and Wilkie, C. (2017). Institutions and the entrepreneurial discovery process for smart specialization. In Kyriakou, D., Martínez, M.P., Periáñez-Forte, I. and Rainoldi, A. (eds) *Governing smart specialisation*, pp. 34–48. London: Routledge.

Sotarauta, M. (2017). An actor-centric bottom–up view of institutions: Combinatorial knowledge dynamics through the eyes of institutional entrepreneurs and institutional navigators. *Environment and Planning C: Government and Policy*, 35 (4), pp. 584–599.

Teräs, J. and Mäenpää, A. (2016). Smart specialisation implementation processes in the north: Lessons learned from two Finnish regions. *European Structural and Investment Funds Journal*, 4 (2), pp. 75–86.

Tsoukas, H. (2003). Do we really understand tacit knowledge? In Easterby-Smith, M. and Lyles, M.A. (eds) *The Blackwell handbook of organizational learning and knowledge management*, pp. 410–427. Malden, MA: Blackwell Publishing.

Virkkala, S. (2002). The Finnish cases: Combining 'top–down' and 'bottom–up' partnership formation. In Östhol, A. and Svensson, B. (eds) *Partnership responses: Regional governance in the Nordic states*, pp. 135–202. Stockholm: Nordregio.

Virkkala, S. and Mariussen, Å. (2013). Theory of organizational knowledge creation as a framework for transnational learning in regional development. In Mariussen, Å. and Virkkala, S. (eds) *Learning transnational learning*, pp. 102–137. Abingdon: Routledge.

Virkkala, S. and Mariussen, Å. (2019a). Emergence of new business areas in regional economies through entrepreneurial discovery processes. In Mariussen, Å., Virkkala, S., Finne, H. and Aasen, T.M. (eds) *The entrepreneurial discovery process and regional development: New knowledge emergence, conversion and exploitation*. Abingdon: Routledge.

Virkkala, S. and Mariussen, Å. (2019b). Self-discovery enabling entrepreneurial discovery processes. In Mariussen, Å., Virkkala, S., Finne, H. and Aasen, T.M. (eds) *The entrepreneurial discovery process and regional development: New knowledge emergence, conversion and exploitation*. Abingdon: Routledge.

Virkkala, S., Mäenpää, A. and Mariussen, Å. (eds) (2014). *The Ostrobothnian model of smart specialisation*. Vaasa: University of Vaasa.

Virkkala, S., Mäenpää, A. and Mariussen, Å. (2017). A connectivity model as a potential tool for smart specialization strategies. *European Planning Studies*, 25 (4), pp. 661–679.

Vissers, G. and Dankbaar, B. (2013). Knowledge and proximity. *European Planning Studies*, 21 (5), pp. 700–721.

Weick, K.E. (2001). *Making sense of the organization*. Malden, MA: Blackwell.

Wenger, E. (1998). *Communities of practice: Learning, meaning, and identity*. Cambridge: Cambridge University Press.

Part III

Macro-level impacts from micro-level solutions

9 Emergence of new business areas in regional economies through entrepreneurial discovery processes

Seija Virkkala and Åge Mariussen

9.1 Introduction

This chapter connects the theory of entrepreneurial discovery processes (EDP) with the literature on cluster evolution. This connection is made possible through the notion of emergence, complexity approach and structuration. The chapter provides a 'stylised story' of how micro-level entrepreneurial discoveries may transform regional economies by creating emergent clusters. The story of this process is summarised in Figure 9.1, and illustrated by a case (see Box 9.1), which is the emergence of the energy technology cluster in Vaasa, Finland.

In Chapters 5 (Lam, 2019, in this volume) and 8 (Virkkala, 2019, in this volume), hybrid knowledge spaces and connections between knowledge spaces through third space are discussed. In this chapter, we take the next step and look at regional economic systems. They consist of firms, networks between firms and related institutions. A distinction is made between two types of complex regional economic systems: static and dynamic. A complex and static regional economy is characterised by fragmentation between knowledge spaces (see Virkkala, 2019, Chapter 8 in this volume) created by a fixed division of labour between different specialised communities of expertise, firms and helices (universities, industries and public sector institutions), created by a one-sided focus on cost-efficient exploitation of existing knowledge, rather than exploration and ambidexterity (in Chapter 10, Nguyen and Mariussen, 2019). A region with a static system is likely to have a few, highly structured connections to the outside world, say, core companies exporting goods or raw material to a fixed set of customers. A complex and dynamic regional economy is open for new knowledge from outside and new combinations of existing forms of knowledge, through various forms of third space connections. For instance, a key enabling technology such as nanotechnology or biotechnology may be provided through transnational relational knowledge spaces and integrated into the regional domain (see Chapter 11, Mariussen et al., 2019). Entrepreneurial actors may even extend the borders of complex systems, by connecting them to other systems.

Structuration theory and complexity approach explain micro–macro interrelations. A successful micro-level entrepreneurial discovery creates a bottom–up (or upward) causation, which is emergence of new business areas. The new business area reinforces this micro-level pattern of entrepreneurship and growth through mechanisms of downward causation such as knowledge spillovers, market entry of firms, and subsequent agglomeration. A new cluster is born. The new cluster can grow and transform itself through selection of related industries which fits into its path, and memory of how to make industrial growth. It contributes to increased diversification and complexity in the regional economy. At the same time, dynamic complexity is necessary for the entrepreneurial actors initiating EDP. Dynamic complexity can be increased by exploring the possibilities of transnational networks. In order to achieve dynamic complexity, public sector organisations should destabilise the system and encourage exploration.

The EDP is expected to drive changes of regional development strategies and regional economic structures. These changes involve self-discovery through regional-level analysis and *complex micro-level dialogues*. According to Aasen (2019) in Chapter 7 in this volume, entrepreneurial discovery involves numerous people being inspired by regional knowledge resources, local characteristics and current trends. During interaction, patterns of discovery may emerge as recurring themes, and also as negotiations over the meaning of such themes. Emergence is one of the key defining characteristics of complex systems.[1] This chapter complements Aasen's in offering a macro perspective on the complexity approach and by examining what comes through the process after discovery.

This chapter explores the concepts of system and emergence developed in complexity approaches, and to that end, both the regional economy and the regional development policy will be interpreted as complex systems. The complexity approach and the notion of emergence will bring deeper understanding of the interrelationships between micro and macro levels in the EDP, in particular, how micro-level discoveries may have macro-level impacts and how these macro-level impacts influence the micro level, in a way which results in self-reinforcing causal loops in the regional economy.

The chapter describes a regional economy as an emerging complex system, and the policy of discovery as a policy system which, under certain conditions, may be able to bypass rigidities and create new synergies. EDP should be seen as a general idea that is an integral part of smart specialisation policy, but it can also be interpreted in a more general sense and as part of a policy of discovery and exploration.

In the next section, we discuss relevant concepts of complexity thinking: specifically, those of system and emergence. The third section will interpret EDP as three forms of emergence in the place-based strategy of smart specialisation when discovery is territorially embedded. However, in some cases there is insufficient complexity or dynamics to enable micro-level dialogues to catalyse discoveries, and the fourth section of the chapter addresses a way to create more dynamics. As shown in Chapter 11 (Mariussen et al., 2019), one solution might be scaling up and building transnational networks to create complexities for discoveries and the emergence of new regional and transregional business opportunities (domains). The last section offers some conclusions on the policy implication of the notion of emergence.

9.2 System and emergence: regional economy and EDP

Complex systems

A system is a group of interdependent elements. The relationships between elements in a social system are non-linear and based typically on sustained interdependence. But what constitutes a system is a matter of judgement by the actors comprised by the system and also its observers. Systems are not discrete entities, and transitions between system and non-system states occur. Observers may include policy actors who contribute to the definition of a system they study.[2] Systems may also be more or less integrated. Mechanisms of integration include the self-referential definitions of members, and members' identities. We may differentiate between strongly integrated, strongly self-referential, and strongly demarcated systems, and weakly integrated, weakly self-referential, and weakly demarcated systems (Morçöl, 2012).

A complex system is open, and it *may let other systems in* (Byrne and Callaghan, 2014: 26). It may also appear to be fragmented. This lack of clear borders makes it into a difficult object. 'A complicated thing can be taken apart into its bits and reassembled from those bits . . . A complex one can't be analysed and integrated either in reality or in mathematical representation' (Byrne and Callaghan, 2014: 4).

Byrne and Callaghan (2014: 17–38) go on to state that complexity rests on a few simple assumptions:

- First, complex systems are not designed top–down, they are the result of self-organisation by many autonomous interrelated decision-makers.
- Second, complex systems have emergent properties in the sense that they have the capacity to change in new directions.
- Third, in order to do so, complex systems are able to create energy, by increasing the system scale.
- Fourth, complex systems are inherently unstable.

It is difficult to determine the boundaries of a complex system because the boundary between a complex system and its environment is usually dependent on the purpose of the analysis, and not on any intrinsic property of the system itself. Openness is an inherent feature of complex systems. These systems also tend to be dissipative in that they interact with their environments. They are likely to experience a continual inflow and outflow of energy, matter, and information.

Social systems may be seen as a result of actors following routinised trajectories between stations or points in time and space (commuting, labour markets, suppliers and buyers in regional clusters) (Giddens, 1984). A region's prior development shapes current and future trajectories and possibilities for structural transformation and innovation. However, dynamic complexity can be created when actors begin to initiate re-articulations of spatial patterns. Individual and collective actors can reflect and re-articulate current stations and make routes for new trajectories possible. The reflexivity may include the spatio-temporal structures of the complex systems and different spatio-temporal horizons of action. When acted upon this could lead to the reflexive reorganisation of spatio-temporal matrices and to changes in strategies. Entrepreneurial actors may initiate processes which change the trajectories and the position of stations. Space is evolving, the structure is changing. These strategies of reflexive reorganisation of horizons of actions differ from a perspective on regional development and cluster evolution, which is seen as unfolding of given technological histories and opportunities within a fixed place.

We can interpret the regional economy as an emergent system. Krugman (1996) described the economic landscape – cities, regions, clusters, industrial districts, centres, and peripheries – as a complex, self-organising system. Bretagnolle et al. (2009) described the urban system as a multi-level system consisting of micro-level basic units (e.g., individuals, firms, and institutions) that are resident in the city. Here, the meso level corresponds to the city (as a geographical entity), and the macro level is the system of cities, made up of a large number of towns and cities that interact under unified control (in a national political territory or a global economic network). This organisation is shaped by interactions operating on different spatial and temporal scales of observation.

The regional economy is an unintended outcome of interactions and decisions made by firms, consumers, inhabitants, citizens, public organisations and institutions. The outcomes of these decisions are systems of cities, rural areas and clusters. Emergence is one way of explaining how structure and form arise in the economic landscape, and why place matters in processes of economic change and evolution (Martin and Sunley, 2013). Accordingly, regional economies can be seen as systems that vary to the extent that there are reciprocal and integrated relations between the elements of the system. The system consists of firms, organisations, as well as actors such as employees and employers from different helices with connectivity and interconnections. The regional economy as a system can be strongly or weakly integrated and demarcated. Entrepreneurial discoveries can occur spontaneously in a regional economy as an entrepreneurial initiative (Foray, 2015: 35), like in the beginning of the energy technology cluster in Vaasa (Box 9.1). However, many regional economies need a policy effort such as Research and Innovation Strategies for Smart Specialisation (RIS3), or similar initiatives, to expand their economy and identify new activities. This is achieved through a differentiation between clusters seen as, on the one hand, results of structural evolution of technological trajectories, and on the other hand, strategies of reflexive reorganisation of horizons of action – in other words, S3. Smart specialisation is based on a policy system that is seen as differentiated from the basic forms of organisation of interests among firms involved in a cluster. A regional strategy may take different clusters and their wider context into consideration. As we will see below, and in Chapter 11, a reflexive reorganisation of space also depends on a differentiation between policy, science-based institutions and the economy – in other words, a triple helix.

The second complex system is accordingly a policy system such as RIS3, which might affect the transformation of the regional economy by establishing new business fields and clusters. The relations among actors involved in this complex system are non-linear and its relations with its elements and with other systems are co-evolutionary. In a policy system, like RIS3 with the EDP as a core method, policies come into being as consequences of the actions and relationships of multiple individual and collective actors. Governmental actors play important roles in policy systems, but they are among many whose actions influence policy outcomes (see Morçöl, 2012), or, in the case of EDP, discoveries. The context of RIS3 as a policy system is a specific region and its characteristics; however, RIS3 is also part of a broader context like the Europe 2020 strategy by the European Union (EU). The boundaries of the RIS3 are not defined *ex ante* but through social construction and by actors, members or observers (typically researchers or reporters) of the regional alliance for discoveries. The activities of organisations in the discovery alliances are more or less integrated (i.e., reciprocated and reproduced across time and space).

Three forms of emergence

Martin and Sunley (2013) differentiate between strong and weak emergence and do so by using a division developed by Deacon (2007) to establish first-, second-, and third-order emergence. In first-order emergence, the micro-level properties spontaneously produce a higher-level structure that is called self-organisation. In second-order emergence, the higher-level structure becomes supervenient as it begins to influence the lower-level properties and serve as an introduction of downward causal effects. These downward effects give an additional dynamic to the upward effects. Third-order emergence extends the second order in two respects, that is, the introduction of selection processes and memory effects. The behaviour of actors incorporates different characteristics, and those characteristics that help them to adapt to the environment will be selected, represented, and remembered. This means that the system will take on an evolutionary character. All lower-level components are, however, not adaptive and some of them may not survive at all; in addition, new components will influence how the macro-structure evolves over time.

Scale is of particular importance to the problem of emergence because an increase in the number of low-level components increases opportunities for iterative interaction. Scale effects also work downwards: an emergent higher-level property, pattern, or element exerts causal power over the lower-level

and development of the new business area or renewal of the existing business area through priorities, projects, and experiments. In addition, specific institutions such as cluster organisations can be established or the existing institutions can redirect their activities to support the emerging domain.

According to the third form of emergence, there will be evolutionary dynamics in the process because of selection and memory. The impacts of the successful EDP and regional strategies might allow a structural change in the regional economy, for example by creating a new growth path through the process of cumulative causation and learning or diversifying the economy (Foray, 2015: 35). Isaksen et al. (2019) (Chapter 2 in this volume) examine the possible outcomes of EDP more thoroughly, by differentiating between path extension, path renewal, and new path creation, using empirical cases. There can be selective sampling of influences that reintroduces the parts into different realisations of the system over time. In the case of disintegration or a weakly integrated regional economy, there might be more integration of the process during the time when the EDP is developed. These forms of emergence are illustrated in the context of the fish-farming by Aasen et al. (2019) (Chapter 12 in this volume) and the experience economy in tourism by Løvland and Finne (2019) (Chapter 13 in this volume).

The general framework is illustrated by Table 9.1.

Table 9.1 Transforming regional economy through three forms of emergence

Forms of emergence	*Characteristics*	*Regional economy* *Role of private entrepreneurs*
First order *Micro level*	**Bottom–up (upward) causation** Aggregated system patterns generated from the micro level	Entrepreneurial discovery of opportunities, based on self-discovery of strengths
Second order *Macro level*	**Downward causal effects** Self-organising emergent phenomena Amplified macro-level structures that reinforce micro-level patterns and configurations	Knowledge spillover, entry of firms, agglomeration
Third order *Structuration*	**Selection and memory** Evolutionary dynamics Selective sampling of influences reintroducing the parts into different realisations of the system over time	Growth through new path creation, path renewal, or path extension Transformation of the regional economy

Source: Based on ideas of Giddens (1984), Cooke (2012), Martin and Sunley (2007, 2013) and Foray (2015)

The role of the public sector in the discoveries

EDP seldom occurs spontaneously and requires policy processes for effective discovery. Public sector organisations are in charge of all emerging elements of the RIS3 (Table 9.2). In the self-discovery phase (the first form of emergence), they should analyse the regional economy and its strengths and opportunities together with universities. They should take the initiative, build connections and partnerships between relevant entrepreneurial actors, and organise the discovery process. Public sector organisations should create conditions of disequilibrium. They have a central role in integrating the relevant entrepreneurial knowledge distributed over firms, universities, clients and users, specialised suppliers and other organisations. After relevant knowledge has been integrated, it should be processed and synthesised in order to formulate and select the key regional priorities for the RIS3. Prioritisation is an interactive process in which public sector organisations assess potential and then empower those actors most capable of realising that potential. Public sector actors are not neutral but select the relevant vertical priorities (Foray, 2015). This can be seen as a process of creating disequilibrium instead of equilibrium. In the case of lock-in, the new domains can be searched by encouraging cross-sectoral cooperation.

In the second phase (downward causation), public sector actors support the emergence and development of the new business area or renewal of the existing business area through priorities, projects and experiments. Determining the policy mix and selecting the projects implementing the strategy can be seen as a process moving from the macro level to the micro level – one in which knowledge diffusion is important. EDP is basically economic experimentation with new ideas and self-organisation.

The third phase includes continuous monitoring of the transformation of the regional economy and experimental learning, which should lead to better governance of the EDP. The process of self-discovery and EDP should be continuous and the implementation of the RIS3 should be evaluated and monitored and the lessons should be learned from the experiments. Finally, the RIS3 and its outcomes should also be evaluated in a broader context, that is, the context of European systems of innovation, as well as the possible context of macro regions.

We can also see the role of the European Commission (EC) from the perspectives of the three phases of emergence. In the first phase the role of the EC or S3 platform is to provide general rules and guidance, encouraging differentiation of regional strategies. The second phase (downward causation) is to encourage more diversified innovation ecosystems.

We can now summarise this discussion based on the literature of clusters and complexity by a stylised model of how EDP creates clusters (Figure 9.1).

In the first phase, a self-discovery in the policy system creates a process of search and disruption in the regional domain, leading to a discovery. This is a process of exploration. In the second phase, the discovery is tested through an industrial pilot, followed by a successful process of upscaling. This leads to

Table 9.2 The role of the public sector in the transformation of regional economy through emergence

Forms of emergence	*Characteristics*	*Economy* *Role of private entrepreneurs*	*Public sector*	
			Operational rules *Role of regional S3 intervention*	*General principles* *Role of EC*
First order *Micro level*	**Bottom–up (upward) causation** Aggregated system patterns generated from the micro level	Entrepreneurial discovery of opportunity, based on self-discovery of strengths	Creation of disequilibrium Analysis, discovery of regional strengths and opportunities Vision, priorities	Common S3 platform with general rules and guidance, encouraging differentiation of regional strategies
Second order *Macro level*	**Downward causal effects** Self-organising emergent phenomena Amplified macro-level structures that reinforce micro-level patterns and configurations	Knowledge spillover, entry of firms, agglomeration	Reinforcing downward causation Compensating the leader, knowledge diffusion and policy mix	Differentiation and interdependence Diversified innovation ecosystems Discovery and enlargement of borders
Third order *Structuration*	**Selection and memory** Evolutionary dynamics Selective sampling of influences reintroducing the parts into different realisations of the system over time	Growth through new path creation, path renewal or path extension Transformation of the regional economy	Experimental learning Monitoring, analysis, better governance	Self-referential ability to self-reproduce and expand

Source: Based on ideas of Giddens (1984), Cooke (2012), Martin and Sunley (2007, 2013) and Foray (2015)

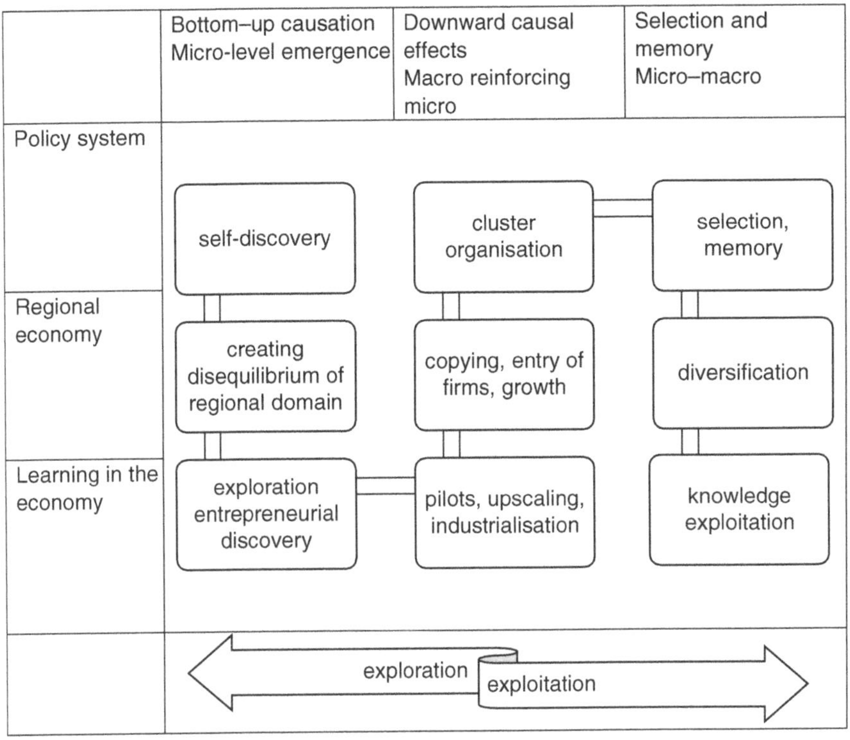

Figure 9.1 The forms of emergence and exploration–exploitation

Source: Own elaboration

entry of new firms, growth, and eventually, in the policy system, setting up of a cluster-supporting organisation. In the third phase, the cluster is institutionalised, it builds on experiences, it exploits existing knowledge, and it has a capacity to extend its own existence, renew itself or go back into a new phase of exploration. The regional economy is diversified and more complex.

Box 9.1 Energy technology cluster in Vaasa, Finland

Energy technology cluster in Vaasa, Finland

The Vaasa area is located on the western coast of Finland, 450 kilometres north-west of the capital Helsinki. The emergence of the Vaasa energy technology cluster has been organic and firm-led: it can be explained as an entrepreneurial discovery in the classical sense and as a process of self-organisation.

(continued)

(continued)

Transnational learning, entrepreneurial discovery and entry of new firms

The history of the energy technology cluster and engineering skills dates back to 1906, when John Wickström started his motor factory with his brother Jacob. John Wickström moved from Vaasa to Chicago to study, and after his studies he established a factory producing boat motors for traffic on Lakes Michigan and Superior. He was an inventor who granted nine patents, also for automobiles.

In Vaasa, and elsewhere in coastal areas in the north, fishing was an important livelihood, but there was no factory to build boat motors; John Wickström saw business opportunities and large virgin markets and moved back to his home country. The motor factory of the Wickström brothers made lucrative engines first for boats, and later motors for sawmills, agriculture machines and the food industry. The successful business attracted other people to the business, and soon the Wickström brothers experienced fierce competition in the region. The factories had a large market; in addition to Nordic countries, the motors were exported to Canada, Spain, Portugal and Japan, for instance.

National entrepreneurship and entrepreneurial discovery in a complex regional domain (first-order emergence)

The second embryonic of the cluster was when the company Wärtsilä came to the region by buying the Onkilahti engineering workshop in Vaasa, with its roots in one of the Wickström brothers' factories, in 1936. Wärtsilä originates from Karelia, where it had a sawmill, iron mill, and a power station. Nowadays, Wärtsilä is a global company providing lifecycle power solutions for the marine and energy markets. Its clients are the marine and oil and gas industry. Wärtsilä is a global energy system integrator offering flexible internal combustion engine-based power plants, utility-scale solar power plants, energy storage and integration solutions, as well as LNG terminals and distribution systems. Wärtsilä Services supports both shipping and power generation companies.

The third embryonic of the cluster was when Strömberg, manufacturer of various electrical appliances, relocated from the capital Helsinki to Vaasa in 1940. Strömberg was acquired by ASEA in 1988, which is today known as ABB. When ASEA entered the Vaasa region, the companies got access to a global marketing network. ABB Vaasa offers solutions for industry automation, and power transmission and distribution, such as energy-efficient motors, low-voltage switches, subsea transformers and grid automation.

Cluster development and cluster organisation (second-order emergence)

The cluster emerged through entry of firms, knowledge spillovers and agglomeration. Since the 1990s, the cluster has evolved around the big firms through spinoffs, the foundation of new firms, and attracting new firms from elsewhere. In this point, the cluster began to influence its members through downward causation, giving dynamics for the upward effects. For instance, the supplier network has been developed because of the needs of near and trustful suppliers. The cluster organisation Merinova was established in 1989 and it led several energy-related sub-programmes of national expertise programmes in Finland from 1995–2014, and later it was active in the sustainable energy solution programme, belonging to the INKA programme. The availability of a strong pool of inputs such as specialised skills and talents has been important, and the educational institutes have adapted to the cluster by suppling skilled workers to the companies. The University of Vaasa established a technical faculty partly to respond to the demands of the cluster.

Memory and selection (third-order emergence)

Increased environmental awareness and legislation after 2000 has given further business opportunities to the cluster, and it has evolved to be the biggest concentration of energy technology competence in the Nordic countries. In 2018, the cluster includes about 140 companies, and the manufacturing goes from simple engines to a wide range of sophisticated power plants (generators) to high-value and high-tech components for appliances that generate actual energy (windmills, power plants, etc.). The cluster evolves now through memory and selection. The first mechanism is the regional diffusion of profitable routines such as new technologies, organisational and managerial innovations, efficient production processes and a subcontractor network. The second selection mechanism is the existing knowledge base of a region, which is an incentive to expansion and further the specialisation, reinforcing path dependence through cumulative causative processes. In 2016, Vaasa Energy Business Innovation Centre (VEBIC) was launched as a multidisciplinary research platform involving all university schools, and offering engine and fuel laboratories. It is hosted by the University of Vaasa in partnership with regional actors and in cooperation with global research partners. VEBIC is part of a cluster policy to enhance research for cluster maintenance and renewal. The regional strategy has supported the growth of the cluster. However, over-specialisation and lock-ins might be future problems in the cluster and continuous entrepreneurial discovery processes at regional level are needed. Smart specialisation strategy aims to diversify the activities based on existing strengths with the help of cross-sectoral platforms.

Sources: Leinamo (2006), Ostrobothnia Chamber of Commerce (2018), Regional Council of Ostrobothnia (2017), Vasek (2018)

9.4 Scaling: discoveries within relational spaces

The complexity approach implies that there has to be a certain level of complexity in the region that enables micro-level dialogues leading to discoveries. The more variety there is of properties such as embodied and embedded knowledge, and the more interaction between them (or the actors), the better are the preconditions for the emergence of new business opportunities and domains. However, even if there is enough variety and complexity in the place-based system, it might still be stable. Destabilisation may be created through transnational learning, which can be initiated by public sector organisations.

For example, regions with economies dominated by exploitation of existing knowledge rather than exploration of new knowledge through discovery might be too rigid and inflexible to change. Networks between people and helices with different types of knowledge may follow strictly standardised definitions. Core companies may be sleeping giants, in that they are large and crucial for the economy, but they focus on exploitation of existing knowledge rather than on exploration. Given these stable frameworks, their regional suppliers may be cultivating and protecting their own unique and internal domains of knowledge defining their position within the network against others. This kind of structure is likely to have clear borders separating insiders from outsiders. Relations are stable and predictable; everybody knows their role in the network. Since the focus is on exploitation, productivity might be high. This type of closed system may seem to be highly integrated and well-functioning, with strong identities among members. Nevertheless, it does not have the dynamics that can support discoveries leading to emerging new opportunities, which would pose a challenge for regional development policy. Nevertheless, the dynamics that can prompt discoveries may have several sources, and not only exogenous ones.

One solution to this problem is the scaling of the EDP and the networks from a regional basis to become interregional and transnational networks (Mariussen et al., 2016). Emergence can occur in a broader transnational context. One example is the EC initiative to construct thematic partnerships between regions, with the aim of encouraging networks to create new institutional frameworks for co-evolution and collaboration between regions (see Mariussen et al., 2019, Chapter 11 in this volume). This effort can broaden the thematic platforms on industrial modernisation, food and agriculture, and energy of the S3 platform. The idea is that the stakeholders in the transnational thematic networks identify shared issues, problems and bottlenecks as well as the methods to address them. This means that new domains might emerge through the entrepreneurial discoveries and interaction of actors in different regions. They form a common transnational knowledge space which has the characteristics of a relational space (see Chapter 8 by Virkkala, 2019, in this volume). This means the networks are based on the cognitive proximity of the participants rather than their geographical proximity. In the transnational discovery process, the fragmented knowledge including the scientific and technological forms embedded in different regions on common issues is first combined and collated, building the new domain (upward causation). In the second phase, the shared new business area (e.g., a value chain) might grow in participating regions through the processes of networks based on pilot-testing in different regions (see Chapter 11), which may lead to knowledge spillovers, the entry of firms, and to agglomeration effects (downward causation). This might extend the innovative ability of both regional ecosystems and the new emerging macro and transnational framework. An example is the development of the European Spallation Source in Scania (Skåne), Sweden, which is a European-level laboratory where firms from all over Europe can experiment with product development (see Chapter 11).

This EDP in relational space requires facilitators; those might be the coordinating partners of the thematic network or the EC – in this case, the S3 platform.

9.5 Conclusion

The complexity approach can serve as a general framework to explain economic development that emphasises the relationships and feedback between activities and actors from different scales. Regional development occurs in the context of both the micro-level interaction of individuals, firms, and organisations as well as that of national and transnational levels of activity. This chapter explored the usefulness of the complexity approach and the concept of emergence in the interpretation of the transformation of the economic landscape through EDP. Both the regional economy and the policies of discoveries or the RIS3 can be seen as complex systems and the transformation of a regional economy can be explained through three forms of emergence. The EDP as a form of emergence was presented in an idealised way; in practice, there are many institutional and other barriers preventing or diminishing the preconditions of the discovery process and its impacts on the transformation of a regional economy.

There are still many open questions around the complexity approach in the context of the EDP. For example, the complexity approach emphasises the endogenous interaction of properties – as does the endogenous approach to place-based development – as a source of emergence, but often the changes are external to the regional economies. Regional economies are open economies and embedded in national or global value chains. The emergence approach can be criticised for not placing sufficient emphasis on design and policy (Cooke, 2012).

The first policy implication of this chapter is that the smart specialisation literature and policy design would benefit from considering a wider variety of properties such as embodied and embedded knowledge, because the more complex the micro-level components are, the greater the connectivity and interaction between them (or between actors), and thus the better are the prospects for the emergence of new business opportunities and domains. The second policy implication is addressed to the regions with complex but stable economies which need to be destabilised for the emergence of new domains. Destabilisation is a challenge for public sector organisations facilitating the RIS3. One way to increase both complexity and destabilisation in regional economies and place-based RIS3s is to encourage transnational learning, which might, for example, come through transnational thematic networks driven by the S3 platform.

Complex policy systems are multi-causal. According to the complexity approach, the outcome of a policy system such as the RIS3 is not linear, and such a policy also often has unintended outcomes (Morçöl, 2012). Moreover, there can be surprising elements owing to an unplanned spatial outcome of a regional development policy like smart specialisation policies, and it is impossible to predict the exact outcomes of policy interventions. However, the discovery process is a combination of deliberate and emergent policy outcomes. Public sector actors have an active role as enablers supporting the discovery process. If there is a negative lock-in in regional economic development due to over-specialisation, the public sector actors should aim to destabilise the static situation and encourage the exploration of new domains. The uncertainty should be acknowledged in the policy design which supports an experimental learning approach through trial and error as a core of EDP and RIS3.

Notes

1 Emergence is also the answer of complexity approach to the central problem of social science, which is the relation between micro–macro or agency–structure, that is, how the properties and actions of agents/actors affect structural properties and vice versa. This is the so-called transformation problem in sociology, aggregation in economics and the problem of social (or public) choice in political science (Morçöl, 2012: 62).

2 According to (Luhmann, 1995), social systems are self-referential, i.e. they determine how the members/actors define themselves.

References

Aasen, T.M. (2019). Approaching entrepreneurial discovery and knowledge conversion from a complexity perspective. In Mariussen, Å., Virkkala, S., Finne, H. and Aasen, T.M. (eds) *The entrepreneurial discovery process and regional development: New knowledge emergence, conversion and exploitation*. Abingdon: Routledge.

Aasen, T.M., Ullern, E.F. and Mariussen, Å. (2019). Science/practice knowledge interaction in the Norwegian fish farming industry. In Mariussen, Å., Virkkala, S., Finne, H. and Aasen, T.M. (eds) *The entrepreneurial discovery process and regional development: New knowledge emergence, conversion and exploitation*. Abingdon: Routledge.

Benner, M. (2017). Smart specialisation and cluster emergence: Elements of evolutionary regional policies. In Fornahl, D. and Hassink, R. (eds) *The life cycle of clusters: A policy perspective*. Cheltenham: Edward Elgar.

Boschma, R.A. and Martin, R. (eds) (2010). *The handbook of evolutionary economic geography*. Cheltenham: Edward Elgar.

Bretagnolle, A., Pumain, D. and Vacchiani-Marcuzzo, C. (2009). The organization of urban systems. In Lane, D., Pumain, D., van der Leeuw, S.E. and West, G. (eds) *Complexity perspectives in innovation and social change*. Cham: Springer.

Byrne, D. and Callaghan, G. (2014). *Complexity theory and the social sciences: The state of the art*. Abingdon, Routledge.

Cooke, P. (2012). *Complex adaptive innovation systems: Relatedness and transversality in the evolving region*. Milton Park: Routledge.

Deacon, T. (2007). Three levels of emergent phenomena. In Murphy, N.C. and Stoeger, W.R. (eds) *Evolution and emergence: Systems, organisms, persons*. Oxford: Oxford University Press.

Foray, D. (2015). *Smart specialisation: Opportunities and challenges for regional innovation policy*. London: Routledge.

Fornahl, D. and Hassink, R. (eds) (2017). *The life cycle of clusters: A policy perspective*. Cheltenham: Edward Elgar.

Giddens, A. (1984). *The constitution of society: Outline of the theory of structuration*. Berkeley, University of California Press.

Isaksen, A. (2011). Cluster evolution. In Cooke, P., Asheim, B., Boschma, R., Martin, R., Schwartz, D. and Tödtling, F. (eds) *Handbook of regional innovation and growth*. Cheltenham: Edward Elgar.

Isaksen, A., Kyllingstad, N., Rypestøl, J.O. and Schulze-Krogh, A.C. (2019). Entrepreneurial discovery processes in different regional contexts: A conceptual discussion. In Mariussen, Å., Virkkala, S., Finne, H. and Aasen, T.M. (eds) *The entrepreneurial discovery process and regional development: New knowledge emergence, conversion and exploitation*. Abingdon: Routledge.

Krugman, P.R. (1996). *The self organizing economy*. Cambridge, MA: Oxford, Blackwell.

Leinamo, K. (2006). Valmistettu Vaasassa. Neljä vuosisataa teollisuutta.

Luhmann, N. (1995). *Social systems*. Stanford, CA: Stanford University Press.

Løvland, J. and Finne, H. (2019). The transformation of Lofoten islands into a year-round experience destination. In Mariussen, Å., Virkkala, S., Finne, H. and Aasen, T.M. (eds) *The entrepreneurial discovery process and regional development: New knowledge emergence, conversion and exploitation*. Abingdon: Routledge.

Mariussen, Å., Hegyi, F.B. and Rakhmatullin, R. (2019). Smart specialisation: Interregional learning via thematic partnerships. In Mariussen, Å., Virkkala, S., Finne, H. and Aasen, T.M. (eds) *The entrepreneurial discovery process and regional development: New knowledge emergence, conversion and exploitation*. Abingdon: Routledge.

Mariussen, Å., Rakhmatullin, R. and Stanionyte, L. (2016). *Smart specialisation: Creating growth through trans-national cooperation and value chains. Thematic work on the understanding of transnational cooperation and value chains in the context of smart specialisation*. Luxembourg: Publications Office of the European Union.

Martin, R. and Sunley, P. (2007). Complexity thinking and evolutionary economic geography. *Journal of Economic Geography*, 7, pp. 573–601.

Martin, R. and Sunley, P. (2013). Forms of emergence and the evolution of economic landscapes. In Cooke, P. (ed.) *Re-framing regional development: Evolution, innovation and transition*. London: Routledge.

Maskell, P. and Malmberg, A. (1999). Localised learning and industrial competitiveness. *Cambridge Journal of Economics*, 23, pp. 167–185.

Massey, D. (1984). *Spatial divisions of labour: Social structures and the geography of production*. London: Macmillan.

Menzel, M.-P. and Fornahl, D. (2010). Cluster life cycles—dimensions and rationales of cluster evolution. *Industrial and Corporate Change*, 19, pp. 205–238.
Morçöl, G. (2012). *A complexity theory for public policy*. New York: Routledge.
Nelson, R.R. and Winter, S.G. (1982). *An evolutionary theory of economic change*. Cambridge, MA: Belknap Press of Harvard University Press.
Nguyen, N. and Mariussen, Å. (2019). Moving beyond related variety: Creating firm-level ambidexterity for economic growth via the entrepreneurial discovery process. In Mariussen, Å., Virkkala, S., Finne, H. and Aasen, T.M. (eds) *The entrepreneurial discovery process and regional development: New knowledge emergence, conversion and exploitation*. Abingdon: Routledge.
Ostrobothnia Chamber of Commerce. (2018). *Coastline* [Online]. Available at: www.coastline.fi/2018/about-coastline/ [Accessed 2018-07-10].
Regional Council of Ostrobothnia. (2017). *Smart specialisation* [Online]. Available at: www.obotnia.fi/regional-development/smart-specialisation/ [Accessed 2018-07-10].
Vasek. (2018). *Energy Vaasa: The Nordic hub for energy technology* [Online]. Available at: http://energyvaasa.vaasanseutu.fi/energyvaasa-shortly/ [Accessed 2018-07-10].
Virkkala, S. (2019). Entrepreneurial discovery processes, knowledge creation and knowledge space. In Mariussen, Å., Virkkala, S., Finne, H. and Aasen, T.M. (eds) *The entrepreneurial discovery process and regional development: New knowledge emergence, conversion and exploitation*. Abingdon: Routledge.

10 Moving beyond related variety

Creating firm-level ambidexterity for economic growth via the entrepreneurial discovery process

Nhien Nguyen and Åge Mariussen

10.1 Introduction

There are two ways of meeting the challenges of restructuring: (1) as reactions to disruptions, market shifts or other types of turbulence that come as a surprise, or (2) proactively, by continuously enhancing the capacity to explore new opportunities and develop new products and areas of business through diversification and innovation (Mariussen et al., 2019). The reactive strategy often involves an over-reliance on the exploitation of existing technologies, markets and products, while the proactive strategy using innovation and a co-creation approach can lead to sustainable development and growth. To proactively restructure the economy, a country should search for the new domains of knowledge, business and industry to confer the ability and capacity to change before the economic situation becomes desperate. The search process is best undertaken jointly between the innovators, that is, innovation firms, entrepreneurs, researchers, and other parts of the innovation system, such as the government and organisations promoting innovation policy. This allows a stronger emphasis on exploration through partnerships between policy-makers, entrepreneurs, and scholars, which is the core idea of the smart specialisation approach.

This chapter discusses a proactive approach to economic restructuring and growth, specifically, smart specialisation. The study begins by introducing several approaches to, and strategies of, economic growth, such as diversification and the complexity model. The complexity concept in this model is one of complicated composition rather than complex systemic behaviour (Price, 2004; see also extensive discussions in Chapters 7 and 9 in this volume: Aasen, 2019; Virkkala and Mariussen, 2019). To facilitate this point of departure the chapter uses secondary data from the *Atlas of Economic Complexity* (Hausmann and Pritchett, 2018) to illustrate a gap in these theories. Next, we use smart specialisation theory to explain this gap, and how its mechanism, the entrepreneurial discovery process (EDP), can contribute to economic growth in advanced countries. One of the important conditions for EDP to work is the ambidextrous capability of firms to explore new domains and exploit current strengths at the same time. Norway is used as an illustration case.

10.2 Economic growth strategies based on diversification

The challenges of economic development lie in 'the formulation of economic theory' and 'the application of policy' which help to understand and solve the core problem of development (Thirlwall, 2003: 21). The essence of economic development is structural change, which 'entails moving workers from traditional, low-productivity activities to modern, high-productivity activities that are quite different in terms of location, organization, and technological characteristics' (Rodrik, 2014: 23). Successful structural transformation requires a growth strategy, but there is no one-size-fits-all blueprint of this nature.

Economic growth could be achieved through the combination of specialisation and diversification based on Rodrik's (2004, 2014) theory. His model of growth is based on the analysis of national sector statistics, with a focus on the balance between specialisation and diversification. According to Rodrik, the driver of growth in a specialised economy is the actions of entrepreneurs (for instance entrepreneurs in an industry producing copper ore) who can apply what they know (such as tacit and codified knowledge of their metal) in a new, related direction, and produce more complex products (such as various copper products). The context of this process of growth is the macro-level structure of the economy, which defines the competences and skills of the entrepreneurs. This national structural macro level creates preconditions for micro-level discoveries, leading to a 'self-discovery' of the hidden possibilities within the existing domains.

Rodrik's theory is referred to both in the economic complexity model (Hausmann et al., 2011) and in smart specialisation strategy (Foray, 2015). The current study examines at these two perspectives to understand which can be beneficial to attempts to devise a proactive strategy of economic restructuring.

Economic complexity or product space theory

Theoretical background

The economic complexity model, originating from the idea of product space (Hidalgo et al., 2007), is developed by Hausmann and colleagues through research on economic development applying export statistics from 128 countries over the last three decades (Hausmann et al., 2013). In this theory, country growth expectations can be derived from two indexes: the Economic Complexity Index (ECI), and the Product Complexity Index (PCI). It addresses growth from the perspective of the potential of a given national economic structure to innovate and grow through diversification or related varieties, which refers to 'industrial sectors that are related in terms of shared or complementary competences' (Pylak and Wojnicka-Sycz, 2014: 2).

The Economic Complexity Index (ECI) is computed based on two main elements (Growth Lab, 2017): the diversity of exported products (a measure of how many different products a country can produce), and ubiquity (a measure of how many countries are able to make those products). Intuitively, the country complexity index or ECI may be seen as an indication of diversification and cross-sector networks in the national economy and systems of innovation. The highest scorer on the ECI ranking in 2016 is Japan, with a score of 2.26. The lowest scorer is Papua New Guinea, with a score of −1.73 (Growth Lab, 2016).

The Product Complexity Index (PCI) is calculated based on how many other countries can produce the product and the economic complexity of those countries. A complex product, therefore, is a product that can be used by many different customers in different sectors. For example, in the *Atlas of Economic Complexity* ranking, the product with highest complexity is 'Endless bands of copper wire for machinery' (HS4 code 7414) with a complexity ranking of 3.51. Copper wire is produced in the metals sector, but it is used in most products involving electrical components across a broad range of sectors. As a comparison, crude oil (HS4 code 2709) has a complexity score of −2.28. Crude oil has only one customer: oil refineries. As oil climbs up the value chain, it can be used to produce products of ever higher complexity, such as plastic, which may be used across several sectors producing complex products, such as vehicles and mobile phones.

Growth by complexity

According to product space theory, countries could grow by increasing their complexity. They can do that by shifting from export of raw materials to export of refined products, based on these raw materials, and by developing horizontal networks between their raw material clusters and other sectors. Countries using this mechanism of growth tend to reduce the relative proportion of raw materials in their exports and instead increase exports of more complex products. Examples of countries that experienced this kind of growth through increased complexity are Denmark and Finland during the 1980s. This was the period when Denmark was able to diversify away from a strong dependency on food (agriculture and fishing) and develop new complex export industries. This took place in sectors which had been a part of the food and maritime industries, such as mechanical industries and chemical industries. These complex products were also enjoying deeper integration into the larger European economy, through Danish membership of the EU. In the case of Finland, the 1980s were the golden years of the pulp and paper cluster, which replaced exports of timber with paper. The pulp and paper cluster was highly diversified and, as in Denmark with the food cluster, the country could foster other export sectors with complex products, such as the mechanical industry, chemicals and ICT sectors.

This theory stays within the original emphasis on growth driven by self-discovery defined by the national industrial structure, which is measured by export statistics. The ability to export a new product successfully proves that the country has acquired new productive knowledge (Hausmann et al., 2013).

The theory holds that countries are more likely to grow successfully if 'they focus on products that are close to their current set of productive capabilities, as this would facilitate the identification and provision of the missing capabilities' (Hausmann et al., 2013: 57). This observation implies that growth in product space is a path-dependent strategy. New technology capabilities and new industry might not have room to be developed (Asheim et al., 2018). This is one drawback of the product space theory of growth.

Another drawback is that the theory does not offer a positive picture for advanced economies: the expected GDP growth to 2020 in advanced economies like Germany, Norway, Denmark, Netherlands, Belgium, and Switzerland lies at the bottom of the growth projection list (Hausmann et al., 2013: 78). Growth expectancy is based on measures of how difficult it is to move from the products the country exports today to related products with higher complexity. This index is a distance to new products from the current export basket of 128 countries. It is based on a strategy of diversification where countries prefer 'easy' targets, or new products, which are most closely related to existing products in the export basket. Therefore, according to this ranking in the 2013 report (Hausmann et al., 2013: 76), the countries with greatest growth expectancy are Uganda, Kenya, Tanzania, Zimbabwe and Madagascar.

This study applies the growth expectancy calculated by the economic complexity model into OECD countries and matches it with country economic performance index (GDP/capita) for 2016. The OECD group is chosen since the organisation is dedicated to promoting economic development, thus OECD countries are good candidates to study an economic growth model. The results obtained are illustrated in Figure 10.1.

The correlation between GDP/capita and expected growth calculated by product space theory is –0.428. Using the complexity index to predict expected growth, Figure 10.1 shows the winners are Turkey and Mexico, which have the highest growth expectancy despite their low GDP/capita. The countries with the lowest expected growth are Germany, Norway and Austria.

Figure 10.1 indicates that only emerging countries are predicted to grow strongly when applying the complexity model, not developed countries. An explanation can be that emerging countries are immersed in rapid processes of industrialisation, and the potential for innovation through related varieties, or discovery of products, which is related to the basket of existing export products, is large. This is why Turkey and Mexico stay on top of the expected growth list. Complexity might be seen as a strategy for growth in emerging economies, where the R&D institutions are weakly connected to firms.

The complexity model of Hausmann shows the growth potential of 'emerging' economies, but it shows how the growth potential of advanced economies would have looked without science to back up innovation. For example, Germany is a developed country where the 'easy' strategy of innovation through related variety/self-discovery *without a science and innovation component* is exhausted. Therefore, if Germany depends only on increasing country complexity without investing in R&D, its expected growth is extremely low, as

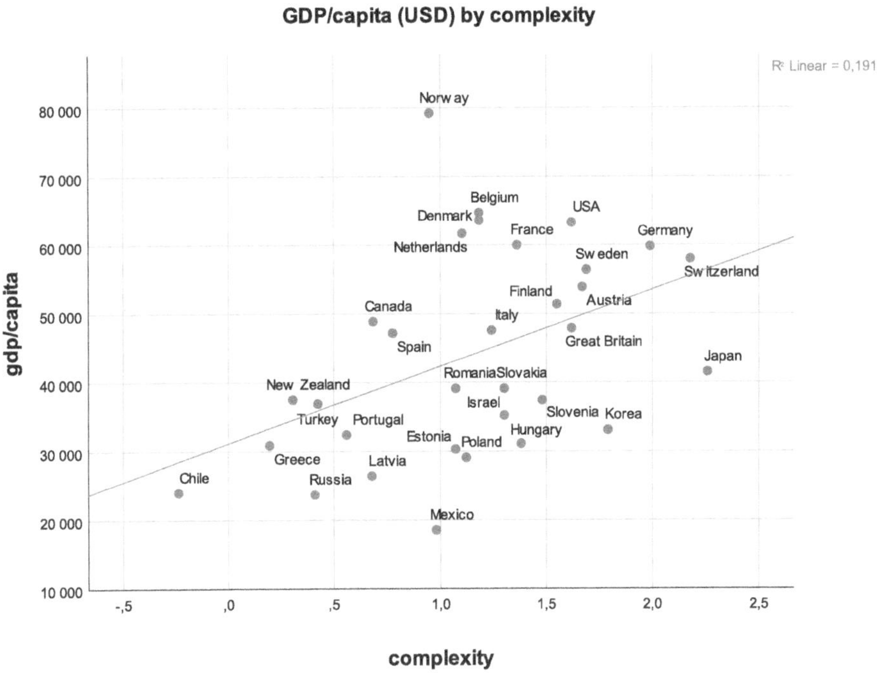

Figure 10.1 Complexity and growth expectancy

Source: *Atlas of Economic Complexity*

shown in Figure 10.1. This is consistent with the idea that the dynamics analysed by the complexity model of growth alone, without the assistance of science and innovation, is driving convergence in the global economy. In emerging economies, such as Mexico and Turkey, innovation and growth through related varieties may go on without R&D policies. But for advance economies, the complexity model might not be a preferable choice due to the low growth expectancy of applying product space strategy.

Smart specialisation strategy and entrepreneurial discovery processes

Theoretical background

The smart specialisation theory of Foray (2015) explains how the basic mechanism of growth through self-discovery drives diversification in advanced countries with firms applying R&D investments. Here, self-discovery and innovation through related variety is backed up through a modern form of R&D policy referred to as smart specialisation and entrepreneurial discovery process (EDP).

The correlation between GDP and firm investments in R&D per capita is +0.600. A correlation of +1 would mean that R&D performed in firms is perfectly correlated with GDP/capita. One implication is that countries with companies that invest heavily and wisely in R&D, such as Switzerland and the USA, are likely to grow, whereas countries with small R&D activities in firms, as in Romania and Mexico, are unlikely to grow.

The outliers are Norway, with 'too much' GDP/capita in relation to the R&D performed in firms, and on the other side Korea and Israel, two countries where several globally leading corporations invest heavily in R&D. The figure illustrates that if Norway did not have advantages from natural resources, the country would either be much poorer, or it should develop a more advanced system of innovation.

Regarding the second question, Figure 10.3 helps us examine the relationship between these two indicators.

The correlation between the complexity index and the R&D performed inside firms per capita is +0.862. Israel and Korea are outliers with massive R&D investments in firms in relation to the level of complexity of their national economies due to their military investment.

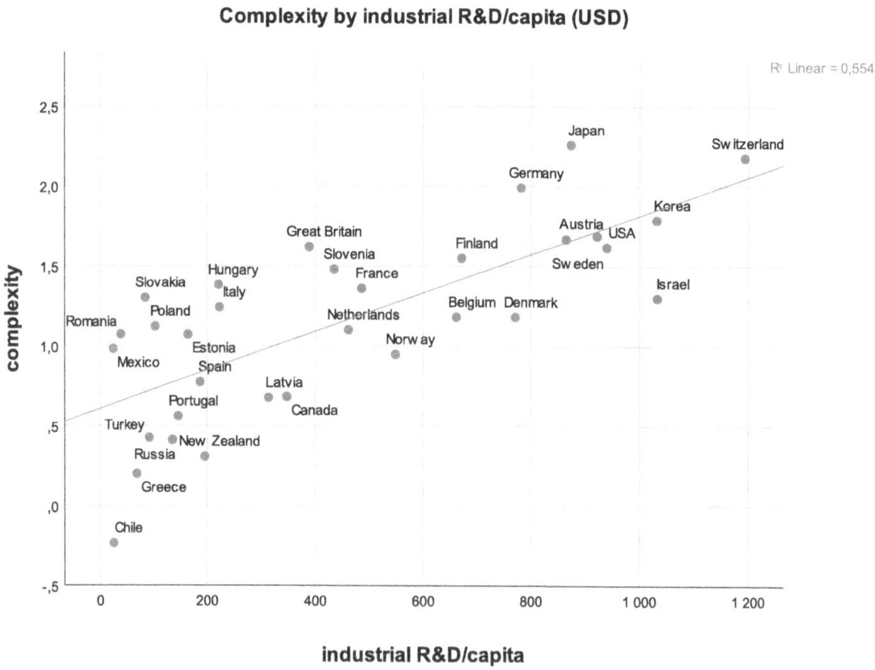

Figure 10.3 Complexity and firm investment in R&D/capita

Source: *Atlas of Economic Complexity* and OECD

In this figure, Norway is no longer an outlier; it fits nicely in together with other advanced processors of natural resources, such as Canada and Netherlands. It seems that Norway has a level of R&D performed in firms which fits appropriately with the level of complexity.

The analysis has shown that Hausmann's model of complexity and the science and innovation policy model of growth driven by R&D investments inside firms are complementary. Complexity and private and public sector investments in R&D are reinforcing each other. This is the basis for Foray (2015) to apply Rodrik's model of growth together with policies promoting national investments in science (science policy) in smart specialisation.

This finding indicates that increased complexity, or innovation through related variety, does require increased R&D inside firms, and the other way around. This combination of the two models of growth is precisely what policies promoting smart specialisation are designed to deliver.

An intuitive explanation is that firms with complex products operating inside complex economies use science to a greater extent than firms with less complex products in less complex economies. It seems that diversification at a high level of economic development requires more science and research inside firms. Complex products made for even more complex products, such as car or computer components, have to be tested and documented, using laboratories and scientific tools of measurement. If they are to be improved or reinvented, the process of innovation is likely to go through R&D. To put this differently, the scope of what is related within a complex economy is broader than in a less complex economy. The combination of innovation through related varieties and science policies promoting innovation is at the core of the smart specialisation strategy.

Supporting conditions for EDP

Smart specialisation's main mechanism for growth is self-discovery via EDP. The 'discovery' in EDP is not an innovation, but an opening of a new area of business opportunities. This area is related to and builds on existing knowledge and industrial resources in combination with external knowledge and resources to open up a new, emerging path of development. Smart specialisation strategy coordinates the search for new business areas; therefore, its nature is explorative rather than exploitative. As we will see below, this has clear policy implications when it comes to public sector involvement. Incentives should only be provided to new activities (Morgan, 2017). The strategy aims to seize new opportunities over time and progressively create new options for economic transformation; therefore, regional policy should regularly change the portfolio of prioritised activities (Foray, 2015). This raises the question of how to balance the tension between changing priorities and policy continuity (Grillo, 2017; Morgan, 2017).

EDP creates a new opportunity to move beyond the limitations of the national economic structure and integrate distant forms of knowledge. Relevant knowledge for the selection to the new business domain may be dispersed, decentralised, divided and in the possession of various entrepreneurial agents such as firms, universities, knowledge brokers, independent inventors and lead users. Therefore, the EDP can only be successful if, first, knowledge can be recombined together by the triple-helix actors (firms, universities and public sectors) and formed into a new knowledge domain, and second, the new knowledge domain can be leveraged into new business opportunities. This requires two fundamental conditions: (1) strong exploration capabilities from innovation actors who, at the same time, know how to exploit their current strength efficiently, and (2) supporting mechanisms for knowledge recombination across actors, sectors, and industries, which should be created through science and innovation policies. The conceptual framework below elaborates on these elements.

10.3 A conceptual framework for economic restructuring and growth

General observations

An economic restructuring process, under our approach, involves diversifying the economy in the direction of complexity by investing in R&D with the support of science and innovation policy. In their theory of economic complexity, which is central to economic growth and development, Hidalgo and Hausmann (2009) refer to capabilities as the building blocks of economic complexity. Capabilities, in this sense, are the inputs required to produce an export product. Felipe and his colleagues (2012) summarise these capabilities as the composition of:

> (i) the set of human and physical capital, the legal system, institutions, etc. that are needed to produce a product (hence, they are product-specific, not just a set of amorphous factor inputs); (ii) at the firm level, they are the 'know-how' or working practices held collectively by the group of individuals comprising the firm; and (iii) the organizational abilities that provide the capacity to form, manage, and operate activities that involve large numbers of people.
>
> (Felipe et al., 2012: 37)

An important realisation from this perspective is that capabilities are created by a combination of an innovation system (a macro level), that is, 'the set of human and physical capital, the legal system, institutions, etc. that are needed to produce a product', and innovation firms (micro level), that is, the technology know-how, working practices and organisational abilities. Therefore, in the process of structural transformation, connecting the macro and micro levels to jointly acquire the capabilities for diversifying the economy plays a central role in the success of restructuring.

Exploration from the point of departure of a single corporate actor may be restricted by the limitations of the corporate knowledge base (the competency trap) and it might start to crowd out exploration, leading to failure in the long term when disruptive innovation comes in. In the theory of smart specialisation and EDP (Foray, 2015), exploration is externalised, and carried on by the powerful wings of science. Through a strategy coordinated by the public sector, universities and industry, the exploration process has the potential to escape from the narrow borders of corporate knowledge bases and national economic structures. Doing so would help to develop cross-sector collaboration, cross-disciplinary and transnational platforms of innovation. A crucial issue is connecting the logic of policy-makers (the macro level) and the world seen from inside firms (the micro level) to discover new opportunities successfully. Success requires better coordination between the micro and macro level, strengthening the emphasis on exploration through partnerships between public policy-makers and the innovators who know the market, and backed by appropriate science and innovation policies researched by academic scholars.

These science and innovation policies need to originate from a thorough understanding of the role of and challenges involved at both the macro and micro levels in order to create successful economic restructuring through joint entrepreneurial discoveries. The macro level, referring to innovation policies, needs to combine both complexity and R&D investment in industry guided by science to create economic growth. The micro level, referring to innovation firms, has moved very rapidly in terms of technology development and innovation strategies because they have to cope directly with the rapid change in the business environment, where they face both internal and external challenges. The internal challenges revolve around internal tensions arising from the two conflicting sets of capabilities – exploiting current core business while exploring new business opportunities – that are certainly difficult to manage. The external challenge revolves around dealing with fast-changing surroundings and navigating the national business system and policies. To resolve the internal and external challenges faced by innovation actors, the innovation system and policies need to devise a strategy to connect the micro and macro levels.

These observations are the foundations for our conceptual framework explaining how the smart specialisation strategy works to connect micro and macro level in the structural transformation process (Figure 10.4).

Conceptual framework

There are three key elements in this conceptual framework (Figure 10.4):

a) Innovation actors (the micro level) need to enhance sets of complex capabilities: such as exploitation capabilities, exploration capabilities, and dynamic capabilities including ambidexterity. An ambidexterity capability helps firms to balance and rebalance the tensions between their exploiting and exploring activities.
b) Innovation system and policies (the macro level) are designed to assist diversifying the economy towards increasing economic complexity via

science-based innovation policies. This includes the supporting institutions and horizontal programmes which help improve the framework conditions and general capabilities.

c) Smart specialisation strategy is the strategy to connect the macro and micro levels. The strategy emphasises entrepreneurial discovery via triple-helix collaboration. This discovery is supported by science-based innovation policies focused on vertical priorities.

Micro level: acquiring sets of complex capabilities

The engine of a country's economic growth is its innovation actors. These actors together create the innovation capacity of that country via their ability to innovate. This ability to innovate is based on sets of complex capabilities, such

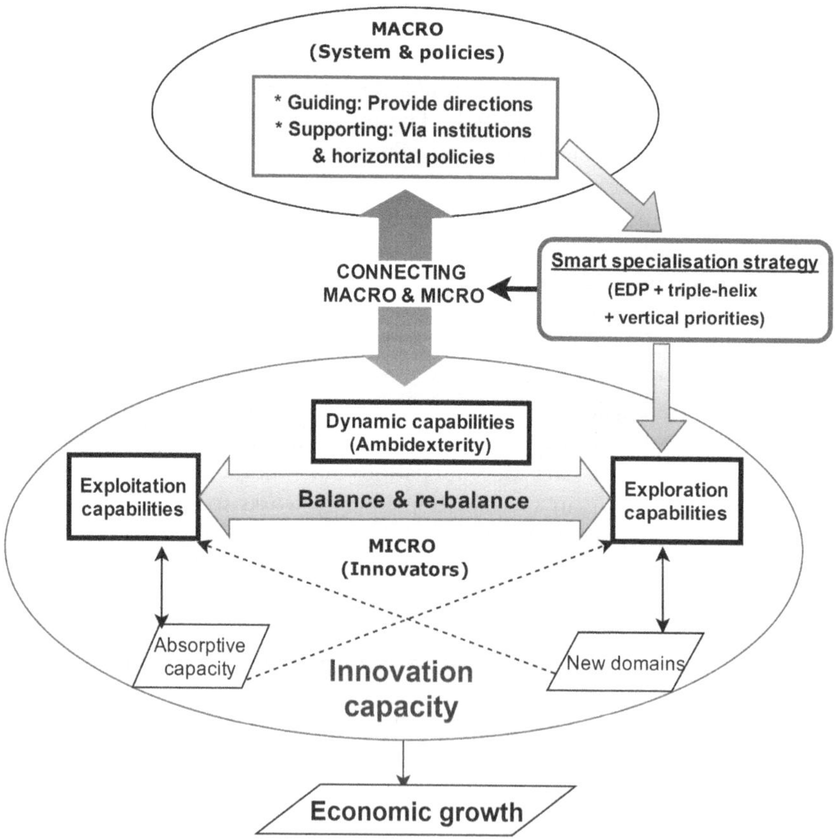

Figure 10.4 Economic restructuring: conceptual framework

Source: Adapted from Mariussen et al. (2018)

as exploitation capabilities, exploration capabilities, and dynamic capabilities, as shown in Figure 10.4.

Exploitation refers to activities focused on the current strength/competitive advantage of the economy, while *exploration* refers to activities developing new knowledge domains that will constitute competitive advantage in the future: 'Exploitation is about efficiency, increasing productivity, control, certainty, and variance reduction. Exploration is about search, discovery, autonomy, innovation and embracing variation' (O'Reilly and Tushman, 2008: 189). Dynamic capabilities, including ambidexterity, are the survival requirements for balancing and rebalancing exploration and exploitation activities at the organisational level.

One important concept that relates to both exploration and exploitation is absorptive capacity, which refers to the ability to recognise the value of new external information, assimilate it and apply it to innovation activities (Cohen and Levinthal, 1990). Cohen and Levinthal pointed out that prior knowledge permits the assimilation and exploitation of new knowledge that suggests two features of absorptive capacity, which are cumulativeness and effect on expectation formation, which 'imply that its development is domain-specific and is path- or history-dependent' (p. 136). This absorptive capacity, developed throughout the exploitation process, is a prerequisite for exploration activities, at both the firm and country levels. To enhance exploration capabilities, the EDP, supported by triple helices as well as science and innovation policy, will result in new domains of knowledge, skills, and business opportunities. New domains should be nurtured and developed until they can be exploited to deliver future growth.

Figure 10.4 illustrates this point by connecting absorptive capacity to both exploitation and exploration capabilities. Meanwhile, the outcomes of exploration capability are new domains that will feed into exploitation capabilities.

The three capabilities combine to form the innovation capacity of innovation actors – which are the engines for economic growth and development.

Macro level: guiding and supporting role of innovation system and policies

It is acknowledged that innovation in an economy 'needs to come from grass roots and not from the top' (Foray, 2015: 37). The role of policy is 'not about telling people what to do, but rather about helping stakeholders to discover what to do and then implementing the necessary sequence of policies according to what has been discovered' (Foray, 2015: 41). In our conceptual framework, the role of the national innovation systems and policies is two-fold:

- *Guiding*: National system and policies must influence the direction in which innovation should be oriented (Foray, 2015). Economic diversification towards complexity combined with science-based policies is a sensible direction.
- *Supporting*: Institutions such as business networks, associations and research laboratories that back start-ups or agencies that facilitate partnerships and

collaboration of small firms are supporting mechanisms that can serve as the locus of entrepreneurial discovery (Foray, 2015). At the same time, horizontal policies for building framework conditions and general capabilities such as improving human capital, accelerating transfer of technologies, creating incubators, upgrading SME capabilities or having a productive university are essential for innovation.

Connecting macro and micro: smart specialisation strategy

The authors propose smart specialisation strategy, at a national level, is the element connecting the macro and micro. This strategy promotes the EDP, based on cooperation between triple helices (government, business and academia), and creates a new process of resource allocation for developing new economic specialties based on vertical priorities. Vertical priorities refer to specific 'selected domains dealing with particular kinds of technology, fields, disciplines, and sub-systems within a sector or at the interstices of different sectors' (Foray, 2015: 39). Using a vertical targeted intervention logic to concentrate resources on a well-conducted EDP can help provide incentives to facilitate the 'emergence and development of "innovation microsystems" dealing with particular market niches' (Foray, 2015: 36) that could lead to structural changes in the economy.

A new regional capacity may be needed to initiate structural changes such as diversification, transition, modernisation, or the radical foundation of industries and/or services (Foray, 2015: 1). EDP defines a process of diversification through concentration of resources and competences in new domains representing possible paths for the transformation of regional productive structures. The transformation of these productive structures and capacities requires new resources, new technologies and new competencies that can be generated within the same area (region or country), although they may also come from outside. When resources are concentrated in the selected domains, new activities can be created to enable and facilitate the transformation and renewal of the economy. This can be the basis for a unique competitive advantage.

In this way, the 'self' in the EDP is a large and heterogeneous set of actors involved in the process of discovering which domains of R&D and innovative activities a region should move into to construct its future. This move should be carried out in partnership between the government, scholars and the private sector. Therefore, the process of entrepreneurial discovery is a central tool to solve an information problem that the government alone cannot solve (Foray, 2015) owing to its strong learning dimension that helps to open and explore new domains of opportunities. This is how smart specialisation strategy can help connect the micro and macro.

Moving beyond related variety: the importance of ambidexterity and knowledge-spanning activities

Related variety (Frenken et al., 2007), consonant with the concept of product space (Hidalgo et al., 2007), refers to 'industrial sectors that are related in terms of shared or complementary competences' (Boschma and Iammarino, 2009; Pylak and Wojnicka-Sycz, 2014: 2). This is the fundamental logic of translating the EDP into structural changes in the case of transition, modernisation and diversification. The fourth pattern of structural change by way of the smart specialisation policy is a radical foundation in which a new domain is founded with no direct link to the existing structures (Foray, 2015), and thus involves opening up new opportunities unrelated to existing productive assets. In this way, Foray resonates well with the call for unrelated variety from Grillitsch and colleagues (2017). That study emphasises the need for path upgrading, path importation, path branching, path diversification, and new path creation as different forms of new path development:

> the combination of unrelated knowledge can lead to the emergence of related industries. At the heart of this argument is the experimental and evolutionary character of new path development. The starting point is the search for competitiveness and high-value creating activities driven by entrepreneurs. In order to become more competitive, entrepreneurs experiment in innovation processes where the combination of unrelated but complementary knowledge offers a high potential for introducing novelty.
>
> (Grillitsch et al., 2017: 10)

This, as shown in the previous section of this chapter, is the logic of advanced economies, which are unable to grow through new re-combinations of existing industrial knowledge. The question is how unrelated variety might be created. This study has shown that there is a clear correlation at the national level between firm investments in R&D and GDP/capita. This indicates that a key factor in generating growth in advanced economies is the presence of science-based knowledge inside firms. Our hypothesis is that firms that invest heavily in R&D will have more opportunities to be exposed to unrelated science-based knowledge from the outside brought into the firm. The unrelated knowledge is absorbed and helps generate processes of knowledge convergence with the existing knowledge base which might lead to the creation of a totally new form of knowledge. This new knowledge may enable the entrepreneurial discovery process.

The importance of ambidexterity

Unrelated variety provides preconditions for technological 'breakthroughs' stemming from combinations across unrelated knowledge domains and technologies (Castaldi et al., 2015). The assumption made in this study regarding the locus for unrelated varieties is R&D activities inside innovation firms. One of the most important preconditions in this case is the ability of the firm to explore new unrelated knowledge (exploration capabilities) while still being able to generate income to survive (exploitation capabilities).

Exploitation is more attractive, profitable in the short term, and far less risky than exploration, and therefore seems easier to implement. Exploration is in contrast risky, uncertain, and a long-term investment, and is thus normally ignored. If there is no action to balance these two activities, exploitation will crowd out exploration (March, 1991). When exploitation crowds out exploration, many firms with strong exploitation capabilities suffer from an innovation dilemma (Christensen, 1997) and are likely to fail when new entrants introduce disruptive innovations. Similarly, countries with strong natural resources might suffer from the resource curse (Ross, 1999) and Dutch disease (Torvik, 2001) and experience slower or poorer economic and political development. This phenomenon can be referred to as a *lock-in trap* or a *competence trap* (Levinthal and March, 1993). As a result, exploration of an unrelated variety knowledge domain will be almost impossible.

To avoid this lock-in trap, balancing exploration and exploitation capabilities is the key element. This requires dynamic capability, which is the ability 'to maintain ecological fitness and, when necessary, to reconfigure existing assets and develop the new skills needed to address emerging threats and opportunities' (O'Reilly and Tushman, 2008). This is the capability to help innovation actors to balance the exploitation and exploration activities by reallocating existing resources and acquiring new skills that will potentially be useful for the future. At the firm level (micro level), this specific dynamic capability of managing both exploitation and exploration is also called *ambidexterity* (O'Reilly and Tushman, 2008). The tension between exploration and exploitation is fundamental and inherent and cannot be resolved permanently. Focusing on either one will ultimately lead to failure. To survive in the long term, it is essential for firms to maintain the balance between them and rebalance when the environment changes. The key to balancing these two activities is integrating mechanisms and strategy that combine the two activities at the level of the firm's top-level management team. Such integration will help facilitate knowledge creation between unrelated new knowledge and existing logics that might entail unrelated varieties.

This is why ambidexterity is crucial in the smart specialisation model and for entrepreneurial discoveries in advanced economies.

The supportive role of knowledge spanning

Unrelated variety requires cross-sector collaboration and interdisciplinary research, which require knowledge boundary spanning.

Boundary spanning is difficult to accomplish owing to the dual challenge posed by cognitive boundary barriers and political boundary barriers. Innovation cross-sector needs both 'actors' and 'objects' in knowledge-spanning activities, in which actors refer to the people who connect different knowledge domains together such as brokers and boundary spanners, while boundary objects refer to scientific instrumentations or exchanging zone where knowledge bridges can be built (Kaplan et al., 2017). Boundary spanners (e.g. a knowledge broker) and boundary objects (e.g. instruments, platforms, space, and zones) are in a symbiotic relationship (Kaplan et al., 2017).

Chapters 5 by Lam (2019) and 6 by Finne and Aasen (2019) in this book contain strong arguments in favour of mobility between sectors, universities and firms (bonding and brokering), in order to facilitate these processes. Lam points out the significance of the hybridisation of borders between different types of knowledge, leading to a third space, a knowledge space crossing institutionalised borders between knowledge spaces. This third space may be created as embodied knowledge in humans who are moving beyond different sectors and helices in their careers. Firms with strategies of ambidexterity may develop hybrid knowledge spaces.

10.4 Empirical illustration case: Norway

Norway is used as a case in point for two reasons. First, the authors collected empirical data to help understand how economic restructuring using the smart specialisation strategy in Norway could be implemented (Mariussen et al., 2018). Second, Norway was ranked the lowest (128th) in the *Atlas of Economic Complexity* (Hausmann et al., 2013: 78) survey in terms growth expectancy using the complexity model. Therefore, Norway as a case is an interesting illustration of how to design an economic growth strategy for an advanced economy.

Structural transformation for economic growth

The economic restructuring process can be implemented by exploration and exploitation activities inside firms as well as in industrial sectors. Using Norway as a case in point, this study illustrates how to apply smart specialisation strategy and the EDP in the process of balancing and rebalancing these parallel activities through integration platforms (see Figure 10.5). These activities are interwoven; for example, exploitation activities at the industrial sector level can include exploration activities at the firm level.

The strategy of changing an economic structure (see Figure 10.5) can be understood as a combination of three parallel processes:

(i) *Exploitation of a country's existing strengths.* The exploited orientation of Norway as a country is based on the existing strengths in the current economy and is built on both exploitation and exploration capabilities of its firms.

Exploiting Norway's existing strength involves working with leading industries such as oil and gas, maritime industries, and aquaculture. Innovation firms in these industries can contribute by (1) strengthening their competence in their existing domains of business, for example, daily operating activities of firms and organisations which bring revenue back to the companies, and (2) conducting exploration activities by recombining knowledge and applying such knowledge recombination to related domains. The exploration activities are directed towards innovation that could resolve societal challenges. Key words to consider in this context are *circular economy, business model innovation, knowledge recombination*, and *climbing in the value chain* through development of more complex products, higher in the value chain.

(ii) *Exploration of new domains and business opportunities*. This orientation requires a joint effort on both the micro and macro levels, through cooperation between industrial entrepreneurs, research institutions and public institutions. The crucial capability for exploration towards unrelated varieties lies at the ability of firms.

Norway should focus on vertical priorities built on breakthrough technologies such as nanotechnology, artificial intelligence, robotics, 3-D printing, quantum computing, biotechnology, and the Internet of Things. These are fundamental, or backbone, technologies in the Fourth Industrial Revolution that are disrupting almost every industry at the global level. Unrelated varieties can happen when the logic of new technologies is applied to existing challenges in a different knowledge domain. One example could be how the medical and oil and gas sectors can innovate together. Two Norwegian companies, Norway Pumps & Pipes and Statoil, have arranged a workshop to explore how technologies and innovation in two different fields (medical, and oil and gas) could be transferred to benefit innovation across both sectors (IRIS, 2018). Here, medical experts and petroleum technologists look for solutions across challenges of pumping crude oil and blood. The medical challenge was vascular flow dynamics – with focus on blood flow restrictions in the lower part of the body. The oil and gas challenge was prediction of particle settling in drilling fluids.

Resource allocation to support this vertical priority focus on medical solutions based on unrelated advanced technologies would be beneficial for the process of exploring unrelated varieties.

(iii) *Balancing exploration and exploitation and connecting the micro and macro through integration strategies*. A capability for ambidexterity requires several mechanisms, but the crucial mechanism to ensure the ongoing success of an ambidextrous strategy is integration.

Coordinating exploration and exploitation demands infrastructure for key enabling technologies, such as digitalisation, automation and software integration to strengthen business activities at the firm level and also the innovation system at the country level (see Chapter 11 in this book). Meanwhile, this infrastructure facilitates the coordination between exploration and exploitation activities in terms of retaining specialised knowledge in exploitation for the purpose of knowledge recombination in exploration. It can also help disseminate best practices of exploration to the exploitation area.

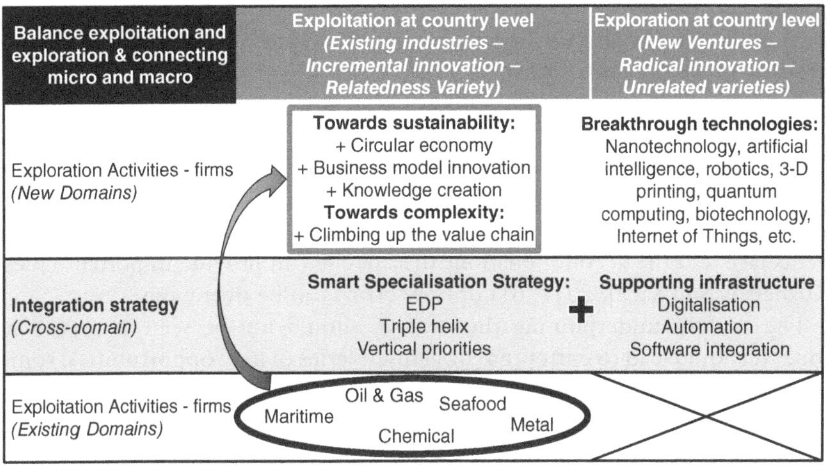

Figure 10.5 How Norway can restructure the economy by balancing exploitation–exploration and connecting macro–micro

Source: Modified from Mariussen et al. (2018: 39)

Crucial conditions: supporting institutions to coordinate the learning process

This section discusses the crucial condition for implementing the above-mentioned strategy. The point of departure of Norway is a sectorised state, with coordinating mechanisms between ministries. Smart specialisation is an experimental process involving public sector authorities, industrial clusters, firms, entrepreneurs, research institutions and researchers. They are expected to be collectively involved in feedback on and learning from their experiments. The authors believe the core coordinating institution should be a public sector institution that can learn and coordinate the joint learning process. The main principles underlying implementing the strategy, which consequently highlight the important role of collective learning and the institution coordinating this process, are discussed below.

The implementation of smart specialisation strategy should not be seen as a state-planned top–down process. It is not based on a rigid application of an equally static set of policy tools, decided once and for all at the beginning of a planning cycle. Neither should it be perceived as an incremental process of implementation, with no long-term vision. What is needed is a Schumpeterian Development Agency (SDA) which learns through monitoring a portfolio of projects (Breznitz and Ornston, 2012).

Implementation of a strategy of smart specialisation can be seen as an experimental *trial and error* process, featuring error detection and correction. It is based on an empirically verified analysis of how existing domains might form the basis of exploration into new related varieties, new sectors and clusters building on domestic strengths. It should also take into consideration how innovating firms and regions in Norway can experimentally access and exploit global networks and systems of innovation which might provide new emerging technologies in areas where Norway is today weak. The approach should be based on diagnostic monitoring where 'careful attention to the problems agents face and the accommodations they devise can provide important clues' (Kuznetsov and Sabel, 2017: 61) of how errors can be overcome.

The analysis underpinning the strategy should not be seen as carved in stone. It should lead to entrepreneurial discoveries of new opportunities, some of them close to home, some based on transnational networks. These discoveries should not be made inside the walls of ministries; they should involve entrepreneurs, science institutions and public sector programme operators and financers. During this experiment, design, visions and long-term goals should be regarded as hypotheses that can be confirmed or rejected during the implementation and monitoring of effects. The closing of this feedback loop, through the analysis of outcomes and the process of learning, where success and failure is used to correct analysis and strategy, is the current agenda of relevant innovation policy research. This suggests a need for built-in feedback loops connecting different process elements: implementation, actual impacts on the innovation ecosystems (to be observed through monitoring and evaluation), the critical analysis of the strategy, as well as design and governance mechanisms. A crucial aspect is research-based learning from experience, which should feed directly into strategy updates and revisions, as some experiments fail, and some succeed. The circle of collective learning is illustrated in Figure 10.6.

This is an experimental trial-and-error process requiring an institution capable of supporting such experiments and coordinating the collective learning process. This coordinating institution could be the Research Council of Norway, or it could also be an institution such as a 'Centre for Innovation System and Policy Research'. Any future research on the coordinating institution should address two crucial questions:

- How can Norway enhance the innovation capacity at the firm level and establish better connections between its triple-helix actors to foster co-creating the EDP?
- How is it possible to reorganise the system of innovation in a way that counters sectorisation and accordingly the exploitation nature of the Norwegian economy?

Summary

The OECD review of innovation policy in Norway in 2017 (OECD, 2017) identified several challenges for the Norwegian economy linked to the issues

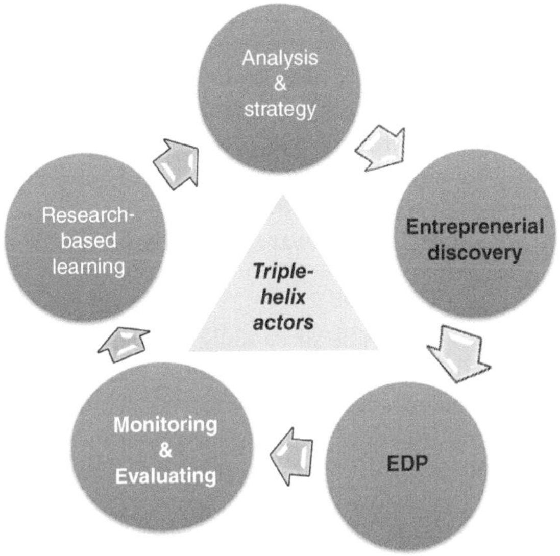

Figure 10.6 Collective learning process in the entrepreneurial discovery process
Source: Modified from (Mariussen et al., 2018: 45)

of too high sectorisation and too much reliance on oil and gas. Overcoming these challenges would apparently require rebalancing the economy in the direction of exploration, thus enabling diversification. A suggestion for restructuring the economy in the direction of exploration through research and innovation (R&I) is smart specialisation based on the EDP. The EDP inherently means focusing on exploration of new growth opportunities and investment in emerging rather than mature markets, through various forms of cooperation between entrepreneurs, public sector policy-makers and academia.

In light of this direction, there should be an institution, preferably a public authority, responsible for connecting the business sector and national-level policy-making on innovation strategy. It is expected to team up with and support entrepreneurs and firms to explore new, as yet unexplored opportunities in the economy. This coordinating institution should be able to act based on an empirically grounded understanding of those market failures that prevent firms from discovering and exploiting new opportunities. In this way, further research and experimentation should contribute to unlocking the hidden potential of the Norwegian economy, while taking account of its current strengths.

10.5 Conclusions

There are two sources of wealth: R&D intensive complexity and R&D intensive exploitation of natural resources.

1 Countries may achieve high levels of GDP/capita through high levels of complexity (diversification), combined with large R&D investments made inside firms and by the public sector in universities, in some cases in synergy with each other. Examples are Switzerland, Germany, USA, Austria, Japan, Korea, Sweden, Finland and others.
2 Countries may have moderate firm R&D investment and nevertheless enjoy incomes from advanced and highly productive export industries based on natural resources, supported by strong science-based sectoral systems of innovation. Examples are Norway, the Netherlands, Denmark, New Zealand and Australia.

These sources of growth can sometimes be successfully combined when countries manage to use the strengths of their resource-based systems of innovation to diversify and develop new export industries. They may also conflict, as when the resource-based clusters dominate other sectors in the labour market, driving out growth and locking supplier industries, such as mechanical industries, into golden cages of well-paid sophisticated products that are removed from other sectors. At the same time a high cost level created by too well-paid raw materials may create labour markets which exclude several manufacturing sectors relying on labour-intensive work and lock the surviving sectors into strategies of increasing capital intensity and deep specialisation, which deter diversification.

A diversification strategy based on product-space complexity might be effective for emerging economies, while diversification via the smart specialisation strategy is more suitable for advanced nations. The EDP is the fundamental mechanism of the smart specialisation strategy, and requires a joint effort between entrepreneurs, researchers, and policy-makers to transform economic structures to embrace innovation, development and growth. The future of economic diversification lies with unrelated varieties, new combinations of so far unrelated knowledge domains (Castaldi et al., 2015), which requires a strong country innovation capacity. Dynamic capabilities at the firm level, especially ambidextrous capacity, is a prerequisite.

References

Aasen, T.M. (2019). Approaching entrepreneurial discovery and knowledge conversion from a complexity perspective. In Mariussen, Å., Virkkala, S., Finne, H. and Aasen, T.M. (eds) *The entrepreneurial discovery process and regional development: New knowledge emergence, conversion and exploitation*. Abingdon: Routledge.

Asheim, B., Fitjar, R., Herstad, S. and Hjertvikrem, N. (2018). *Diversity and beyond for new path development: Broadening the scope for new perspectives on innovation theory and policy*. Occasional report. Oslo: Norges forsknngsråd.

Boschma, R. and Iammarino, S. (2009). Related variety, trade linkages, and regional growth in Italy. *Economic Geography*, 85 (3), pp. 289–311.

Breznitz, D. and Ornston, D. (2012). *Scaling up and sustaining innovation policies and projects: Schumpeterian development agencies in small open economies*. [World Bank] Working Paper. Washington, DC: World Bank.

Castaldi, C., Frenken, K. and Los, B. (2015). Related variety, unrelated variety and technological breakthroughs: An analysis of US state-level patenting. *Regional Studies*, 49 (5), pp. 767–781.

Christensen, C.M. (1997). *The innovator's dilemma: When new technologies cause great firms to fail*. Cambridge, MA: Harvard Business School Press.

Cohen, W.M. and Levinthal, D.A. (1990). Absorptive capacity: A new perspective on learning and innovation. *Administrative Science Quarterly*, 35 (1), pp. 128–152.

Felipe, J., Kumar, U., Abdon, A. and Bacate, M. (2012). Product complexity and economic development. *Structural Change and Economic Dynamics*, 23 (1), pp. 36–68.

Finne, H. and Aasen, T.M. (2019). The bond, the bridge and the broker. Knowledge conversion in the university–industry nexus. In Mariussen, Å., Virkkala, S., Finne, H. and Aasen, T.M. (eds) *The entrepreneurial discovery process and regional development: New knowledge emergence, conversion and exploitation*. Abingdon: Routledge.

Foray, D. (2013). The economic fundamentals of smart specialisation. *Ekonomiaz*, 83 (2), pp. 54–78.

Foray, D. (2015). *Smart specialisation: Opportunities and challenges for regional innovation policy*. London: Routledge.

Foray, D. and Rainoldi, A. (2013). *Smart specialisation programmes and implementation*. Luxembourg: European Commission.

Frenken, K., Van Oort, F. and Verburg, T. (2007). Related variety, unrelated variety and regional economic growth. *Regional Studies*, 41 (5), pp. 685–697.

Grillitsch, M., Asheim, B. and Trippl, M. (2017). *Unrelated knowledge combinations: Unexplored potential for regional industrial path development*. Papers in Innovation Studies 2017/10. Lund: Lund University, CIRCLE.

Grillo, F. (2017). Structuring the entrepreneurial discovery process to promote private–public sector engagement. In Kyriakou, D., Martínez, M.P., Periáñez-Forte, I. and Rainoldi, A. (eds) *Governing smart specialisation*, pp. 62–79. London; New York: Routledge.

Growth Lab (2016). *Country complexity rankings (ECI)*. Cambridge, MA: Harvard University, Center for International Development. Available at: http://atlas.cid.harvard.edu/rankings.

Growth Lab (2017). *Glossary*. Cambridge, MA: Harvard University, Center for International Development. Available at: http://atlas.cid.harvard.edu/learn/glossary#economiccomplexity.

Hausmann, R., Hidalgo, C.A., Bustos, S., Coscia, M., Chung, S., Jimenez, J., Simoes, A. and Yıldırım, M.A. (2011). *The atlas of economic complexity: Mapping paths to prosperity*. Cambridge, MA: Harvard University, Center for International Development.

Hausmann, R., Hidalgo, C.A., Bustos, S., Coscia, M., Simoes, A. and Yildirim, M.A. (2013). *The atlas of economic complexity: Mapping paths to prosperity*, 2nd ed. Cambridge, MA: MIT Press.

Hausmann, R. and Pritchett, L. (2018). *The atlas of economic complexity [database]*. [Cambridge, MA]: Harvard's Center for International Development (CID)'s Growth Lab. Available at: http://atlas.cid.harvard.edu/.

Hidalgo, C.A. and Hausmann, R. (2009). The building blocks of economic complexity. *Proceedings of the National Academy of Sciences*, 106 (26), pp. 10570–10575.

Hidalgo, C.A., Klinger, B., Barabási, A.-L. and Hausmann, R. (2007). The product space conditions the development of nations. *Science*, 317 (5837), pp. 482–487.

IRIS (2018). *Medical and oil & gas innovate together*. International Research Institute of Stavanger. Available at: www.iris.no/home/medical-and-oil-gas-innovate-together.

Kaplan, S., Milde, J. and Cowan, R.S. (2017). Symbiont practices in boundary spanning: Bridging the cognitive and political divides in interdisciplinary research. *Academy of Management Journal*, 60 (4), pp. 1387–1414.

Kuznetsov, Y. and Sabel, C. (2017). Managing self-discovery: Diagnostic monitoring of a portfolio of projects and programs. In Radosevic, S., Curaj, A., Gheorghiu, R., Andreescu, L. and Wade, I. (eds) *Advances in the theory and practice of smart specialization*, pp. 51–72. London: Academic Press.

Lam, A. (2019). Career mobility, hybridity and knowledge combination: A 'third space' perspective. In Mariussen, Å., Virkkala, S., Finne, H. and Aasen, T.M. (eds) *The entrepreneurial discovery process and regional development: New knowledge emergence, conversion and exploitation*. Abingdon: Routledge.

Lavie, D., Stettner, U. and Tushman, M.L. (2010). Exploration and exploitation within and across organizations. *Academy of Management Annals*, 4 (1), pp. 109–155.

Levinthal, D.A. and March, J.G. (1993). The myopia of learning. *Strategic Management Journal*, 14, pp. 95–112.

March, J.G. (1991). Exploration and exploitation in organizational learning. *Organization Science*, 2 (1), pp. 71–87.

Mariussen, Å., Nguyen, N. and Løvland, J. (2018). *Smart economic restructuring in Norway: Connecting micro and macro*. Nordland Research Institute.

Morgan, K. (2017). Speaking truth to power: The political dynamics of public sector innovation. In Kyriakou, D., Martínez, M.P., Periáñez-Forte, I. and Rainoldi, A. (eds) *Governing smart specialisation*, pp. 49–61. London: Routledge.

O'Reilly, C.A. and Tushman, M.L. (2008). Ambidexterity as a dynamic capability: Resolving the innovator's dilemma. *Research in Organizational Behavior*, 28, pp. 185–206.

OECD (2017). *OECD reviews of innovation policy: Norway 2017*. Paris: OECD.

Price, I. (2004). Complexity, complicatedness and complexity: A new science behind organizational intervention? *Emergence: Complexity and Organization*, 6 (1–2).

Pylak, K. and Wojnicka-Sycz, E. (2014). *Related variety in the development of less developed regions*. Presented at Regional Studies Association European Conference 2014. Izmir, Turkey.

Rodrik, D. (2004). *Industrial policy for the twenty-first century*. Faculty Research Working Papers Series. Cambridge, MA: Harvard University, John F. Kennedy School of Government.

Rodrik, D. (2014). The past, present, and future of economic growth. *Challenge*, 57 (3), pp. 5–39.

Ross, M.L. (1999). The political economy of the resource curse. *World Politics*, 51 (2), pp. 297–322.

Thirlwall, A.P. (2003). *Growth and development: With special reference to developing economies*, 7th ed. London: Palgrave Macmillan.

Torvik, R. (2001). Learning by doing and the Dutch disease. *European Economic Review*, 45 (2), pp. 285–306.

Tushman, M.L. and O'Reilly, C.A. (1996). Ambidextrous organizations: Managing evolutionary and revolutionary change. *California Management Review*, 38, pp. 8–30.

Virkkala, S. and Mariussen, Å. (2019). Emergence of new business areas in regional economies through entrepreneurial discovery processes. In Mariussen, Å., Virkkala, S., Finne, H. and Aasen, T.M. (eds) *The entrepreneurial discovery process and regional development: New knowledge emergence, conversion and exploitation*. Abingdon: Routledge.

11 Smart specialisation and interregional learning via thematic partnerships

Åge Mariussen, Fatime Barbara Hegyi and Ruslan Rakhmatullin

11.1 Introduction

The smart specialisation approach grew out of a critical review of policies of the past, such as the national systems of innovation, or the NIS policies of the 1990s. According to NIS policies, all countries should go in the same direction, and hunt leading scientific achievement in identical 'high tech' sectors. This led to the creation of 'micro-clusters' and fragmentation of European R&D resources. This is why Foray in his 2015 book wrote:

> If accomplished properly through an entrepreneurial discovery process, the smart specialisation strategy should logically identify not necessarily the hottest domains in nanotechnology/biotechnology/ICTs but rather the domains where new R&D and innovation activities will complement the region's other productive assets to create future domestic and interregional competitive advantages.
>
> (Foray, 2015: 5)

When the smart specialisation approach was introduced and applied, emphasis was put on place-based development, and accordingly entrepreneurial discoveries of new business opportunities based on the regional domains. As shown in section 11.2 of this chapter, analysis of experiences from this first period has now encouraged emphasis on transregional thematic partnerships, providing R&D input to regional domains and strategies. This is not a 'back to the nineties' strategy where all regions are supposed to grow similar small-scale applications of high-tech clusters. Instead, it is a question of developing new applications of key enabling technologies (KETs) inside already existing regional domains, in cooperation with innovation leaders and clusters with core KETs.

This strategy faces three specific challenges (Mariussen et al., 2016):

- Challenge 1: How to develop a stronger place-based regional innovation ecosystem through improved internal connectivity between existing industrial and knowledge provision strengths.

- Challenge 2: How to grow a larger, stronger and more dynamic regional innovation ecosystem by opening it up and connecting it to macro-regional and European knowledge networks and systems of innovation.
- Challenge 3: How to create economic growth through innovation expanding across borders, in ways which enable new entrepreneurial discovery processes.

As illustrated by the example of European Spallation Source (ESS) presented later in this chapter, solving these challenges seems to rely on synergies where strong regions provide access to KETs, and other regions apply these technologies within their domains. Section 11.3 presents a conceptual framework for how the challenges may be understood through the concepts of regional and relational knowledge spaces as well as third space introduced in other chapters of this book.

So what are the multi-level governance mechanisms and systems of planning for integrating regional S3 partnerships and transnational networks in ways which enable entrepreneurial discovery processes?

This is discussed in section 11.4. The section explains how potential networks are identified and validated through an analysis which includes and matches regional domains and the emerging domains of transregional networks. The approach is based on the achievements of the first phase of regional smart specialisation planning. This involves scoping, mapping and monitoring.

How can the outcomes of these experiments be institutionalised?

Section 11.5 presents examples of the new forms of transnational governance. The discussion is summarised in section 11.6, which presents a case of institutionalisation through a new way of co-managing a knowledge commons in photonics.

11.2 Place-based learning and thematic partnerships

As discussed in the introduction of this book, the initiative of smart specialisation strategies (S3) which was launched in 2011 and made a part of cohesion policy in 2014 had a main focus on place-based learning. The implementation of this policy throughout 2014–2016 went through evaluations and analyses that were published in 2016–2017. The focus on interregional learning via thematic partnerships explained below is a result of this learning process. Here, the focus is on R&D that complements regional competitive advantages.

The European Commission suggests in a Communication (COM(2017)376) that Europe's competitive edge is increasingly dependent on its ability to facilitate new models of regional-level growth and target investments in strategic areas with significant growth potential and high added value. Furthermore, the Communication outlines four specific areas to be addressed: (1) further reform of the research and innovation systems within regions; (2) increase cooperation in innovation investments across regions; (3) leverage research and innovation in less developed and industrial transition regions; and (4) harness synergies and complementarities between various EU policies and instruments.

New and existing networks of transnational learning can help regions to tackle various obstacles linked to the implementation of S3s. In fact, earlier research suggests (Mariussen et al., 2016) that interregional learning can support the knowledge bases and S3s of regional innovation systems, enhancing the potential for upgrading products, improving participating regions' position in global value chains, and leading to new entrepreneurial discovery processes (EDPs). As a result, new paths of development could be created through transnational collaboration on policy tools, effectively leading to transnational joint strategies of innovation.

One driver behind transnational and inter-regional collaboration in the S3 context relates to an attempt to overcome the recognised *lack of public investment in research and innovation*, while aligning various S3 agendas through joint initiatives in order to overcome capability failures hindering innovation. Regions and countries working together to implement their smart specialisation strategies can combine complementary strengths, exploit their competences in research and innovation (R&I), acquire necessary research capacity, overcome lack of critical mass as well as fragmentation and access to global value chains.

The European Commission (COM(2017)376) suggests that linking innovation actors with relevant industrial stakeholders at the regional level and across the EU could help to explore complementarities in the development of products and process design. This is then expected to enable the creation of new EU-wide value chains by encouraging investment synergies between the private and public sector. Smart specialisation should be seen as 'a new and different way of working together, which ensures stronger local and regional participation in decision making, and whose potential can be scaled-up for the benefit of the EU's regions and the EU as a whole' (p. 11). This means coordination between EU cohesion policies (smart specialisation) and industrial policies promoting key enabling technologies (KETs).

Industrial policies

The Commission aims to support the modernisation of Europe's industry in order to ensure the EU's global competitiveness. This ambitious objective is now encouraged by a number of EC Directorates-General (DGs) through a focused alignment of their multi-level policies. These DGs are now aligning their efforts aiming to support new strategic growth areas including those linked to the development in a number of strategic, cross-cutting areas (COM(2012)341) such as key enabling technologies (KETs) including advanced manufacturing, clean vehicles and transport, bio-based products, construction and raw materials, and smart grids. These and other technologies are now recognised as the means to address important societal challenges, by facilitating new ways to new products and services and effectively leading to smart, sustainable and inclusive growth.

In its 2014 Communication *For a European Industrial Renaissance* (COM(2014)14), the EC recognises that fostering growth and competitiveness to sustain and strengthen recovery and to achieve the goals of the *Europe 2020* agenda have effectively become the top priority for the Commission and EU Member States. It is further acknowledged that Europe's mid- and long-term competitiveness is linked to the extent to which the European industries are able to take advantage of these new technical opportunities. To address this particular challenge, the EC encourages its Member States and regions to consider supporting potential spillover effects of KET-based solutions and, as a result, strengthen existing and possibly develop new European industrial value chains.

KETs and regional strategies

One way this could be done is through the integration of these technologies into national and regional RIS3 strategies. While generally KETs are technology- and research-intensive, various regions are able to participate in KET-related activities in different roles. The S3 framework, coupled with an increase in interregional connectivity, can give rise to cooperation in deployment, diffusion or even co-innovation of applications. Such dynamics may be distributed between regions specialised in basic inventions and regions investing in specific application domains.

In addition, the adoption of new digital technologies can result in increased productivity of European Industry. Various EU policy-makers agree that their transformative power and growing impact across all sectors can help redefine traditional business and production models while resulting in a range of new product and service innovations (also known as *servitisation of industry*).

The European Commission offers a list of additional actions that recognise the important role of industry for creating growth and jobs. These actions highlight the ambition to mainstream industrial competitiveness in other policy areas, use the existing instruments for regional development to support innovation, skills and entrepreneurship as well as facilitate the integration of EU firms in global value chains. The European Commission also commits to working towards implementing the instruments of regional development with national and EU instruments in support of innovation, skills, and entrepreneurship to deliver industrial change and boost the competitiveness of the EU economy. It urges its Member States and regions to encourage investment while doing more to facilitate the integration of EU firms in global value chains to boost their competitiveness and ensure access to global markets on more favourable competitive conditions.

This position was further strengthened by the Communication on *Digitising European Industry* (COM(2016)180), which promoted digital transformation and recognised key challenges such as funding, ICT standardisation, big data and skills. While the Communication further stresses the increasingly important role of the manufacturing industry in Europe, it points out that a new industrial revolution is in fact driven by new generations of technologies including digital technologies such as big data. Hence, advances in new technologies (such as the Internet of Things, 5G, cloud computing, data analytics and robotics) pave the way for new and transformed products, processes and business models in all sectors, ultimately creating new industrial patterns as global value chains shift.

Cohesion policies and thematic S3 platforms

Many of the strategic technology areas outlined by the Commission in the two Communication documents are closely intertwined with the areas of investment for the Cohesion Policy 2014–2020. The European Commission (COM(2011)614) invites Member States and regions to take these policy synergies into account in their industrial policies, as well as in their strategies for social cohesion and economic development of their regions. The EC further encourages regions to seek synergies between various EU instruments, including Horizon 2020 and the EU Structural and Investment Funds (ESIF).

In 2016, the European Commission launched three thematic platforms to support activities falling into the following areas: agri-food, energy, and industrial modernisation. The three platforms aim to support EU regions committed to co-invest in these new strategic growth areas. To align European initiatives, fragmented efforts would need to be connected with the thematic platforms and their regional partnerships, to facilitate the commercialisation and upscaling of interregional innovation projects and to incentivise joint business investment. And as such, the new thematic partnerships could then also be used to deepen cooperation between various types of regions including the less developed regions, regions in industrial transition and more advanced ones, to facilitate their industrial and technological transition. As of 2018, these thematic smart specialisation platforms have brought together over 100 regions working in over 25 interregional partnerships in a broad range of areas to foster innovation and business linkages along value chains in view of developing joint investments.

A good practice: European Spallation Source (ESS)

When it comes to the frontrunners, advantages of scale are sometimes crucial. The European Spallation Source (ESS) started as a project in the context of the Öresund region (Denmark and Sweden) aiming to create a critical, large-scale scientific infrastructure. Because of the scale of these investments, moving to the European level was an obvious choice. Today, a key European institution is developed in Skåne and Copenhagen under the European Research Infrastructure Consortium (ERIC) legal framework created by the Commission in 2009 to facilitate the joint establishment and operation of pan-European research infrastructures.

Here, Spain has an important position, both as a country with many industrial and academic users of these new instruments, and as a contributor to their construction.

Box 11.1 The European Spallation Source

Case: The European Spallation Source

The European Spallation Source (ESS) is a multi-disciplinary research facility being built in Skåne region, while its data management and software centre in Copenhagen. The facility is to be built to operate the world's most powerful neutron source, enabling scientific breakthroughs in material, energy, health and environment-related research. The need to build such a ground-breaking facility was defined 20 years ago.

As part of the design and development work, the ESS is collaborating with leading laboratories, institutes and research facilities within partner countries. Fifteen other European Member States, including Spain, and, at the regional level, the Basque Country, are participating with in-kind contributions. At the Monitoring Committee of the 2014–2020 Spanish Multiregional Operational Program that took place in May 2017, the proposal for 8.47 million euros out of the 55 million euros of total Spanish investment in the ESS until 2020 was accepted.

The project stands as a unique example for using funds outside of a specific programme area named above. An assessment has been made of the opportunities and benefits of such contribution and its effects on the regional economy. The contribution of Spain at national level and the Basque Country at regional level presents a clear case for the rationale of a joint investment that contributes to a European research project that joins strength and avoids fragmentation and duplication of efforts, along the basic principles of S3.

Source: Authors' own compilation

In this case there is a synergy between the Basque region and the ESS facility in Skåne, Sweden. Spain gives contributions in kind to the construction of the ESS, and several Spanish firms and institutions will get access to use the instruments in their product innovation processes.

Let us briefly summarise in a stylised form how this extension of the scope of entrepreneurial discoveries from regional domains and innovation ecologies into transnational innovation ecosystems of thematic partnerships may be understood. An innovation ecosystem is a network of institutions and actors that enables certain forms of innovation, because the actors involved share certain forms of knowledge, which makes up the domain of the ecosystem. Many regional innovation ecosystems are regarded as relatively stable through time. In looking at them from a dynamic perspective, we will focus on the relation between multi-level governance, learning and new knowledge creation through entrepreneurial discoveries in the process of aiming to reach their objectives of realising joint investment projects. The concept of a knowledge space refers to shared knowledge. As illustrated by the ESS example above, the 'space' of shared knowledge is not necessarily embedded in a single region.

11.3 Theoretical framework: knowledge, governance and institutionalisation

Knowledge is shared understanding between people with a common practice and the context where it can be applied. Virkkala refers to shared knowledge as knowledge spaces (see Virkkala, 2019, Chapter 8 in this book). Examples are communities of practice and expertise (such as engineers who share the knowledge of programming a 3D printing machine), or corporate, regional and cluster domains (shared knowledge which is the competitive advantage of a company, a region or a cluster).

Knowledge spaces may be integrated into overlapping or hybrid spaces (as in cross-disciplinary or cross-sector knowledge), or separated as specialised knowledge by borders (such as borders between disciplines, sectors and helices). Hybrid spaces enable more sophisticated processes of innovation, because they open up more knowledge combinations. A hybrid space may include different specialists sharing the knowledge of a wider field of practice. Borders between knowledge spaces may be closed or opened. The question is how borders between knowledge spaces can be opened up in order to create more hybrid knowledge spaces, where different forms of knowledge may be connected. This is particularly relevant in the context of thematic partnerships.

Knowledge may be connected and form knowledge spaces:

1 through organisational relations, such as inside a company or inside an organised network, a cluster, a regional partnership or a thematic network which creates mechanisms of knowledge transfer and knowledge sharing;
2 through various forms of dialogue which results in knowledge sharing, often taking place in a physical space, a seminar room, a factory floor, a classroom or through other forms of physical proximity. In the case of the ESS, a core physical meeting place is the laboratory in Skåne;
3 through transnational, professional or scientific communities of practice and expertise. One example is the ESS community which allows sharing the knowledge of how neutrons may be used to develop new products within material, energy, health and environment-related research and industrial testing.

These three ways of connecting knowledge may be territorially embedded, and create regional domains, or, as illustrated by the ESS, they may be independent of territory. We refer to these connections as relational knowledge spaces.

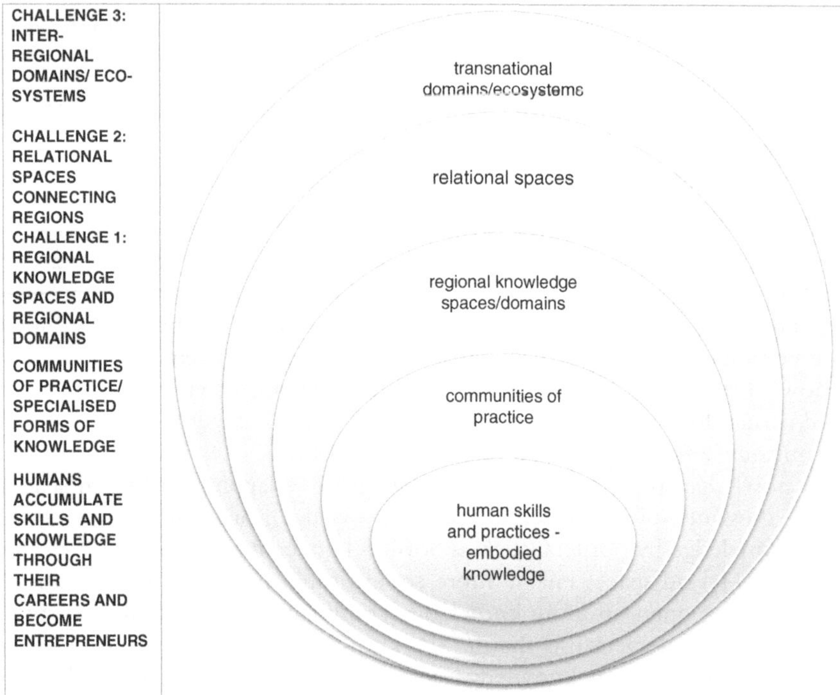

Figure 11.1 Fragmentation between knowledge spaces
Source: Authors' own compilation

We make a distinction between regional knowledge spaces, which provide regional domains, and relational space, which is the building block of transnational domains and innovation ecosystems. Below, we will see that transnational platforms represent closely linked regional knowledge spaces, through processes of scoping, mapping, and matchmaking, so as to ensure integration of new innovation ecosystems, combining regional and relational space.

The question of governance discussed below becomes: how do we combine regional knowledge with knowledge from the thematic platforms to create knowledge-enabling collaboration in wider transnational and macro-regional strategic frameworks leading to institutionalisation of knowledge and structures?

The crucial process is to be able to cross borders between knowledge spaces. A point of departure is human skills. In Chapter 5 of this book, Alice Lam (2019) explains the significance of mobility of humans across borders between knowledge spaces, such as moving between helices (university–industry careers), between sectors and between disciplines/professions. Stakeholders with expertise from different knowledge spaces grow unique 'third spaces', where borders may be crossed. Accordingly, under favourable institutional

Table 11.1 Challenges and examples of a solution

Challenges	*Knowledge spaces*	*Example*
Challenge 1: How to develop a stronger place-based regional innovation ecosystem	Regional knowledge space	The Basque government promotes collaboration between Basque agents and companies working on particle acceleration and neutron in cooperation with the ESS
Challenge 2: How to grow a larger, stronger and more dynamic regional innovation ecosystem by opening up	Relational knowledge space (thematic platform)	The transition from the Swedish–Danish ESS AB to the transnational ESS under the ERIC legal framework, created by the Commission
Challenge 3: How to create economic growth through innovation expanding across borders	Shared knowledge (hybrid third space)	Expected future EDP, combining ESS instruments and technologies, including emergence of new clusters and regional growth

Source: Authors' own compilation

conditions, they may be able to act as entrepreneurial 'translators' between different knowledge spaces, developing new ways of working together, based on new knowledge combinations feeding new ideas.

This ability to cross borders between knowledge spaces is important in the creation of hybrid regional and transnational domains which are able to integrate and connect thick layers of knowledge spaces, creating regional domains where different stakeholders are working closely together in producing complex products. Integration of these hybrid knowledge spaces may be seen as an outcome of a series of successful micro-level entrepreneurial achievements enabled by adequate forms of governance.

Discoveries of new combinations of knowledge are regularly made by entrepreneurs, skilled and active 'translators' operating in a third space. Through dialogue (see Chapter 7 in this book (Aasen, 2019)), these discoveries may emerge as new ideas. At first, these ideas might not yet be recognised as innovations but as potential solutions or possibilities. If they are supported by legitimacy, power, people or structures with authority, and adequate governance mechanisms are in place, they might become 'prototypes' which are tested in practice.

If a successful test is to be scaled up, its success is likely to provide a feedback learning loop. The relations in the innovation ecosystem which created it may be made stronger, deeper and more long-lasting.

The aforementioned Communication by the Commission on *Strengthening Innovation in Europe's Regions* (COM(2017)376) proposed the launch of a pilot action on further supporting innovation projects proposed by interregional partnerships to strengthen particularly commercialisation and scale-up activities and foster investments. The objectives of the pilot action are threefold – see Box 11.2.

The impact of a successful experiment might be institutionalisation of a new innovation ecology, kept together by hybrid knowledge spaces. Governing these processes depends on the right methods of scoping and mapping, on bringing the right stakeholders together, and on an adequate system of assessment that is able to identify achievements in reaching milestones, as well as signal failures that should be avoided or not be repeated.

Box 11.2 DG REGIO pilots

Case: DG REGIO pilots

This DG REGIO pilot builds on close collaboration between the European Commission, and associated Member States or regions on the basis of eight thematic partnerships involving policy-makers, researchers, businesses and other innovation actors. The pilot action builds on the work already undertaken under the thematic smart specialisation platforms and provides a more tailored approach to support concrete actions during the commercialisation and scale-up phase.

Thus the aim of this pilot project is to commercialise and scale up 'bankable' interregional projects in priority sectors such as big data, bio-economy, resource efficiency, connected mobility, health and active ageing or cybersecurity. ('Bankable projects' should be understood to mean fundable projects which could not be implemented without EU support. The term 'bankable projects' could be defined in the regulation as 'projects that secure financial balance through aid provided under European instruments'. (Source: https://eur-lex.europa.eu/legal-content/EN/TXT/?uri=CELEX%3A52010AE1188)

This pilot is also to test new approaches to interregional cooperation and provide the European Commission with evidence to feed into the reflection on smart specialisation after 2020.

Eight interregional partnerships are currently receiving this tailored support: four partnerships under the industrial modernisation platform, two partnerships under the agri-food platform, and two partnerships under the energy platform.

Source: Authors' own compilation

The leap from challenge 1 to challenge 2 and 3 means that the regional, place-based knowledge space is opened up for *relational transregional spaces.* A relational space (Virkkala, 2013: 62) is a knowledge space as defined above that does not depend on place-based regional proximity. It may still rely upon networks of organisations and transnational communities of expertise.

As demonstrated below, this involves consultations between partners, definitions of aims, and setting-up of relevant governance structures which, again, are built on multi-level governance, with institutional frameworks that enable stakeholders to come together and make entrepreneurial discoveries.

11.4 Connecting RIS3 and thematic S3 platforms

The existence of research and innovation strategies for smart specialisation (RIS3) is a legal precondition or *ex ante* conditionality for using the European Regional Development Fund (ERDF) in the funding period 2014–2020. Over 120 RIS3 strategies are currently being implemented. These have been designed following the same principles and methodology establishing national and/or regional priorities for research and innovation investment priorities. It is estimated that over 40 billion euros – that accounts for more than 65 billion euros with national co-financing – are allocated to regions and Member States through the European Regional Development Fund (ERDF) that will fund these priorities.

The S3 approach is characterised by the identification of strategic areas for intervention based both on the analysis of the strengths and potential of the economy and on a process of entrepreneurial discovery with wide stakeholder involvement. It embraces a wide view of innovation that goes beyond research-oriented and technology-based activities and requires a sound logic of intervention supported by effective monitoring mechanisms.

Many regions implement certain elements of their regional RIS3 strategies through the activities supported under the three thematic smart specialisation platforms. Many of these elements are carried out through interregional partnerships connecting regional knowledge spaces to realise joint investment projects. They support the development of European ecosystems of interregional collaboration linked to specific areas of S3, thus their joint efforts go beyond interregional learning, but build on it – and intend to realise joint investment projects.

The European Commission recognises how interregional collaboration contributes to reshape EU-wide value chains and contribute to a more effective innovation policy (COM(2017)376: 6).

The thematic S3 partnerships may be seen as an approach within this experiment. Each partnership starts with a definition of one or more S3 priority-related sub-areas offering all or most partner regions significant opportunities for regional investments. These interregional thematic partnerships represent joint transnational networks of knowledge and expertise that aim to develop and enhance global value chains in Europe.

The collaboration between participating actors promotes an understanding and provides a reflection on the competitive position of a region with regard to other regions' capabilities and gaps in specific sub-areas.

Since the launch of the three thematic platforms on agri-food (Ciampi Stancova and Cavicchi, 2017), energy (Gómez Prieto et al., 2017) and industrial modernisation (Hegyi and Rakhmatullin, 2018), a total of 26 qualified partnerships are now (as of July 2018) developing their activities in line with the workflow proposed by the European Commission. This high number of partnerships and participating regions confirms that there is a will and need of working together to align innovation roadmaps across European policies and territories. The learning of the thematic platforms is accordingly incorporated into the monitoring and evaluation activities of the S3 implementing bodies.

Connecting regional knowledge spaces through thematic partnerships

Figure 11.2 depicts how the steps of the RIS3 methodology feed into the workflow of thematic S3 partnerships. The thematic platforms guide the partnerships through a structure that generates the stream of bankable projects that follows a methodological workflow defined by the thematic platforms.

Generally, thematic S3 partnerships are linked to regional S3 priority areas (Figure 11.2, step 1) and their intention to translate a specific S3 area into concrete investment projects through connecting regional knowledge spaces. The scoping phase (Figure 11.2, step 1a) serves to elaborate on the thematic area for co-investment as well as to define the mission, vision, target markets and sub-themes of the partnership. It is then followed by a comprehensive mapping exercise (Figure 11.2, step 2) that identifies existing (or even missing) regional knowledge domains and competences of stakeholders in the participating regions. During matchmaking (Figure 11.2, step 2), potential business opportunities are examined to identify concrete areas for investment projects, effectively connecting relational spaces across regions. Business actors are then to support the regional authorities in their efforts to develop a business plan and explore funding opportunities for financing their projects (Figure 11.2, step 3), while identifying synergies among various funding sources. Finally, the investment projects (Figure 11.2, step 4) phase is about facilitating discussions with private investment organisations and final preparatory steps, including any refinements of investment projects and submissions for financial support.

This process can and should potentially feed crucial information and data back to each region's S3 monitoring and evaluation framework (built as part of RIS3). Being proactively involved in a thematic S3 partnership allows regional authorities to gather various empirical information about any weak or missing competences (in terms of research and innovation capacities and capabilities), available facilities, skills or business networks linked to a specific thematic sub-area, verifying or checking the feasibility of S3 priorities identified during the RIS3 design phase.

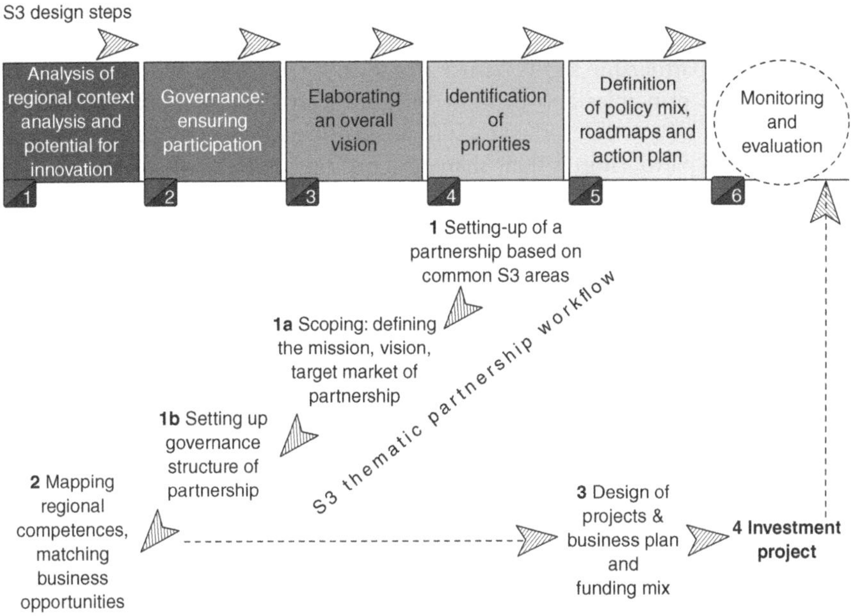

Figure 11.2 How the results of the thematic S3 platforms feed back into RIS3

Source: Authors' own compilation

Governance principles

A key aspect of S3 is linked to putting in place a tailor-made governance structure to facilitate RIS3 implementation including the development of a sound monitoring and evaluation framework. The governance structure shall reflect the applicable regional context. It refers to the design and implementation (and review) of the RIS3 process, defining who is involved and the structures that are in place. As stated in the RIS3 implementation guide (Gianelle et al., 2016: 37), a central challenge during the implementation of smart specialisation strategies is being able to follow a structured process that involves a broad range of actors.

Using the term governance recognises that effective strategies are not implemented exclusively by national or regional authorities; rather, executive power is shared with innovation actors, networks and indeed civil society more widely.

The seven principles of good RIS3 governance can be easily translated to the context of interregional thematic partnerships (Gianelle et al., 2016):

- leadership and participation;
- cohesion to implement a collective vision;
- independence and transparency;
- integrated implementation;
- embedding S3 in regional policy-making;

- multi-level governance; and
- reflection and learning.

Setting up a partnership's governance structure is part of the scoping phase. In line with the principles above, most thematic partnerships are led by one or several regions (1), while other regions are participating partners. The starting point of each partnership is their shared S3 priority area (5), within which they define the mission and the vision of the partnership in reference to the second principle on collective vision (2). The governance structure of each partnership is an agreed structure among partners of the partnership (3) with the aim to facilitate the realisation of joint investment projects linked to their thematic area of RIS3 (4). Furthermore, thematic partnerships work along the alignment and cooperation of innovation actors, competences and investments to generate and facilitate the flow of investment projects. The multi-level governance (6) is present on various levels. Within each partnership, there are partnership-level governance mechanisms set up; furthermore, specific sub-themes have their own governance structures with their leaders.

Box 11.3 Textile innovation partnership

Case: Textile innovation partnership

The thematic S3 partnership on textile innovation is building on a sectoral transregional, bottom–up initiative from regional stakeholders to leverage textile innovation through collaboration. The RegioTex initiative has the support from regional authorities and stakeholders to address common challenges and to facilitate an open and collaborative innovation environment between regional textile and clothing industry clusters and other stakeholders across Europe. The objective of the initiative is to concentrate innovation efforts and resources into knowledge, technology or market domains in which participating regions and actors have comparative advantages and market opportunities. Building on the previous work of RegioTex, all participating regions of the initiatives agreed to join the Smart Specialisation Platform on Industrial Modernisation at its official launch in June 2016, and since then have been actively contributing to the learning process at platform level.

Objectives addressed by the partnership require collaboration and a European-wide perspective to enable to sector to reinvent itself. According to the recent press release by the partnership, the sector is regaining a leading position in the EU industrial landscape and is experiencing an impressive industrial renaissance through investments into modern manufacturing and service facilities and technologies that are creating safer and higher-added-value European jobs.

To achieve these, challenges of the sector have to be addressed jointly, resulting in joint textile innovation infrastructures, better industrial innovation performance, stronger industrial investments, enhanced job creation and an overall repositioning of the sector through which young talents can be attracted. Figure 11.3 presents the objectives of the S3 partnership on textile innovation, reflecting the challenges of the market.

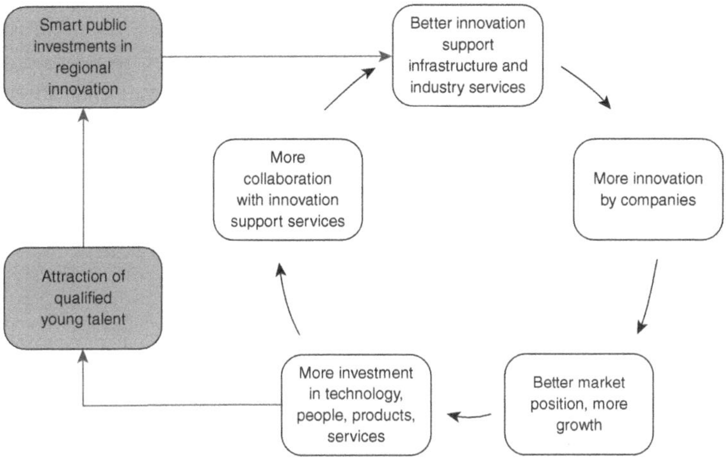

Figure 11.3 Objectives of S3 partnership on textile innovation

Source: European Textile Platform (www.textile-platform.eu/regiotex-regional-investment/)

The governance structure of the textile innovation partnership allows formal commitment from regional governments as active participants and as observers. As of 2018, the share of the partner and observer regions in the general employment in the textile and clothing sector constitutes 28 per cent of employment in the textile industry and 23 per cent in clothing, formulating the partnership as an important player in the modernisation of the sector in Europe.

The governance structure allows each active partner to delegate one high-level regional policy representative to the high-level group, which provides the strategic direction and political backing of the overall initiative and approves the operational action plans and strategic projects. The support group is made up of three to four operational sectoral experts from all active participant regions and observer regions. The support group is – among other things – responsible for mapping stakeholders, and for preparing and implementing operational action plans and projects. The strategic projects are inspired by regional, national, and European sectoral strategies, defined by regional sectoral experts and led by active regions, thereby contributing to a continuous engagement and dialogue between key stakeholders. (For further information, please visit partnership page: http://s3platform.jrc.ec.europa.eu/textile-innovation.)

Source: Authors' own compilation

As part of the multi-level governance, a steering committee is set up to govern and monitor the progress of the thematic platforms. In the steering committee, lead regions represent partnerships. The objective of the steering committee is to ensure the efficient functioning of the thematic initiatives and to monitor the implementation of the platforms' activities, to resolve potential issues and provide strategic guidance. The S3P – Industrial Modernisation, for example, is governed by over 20 lead regions representing 16 qualified partnerships and four Directorates of the European Commission, namely DG Internal Market, Industry, Entrepreneurship and SMEs (DG GROW), Regional Policy (DG REGIO), Research and Innovation (DG RTD) and Joint Research Centre (JRC).

The thematic partnerships show different structures, given that they all have to reflect specificities of their thematic area. This is explained below.

A stronger place-based regional innovation ecosystem through improved internal connectivity (challenge 1)

The workflow step of scoping the thematic platforms requires various activities that support connecting and reconnecting actors of the innovation ecosystem. In the phase of setting up a partnership (for further information on the partnership, please visit the partnership page: http://s3platform.jrc.ec.europa.eu/photonics), regions having an interest in jointly investing in an area submit an expression of interest form. To qualify as a partnership, regions participating have to confirm a number of key elements that require a vision on how regional actors with specific knowledge domains would join and contribute to the development of new value chains. The following example is the expression of interest of setting up a partnership in the field of photonics:

S3 Photonics partnership

Europe in general, and in particular the Netherlands, has invested both academically and commercially in the field of integrated photonics (e.g. TriPleX™ technology and Indium Phosphide (InP) technology). The basis of the investment thesis to date was to establish platform technologies that may enable economies of scale in photonics. The leader of the partnership is a cluster organisation, PhotonDelta, responsible for building a global 'end-to-end ecosystem' of researchers, chip designers, foundries, corporates, investors and software/hardware developers. The initiative has been founded to accelerate the growing international business demand for photonics technologies. It is an open, collaborative network of trusted partners. Through the partnership, the participants wish to address the challenges to determine the supply chains for key product domains and to identify the unique capabilities and the weak spots in the clusters related to market potential. All participants in the partnership have business clusters and/or civil society organisations as part of their organisation, and since the partnership qualified in September 2017, there is a growing interest for participating across the EU, and thus, the partnership is expanding greatly.

The qualification of a partnership is followed by the scoping phase (Figure 11.2, step 1), which is elaborated in a scoping note that serves the purpose to elaborate on the thematic area for co-investment: on its mission, vision and target markets. The scoping exercise is based on a general understanding of the sector or domain, including main processes, challenges and value chains followed by the analysis of interest and objectives of lead regions, looking at strategic documents that provide information on actual and future activities in the field. The analysis of strategic documents – which shall be grounded on thorough analysis of strength and potentials and entrepreneurial discovery processes – results in the identification of preliminary project ideas. Gathering all this information, furthermore executing the interviews and surveys with stakeholders, provides a strong basis for intra-regional learning. Figure 11.4 provides an overview of the scoping process and an overview of the sources of analysis to be performed.

Further potential interested regions can be identified based on the preliminary project ideas along the analysis of smart specialisation priority areas. The preliminary and refined project ideas are to be validated in the course of later activities after having performed qualitative and quantitative analysis and mapping activities.

Thus, the scoping exercise aims to identify the opportunities and challenges in the targeted domains or value chains and is expected to result in the definition of sub-themes in which the partnerships wish to pursue further work and investment. Figure 11.5 shows the pilot areas defined by the partnerships in the scoping phase for the partnership under the S3P – Industrial Modernisation.

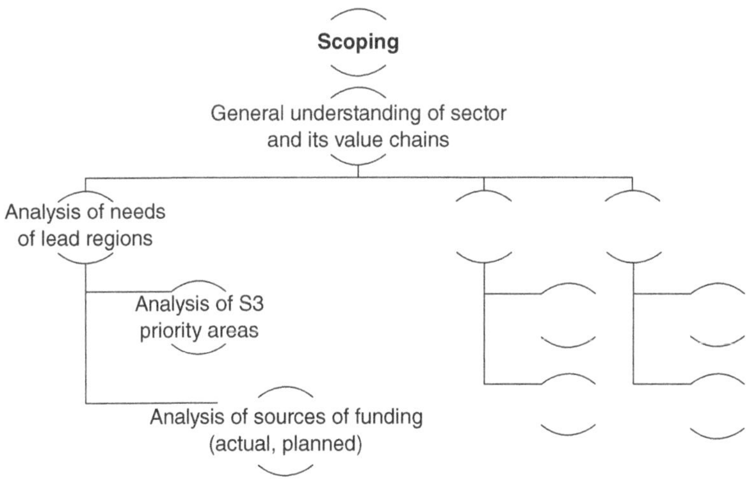

Figure 11.4 Scoping exercise of thematic S3 partnerships

Source: Authors' own compilation

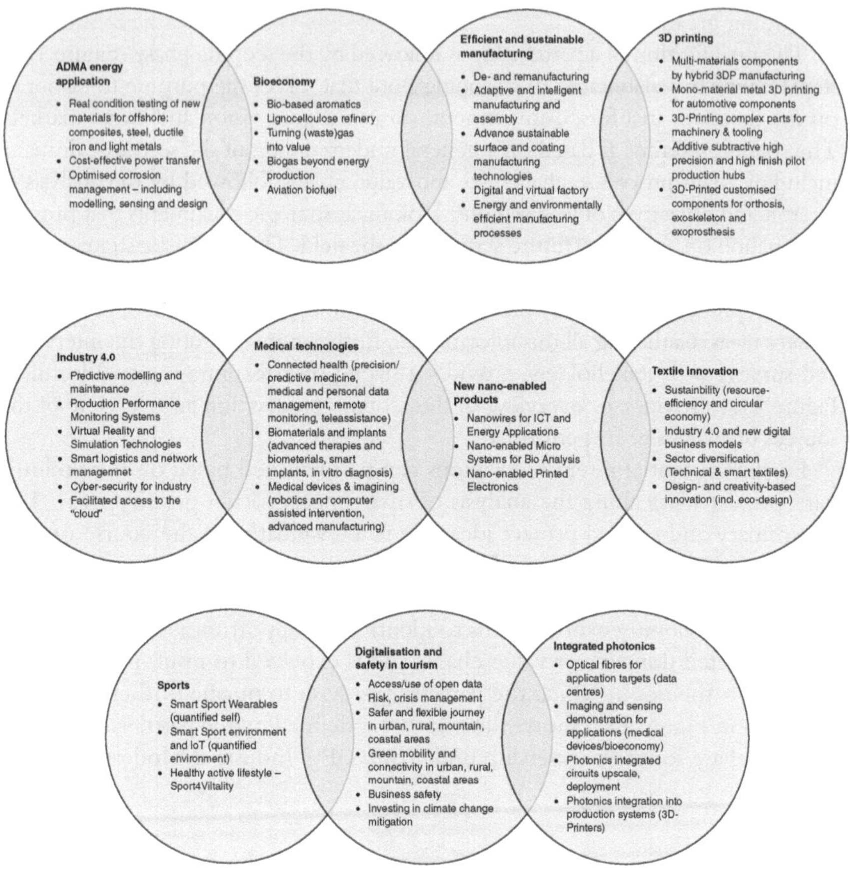

Figure 11.5 Pilot areas of S3 partnerships

Source: Authors' own compilation

As the partnerships advance along the defined workflow process, specific sub-themes in which they intend to realise joint investment projects are becoming increasingly more defined. This definition is a result of comprehensive analysis of specific markets and its trends, followed by mapping of stakeholder capabilities and competency gaps.

A more dynamic regional innovation ecosystem through connecting to knowledge networks and systems of innovation: mapping (challenge 2)

One novelty linked to the concept of smart specialisation is the so-called 'outward-looking dimension'. This requirement invites regions to explore potential synergies with other regions across the European Union. As discussed earlier, the first part of the scoping phase is effectively an assessment of the existing regional assets, which is about 'looking inside the region'. However, many thematic S3 partnerships require strategic decisions taking into account the region's relative position to other regions, thus looking beyond regional boundaries. Through this, regions' competitive advantages may be identified through systematic comparison with other regions. Furthermore, a region has to be able to identify relevant linkages and flows of goods and services and knowledge, as well as the position of regional businesses within international value chains – that is, links between regional knowledge spaces.

Along the sub-themes defined, thematic S3 partnerships map existing and missing competences in each region in terms of research and innovation capacities, infrastructure, skills and businesses. In this exercise, it is very important to involve local stakeholders to explore the business opportunities and to explore concrete areas of investment. This phase involves a great amount of learning of regional assets and building and strengthening of regional networks and the ecosystem as a whole. The result of the exercise is a collection of data that provides valuable information for S3 implementing bodies and that should lead to institutionalisation of relational spaces. The mapping exercise shall provide information about business and research actors of the field present in the region, also providing information regarding which part of the value chain they operate in, their strengths and collaborations.

Mapping actors strongly builds on the analysis performed as regards the sector/area. Figure 11.6 depicts examples of data that may be gathered from stakeholders in the mapping exercise.

These mapping phases shall be followed by workshops and in-depth interviews with regional stakeholders and/or surveys conducted within regions.

Mapping actors of the High-Performance Production through 3D Printing partnership[1]

This thematic area deals with the implementation of synergies in new 3DP value chains across regions based on smart specialisation priorities defined by the regions. The key objective of the partnership is to identify opportunities for joint demonstration between participating regions, based on a solid mapping exercise and on the defined complementarities between existing demonstration facilities and company needs. The partnership is a Vanguard Initiative Pilot Project that targets the accelerated deployment of new 3DP applications. As a result of this mapping exercise, a total of over 1,300 actors and their

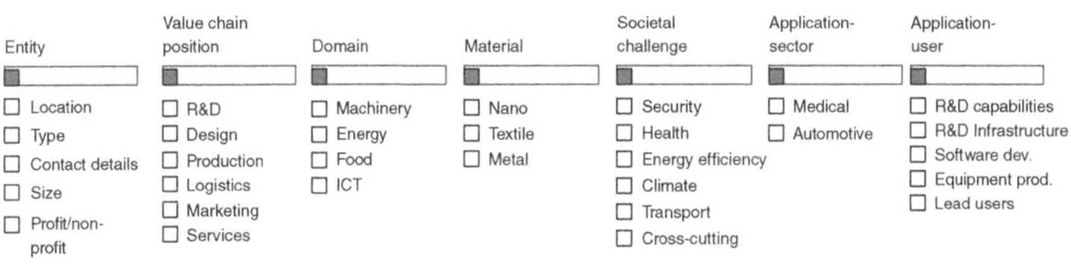

Figure 11.6 Mapping exercise by thematic S3 partnerships

Source: Authors' own compilation

competences have been identified and mapped. Furthermore, this mapping exercise identified over 800 relevant companies. Finally, participating regions have also mapped their existing training capabilities across all participating regions. As a result, partner regions are currently developing an integrated training course (Additive Manufacturing Technologies) that would provide regional actors with any key but currently missing competences.

During the mapping phase, partner regions work together to identify opportunities for joint demonstration based on a mapping exercise and detected complementarities between existing demonstration facilities and company needs. Subsequently, an analysis of the mapping results allows identifying first 'matches' and areas for potential cross-regional, joint demonstration. Further analysis of these areas (through bilateral and multilateral contacts with regional experts and discussion during plenary meetings) generally leads to the identification of a number of cases for cross-regional joint demonstration.

Box 11.4 High-technology farming mapping methodology

Case: High-technology farming mapping methodology

Partner regions carried out an initial mapping exercise via an extensive survey among regions. Generally, the use of mapping and consequent interviews with actors has provided partner regions with new insights on the needs from different sectors and technology segments. The survey-based mapping activity was a good starting point for a broad involvement of different stakeholders from the business sector.

In case of the High-Technology Farming Partnership, it was decided to pilot a new mapping approach by using comprehensive databases of firms representing specific industry value chains. Using such comprehensive databases with the firm-level data is not just a critical tool for identifying any relevant business actors across partner regions (to be involved in various matchmaking activities during the 'connect' phase) but also an essential step towards scaling up from single demonstration projects to integrated capabilities and global competitive advantage in emerging industries. While the piloted mapping method is quite complex, it allowed mapping strategic concentrations of capabilities and areas of firm specialisation and diversification across sectors. The mapping exercise showed how farming companies vary across different farming value chains, and that many technology companies based in partner regions deliver multi-sectoral technology solutions. Furthermore, this additional exercise allowed identifying cross-regional value chain segments that contain firms that have diversified across both – farming and technology activities.

Source: Authors' own compilation

In some emerging thematic areas, involving the right regional business actors requires more global value chains (GVC) insights and a comprehensive understanding of the concentration of capabilities across partner regions and clusters. Furthermore, it requires understanding any backward and forward linkages that are taking place across sectors and between core and periphery actors, and the distribution of these capabilities across SMEs, medium and large firms.

Yet, the regional diversity among partners is substantial – both in terms of concentration of firms in value chain segments and the diversification across segments. The diversity across regions is a result of a number of factors including the structure of regional economies, firms' reporting requirements, and the selection of strategic priorities in farming.

By applying this approach to as many European regions as possible, the comparative advantage of the emerging industrial niche in partner regions can be assessed. The results of this analysis can help regional authorities assess their degree of participation in the industry value chain in order to establish those locations that serve as its main sources of inputs and destinations of its outputs. At the same time, the analysis can reveal where along the value chain the industry is positioned and the extent of that positioning. Thus the analysis points to opportunities for maintaining, extending and deepening the region's positioning on the global value chain (GVC). By applying a similar analysis to as many European regions as possible, a partnership can ascertain who occupies significant parts of the industry value chain, and how strong their positions are and whether those clusters of GVC activities in these other competing regions/countries are similar/complementary to their own activities. Taking account of the identified linkages, this can indicate whether there might be opportunities to capitalise on complementarities in other locations and the development of interregional/ trans-European linkages.

The results of the mapping activity shall be reviewed regularly as markets are changing. For example, the photonics product lifecycle has dropped from 20 years to approximately five years, which has to be reflected in the strategic documents. In case of an existence of a sound monitoring and evaluation system, the strategic management tool of RIS3 monitoring signals in time the need to review RIS3 strategy. Reality-checked/reviewed RIS3 priorities allow the identification of complementing research and innovation activities that combine complementary strengths, the exploitation of R&I competences, acquisition of missing research capacity from other regions, overcoming lack of critical mass as well as fragmentation, which lead to strengthening of European part of value chains.

Innovation expanding across borders (challenge 3)

As a recent paper on transnational cooperation and value chains (Mariussen et al., 2016: 17) states, 'the next technological revolution will depend upon multiple innovations across many industrial areas linked to emerging value chains with several technological components, joined in new ways'. Thematic S3 partnerships have the capacity to provide these by driving firm-level competitive advantage through integrating global and local competitive and comparative advantages (firm- and location-specific advantages).

Once the results of the mapping exercise are ready, partner regions can move on to the next step, which is about matching complementary innovation activities while starting to define specific investment projects. Here, matching of business opportunities is effectively an analysis of complementarities and challenges as well as mobilisation of entrepreneurial actors.

Matchmaking events

Having a solid interregional governance structure generally facilitates further experimental work as part of the actual projects. Here, communities of practice and expertise provide a shared knowledge space between experts, across borders between regions and countries. These emerging knowledge spaces are facilitated through matchmaking events, as illustrated above.

The matchmaking events of the partnerships are organised at the sub-theme level with the objective to define concrete business cases at the end of each matchmaking exercise.[2]

Box 11.5 High-Performance Production through 3D Printing Partnership

Business cases identified in the matching phase of the High-Performance Production through 3D Printing Partnership

Building on the mapping activity performed by the partnership, in total close to 30 business cases have been identified under the sub-themes of the partnership. Most of the business cases are related to the sub-themes on '3D printed hybrid components' and the 'additive-subtractive pilot lines'. Taking the example of the latter sub-theme, the main aim of this platform is to offer companies – including SMEs – easy access to fully integrated additive and subtractive technology production flows. Up to date, 20 concrete user cases from industrial companies in seven participating regions have been identified. The business cases cover a wide range of sectors, such as aerospace, automotive, machinery and tooling, packaging, and electronic equipment.

For further information, please see partnership page: http://s3platform.jrc.ec.europa.eu/high-performance-production-through-3d-printing

Source: Authors' own compilation

Matchmaking events have been organised to address specific challenges of partnerships:

- Digitalisation in fashion for European SMEs, organised to support the textile innovation partnership;[3]
- Application of advanced technologies in tourism and sports, organised to support the matching phase of the sports and digitalisation and safety of tourism partnerships;[4]
- Challenges connected to the commercialisation of nanowire technology, organised to support the new nano-enabled products partnership;[5]
- 'Block chain in Tourism' conference will bring together new and emerging technologies, and business models to respond to the key shifts that will occur soon in the online tourism industry to support the Safety and Digitalisation in Tourism Partnership;[6]
- 3D medical event to support the Medical Technologies Partnership;[7]
- Bio-aromatics to support the Bio-economy Partnership;[8]
- 3D printing to support the 3D Printing Partnership;[9]
- Photonics to support the Photonics Partnership;[10]
- Industry 4.0 and human-robotics cooperation to support the Industry 4.0 Partnership.[11]

11.5 Examples of transnational governance

A good governance structure should involve relevant actors and stakeholders representing regional or national governments and cluster or other intermediary organisations. The actual project implementation takes place through pilots and business cases which are to be managed by firms and other actors.

As illustrated in Figure 11.7, positions of the stakeholders might shift. In the case of textiles, the thematic platform experts are located as a support group between a 'high-level group' with regional representatives and an operational strategic project level inside the regions. In the case of photonics, the EU Commission is placed at the top, with two industrial steering committees, one with responsibility for volume producers, and one with service providers. This indicates that there are two knowledge spaces, with a bridge between them, which is the value chain between service/software providers and producers of printed 3D products. Producers running 3D machines are likely to have in-depth knowledge of their users, such as the need for new parts among manufacturers of expensive and fast cars, or hospitals needing new body parts. Service providers are software developers making machine-specific tools with broader sets of application. Projects are inside the countries.

The Photonics Partnership shows a different structure with two distinct committees: one on application readiness and the other on volume manufacturing competency.

Box 11.6 Photonics Partnership

Case: Governance structure of the Photonics Partnership

The partnership has set up two steering committees made up of partners proposed by partnership members. The two committees are to steer the network and their projects.

Source: Authors' own compilation

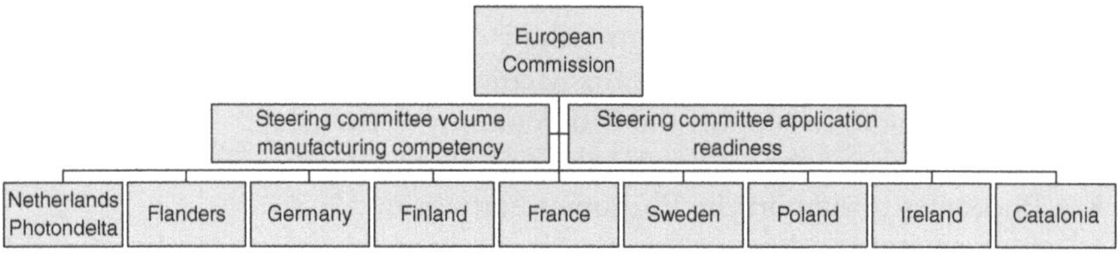

Figure 11.7 Governance structure of the Photonics Partnership

Source: Scoping note of the partnership

Various forms of governance structures have been agreed in the existing thematic S3 partnerships. Importantly, many of these guarantee and pursue an ongoing contact with relevant S3 implementing bodies, provide feedback on their activities, and, thus, contribute to the monitoring and evaluation of various aspects of RIS3 implementation.

As markets are changing, monitoring and evaluation activities shall reflect if the priorities and the policy instruments defined in the strategies are still appropriate to reach the objectives of smart specialisation – that is, to confirm if the strategies are built on competitive advantages that develop and match research and innovation strengths and business needs while intending to identify new and emerging market opportunities and simultaneously trying to avoid duplication and fragmentation of efforts.

Box 11.7 Network management of Traceability and Big Data Partnership

Case study: Network management of Traceability and Big Data Partnership

The Traceability and Big Data (TBD) thematic partnership focuses on the creation of an ecosystem to support innovation and digitisation of the agri-food sector in Europe. The partnership is working towards setting up a successful framework towards digitisation of agri-food value chain using digital technologies and, additionally, to generate value out of data and bring more efficiency, a better balance and transparency to agri-food value chains.

The TBD Partnership is led by Andalusia (ES) and Emilia-Romagna (IT). As of July 2018, regional authorities from a total of 20 European regions have committed to working together towards smart specialisation investments in joint demonstration projects to increase public and private funding in this area by promoting new interregional agri-food value chains. The activities supported by the partnership involve all triple-helix actors, including regional governments, knowledge centres and private companies from both the agri-food and technological sectors in each region, in line with the objectives of the RIS3 strategies of participating regions.

Regions involved in the TBD Partnership have built a solid action plan that incorporates a governance and management framework, a code of conduct as well as a framework of governing principles of the interregional ecosystem. These principles cover strategic vision, open and inclusive approach, transparency, trust and loyalty, outcome-focused, mutual respect, equality-focused, reliability and responsibility, and participatory methodology.

The current governance and management (G&M) framework was formally approved by member regions on 2 June 2017. The G&M architecture allows for different levels for decision-making and monitoring of partnership strategy and results. It is sufficiently versatile in that it defines key functions to be performed and important objectives to be pursued at different levels, yet without going into an exhaustive description of functions and tasks. The framework outlines the relationship between all members while facilitating a more flexible implementation of tasks and a delivery of consistently high-quality results.

Source: Authors' own compilation

While the development of a solid governance model required significant efforts during the early stages of this partnership, participating regions can progress faster while helping all members improve accountability, manage risks and rationalise their working arrangements. Furthermore, well-defined governing principles have proved particularly useful for any new member regions considering joining the partnership.

11.6 Summary discussion and a case of institutionalisation

First, what are the multi-level governance mechanisms applied by the Commission, regions, industrial actors and other stakeholders for integrating regional S3 partnerships and transnational networks in ways which enable entrepreneurial discovery processes?

Table 11.2 Organising partnerships: structure of ecosystem and role of regions

Partnership	*Role of regions*	*Structure of ecosystem*
ESS	Basque regional and national coordination	Centralised and open to members Institutionalised framework provided by the Commission (ERIC) for building and managing the R&D infrastructure centre, including states and regions as partners
Photonics	Cluster organisation as leader	Large investments in platform technologies, an 'end-to-end' diversified ecosystem, with an institutionalised mechanism for knowledge sharing (a knowledge commons)
Textile, food	Strong role for regions	Co-creation of joint innovation infrastructure. Open and distributed knowledge, with universities as core knowledge providers and a wide variety of firms and clusters joining regions with strong economic and scientific potential in the sector

Source: Authors' own compilation

There is a wide variety in forms of organisation that to a large extent reflects differences between technologies and the structures of innovation ecosystems, with an impact on the position of key stakeholders, such as clusters and regions.

The organisation of partnerships was a bottom–up process, where different stakeholders were included. The organisational maps presented above indicate the power and legitimacy of the core stakeholders in these new, hybrid forms of regional and transnational networks of learning.

The organisational maps shown above may also be seen as institutionalisation of a series of transregional physical meetings. Here, key stakeholders with core positions in supporting institutions meet to exchange information and generate a common understanding of achievements and challenges. The analysis, monitoring and governance described above feed information into these meeting places and provide a common platform for dialogues, and the emerging transnational relational knowledge space. At this level, learning also means feedback learning loops into decisions of adjustments and corrections of strategies. These groups may also be seen as a strategy of connecting the partnership with key external stakeholders, such as industrial actors and governments, with a potential capacity to provide future resources and legitimacy to make decisions regarding the ongoing pilot experiments.

Not surprisingly, the balance between the relational knowledge spaces of the industrial networks and the regions varies considerably between different technologies. For example, regions have a core position in textiles and agricultural networks, and they are not as visible in other partnerships, such as photonics. This is not surprising. Textiles and agriculture traditionally have deep roots in regional knowledge spaces and innovation ecologies as well as firm positions in regional domains. Domains such as photonics and 3D printing are early, emerging components of what might become a new technological paradigm. In this early phase, the value chain is only rudimentary, the innovation system is open and experimental, and there is a lot of knowledge sharing. Products are expensive. One might expect that this kind of relational industrial network will discover the need for regional embedding if or when their technologies start to become more cost-efficient. If so, they are likely to start growing and diffusing further into new markets. At that point, embedding in a regional domain might become more relevant.

There are important synergies and differences between clusters and regional smart specialisation institutions. Clusters may often be controlled by their core stakeholders, firms and other relevant institutions and helices, and their day-to-day needs. Particularly small and medium-sized firms in agriculture (SMEs) easily get caught in short-term considerations and exploitation of existing technologies, instead of exploration for new opportunities. They may be hard to involve, and methods of consultation and co-creation seem to be relevant.

Regions with smart specialisation strategies have the capacity to look across clusters and sectors and discover problems that can only be solved through long-term strategies. This might sometimes be a hard sell to SMEs. The planning horizon is different, and expectations are sometimes hard to align. By connecting regions and clusters in the context of a thematic partnership which aims to strengthen the cluster, some of these issues may be overcome. First, the thematic partnership may have the potential to give the cluster a stronger voice inside the region. Second, the partnership may add more depth and flexibility to the strategy, through wider networks of learning as well as through experimental pilots, which connects more knowledge and makes the space more hybrid.

How can new potential networks of innovation business opportunities be identified and validated through an analysis that includes and matches regional domains and the emerging domains of transregional networks?

So far, the provided tools of transnational governance build on the methods of scoping, mapping, discussions (consultation) and matchmaking described above. In doing this, the S3 platform has been able to use and build on the extensive analysis undertaken during the development of the regional S3 strategies in a systematic way. This effort is now providing a platform for monitoring, evaluation and learning from the ongoing transnational experiments.

Third, how can the outcomes of these experiments be institutionalised?

One of the findings presented in this chapter is a new way of co-managing knowledge commons. This chapter also presents an ongoing attempt to trigger industrialisation projects, through pilots, with a potential to result in institutionalisation.

Box 11.8 Photonics Partnership's innovation model

Case study: Photonics Partnership's innovation model

The Photonics Enabled Products Partnership, led by PhotonDelta, is recognised as one of Europe's leading innovation hubs linking research and development to business practices. PhotonDelta is an initiative of Eindhoven University of Technology and strongly supported by the Province of Noord Brabant and Brainport Development. Their main mission is to amplify initiatives between industry, research institutes and governments and through the thematic S3 partnership to amplify it at European level. Through the partnership, a shared vision can be agreed upon to identify the crucial technologies and make the necessary strategic investments to reach the potential offered by photonics.

> Being a member of the PhotonDelta cooperative gives you fast-track access to relevant IP before that intellectual property is published. That's a clear strategic advantage you can't achieve alone.
>
> (Dr Anna Nikiel, PhotonDelta)

To facilitate a faster process of collaborating, the partners offer an initiative to co-manage knowledge commons. To leverage knowledge and practical experience financed from public funds and to accelerate technology transfer, PhotonDelta has created the first secure IP cloud, in which research results are accessible for members before publication, thereby contributing to building strong competitive advantages for the community. It grants access to relevant IP before IP is published to provide SMEs a clear strategic advantage that they could have not achieved alone, but only through collaboration. The IP cloud of PhotonDelta also offers companies the opportunities to post anonymous calls for technology solutions and expertise in a secure network.

The fast-track PhotonDelta innovation model replaces the classical technology transfer process, which takes years, with a model that evaluates ideas, discusses with academics and prepares the bid within two months, followed by a one-week period of evaluation.

The partnership believes that the photonics community needs to understand the impact of a new European unitary patent system that allows European photonics SMEs to receive technology licences, to simplify administration and to have a cheaper access of validating patents. Because of the complex nature of these nano-technologies, Europe needs an interregional collaborative approach if it wants to scale up Photonics companies. The partners want to

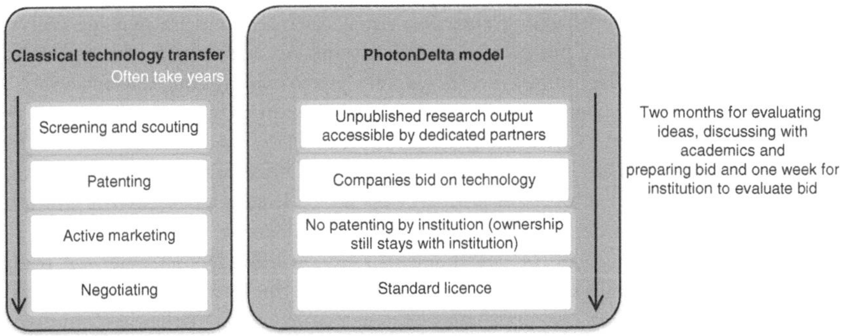

Figure 11.8 PhotonDelta innovation model

Source: PhotonDelta website, https://photondelta.innogetcloud.com

maintain their lead in the development of photonic integrated chips. Scaling up to volume-manufacture of chips and products is important for a financially, socially and environmentally sustainable industry. Given the product lifecycle in photonics, which has dropped from 20 years to approximately five years, SMEs need an independent, trusted, 'hands-on help' to accelerate their time to market that is supported by the co-management of knowledge commons.

Notes

1 For further information, please see partnership page: http://s3platform.jrc.ec.europa.eu/high-performance-production-through-3d-printing
2 Matchmaking events have been organised in the frame of the Watify, which is an awareness-raising campaign funded by the European Commission to support the EU efforts to stimulate the modernisation of Europe's industry.
3 https://watify-bologna.b2match.io
4 Please see further information about the event here: https://watify-rovaniemi.b2match.io
5 Please see further information about the event here: https://watify-lund.b2match.io
6 Please see further information about the event here: http://www.blockchain-tourism.com
7 Please see further information about the event here: https://3dmedicalconference.com
8 Please see further information about the event here: https://watify-antwerp.b2match.io
9 Please see further information about the event here: https://ec.europa.eu/growth/tools-databases/dem/watify/connecting/watify-events/3-d-printing-vanguard-watify-matchmaking-event
10 Please see further information about the objectives of the event here: https://watify-florence.b2match.io
11 Please see further information about the objectives of the event here: https://watify-industry-4-0.b2match.io

References

Aasen, T.M. (2019). Approaching entrepreneurial discovery and knowledge conversion from a complexity perspective. In Mariussen, Å., Virkkala, S., Finne, H. and Aasen, T.M. (eds) *The entrepreneurial discovery process and regional development: New knowledge emergence, conversion and exploitation*. Abingdon: Routledge.

Ciampi Stancova, K. and Cavicchi, A. (2017). *Dynamics of smart specialisation agri-food trans-regional cooperation*. Luxembourg: Publications Office of the European Union.

COM(2011)614 (2012). Cohesion policy 2014–2020: Investing in growth and jobs. *COM*. Brussels: Commission of the European Communities.

COM(2012)341 (2012). A European strategy for key enabling technologies – A bridge to growth and jobs. *COM*. Brussels: Commission of the European Communities.

COM(2014)14 (2014). For a European industrial renaissance. *COM*. Brussels: Commission of the European Communities.

COM(2016)180 (2016). Digitising European industry reaping the full benefits of a digital single market. *COM*. Brussels: Commission of the European Communities.

COM(2017)376 (2017). Strengthening innovation in Europe's regions: Strategies for resilient, inclusive and sustainable growth. *COM*. Brussels: Commission of the European Communities.

Foray, D. (2015). *Smart specialisation: Opportunities and challenges for regional innovation policy*. London: Routledge.

Gianelle, C., Kyriakou, D., Cohen, C. and Przeor, M. (eds) (2016). *Implementing smart specialisation: A handbook*. Brussels: European Commission.

Gómez Prieto, J., Periañez-Forte, I. and Martinez, M.P. (2017). *Capitalising on smart specialisation and Interreg, the case of energy: An overview of synergies between two instruments of the EU Cohesion Policy*. JRC Technical Reports. Sevilla: EC-JRC.

Hegyi, F.B. and Rakhmatullin, R. (2017). *Implementing smart specialisation: Thematic Platform on Industrial Modernisation*. Luxembourg: European Commission.

Lam, A. (2019). Career mobility, hybridity and knowledge combination: A 'third space' perspective. In Mariussen, Å., Virkkala, S., Finne, H. (eds) *The entrepreneurial discovery process and regional development: New knowledge emergence, conversion and exploitation*. Abingdon: Routledge.

Mariussen, Å., Rakhmatullin, R. and Stanionyte, L. (2016). *Smart specialisation: Creating growth through trans-national cooperation and value chains: Thematic work on the understanding of transnational cooperation and value chains in the context of smart specialisation*. Luxembourg: Publications Office of the European Union.

Virkkala, S. (2013). Geographical perspectives: regional development and transnational learning. In Mariussen, Å. and Virkkala, S. (eds) *Learning transnational learning*, pp. 51–101. Abingdon: Routledge.

Virkkala, S. (2019). Entrepreneurial discovery processes, knowledge creation and knowledge space. In Mariussen, Å., Virkkala, S., Finne, H. (eds) *The entrepreneurial discovery process and regional development: New knowledge emergence, conversion and exploitation*. Abingdon: Routledge.

Part IV

Lessons from systems of innovation

12 Science–practice knowledge interaction in the Norwegian fish farming industry

Tone Merethe Aasen, Eli Fyhn Ullern and Åge Mariussen

12.1 Introduction

The context for this chapter is the salmon farming industry in Norway, which, over the past decades, has grown tremendously. The long, sheltered Norwegian coastline, with its favourable currents and water temperatures, has, since far back, formed the basis for strong local societies along the coast, and, more recently, has opened for a prosperous aquaculture industry. Today, there are more than a thousand fish farms from the south to the far north, producing salmon, rainbow trout and other marine fish species. They deliver their products to more than 100 countries, and jointly hold close to a 60 per cent share of the global market. Farmed salmon and other marine species have grown to be among the biggest Norwegian export industries, with important spinoff benefits for the coastal communities, supplier industry and Norwegian fishing industry in general (Winther et al., 2017). The extraordinary results can be explained by the industry's capacity of converting new ideas into practice (Stensvold, 2015), but also by outstanding research initially performed by agricultural researchers.

The chapter is based on empirical evidence from the Trøndelag region in Mid-Norway, developed as part of the research initiative 'Regional innovation through situated knowledge conversion'.[1] Empirical data were collected through semi-structured, step-stone interviews with 15 key respondents in the fish farming industry, related research communities, and public support systems. The ambition of the research was to explore how existing networks and systems of innovation, including policy instruments, contribute to the development and exploitation of new, science-based knowledge. Today, the fish farming industry faces the challenging situation of high commodity demand and increasing costs, combined with increasingly strict environmental restrictions on a production environment that is vulnerable in many ways: fish health, environment, volume, slaughter, transportation and revenue. Despite many excellent research communities, research is lagging behind when it comes to solving the challenges. Implicitly, the industry needs to turn its attention in new directions.

The questions emerging during the project were: which role does research-based knowledge play in processes of knowledge conversion, and what are the possible relationships between such processes and entrepreneurial discoveries?

12.2 Entrepreneurial discovery and knowledge conversion

Entrepreneurial discovery processes are explained throughout this book, yet a few characteristics of significance to this chapter should be emphasised. First, it should be remembered that entrepreneurial discovery is defined as the phase that precedes the structured, visible phases of innovation (Foray, 2016; Piirainen et al., 2017), also referred to as the fuzzy front end of innovation (Shiba et al., 1993), or the gestation phase (Van de Ven et al., 1999). Although elaboration of the concept is still in progress, it can fruitfully be framed as processes of exploration and imagination creating new ideas about possible futures based on combinations of different types of knowledge, information and fantasies. Selection of a desired future forms a basis for new action: that is, experimentation and development. Implicitly, the objective of entrepreneurial discovery is not to favour innovation in specific companies, but to incite the development of collective action and experience on a regional level, with the intention of identifying new opportunities. Second, entrepreneurial discovery allows for actors to re-orient and renew themselves and will therefore increase the probability for innovation. Thus, entrepreneurial discovery can be conceptualised as 'opportunity recognition' (e.g. O'Connor and Rice, 2001; Park, 2005; George et al., 2016), where the domain of opportunity is created through new combinations of separate domains of knowledge (Foray, 2015). The recognition of opportunity has also been connected to the identification of a 'fault' or an 'imperfection', which can be addressed through the invention of new resources (Kirzner, 1997).

While the purpose of entrepreneurial discovery is new activity, innovation is the translation of that discovery into real economic convergence (Foray, 2017), resulting from a group's or companies' successful exploration and exploitation of the recognised opportunity. Thus, a discovery can be the source of many lines of innovation. George et al. (2016) further suggest that the concept of opportunity recognition involves diverse processes for creating value. The interplay of such processes, nationally and globally, can be considered as the engine of market dynamics, where individual and regional initiatives are interlinked.

Entrepreneurial discoveries are characterised by strong learning dimensions (Foray, 2015). To follow the reasoning of Nonaka and Takeuchi (1995), learning is the result of destabilisation of an accepted 'truth', and the movement from old 'know-how' to new 'know-how'. This process implies the input of new, explicit knowledge perceived as relevant (Nonaka and Toyama, 2003). A principal idea of this perspective is that to be of use in a specific context, explicit knowledge must undergo a conversion. As discussed by Aasen (2019) (Chapter 7 in this volume), knowledge conversion can be understood as a key concept, core to entrepreneurial discovery as well as to the subsequent events leading to the perceived existence of an opportunity for profit on the part of many people, and further actions on that perception. The research of Nonaka and von Krogh (2009) suggests the concept of 'knowledge conversion' is composed of two elements. The first is individual knowledge expansion, coming about through combination of own knowledge with that of others. The second is group knowledge dynamics, energised by the interaction between explicit and tacit knowledge along the continuum (Janhonen and Johanson, 2011). In these processes 'tacit and explicit knowledge mutually enhance each other towards increasing capacity to act' (Nonaka and von Krogh, 2009: 638). The outcome of the knowledge-conversion processes is dependent on the process participants, because it is the interpretation of the knowledge into the context which is the important step. The 'medium' of interpretation is tacit knowledge, which could also be referred to as (non-articulated) experience. As pointed out by Janhonen and Johanson (2011), knowledge-creation and codification processes do not necessarily lead to performance improvement or value creation. Companies' competitive advantages depend not only on knowledge creation but more importantly on knowledge conversion, diffusion and application. Thus, to be useful, the resulting ideas must then be articulated, shared, accepted and acted upon.

12.3 The Mid-Norway salmon farming case

Like the rest of the country, fisheries and fish farming represent significant export values in Mid-Norway, and is acknowledged as a cornerstone in the economic activity of the region far into the future. From the modest beginning, nearly 30 years ago, fish farming has grown into a multi-billion-euro industry creating local value for the 32 coastal municipalities in the region. The region contributes to about 25 per cent of the total sales value of farmed salmon in Norway. The industry is dominated by three large, national salmon farmers with activity in many locations all along the coast, accompanied by many small, local farmers, and sub-suppliers. A total of 18 companies produce edible salmon and rainbow trout, while 19 companies produce young fish. Most fish farming companies, both large and small, are family owned. In 2014 there was a total of 216 licences in the region, in 152 locations. 168 licences were granted to produce edible fish, eight for broodstock, and 36 for young fish. In addition, there were 13 R&D licences, as well as a few exhibition and educational licences.

In many ways, focusing a case of Norwegian salmon farming on one region may seem to be a redundant delimitation, as this has indeed become a national industry. The large fish farmers dominating regional activity are established in several Norwegian regions. Yet, more than anywhere else in the country, the climate for entrepreneurial discovery and innovation in Mid-Norway should be favourable, with the combined and strong presence of fish farmers, suppliers, finance companies, public support, and strong education and research institutions.

The county municipality of Trøndelag has taken an important role in the development of the regional fish farming industry, as a connector, coordinator and initiator of development activities. The connection between the county and the industry is close. Furthermore, actors from education and research are well integrated with the industry, and the approach they have developed to cooperation serves as a model for other regions. There are two upper secondary schools offering high-quality education within aquafarming in close cooperation with the industry, and the students are very popular. Both high schools and the industry are granted education and information licences to educate pupils, students, and the public. Moreover, the regional fish farming industry finances a professorship at the Norwegian University of Science and Technology (NTNU) in Trondheim. SINTEF, which is the largest independent research organisation in Scandinavia, is also situated in Trondheim, and is a key partner for the industry. Among other important partnerships is a centre for research-based innovation, Exposed, aiming to enable a sustainable expansion of the fish farming industry.

The Mid-Norway fish farming case was framed as a case of exploring the role of research-based knowledge in processes of knowledge conversion, and the potential importance of this for innovation in the regional salmon farming industry. Entrepreneurial discovery emerged during the project as a significant concept, in part justified by a growing regional interest in smart specialisation strategies.

A reason for the original framing of the case was that from the very beginning of the Norwegian aquaculture adventure, the research community cooperated closely with the emerging industry. During the first years of salmon farming, several biological and technological challenges were overcome, such as the development of dry feed and onshore rearing of young salmon (i.e. smolt) (Aarset, 1998). This fundamentally advanced salmon aquaculture. Today, there is an increasing recognition of the need for research-based knowledge within the fish farming companies, gradually leading to the employment of more people with higher education at the academic level, facilitating knowledge transfer.

When studying actors in the regional fish farming economy, our original assumption was that the dynamics between industrial actors and research and education communities were empirically accessible in two ways: (1) through networks and systems of innovation providing flows of codified/research-based knowledge, and (2) through micro-level processes of converting and applying this knowledge through combinations of research-based knowledge with various forms of tacit knowledge. As distinct from mainstream studies, systems and networks of innovation were viewed as sources to, as well as results of, such. A second assumption was that knowledge conversion is the result of localised interaction between groups of people with different forms of knowledge. The concept of 'ba' (Nonaka and Takeuchi, 1995; Nonaka and Konno, 1998; Mariussen, 2013) was adopted to enable a discussion about how the many actors in and related to the aquaculture industry share, combine, and convert knowledge in different forms and from different sources in interactive processes of learning and innovation.

12.4 Framing the case: a glance in the mirror

The government's vision is that Norway is going to be the world's leading seafood nation. This is a realistic vision, given the favourable national conditions. But to realise this vision, the industry is dependent on a high rate of innovation and a growth in productivity. Although Norway is among the main global producers of salmon, productivity of salmon farming has gradually stagnated in recent years. This is linked to biological challenges, and to the decreasing availability of new fish farm areas (Asche et al., 2012; Almås and Ratvik, 2017).

Fish farming in Norway has a long history, which we suggest may be divided into five phases: *experimental, pioneering, regulation, industrial,* and *sustainability.* Table 12.1 shows important milestones of the four latter phases, and the roles of the triple-helix actors (Etzkowitz and Leydesdorff, 2000) in this.

Experimental fish farming was performed already around 3500 BC, in China, with the farming of common carp. In Norway, rainbow trout was cultivated in fresh water in 1901 (Hindar et al., 1996), and at that time, some also managed to produce smolt for introduction into rivers. In the 1930s, research experiments were performed on the survival of captured saltwater fish. However, the real adventure of Norwegian aquaculture was initiated decades later, in the mid-1960s, by Professor Skjervold at the then Agriculture School at Ås (Now: *Norwegian University of Life Sciences*). At the time, he was already internationally recognised for his research on the breeding of sheep and cattle. In 1965 he started to use fish as model animals, but soon realised that this could be developed into an industry for coastal farmers. An institute for aquaculture research was established, headed by Professor Skjervold, and this institute became central for the development of the fish farming industry in Norway. By combining research-based knowledge on stock breeding with the long traditions of fisheries, the idea that fish could be grown in a net pen emerged. This was the entrepreneurial discovery that launched the Norwegian fish farming industry.

Four years later the first successful tests of net pen salmon farming in sea water were accomplished, and the first fish farm was built in the north-western part of Norway soon after that. Research to deal with the problem of diseases of hatchery-produced fish was also started in this period.

In the wake of the *pioneering* activities, the seeds of the current industry were planted, primarily as a government-supported activity to strengthen the economy of rural fishing. The first 'licence to operate' system was introduced in 1973. Like trout, cod, herring, halibut and other fish species, salmon was then traditionally harvested as an important food source, yet the catch of wild salmon was rather modest compared with many of the other fish species (Liu et al., 2011). In the 1960s, declining wild fisheries thus threatened the basis of existence of most coastal communities. Since then, the Norwegian farmed salmon as we know it today has been developed through systematic breeding, as well as determined cooperation. The Norwegian Fish Farmers Association was established in 1970 to promote the economic, technical, social and cultural interests of fish farmers. Eight years later, a fish farmers' cooperative was established as a joint sales channel. The cooperative was liquidated in 1991, the same year as the Norwegian Fishing Industry Federation was established. Four years later, the federation merged with the Norwegian Fish Farmers Association to form the Norwegian Seafood Association. The aim of this association was, and still is, to attract the fishing, aquaculture and seafood processing industry of Norway to promote their common interests. During these years, governmental *regulations* started to proliferate, and were gradually accompanied by an international body of rules.

Apart from a period of depression in the late 1980s, the aquaculture *industry* has experienced remarkable growth. Norwegian salmon farming has undergone several structural and technical changes on the way. In only a few decades, it has dramatically expanded to the extent that it has replaced wild salmon in production and markets and changed the dynamics of the whole seafood industry, both in Norway and worldwide. The industry has grown tremendously in recent years, and in 2013, seafood was the fourth largest export business in Norway (behind oil, gas and metals).

Today, Norway has a diversified system of commercial licences, including green licences, licences for increase in production, land-based aquaculture, licences for young fish and licences for flexible production capacity. 'Green licences' were introduced in 2013 to develop a more *sustainable* industry. Such licences are granted to fish farmers as a means of stimulating new technological solutions or modes of operation. There are presently more than 45 green licences in Norway. In addition to the commercial licences, the government has also introduced a set of special licences. These licences include broodstock production, research and development licences, educational licences and exhibition licences.

Research licences have been a government instrument to increase and strengthen the development of the fish farming industry through research since 2005. One year earlier the industry itself had established the Norwegian Seafood Research Fund, financed through an R&D levy on exports of all seafood (which is currently 0.3 per cent). Based on evaluation of the potential of results for the industry, the fund has prioritised and financed a broad range of biology-related R&D projects.

As for the research licences, they are available to public or private research institutions at university or university college level. The orientation of the projects that have been granted a research licence has been mostly towards biological challenges. The projects have a set timeframe, and the results are expected to be widely available to the public. Research licences cannot be converted to commercial licences. As of January 2017, there are 90 research licences in Norway.

In November 2015, development licences were launched as a temporary tool to stimulate technological innovation in a period of considerable biological challenges. The ambition was to develop projects contributing to significant investments in the industry. While the research licences mainly set focus on biological problems, these licences were aiming at the development of new

Table 12.1 Triple-helix actors in Norwegian fish farming and their role over time

		Industry	*Government*	*Public R&D*
2020	Sustainability	Towards new entrepreneurial discoveries through experiments with potentially disruptive breeding systems	2017: Stricter climate regulation and a traffic-light system regulating production volumes in coastal zones	Public R&D expenditure to aquaculture to continue to increase
2015			2015: Development licences 2013: 'Green' licences	
2010		The year-on-year increase in industry R&D expenditure approaches 30%	2012: Revision of Aquaculture Act to further strengthen sustainability focus	
2005	Industrialisation		2006: The Aquaculture Act 2005: The Food Safety Act 2004–2008: Several rules and regulations introduced	2005: Research licences introduced to strengthen fish farming through research An average of 5% annual increase in R&D funding
2000		2004: Strengthened focus on research through the Norwegian Seafood Research Fund		
1995		Mergers and restructuring 1995: Norwegian Seafood Federation		
1990	Regulation	1991: The Norwegian Fishing Industry Federation		1993: The Research Council of Norway
1985		Depression due to a combination of economic, structural and biological factors	The Fish Farming Act 1985: Introduction of revised, market-oriented licence system	Research expands into several programmes on diverse biological aspects
1980				1983: First public research programme: 'Healthy fish'
1975		1978: Fish farmers' sales cooperative The first fish farm is built	Introduction of 'owner–operator' licence system	1972: Norwegian fishery research council
1970		1970: The Norwegian Fish Farmers Association		
1965	Pioneering	Fish farming developed in the coastal regions by pioneers with experience from fisheries	Focus on strengthening the economy of rural fishing	Fragmented organising of multidisciplinary-oriented public R&D strategy

Source: Own elaboration

technologies and equipment of benefit to the total fish farming industry. After the project period is over, a development licence can be converted into a commercial licence.

The modern Norwegian salmon aquaculture industry is a highly capitalised, vertically integrated and export-oriented industry. There is a total of 1,300 fish farming licences in Norway today. Although there are still several small fish farmers running their business along the coast, the industry is in the main owned and controlled by a few multinational companies. Most of these companies, small or large, are still family owned. The industry is a significant contributor to the Norwegian economy and creates important employment opportunities in many rural coast communities. This is true, at least, for the farming of salmon. When it comes to culturing trout, current knowledge has so far shown to be inadequate for successful development of an industry of the same magnitude.

The fish farming industry is among the most innovative industries in Norway, profiting on own skills, and on world-leading national expertise. Salmon companies have expanded abroad, and Norwegian fish farming is established in countries such as Canada and Chile. Since the entrepreneurial discovery in 1965, the Norwegian salmon farming industry has grown into a major player in the global market.

12.5 Entrepreneurial discovery interpreted

Taking salmon farming in Mid-Norway as our point of departure, and looking upon the historic and present development of Norwegian fish farming, how could the concept of entrepreneurial discovery be interpreted?

We have already pointed at the ground-breaking research of Professor Skjervold as the entrepreneurial discovery launching the Norwegian aquaculture adventure. By applying his experiences with breeding methods for cattle to develop a similar breeding programme for fish, he rendered possible the future of Norway as a world-leading producer of farmed fish. The discovery was followed by experimentation and development resulting in several related varieties with input from many actors, which supported it and moved it into the booming industry of today. Hence, the initial discovery set off an entrepreneurial discovery process, which presently, more than 50 years later, is still ongoing. Over time, the scope, attention and intensity of the process has changed, in response to the evolving environment. In line with Foray (2016), the discovery has become the source of manifold innovations. As part of this process, strong clusters have been formed between the industry, public actors, and research and education institutions.

The role of government

From being a marginal industry forwarded by visionary individuals, the government has taken an important role in the development of the Norwegian aquaculture industry (cf. Table 12.1). In the beginning, production licences, i.e. access to coastal zone areas, were allocated in accordance with a strict regional development regime. Only residents who were both owners and operators of a farm could be issued a licence (Liu et al., 2011): one licence to each owner. This effectively made fish farming a rural industry of small, family-owned businesses targeting the local markets. A reorientation of government policy in the mid-1980s was made to promote a profitable industry, able to compete in the global market. The shift was accompanied by a more market-oriented licensing system, and the strict rules on ownership were substituted by regulations allowing multiple licences per owner and farm sites at any locations. The fragmented ownership structure soon resulted in overproduction and spreading of fish diseases, and market prices for salmon fell. This coincided with an increase in bank interest rates. On top of this, the industry was inexperienced in dealing with international competition, and in the late 1980s many fish farmers went bankrupt.

Despite challenges, prospects for high profitability and further expansion soon brought about comprehensive structural changes. In the early 1990s many of the local small-scale farms started to merge, and over time restructured and grew into large, multinational enterprises. Market demands increased and expanded, followed by a further governmental liberalisation on capacity, and the emergence of new technologies.

The first Aquaculture Act was passed in 1985, with a focus on incorporating all national enterprises into the licensing system and ensuring that new aquaculture activities were established in a responsible manner. Twenty years later the industry had grown substantially, and a new Aquaculture Act was adopted, adapting for profitability and competitiveness within a framework of sustainable development. As the need for sustainable development was increasingly acknowledged, the Aquaculture Act was further revised a few years later to restrict the maximum allowable biomass in a specific location.

In addition to the Aquaculture Act, a comprehensive body of rules has been developed during the last 15 years to ensure sustainable industry development and safe food. In 2017, a new and stricter climate regulation was passed, entailing environmental commitments, frames and systematics, making further demands on the fish farming industry. The regulation is accompanied by a 'traffic light system' regulating production volumes in the coastal zones, and thus will be a determinative factor for future growth.

From playing a very modest role in the early phase of the entrepreneurial discovery process, the government has taken an important position in relation to Norwegian aquaculture industry: as regulatory environment, as regional developer, as driving force for innovation, and as source of R&D funding.

The role of public research

The first public aquaculture-related research programme, 'Healthy fish', was initiated in 1983, and during the next ten-year period, research expanded into several research programmes focusing on diverse aspects of fish farming, including fish feed and water quality. At the time, there were five independent research councils: science and technology (established 1946), social sciences (1949), agriculture (1949), fisheries (1972) and applied social sciences (1987). The five councils were merged into the Research Council of Norway in 1993. The merger was made to strengthen the state-led R&D strategy, which emphasised the need for combination of knowledge from separate domains, but which suffered from the fragmented research structure (Mariussen, 1992). The establishment of a joint Research Council of Norway enabled the integration of research areas into multidisciplinary programmes providing extensive funding to a wide range of supporting sectors.

Since the 1990s, restructuring and vertical integration of companies, accompanied by changing ownership models and close cooperation with public authorities, have substantially impacted the extent and orientation of R&D in the industry. Today, Norwegian marine research amounts to about 500 million euros (Sarpebakken and Ubisch, 2017), of which about one third of the resources are spent within the field of aquaculture (Nærings- og fiskeridepartementet, 2015). Substantial R&D efforts are presently made to improve solutions for breeding, feeding, and heeding the fish (from disease) and its environment. Among other effects, public-funded aquaculture-oriented clusters have emerged, gathering fish farmers, suppliers, researchers, education institutions, and authorities into the same arenas. R&D efforts are supported by public priority programmes and framed by the scope of research licences. In their 'Master plan for marine research' (Nærings- og fiskeridepartementet, 2015), the Ministry of Trade, Industry and Fisheries still underlines the importance of research collaboration across traditional disciplines, and the need to transform research into commercially valuable solutions.

Research as basis for industrial development

At present, the Norwegian fish farming industry profits from favourable regulations, environment- and health-oriented consumers, technological advancements and a growing seafood demand. Compared with most other industries, profit margins are currently high. In many aspects, the modern salmon industry can be compared with the petroleum industry. They are both commodity producers, and as such, the core interest of the industry is, and would naturally be, to optimise the value of the commodity, i.e., to produce as much as possible as efficiently as possible. Value creation is based on the ownership of production licences, and not on technology ownership. The strategic focus of the large fish farmers is on production, logistics and market development, of which the first two in many cases are developed by suppliers, with or without the support from research communities. Thus, as in the petroleum sector, experimentation, research and knowledge development have chiefly been within the primary, upstream production, and to a much lesser extent focused on downstream activities and differentiation. On top of this, regulations of trade and rates of tax on processed seafood, particularly towards the EU market, represent weak incentives for increased differentiation and value creation in Norway.

Empirical evidence from our Mid-Norway case suggests that the strategic importance of research varies within companies. This may seem a surprising finding, as, roughly seen, research collaborations are about experimental development aimed at the growth of the feeding and breeding core segments of the industry. Even more surprising was that the majority of respondents claimed that, so far, learning and knowledge development in the business had largely been based on experience rather than on research. These views were partly explained by the industry themselves, reporting a lack of strategic foundation of research initiatives in their companies. But in the end, it is also a question about money and strategy. For the small companies, a main challenge is that their resources are sparse, and it is challenging for them to enter into long-term, resource-demanding R&D projects. Thus, they tend to rather partner up with suppliers and use their technologies. Therefore, they can be seen as 'unconscious' consumers of research, as customers of actors exploiting new knowledge. In line with a tradition of sharing, the small fish farmers exchange experiences with each other, and oftentimes choose the solutions that 'work for their neighbour'.

As for the large enterprises, they are gradually becoming less embedded in their region and community of origin, their focus being on global markets, cost leadership and rapid upscaling of production. Competition is about the ownership and development of new fields for fish farming: abroad, further north, further offshore, or on land. Most of these enterprises establish their own R&D departments, and strong research communities based on collaboration between research institutes and company-internal researchers have emerged in recent years. Their attention is on solving the key challenges of primary production, such as fish diseases, shortness of feed, and environmental effects. A potential consequence is that the large enterprises may be 'locked in' by their strong focus on competitive growth, and their fading interest in novel, regional domains. While important in very many aspects, the formation of strong communities of interest with a rather uniform focus on biological and veterinarian knowledge thus appears to also inhibit the open flow of knowledge and experience of relevance for entrepreneurial discovery, knowledge conversion and widespread innovation.

Our empirical evidence confirms that interaction between important actors within the Mid-Norway salmon farming industry is close and rich, and that there is 'almost no distance' between research and the industry. Contrary to this, respondents suggest that a lack of cooperation in the fish farming industry may be one of the main threats to further entrepreneurial discovery, opportunity recognition, and innovation. One explanation given is that in spite of the many meeting arenas, there are gaps between the industry, the authorities, and research communities, who continue to 'talk different languages'. Another explanation has to do with development horizon and frame conditions. Up to now, the fish farming industry has been characterised by short-term strategies, and accordingly, has been reluctant to enter long-term (i.e. three to four years) research collaborations. A third explanation is related to culture and company size. While the larger fish farmers are acknowledged for contributing to research-based knowledge, internally or in partnership with research and education institutions, they are credited less for sharing their knowledge and partnering for innovation. This is in line with the above discussion about communities of interest, which by some are referred to as 'communities of vested interests and knowledge protection', rather than of knowledge sharing and conversion. The smaller fish farmers, on the other hand, who more rarely participate in research initiatives, still have a reputation for sharing both knowledge and experience.

Entrepreneurial discovery processes and knowledge production

Ignoring the differences between large and small fish farmers, entrepreneurial discovery processes can be regarded as clusters of triple (or quadruple) helix actors pursuing shared visions of a desirable future in processes of simultaneous cooperation and competition: co-opetition (Carayannis et al., 2018). The concept of 'triple helix' refers, among other things, to the ideas of 'Mode 1' and 'Mode 2' knowledge production (Gibbons et al., 1994; Etzkowitz and Leydesdorff, 2000), which, simplified, can be understood as being about 'solving a problem' versus 'solving the problem'. Traditionally, university research is based on the norm of open science and produced in accordance with a Mode 1 knowledge production model. Industrial research, on the other hand, is based on the norm of proprietary science, implying that a Mode 2 knowledge production model is adopted when a specific problem needs to be solved. This alternative mode of knowledge production can be characterised as an outcome, and thus, regarded as an emerging system (Etzkowitz and Leydesdorff, 2000). Gibbons et al. (1994) mention that Mode 1 knowledge production can of course result in practical applications, but as opposed to the outcomes of Mode 2 these will be separated from the actual knowledge production in space and time.

Seen from a Mode 1 perspective, the role of R&D in fish farming industry innovation would be as an arena for knowledge transfer from research to industry (Hessels and van Lente, 2008), independent of the level or intensity of interaction. Knowledge, if made public, can be exploited and capitalised on by everybody. As different target groups are likely to make use of new knowledge in ways unknown at the start of research projects, this may also induce innovation in unforeseen areas. If, however, R&D-based knowledge production is interpreted from a Mode 2 perspective, triple-helix partners should share knowledge and experience, and jointly convert it into new opportunities. In this case, innovation could be understood as communicative processes influenced by, but also influencing, the actors engaged in the development, exploration and exploitation of new knowledge and technologies. Such processes do not evolve in a vacuum but will be affected by external factors such as public opinion, political discourses, and scientific breakthroughs. Implicitly, all partners, whether researchers, representatives from the fish farming industry, or the government, need to engage in joint scientific discussion as a basis for the co-production of new knowledge and innovation, as two aspects of the same process.

Approaching knowledge from different perspectives (Mode 1/Mode 2, and the more recent Mode 3 suggested by Carayannis et al. (2018), involving knowledge clusters and innovation networks) implies different expectations about interaction and innovation. As an example, (Lam, 2011: 137) states that:

> If firms are therefore to seek to anchor their R&D activities in academic knowledge networks which are the cutting edge of new knowledge and research potentially ahead of their commercial competitors, then they have to find a way of getting scientists to draw on their Mode 1 knowledge and apply it in a Mode 2 environment, and they have to help to shape the competencies acquired by scientists so that they can function easily in this manner.

Seen more generally, the aggregated knowledge, developed through (interdisciplinary) research and altering practice must be examined in an open, trusting dialogue between stakeholders. A possible way to bridge the distant–close triple-helix relationships described by our respondents could be to develop a collective framework for such dialogue, and its influence on knowledge development and conversion into new knowledge domains. However, there may be a need to differentiate between mature and emerging knowledge areas. As an example, we suggest that the current faltering cooperation between fish farmers on sustainable farming systems should be discussed from a different perspective than more mature problems, like feed and fish health (Foray, 2015). An obvious question is whether increased cooperation on innovation within the industry would be more cost-efficient, yet the immature state of the particular field probably calls for a period of experimentation in many directions, leading to a variety of solutions that, over time, will converge towards a dominant design (Utterback and Abernathy, 1975).

12.6 Final reflections

The focal point of interest in the Mid-Norway case study was the role of research-based knowledge in processes of knowledge conversion, and the possible relationships between such processes, entrepreneurial discovery and innovation. The study points towards some important insights. Importantly, the emergence of the world-leading Norwegian salmon farming industry can be attributed to a single entrepreneurial discovery, triggering diverse processes involving a large number of triple-helix actors which in different ways are interrelated. Despite comprehensive clustering and interaction between the various actors, knowledge development processes still appear fragmented. The prolonged focus on fish health, feed and water quality has resulted in world-leading expertise within the fields of aquaculture-related biology and veterinary science, yet core challenges remain to be solved.

Another insight is that authorities' regulation regimes paradoxically affect innovation and regional development in both productive and unproductive ways. As an example, the research licences system is perceived to be as much a restraint as an enabler of entrepreneurial discovery and innovation, being used as much for curiosity-driven, basic research as for the solving of urgent challenges inhibiting industrial growth. Seen from the perspective of innovation, this makes demands on the framing of R&D deliverables, which should reflect a movement from basic research towards demonstration of the potentiality of the new knowledge in solving the challenge. Incidentally, this claim supports the Mode 2 call for additional ways of evaluating research quality.

On the other hand, the recent development licences system has enabled the destabilisation of several 'truths' about fish farming, and by this has opened the way for a broad range of potential discoveries. Interpreted in the contradictory lights of global population growth and demands for proper, environmentally responsible production, 'sustainability' and 'circular economy' have become key innovation drivers in the industry. Rapidly increasing interest is, among other areas, in technological solutions opening for new fish farming systems. An example is the current search for more sustainable caging of the fish, either in open ocean systems further off the coast, or in closed systems offshore or onshore. At present, several solutions are tested in parallel, headed by different fish farmers in cooperation with various sub-suppliers and research partners. An example is the gigantic ocean net pen currently being tested some miles off the coast of Mid-Norway. The experiments imply the combination of knowledge from aquaculture with that of the offshore petroleum industry. The social role of entrepreneurial discovery in this is that it will inform industrial actors and other interested parties that certain combinations of knowledge domains are more likely to open new opportunities than others (Foray, 2016).

The predominant need of the fish farming industry is to create new paths to growth. To succeed, several questions remain to be answered. The most important of these probably are how public authorities, researchers and the industry itself can incite to entrepreneurial discovery, and how new opportunities may be explored to the combined benefit of the industry and the region(s) in which a particular company is situated. Broad experience can be found in the industry, and important scientific knowledge is developed in the research communities, in and external to the salmon farming industry. Reinventing the way science and experience is recognised, combined, transformed and discovered as opportunity will be key to triggering novel, pathbreaking entrepreneurial discovery processes.

Note

1 Thank you to Jarle Løvland, Nordlandsforskning, for helpful comments on the preliminary manuscript.

References

Aarset, B. (1998). Norwegian salmon-farming industry in transition: Dislocation of decision control. *Ocean & Coastal Management*, 38 (3), pp. 187–206.

Aasen, T.M. (2019). Approaching entrepreneurial discovery and knowledge conversion from a complexity perspective. In Mariussen, Å., Virkkala, S., Finne, H. and Aasen, T.M. (eds) *The entrepreneurial discovery process and regional development: New knowledge emergence, conversion and exploitation*. Abingdon: Routledge.

Almås, K.A. and Ratvik, I. (2017). *Sjøkart mot 2050 – Tiltak for utvikling av biologisk baserte marine næringer mot 2050*. SINTEF Ocean.

Asche, F., Roll, K.H. and Tveterås, R. (2012). FoU, innovasjon og produktivitetsvekst i havbruk. *Magma*, (1), pp. 23–31.

Carayannis, E.G., Grigoroudis, E., Campbell, D.F.J., Meissner, D. and Stamati, D. (2018). The ecosystem as helix: An exploratory theory-building study of regional co-opetitive entrepreneurial ecosystems as quadruple/quintuple helix innovation models. *R&D Management*, 48 (1), pp. 148–162.

Etzkowitz, H. and Leydesdorff, L. (2000). The dynamics of innovation: From national systems and "Mode 2" to a triple helix of university–industry–government relations. *Research Policy*, 29 (2), pp. 109–123.

Foray, D. (2015). *Smart specialisation: Opportunities and challenges for regional innovation policy*. London: Routledge.

Foray, D. (2016). On the policy space of smart specialization strategies. *European Planning Studies*, 24 (8), pp. 1428–1437.

Foray, D. (2017). The concept of the 'entrepreneurial discovery process'. In Kyriakou, D., Martínez, M.P., Periáñez-Forte, I. and Rainoldi, A. (eds) *Governing smart specialisation*, pp. 5–19. London: Routledge.

George, N.M., Parida, V., Lahti, T. and Wincent, J. (2016). A systematic literature review of entrepreneurial opportunity recognition: Insights on influencing factors. *International Entrepreneurship and Management Journal*, 12 (2), pp. 309–350.

Gibbons, M., Limoges, C., Notwotny, H., Schwartzman, S., Scott, P. and Trow, M. (1994). *The new production of knowledge*. London: Sage.

Hessels, L.K. and van Lente, H. (2008). Re-thinking new knowledge production: A literature review and a research agenda. *Research Policy*, 37 (4), pp. 740–760.

Hindar, K., Fleming, I.A., Jonsson, N., Breistein, J., Sægrov, H., Karlsbakk, E., Gammelsæter, M. and Dønnum, B.O. (1996). *Regnbueørret i Norge: forekomst, reproduksjon og etablering*. Trondheim: NINA.

Janhonen, M. and Johanson, J.-E. (2011). Role of knowledge conversion and social networks in team performance. *International Journal of Information Management*, 31 (3), pp. 217–225.

Kirzner, I.M. (1997). Entrepreneurial discovery and the competitive market process: An Austrian approach. *Journal of Economic Literature*, 35 (1), pp. 60–85.

Lam, A. (2011). University–industry collaboration: Careers and knowledge governance in hybrid organisational space. *International Journal of Strategic Business Alliances*, 2 (1–2), pp. 135–145.

Liu, Y., Olaussen, J.O. and Skonhoft, A. (2011). Wild and farmed salmon in Norway: A review. *Marine Policy*, 35 (3), pp. 413–418.

Mariussen, Å. (1992). *Fra vann til hav: prosessevaluering av havbruk som forskningspolitisk hovedinnsatsområde*. Trondheim: Norges fiskeriforskningsråd.

Mariussen, Å. (2013). Sociological preliminaries: The societal context of transnational learning. In Mariussen, Å. and Virkkala, S. (eds) *Learning transnational learning*, pp. 13–50. Abingdon: Routledge.

Nonaka, I. and Konno, N. (1998). The concept of 'Ba': Building a foundation for knowledge creation. *California Management Review*, 40 (3), pp. 40–54.

Nonaka, I. and Takeuchi, H. (1995). *The knowledge-creating company: How Japanese companies create the dynamics of innovation*. New York: Oxford University Press.

Nonaka, I. and Toyama, R. (2003). The knowledge-creating theory revisited: Knowledge creation as a synthesizing process. *Knowledge Management Research & Practice*, 1 (1), pp. 2–10.

Nonaka, I. and von Krogh, G. (2009). Tacit knowledge and knowledge conversion: Controversy and advancement in organizational knowledge creation theory. *Organization Science*, 20 (3), pp. 635–652.

Nærings- og fiskeridepartementet (2015). *Masterplan for marin forskning*. Oslo: Nærings- og fiskeridepartementet.

O'Connor, G.C. and Rice, M.P. (2001). Opportunity recognition and breakthrough innovation in large established firms. *California Management Review*, 43 (2), pp. 95–116.

Park, J.S. (2005). Opportunity recognition and product innovation in entrepreneurial hi-tech start-ups: A new perspective and supporting case study. *Technovation*, 25 (7), pp. 739–752.

Piirainen, K.A., Tanner, A.N. and Alkærsig, L. (2017). Regional foresight and dynamics of smart specialization: A typology of regional diversification patterns. *Technological Forecasting and Social Change*, 115, pp. 289–300.

Sarpebakken, B. and Ubisch, S.S. (2017). *Ressursinnsatsen til marin FoU og havbruksforskning i 2015*. Oslo: NIFU.

Shiba, S., Graham, A. and Walden, D. (1993). *A new American TQM: Four practical revolutions in management*. Portland, OR: Productivity Press.

Stensvold, T. (2015). *Slik skal «Norges viktigste vekstnæring» bli enda viktigere. (Interview with SFI Exposed)*. Available: www.tu.no/artikler/slik-skal-norges-viktigste-vekstnaering-bli-enda-viktigere/196893.

Utterback, J.M. and Abernathy, W.J. (1975). A dynamic model of process and product innovation. *Omega*, 3 (6), pp. 639–656.

Van de Ven, A.H., Polley, D.E., Garud, R. and Venkataraman, S. (1999). *The innovation journey*. New York and Oxford: Oxford University Press.

Winther, U., Tiller, R., Ratvik, I., Bull-Berg, H., Vik, L.H. and Grindvoll, I.L.T. (2017). *Ringvirkningsanalyse for teknologi- og serviceleverandører til sjømatnæringen – leverandører, utviklingstrekk og eksport*. Trondheim: SINTEF.

13 The transformation of Lofoten islands into a year-round experience destination

Jarle Løvland and Håkon Finne

13.1 Introduction

The Lofoten islands are an iconic tourist destination in Norway and one of the most attractive ones in the country. Their original attraction stems from a unique nature, breath-taking scenery and a cultural heritage related to fisheries, the region's primary source of livelihood and wealth. Over a period of ten years around the turn of the century, the Lofoten tourist industry changed from scattered providers of basic services for island visitors in the summer season to a well-organised destination offering a wide variety of year-round experiences for an ever-increasing number of individual customers.

In retrospect this transition can be characterised as quite unique and very unexpected, and some have also explained it as 'sheer luck'. Serendipity notwithstanding, when looking into the process and the details, it becomes evident that other and more convincing explanations can be offered. In line with the framework offered in this book (notably Chapter 9 by Virkkala and Mariussen, 2019a), we argue that the new and successful character of the tourist industry in Lofoten, particularly as concerns its constitution as a *destination*, has emerged through complex interactive processes (Byrne and Callaghan, 2014) and that it can be understood as an entrepreneurial discovery process (EDP) involving a self-discovery (see Chapter 1, Virkkala and Mariussen, 2019b for further detail) of what it involves to be living successfully off an experience economy.

13.2 Innovation theory for tourist destinations

Smart specialisation strategies tend to focus on technology-driven industries and their related activities, as do most innovation policies, path-dependent as they seem to be on their theoretical and empirical origins. Are they equally relevant for tourism in the transformation from a service industry to an experience industry?

These strategies rely on understanding economic development in general and innovation in particular. It is true that both the innovation management literature, which aims to understand innovation from the innovator's point of view, and the innovation systems literature, aimed at innovation policy-makers, both early had a preference for technology as the proper content of innovation and that the job for either was to harness its power for individual or social economic benefit, with science somewhat autonomously moving the boundary for technological possibilities. Increasingly, however, a wide array of social, territorial, economic, and even political modernisation and restructuring processes have been linked to innovation processes at the core (Mabogunje, 1980; Brandão, 2014). The micro-oriented and the macro-oriented literature have been broadening their scopes significantly over time and can in some respects be seen to overlap in their current concern with knowledge from all sources and in all forms, connectivity and interaction in a wide network of private and public actors, individual as well as institutional, organisational and governance issues in hierarchies, markets and networks, the embeddedness of activity in social, cultural and territorial space, and explanatory models that see the same processes behind both structural and institutional inertia and change.

Studies of innovation in tourism are growing, building on the general innovation concepts referred to above, as well as on the specificities of tourism and the place-based innovation of destinations. A current taxonomy of innovations in tourism ranges over product/service, process, organisational, marketing, institutional and community-based innovations (Brandão, 2014; Hall, 2009; Hjalager, 1997, 2010; Hjalager et al., 2008). To this has recently been added reverse business and community innovation. This addresses the dual role and resource dependency found in tourism destinations, making it necessary to create innovations that bring benefits to local communities and other industries present. Examples of such innovations can be establishing new capacities and businesses for services and accommodation when addressing multi-season tourism development, giving benefits to local society through the labour market, new jobs and improved quality of life for the local community. Business innovations such as new experience-based products and activities can similarly support supplier companies locally.

Applying this increased and systemic complexity perspective on tourism, it becomes important to address the role of innovation in governance relations between regional and local development actors on one hand, and the stakeholders of the tourism destinations on the other. In this perspective local innovation networks and clustering processes are important to allow for wide public participation as a social innovation in tourism. In a recent study of the role of innovation in tourism industry and destinations in Portugal, Brandão (2014) argues that the social innovation within territorial and tourism innovation systems is embedded in local communities, institutions and norms. To support the local and social innovation needed, it becomes important to engage local residents and actors in new dynamics, as well as support new structures in planning, management and governance.

According to Bonetti et al. (2006), regional innovation systems of tourism share some common perspectives on the innovation processes and outcomes of particular significance. Compared with many other industries that rely more on industry-specific assets, solutions and regulations and technology-specific (national) innovation systems, tourism is particularly dependent on factors that frequently vary between regions and can benefit more from well-functioning regional innovation systems. Incremental innovation strategies in a long-term perspective of sustainability of the local resources that attract and serve tourists depend not only on intimately local knowledge but also on the legitimacy of using local commons and infrastructure for large numbers of visitors. A factory can contain its production process, but a tourist destination has to give its clients wide access beyond the coach and the suite. Innovation in tourism needs to access social, political and cultural capital resources that will determine the success of the innovation at the destination level. If the strategy of innovation in tourism is regionally relevant and embedded, it will strengthen the social, political and cultural capital base of the region. Brandão (2014) therefore argues that the concept of regional innovation systems perhaps is the most adequate as a framework to understand the innovation processes of tourism destinations.

13.3 How Lofoten transformed itself

More tourists, less profitability

The six municipalities of the Lofoten region have a population of about 24,000 inhabitants and currently cater for half a million overnight stays per year. The archipelago's location north of the Vestfjorden basin, combined with the warm Gulf Stream coming along the Norwegian coast, have created a very productive and unique natural environment for fish species and fishing activities. Every year in the winter season from December to March, the Arctic cod come south from the Barents Sea for spawning along the Norwegian coast from Finnmark to Lofoten. This natural and sustainable bioproduction system has been a major resource and driver for developing the coastal communities and their culture in northern Norway for centuries. The abundance of marine fish resources has created wealth by export since the Middle Ages, and products based on Arctic cod today are still among the most important seafood products from Norway because of their unique taste and quality and export lines maintained over hundreds of years. The export has traditionally gone through traders further south, but also local entrepreneurs have developed strong business and cultural relationships with continental and Mediterranean customers. Fisheries still make up a staple activity in the region but growth in *employment* needs to come from other sources.

Norwegian and foreign tourists have come to visit the islands in increasing numbers over several decades, but they have primarily arrived in the summer time, to enjoy the scenery of the steep, green-clad mountains diving directly into the fjord with their vast nesting cliffs, and to lead the calm life and mingle with the fishermen on the brim between the frothing sea and the inhospitable rocks, all under the midnight sun. The locals have extended their hospitality to the visitors and have been able to build small part-time business activities to serve them with transportation, lodgings, meals and other amenities, but much of the capacity required to accommodate the growing number of tourists has been built by extra-regional corporate actors mostly intent on high-volume service production. In 1992 the local tourism industry and the municipalities of Lofoten formed a joint destination management organisation (DMO), Destination Lofoten, to provide sales and marketing services to its members, for inducing more tourists to visit the attractive landscape with their significant culture and history related to fisheries.

Based on the high attraction of the destination, the number of visitors was significant and growing, but with severe limitations related to handling visitor-driven activities in a short summer season. The tourists paid for coach and suite, but they came for self-organised outdoor activities. Cruise tourism was also growing, and the concentrated volume of shore excursions in the region created high activity in the summer season, but with low profitability and a very cost-oriented competition among the actors with marginal profits as a result. Although Lofoten as a region had created external cultural and economic ties to important European and Mediterranean visitor countries based on export of stockfish and other seafood products, the tourism industry organisation at the destination appeared very fragmented, the suppliers of tourism products were highly dependent on local infrastructure and external resources, and their business model did not allow for a sustainable long-term development. The competitive situation was based on service production related to transport, food and accommodation, with limited opportunities for local differentiation or focus strategies. The seasonality of the tourism with part-time employment and high turnover also effectively limited building of new and relevant competences within the companies. The region's limited population size and air travel availability prevented access to new (and more profitable) business segments related to conferences and arrangement, as might have been the case for a more central tourism destination. Improvements had to be made within the leisure market related to vacation and holiday activities.

A turning point for tourism research in the region

By this time relevant research and new knowledge was starting to emerge internationally. Especially Pine and Gilmore's (1999) model of the progression of economic value creation, from undifferentiated extraction and production of commodities to goods, services and finally into staging experience production and transformative interactions with individual and demanding customers, gained widespread attention and diffusion. Basically, growing population segments are seeking authentic experiences to enrich their lives and are willing to pay quite well for them if they are sufficiently well staged. The emerging experience economy seemed to hold important preconditions for improving the business model and economic activities in destinations where tourism formed a growing and increasingly important basis for the local economy.

Relevant R&D institutions, both regionally and nationally, did not pick up these new ideas right away. Instead the focus of tourism and hospitality research was directed towards service quality and marketing, and the general problem of creating a viable funding of infrastructure for tourism remained unaddressed and unsolved. In 2001, however, the Research Council of Norway launched a national R&D programme called 'Value Creation 2010'[1] for enterprise development in firms and regions with little or no absorptive capacity (Cohen and Levinthal, 1990). At that time, the R&D partners of the greater region (Nordland county) gave high priority to the key challenges of inadequate infrastructure and the need for more sustainable business models for tourism. Dense interaction with the industry and other relevant actors in the region was a strict requirement for the funding.

In their subsequent interactions with the industry, the researchers developed a joint understanding with the industry of the potential value of delivering (and charging for) experiences, not just services.

Mobilising for collective action and connectedness

Based on their local experiences and inspired by the new ideas of staging locally embedded unique experiences for international customers, a group of leaders from major tourism enterprises in the Lofoten municipality of Vågan started informal strategic discussions on how this situation could be improved. They also discussed the need for rethinking their strategy to improve profitability in their operating activities. The process was initiated by the leader of a new tourism activity spun out from a traditional fish processing company with a long history and relationships to the seasonal spawn fishery activity of Arctic cod in Lofoten. Spartan housing facilities ('rorbuer'), used to accommodate fishermen from other regions during the winter fisheries, now formed the basis for new tourism activity. To live in authentic fishermen's quarters had a value in itself. The housing capacity was an asset for prospective business development, but the market orientation was not established from the start. Gradually the companies in the eastern part of the region engaged in closer cooperation arrangements and networking activities related to finding a new and more viable platform for business and what later came to be known as destination development.

One of the early activities was simply called 'The low season project', focusing on the key problem of the seasonal (summer) tourism, and how the business activity could be transformed into a full-year activity by cooperation and innovation. The project led to an increased level of interaction between more than ten companies. The outcomes of the project included building a more formal platform for strategic dialogue and development at the destination level. At the same time, the project created trust-based relations among the companies and new leadership roles in the dialogue with municipalities and public sector development actors relevant to support the strategic reorientation needed in tourism and destination building.

The networking experiences from this project paved the way for the next step, which was called 'Lofoten Winter', focusing on creating winter and full-year tourism activity (Løvland et al., 2014). The project started in 2004 and there is still development activity at the destination today that is a direct continuation of this project. The main goal for the project was to create increased profitability through winter and experience-based tourism in Lofoten. In parallel with the local emergence process of an experience-based business platform for tourism, regional development actors such as the Nordland county administration in cooperation with national institutions at the regional level for cultural heritage management launched a generic strategy to support tourism development based on the coastal culture heritage, local food and natural phenomena available. In two periods from 1992 to 2010, the artwork project 'Sculpture landscape Nordland' was implemented, employing international sculpture artists in developing and deploying 35 installations in 34 of Nordland's municipalities. The project was bold and created both high levels of engagement and conflict, but in the end, it obtained local and international recognition. Today it appears highly appreciated with international appeal and provides a strong 'reason to go' for modern cultural explorers in tourism.

In 2004 a new source of funding for regional support to innovation processes was made available through a regionally differentiated payroll tax system. This new funding source was used in Nordland to support innovation activities, knowledge support and research in order to stimulate new economic activity and to build new capabilities in relevant industries and regions, rather than to compensate for, for example, the higher transportation costs associated with a peripheral economy.

The Nordland county council prioritised attention to the growing regional tourism economy, and in 2006 an ambitious and thorough development project was initiated to create a new master plan and strategy for tourism development, using these funds. The timing of the fresh economic resources was perfect in order to link with the ongoing network building between the local tourism enterprises in their search activity and strategic product and business model innovation process. The planning process in the six municipalities was governed by their political partnership 'Lofotrådet' (the Lofoten Council). In addition to verifying external contingencies for a tourism strategy, the process furthered the established division of labour and responsibilities between the different parts and municipalities of the islands. The eastern part (Vågan) should focus on experience and nature-based activity tourism, whereas the western municipalities should develop their stronger position on cruise tourism. Creating food tourism and regional branding was organised as a shared area for strategic development in the whole region. This regional division of labour and the master plan process behind it became a very necessary precondition to support shared knowledge and at the same time allow for the use of complementary competences and reduced internal rivalry.

Boundary spanning and opening of entrepreneurial discoveries

From the experience of the central tourism companies in eastern Lofoten it became evident that the destination development was dependent on identifying an innovative product development to provide a bookable experience core product that could be offered on a year-round basis. A strong inspiration came from Finnish Lapland, where the regional winter tourism was reinventing itself and branded Rovaniemi and its surroundings 'The Santa Claus town', with a growing number of tourists coming from new overseas markets worldwide, ready to pay quite well for the experience.

The Lofoten Winter project organised strategic cooperation between 25 tourism enterprises in eastern Lofoten (in the municipality of Vågan mainly), with shifting activities and focus through three stages:

1 Entrepreneurial discovery and integration with masterplan for tourism development (2004–2007);
2 EDP meets challenges (2008–2010);
3 EDP challenges and consolidation (2010–2016).

Although the three stages are somewhat overlapping, they indicate the time frame for the emergence of the entrepreneurial discovery itself, and how the process developed and started to institutionalise a new platform for Lofoten as a year-round experience-driven destination – a process that is still ongoing. In the following we go into more detail about the emergence of the new destination and the role of new emerging knowledge support to this process.

The entrepreneurial discovery: discover the whales

In Tysfjord (in a neighbouring region across the fjord), the development of orca whale watching had been established from 1990 as a very powerful new attraction with a growing number of customers. A cooperative arrangement was established with the orca whale watching company in Tysfjord, and a new branch of the activity was opened in Lofoten, providing a long-awaited platform and reason to go for new experience-based attraction and winter tourism in the season from November through the winter months. In addition, the industry network was strengthened by new entrepreneurial actors having skills in nature-based activities and strategic leadership resources needed for taking the destination in a new direction. The new actors with complementary core competences in concept and product development of new nature-based activities quickly became central in the innovation process at the destination.

Up to 2008, RIB (rigid-inflatable boat) safaris for watching whales and other natural features grew in activity and economic significance during the second stage of the Lofoten Winter project. But around 2006 the rebuilding process of the herring stock, spawning in the Vestfjorden basin and feeding the orca whale, reached a higher level and took a new geographical distribution pattern further to the west in the basin, towards the neighbouring region Vesterålen. The change was to be expected based on existing marine research knowledge, but still came as a surprise when it happened – although the signs had been visible since 2003. The region's natural resource was not depleted; it had simply moved. This turn had a negative effect on the orca activity in Lofoten and triggered a new entrepreneurial search for a new core product for destination development and innovation. For the Lofoten Winter network, the activity in the third stage now was oriented towards a new strategic direction that both led to successful new experience product development and increasing challenges in the network cooperation.

Emerging knowledge support activities, networking and R&D mobilising (2007–present)

When Lofoten emerged as an experience-based destination, the actors in the tourist industry mostly used their own experiential knowledge. True, some inspiration had come from Harvard (Pine and Gilmore's ideas had diffused quite widely) and from Finland, but there was no or little direct contact with research. Innovation-relevant knowledge came from doing the job, using the solutions and interacting with customers and competitors.

In relation with the making of the Santa experience in Finland, Lapland University had played an important supporting role by developing and applying experience design methods with innovators in the tourism industry. The Finnish so-called LEO methodology in experience design, product and enterprise development soon became known and formed the standard for similar initiatives in the Nordic countries. The regional partnership of Nordland county administration joined forces with the regional branch of the innovation agency Innovation Norway, structuring short courses in applying the LEO methodology for enterprises and facilitators. In this way the development regional actors in Nordland took an important initiative and provided necessary support to this practice-based knowledge platform in the tourism destinations with relevant R&D partners, methods and knowledge for application. Based on the experiences from the early stages of the process in Lofoten, the inclusion of R&D-based knowledge partners seemed very relevant to reduce the possible lock-in problems in the strategic discovery process, even if their knowledge and research in the early stages of cooperation was not regarded as highly relevant. Establishing connections with research was also important to address the need for ambidexterity capabilities in the tourism companies to shift the balance in knowledge from exploitation towards exploration of strategic opportunities to enter the experience economy.

Following this initial effort to increase relevant new knowledge and core competences in the tourism companies at the Lofoten destination, the regional development agents also initiated a new regional cluster development project under the national Arena cluster programme of Innovation Norway. In this process R&D partners such as the Nordland Research Institute and Nord University were invited to participate in the early mobilising effort for recruiting companies to the cluster project 'Innovative Experiences', together with a very competent consultant and facilitator who also had long experience from tourism and destination development in other parts of the country. The network project started in 2008 with companies from the northern part of Nordland, and the core partners came from Lofoten Winter and their efforts to shift into a year-round experience-based destination. The cluster project created an important new meeting point between companies and research, where the R&D experience design and production LEO methodology was used to create a new knowledge platform for experience design and product development in the participating companies. The project and the facilitation process also balanced the competence-building capabilities with usefulness for the participants, as they could master a common method and language that was used to visit each other and act as 'critical friends' in helping the companies to improve the experience quality and their business model.

In addition, the 'Innovative Experiences' project also had an ambition to structure the cooperation and use of shared knowledge and methods to support network-based product development and innovation. This was important for the move from loose competence network activity towards aligning companies from different activity areas into network cooperation to deliver composite attractive and world-class experience products that could create a powerful 'reason to go' factor for international guests, compared with similar leading nature-based destinations. The network cooperation soon proved very useful and stimulated building of trustful relations among the companies. After two years of cooperation, the cluster partners entered into integrated product development processes.

The cluster project management and the R&D partner also facilitated a foresight process, identifying the major drivers that were considered to affect future development of tourism and destination development. The foresight process and findings provided important shared analysis, memory and visions necessary to create a roadmap for action that could lead to early warning towards lock-in tendencies – and give strategic input to possible growth areas and business model development at the destination level. Trust and increased network interaction among the companies gave important input to enter integrative strategic cooperation, reducing the risk of entering into internal price-driven competition, undermining the unique and heterogenous resource advantages present at the destination level. Instead of cannibalism, this allowed for the professionalisation of the new and fast-growing segments of tourism within nature-based activities and experience product development. The networking and cooperation gave new experience-based entrepreneurs the chance to enter into cooperative agreements with the major service providers within transport, accommodation and food, whose scale and capacity formed new market opportunities important for the start-up stage and early consolidation.

As a result of the high level of destination development activity and an increasing number of experience-oriented product developments, Lofoten became an even more attractive destination for new external actors. An important step in this development was when the major Norwegian hotel chain Thon decided to have a new conference facility in Svolvær in Lofoten, and this was co-located with the new regional facility for cultural activities, 'Lofoten Culture Hall'.

However, the challenges of funding this infrastructure also illustrated some of the systemic problems of tourism destinations like Lofoten, with high resource dependencies in necessary infrastructure in a fragmented industry. The cooperation with local and regional municipalities and development agents proved important to overcome this obstacle.

The cooperation between public and private interest in establishing the hotel and conference facility allowed for creating linkages to the growing interest in cultural experiences internationally, while supporting the transition from being a summer leisure destination into a full-year destination, supporting the growth of business-related experience production. For the existing networks within experience production, the new convention hotel was important to create the necessary scale and focus in the development of more professional actors and a clearer division of labour on the supply side – reducing the risks of rivalry and competitive disadvantages towards other growing destinations.

At the same time, a growing interest in establishing more supplier industries and enterprises to the petroleum offshore industry moving towards Lofoten meant that the competition of control and access of natural resources became more intense. The industry clusters teamed up with other regional development actors in communicating the positive and fast-growing local effects from the experience-based tourism. In this respect the emerging new industry with R&D support provided input to national policies and supported a strategic and regional perspective on balancing the interest of local and diverse stakeholders. This was important in order to avoid a lock-in situation and secure sustainable use of the ecosystem services of marine and terrestrial natural resources and areas in the coastal zone, where Lofoten was a strong symbol of the important values and resources at stake.

Emerging relevant knowledge support

The cluster and network cooperation also became an important platform to shape the institutional organisation of R&D support from the universities and academia, particularly through the R&D programme 'Northern Insights' (2009–2017), focusing on experience design in destinations in northern Norway. The 'Innovative Experiences' cluster thus took initiatives to providing a new R&D-based hub called Novadis at Nord University and Nordland Research Institute, to facilitate access to relevant multidisciplinary research and education, strongly supported by the Nordland county administration through their partnership with the Research Council of Norway in the aforementioned VRI programme for regional research and innovation.

A third form of network organisation was the cooperation within the DMO (Destination Lofoten), which both served as a loose network of related stakeholders to the economic activities in the region stemming from tourism, as well as being a service provider for generic marketing and destination branding. However, with the shifting focus from generic and common mass marketing to incremental and targeted individual high-quality deliveries, this transformed the need for generic marketing services from Destination Lofoten. The need for some form of network organisation at the destination level was acknowledged by the industrial actors. The DMO was central in developing the masterplan process, but later the destination organisation played a minor and shifting role in connection with the innovation and strategic development processes taking place in the Lofoten Winter project and the Innovative Experiences cluster. In the beginning the DMO was bypassed in the direct cooperation between the companies, as their activities did not seem relevant for the core companies. Gradually the DMO company was integrated more systematically in the overall strategic development of Lofoten as a destination, and in 2014 the revision of the masterplan underpinned a more central role when deciding the focal areas for strategic action and coordination.

New arenas – the experience conference

As a result of the combined network and strategic development work being organised by the regional development actors, municipalities and tourism enterprises, the cluster project Innovative Experiences in 2008 organised the first major conference within experience tourism in northern Norway. During the first years the experience conference alternated between Lofoten, Narvik and Bodø (the administrative seat of the county council) and became an important arena for networking and mobilising the growing interest in experience-based tourism. It also had played an important role in setting the agenda for industry-related policy areas and strategies.

Offering new R&D, knowledge and perspectives on tourism, the conference became an important arena for exchanging ideas, knowledge and inspiration in entrepreneurial development and product innovation within activity-based experiences rooted in nature and cultural resources. From 2014 the conference became the Norwegian Experience Conference, aiming to be an arena for knowledge-based innovation and experience tourism development for the whole of Norway.

A key to maintaining the importance of this arena has been the ability to link and combine practice and R&D-based expertise and interest with relevant perspectives for strategic development for the new emerging industry. Another important condition has been staging the conference in the autumn, when the production activity within tourism (still) is somewhat lower than the rest of the year. This formula has been critical in keeping it relevant and attractive both to former and new participants, always finding something useful and building important networks for their own development purposes.

Gradually a platform for exchange of knowledge and collaboration between industry partners, academia, regional and national development actors has been established both through the clustering and networking activities. During this process both the experience conference and the active involvement of and from the DMO in Lofoten has given significant contributions in transforming the destination and stakeholders into a knowledge-based and strategically coordinated partnership. Given the challenges of both fragmentation and resource dependencies, the institutional support of the experience conference has been instrumental in diffusing both practical solutions and research findings. Thus, although the resources and solutions vary between destinations, the emerging competences support activities in experience design and quality development of tourism products and enterprises across the country. Here we see research and industry intertwining in forming the co-production of Lofoten as a competitive, experience-delivering destination.

The experience-based year-round destination

New structures and models of both operation and development have emerged, but is the industry more successful?

As the overview of some of the emergence processes and interactions shows, Lofoten as a destination has undergone a major development during the past decade. This is also clearly demonstrated in the tourism statistics for incoming tourism development and the related product development that has been a result of the innovative activity and co-production among many different actors and stakeholders, both at the destination and in Nordland as a region.

Destination development

The development in the number of visitors to Lofoten does to some degree reflect the static situation described as the point of departure for the self-discovery process that led to the transformation towards a year-round experience destination. Interestingly, the number of winter tourists has increased steadily over the last decade, regardless of recession-induced dips in the total numbers. This indicates that the efforts have had a positive effect on the overarching goal of a seasonally more balanced load (Finne, 2017). The global petroleum crisis hitting Norway hard in 2014 has boosted Norwegian tourism in general by improving currency and purchasing power in important incoming markets, but when comparing with other regions the development of Lofoten has been above average among comparable Norwegian destinations.

Full-year experience product development escalating

According to a competitive analysis and comparison of nature-based tourism in northern Norway with the most relevant competing destinations in Nordic, European and overseas, the conclusion was that the challenge seemed to be the ability to transform superb resources into world-class products and to mobilise the partners to take part in co-production of complex and export-ready packages (Løvland et al., 2013). The key to this positive development has been the ability of core industry partners to engage with local municipalities, regional development partners with active support from applied R&D and education to convert the spectacular cultural and natural resource base into individual and bookable experience products, available throughout the whole year. This allows for co-specialisation among producers and improved profitability, both through scale and scope economics related to new network business models.

In the period from 2004 onwards, a large number of new nature-based experience products were designed and launched. The Lofoten Winter project organised the core network of enterprises taking part in this development, with a special focus on new winter products. In addition to whale watching being the core product innovation, other nature-based products and experiences were developed and launched commercially. New activities such as kayaking, bicycling and randonné skiing were brought to the market within a few years, and with the build-up of new hotel services in Vågan with full-year activity, this stimulated activity-based entrepreneurs to bring new products forward and establish a better-coordinated supply of experience packages also through the traditionally low winter season.

The new facilities also attracted new segments of the business market, and the combination with cultural experiences created external resource linkages that made it possible to develop new events targeting new segments.

Gradually the geographical area for experience deliveries was extended from the core area in central and eastern Lofoten (Svolvær and Leknes area) to new areas. In Gimsøy, a new world-class golfing experience was developed in close cooperation with leading international partners, placing the new facility among Europe's and the world's most spectacular links golf courses. The golf activity was bundled with natural phenomena, offering golf experiences to all segments with midnight sun in the summer and the Northern Lights in the winter season. Internationally this links facility is attracting growing interest and standing.

Based on the core activity of the Viking museum Borg in western Lofoten, new outdoor experience-based activities were launched, bridging with other local partners. A combined food trail was established, linking with the Viking history of the region and the museum, which also developed a number of new activities linking with the growth of the international explorer cruise segment. As a result, this stimulated an extension of activity into the winter season as the interest in winter cruises was growing and resulted in increasing numbers of visitors and new customer groups in the traditionally low season.

At the same time, new and more individual tourism emerged, based on the adoption of new social media and increasing mobility among tourists. Internationally the term 'going with the locals' gained importance in providing less staged and more authentic experiences for visiting guests, both for leisure and corporate visitors. In Lofoten the development can be seen with a rapidly growing number of AirBnB offers, powered by the high interest in the iconic region. Around 2016 the small municipalities of Lofoten had among the highest share of AirBnB offers per capita in Norway (Vinogradov and Strømmen-Bakhtiar, 2017).

Other nature-based activities were introduced and established ones were developed further. Birdwatching and nature safaris soon became part of the new portfolio of winter products emerging. With the increasing network activity among the local experience enterprises, new actors were attracted and started businesses not present before.

Arctic cod fishery is the basis for the history and economy of Lofoten and many coastal communities in northern Norway. In 1991 the first 'World championship in arctic cod fishing' was organised as a new winter event. The cultural heritage related to the fishery was present in the initiatives leading to increased networking activities and the priorities of the master plan for destination development launched in 2006, but did not gain full momentum until the process matured. The increasing experience-based product development at the Lofotr Viking museum, the ongoing consolidation of the Norwegian museum sector to the new Museum North, led to new momentum in the work to establish a new cultural heritage centre in Lofoten. The centre had the Norwegian name for Arctic cod, 'Skrei', and was launched as a national centre with the support from the Norwegian Ministry of Fisheries.

Another element in developing year-round experiences was related to developing and branding new and extreme sports events with Lofoten as the arena. In 2000 the first 'Arctic Challenge' snowboard event was arranged in western Lofoten by the world-leading snowboarders Terje Håkonsen and Daniel Franck. The arrangement was a kind of self-organised alternative championship between the best riders in the world, and Lofoten was the stage for this winter event until 2005, when it was moved to Oslo. The branding effect of the Arctic Challenge was important in building new extreme winter activities.

At Unstad in western Lofoten a small group of surf amateurs and enthusiasts, since 1990, developed a limited surf activity, utilising the special natural conditions here. Especially in the fall and winter season the conditions for building huge waves are favourable and attract surfers internationally in growing numbers – as well as during the winter. Surfing and kite-surfing under the Northern Lights have become new elements on the bucket list for surf enthusiasts from all over the world.

In 2013 a new bicycle race event took place: the Arctic Race of Norway was launched by the sports event giant ASO (also staging the Tour de France arrangement) together with Norwegian partners. They wanted to expose the Arctic landscape inside the Arctic Circle as the stage for the new event. The first stage of this race took place in Lofoten and the neighbouring archipelago region of Vesterålen and proved very promising, even when comparing with the much more established Tour de France.

Based on the growing and successful sports events, local entrepreneurs from the experience-producing companies in Vågan started developing new and even more extreme sports experience events, using the Lofoten nature in destination branding. The preparation included building supplier networks for conferences and events, and was followed by the development of a new extreme sports event called the Arctic Triple in 2016. This race included a ski mountaineering event in the winter (Lofoten Skimo), the Lofoten Ultra trail going through Lofoten in the summer, finishing with the Lofoten Triathlon in late summer.

13.4 Reflections on the co-emergence of destination transformation and knowledge support

We can clearly classify the overall process in Lofoten as a *process of self-discovery*. In Rodrik's original formulation, this is a process whereby actors discover how they can produce a certain class of products successfully in commercial terms, and the solutions spread locally to other actors, with a significant spillover effect from the first successful mover to new entrants in the industry. A mere scan of the preceding chapter shows how widely the range of new experience products has proliferated in a region where all experiences some 20 years ago were staged by the tourists themselves, for themselves. Additionally, the new products are not only copies or near copies of those that have already proven their success, but are closely or remotely related ones.

It also qualifies as an entrepreneurial discovery process in the Foray sense of the term as a process involving multiple actors that could not possibly arrive at the discovery alone. Then, what was the discovery? It has three components.

First is the discovery of the untapped economic potential in providing experiences rather than services – which is the core of the experience economy. This is a cognitive aspect, but it obviously has some major consequences for practicalities. Services are of course still required but they are integrated in something with a greater economic potential. Some services also had to change character, such as the marketing service of the original destination management organisation.

Second is the realisation that all these new offerings will hardly be possible – to develop, to produce, or to sell – unless there is a development of the destination as a whole on which all these activities can stand. This is of course a *post factum* description: the collaboration began as a simple coordination of actors with similar concerns and the new layers of benefits arising from the progressive consolidation of cooperative arrangements were hardly imaginable before they were at least actually emerging.

The importance of the destination as a crucial object of interest is also underlined by the need to manage shared infrastructure and other common goods and services in a balance between residents and visitors.

In fact, this is not only a realisation of the importance of the destination level but actually a redefinition of what a destination is.

Third are the changes in the industrial organisation. It used to be a dispersed set of service providers with differing quality levels and differing attitudes towards customers, and essentially competing on price, despite the growth in visitor numbers. Other actors have come in that sell other products, but the main issue here is that all the small actors have been forced into more or less stable and tightly linked production networks, or composite value chains. And, of course, the intended and successful move towards year-round business also changes the character of working in the tourism business.

In one way this story differs from Rodrik's original conception of a self-discovery. He emphasised the discovery of an appropriate cost structure. Obviously the stable production networks at destination level and their provision of basic services is important in this respect. The move from a fragmented service industry to a more tightly knit destination organisation means more for the cost structure than just being able to benefit from the scale of some underlying operations. However, even if cost is obviously important, discovering the *value structure* or perhaps the income structure is probably more important in this case. This has two aspects. One is the discovery of what it means to provide for experiences rather than (or on top of) services. The other one is the value added by belonging to a destination that may have a visible brand around the world as a reliable place to go for the experience that gives one the 'reason to go'.

The consolidation can be said to have some characteristics of the stages of a process of emergence of a cluster: rivalry, network cooperation on joint challenges, cooperation on knowledge and innovation, attracting resources of shared interest, and strategic knowledge cooperation (Smith, 2009). The first cooperative effort reduced rivalry by essentially agreeing on a division of labour between the islands but did not improve the firms' ability to improve their structural position nor to reduce their path dependency. The whale watching product moved the cooperation out of the shared concerns zone and into significant attempts at collaboration in innovation – which proved a successful turning point for the entire industry in the region and set a pattern for future work. Together with the mobilisation and joint work on the master plan, the foresight exercise and the attraction of a very knowledgeable consultant, the cooperation gained momentum and resulted in an even tighter network and more extensive trust relations upon which future efforts could build. The establishment of enduring relations to research and the successful launching of the national conference series, then, could be said to have moved the Lofoten tourist industry and its partners over in a national strategic position with prospects of also gaining access to more R&D resources for future development.

In summary, then, we could say that the story is one of smart specialisation – and it is, in fact, one of the pillars of the more recent decision of the Nordland County Council to actually establish its own *strategy* for smart specialisation (Nordland County Council, 2015).

13.5 Final remarks

The clustering dynamics perspective offers useful insights from the actor perspective, underpinning how timing and overlapping activities of partners engaging in different and parallel network initiatives resulted in the accumulation of necessary resources and skills needed to break out of the structural limitations and path dependencies found at the destination around 2000. This provides some necessary, but not sufficient, preconditions for the path renewal and creation observed.

On the other hand, the emergence and complexity perspective deals with the apparent systemic and functional logics, guiding the emergence of a new experience-based destination structure and the EDP. Referring to the initial clustering stage, this might be characterised within the framework of knowledge creation and EDP, following Martin and Sunley (2013), with emphasis on knowledge fragmentation at the micro level. The initial changes and the initial entrepreneurial discovery mainly came about through the role of private entrepreneurs of the tourism industry in Lofoten, but this effort was highly related to and dependent on the actions of public sector actors, especially at the regional level in Nordland. The active intervention from the regional development actors as Nordland County Council and administration together with the regional branch of Innovation Norway complemented and governed the systemic process towards addressing the new foundations in experience design and necessary R&D support to the destination strategy development through the masterplan process, which itself created the wider context for enhancing the transformation process.

Gradually more second-order effects through downward causation can be observed in the next stage, from 2007 onwards, when the process was increasingly supported by research and the development of applied methods and knowledge. In this stage this also led to the inclusion of the experience economy approach in regional planning and strategies. At the same time the development actors at the regional level gradually became more concerned about the dissemination of new and relevant research and practice-based knowledge in experience design and production to other destinations than Lofoten, thus exploring how this knowledge could be relevant to new destinations and resource configurations. In this period the focus shifted towards bringing out the potential of the promising coastal region Helgeland further south.

With increasing R&D knowledge as well as new institutional platforms such as a new national programme of experience tourism research (Northern Insights), localised in Nordland and northern Norway, the Novadis knowledge centre and the joint innovation arena Norwegian Experience Conference, the experience tourism and economy in Lofoten and Nordland had created the necessary structures to go further in the transformation of the regional economy. This process gradually has led to the integration with the smart specialisation process in Nordland mentioned above, starting around 2013. Based on the knowledge platform created through the co-emergence process of transforming Lofoten as a destination, the smart specialisation strategy provided new tools to the tourism industry, destinations and the regional partnership to address further development and recombination of the core competencies into new and full-year experience activities.

The observed transition process of Lofoten as a tourism destination also has demonstrated the relevance of specific mechanisms in spatial innovation in tourism destinations pointed out by Brandão (2014) and Bonetti et al. (2006). This especially deals with the necessity to develop local strategies for tourism innovation that are locally and socially embedded and thus able to draw upon a wide range of physical, social and cultural capital and, over time, mobilise broad participation among key stakeholders, both at the regional and destination level. The described strong local and regional networks have played important roles in creating the required memory and priorities to produce a wide range of different innovations, and also contributed to a wider accumulation of capital in all forms – physical, social and cultural.

As an epilogue to the Lofoten case, it may be observed that the quite successful and long-term innovation process has created new structures and preconditions for future and sustainable growth of the destination. However, the complexity perspective still reminds us that the outcomes so far give opportunities for continued path renewal and path creation. When observing the ongoing innovation process today, the basic challenges of fragmentation and lack of coordination in implementing place-based strategies of experience tourism in Lofoten and elsewhere remain, since much of the gradual change takes place within project frameworks rather than long-term strategies and support. Hopefully the present and more robust knowledge base can provide a sufficient fundament to handle the necessary and strategic market orientation while continuing the entrepreneurial discoveries needed for path renewal and creation. The ongoing implementation and learning process of the regional smart specialisation strategy in Nordland, with linkages to local destination innovation strategies in Lofoten and other tourism destinations, provides an important strategic and structural framework and guidance to support relevant and long-term innovation, both in tourism and in bringing the local communities and other local industries into the necessary transformation process.

Note

1 The Value Creation 2010 programme was merged in 2007 into the VRI programme (Sörvik and Midtkandal, 2017), the council's programme to support research and innovation in the regions of Norway for the next ten-year period up to 2017.

References

Bonetti, E., Petrillo, C.S. and Simoni, M. (2006). Tourism system dynamics: A multi-level destination approach. In Lazzeretti, L. and Petrillo, C.S. (eds) *Tourism local systems and networking*, pp. 111–133. Oxford: Elsevier.

Brandão, A.F.F.A. (2014). *Innovation in tourism: The role of regional innovation systems*. Aveiro: University of Aveiro.

Byrne, D. and Callaghan, G. (2014). *Complexity theory and the social sciences: The state of the art*. Abingdon: Routledge.

Cohen, W.M. and Levinthal, D.A. (1990). Absorptive capacity: A new perspective on learning and innovation. *Administrative Science Quarterly*, 35 (1), pp. 128–152.

Finne, H. (2017). Gir smart spesialisering resultater? *Plan*, 48 (2), pp. 8–13.

Hall, C.M. (2009). Innovation and tourism policy in Australia and New Zealand: Never the twain shall meet? *Journal of Policy Research in Tourism, Leisure and Events*, 1 (1), pp. 2–18.

Hjalager, A.-M. (1997). Innovation patterns in sustainable tourism: An analytical typology. *Tourism Management*, 18 (1), pp. 35–41.

Hjalager, A.-M. (2010). A review of innovation research in tourism. *Tourism Management*, 31 (1), pp. 1–12.

Hjalager, A.-M., Huijbens, E.H., Björk, P., Nordin, S., Flagestad, A. and Knútsson, Ö. (2008). *Innovation systems in Nordic tourism*. Oslo: Nordic Innovation Centre.

Løvland, J., Fabritius, M.K. and Madsen, E.L. (2014). Erfaringer fra bedriftsnettverket Lofoten Winter. *Arbeidsnotat*. Bodø: Nordlandsforskning.

Løvland, J., Jervan, B., Mackay, M., Bergsli, M., Fabrititus, M.K. and Bulanova, O. (2013). *Markedsanalyser for NordNorsk Reiseliv. Turoperatøranalyse*. Bodø: Nordlandsforskning.

Mabogunje, A.L. (1980). *The development process: A spatial perspective*. London: Hutchinson.

Martin, R. and Sunley, P. (2013). Forms of emergence and the evolution of economic landscapes. In Cooke, P. (ed.) *Re-framing regional development: Evolution, innovation and transition*, pp. 73–94. London: Routledge.

Nordland County Council (2015). *Innovative Nordland. Innovation strategy for Nordland 2014–2020*. Bodø: Nordland County Council.

Pine, B.J. and Gilmore, J.H. (1999). *Experience economy: Work is theatre and every business a stage*. Boston: Harvard Business School Press.

Smith, M. (2009). Exploratory techniques for examining cluster dynamics: A systems thinking approach. *Local Economy*, 24 (4), pp. 283–298.

Sörvik, J. and Midtkandal, I. (2017). Continuous priority setting in the Norwegian VRI programme. In Kyriakou, D., Martínez, M.P., Periáñez-Forte, I. and Rainoldi, A. (eds) *Governing smart specialisation*, pp. 156–178. London: Routledge.

Vinogradov, E. and Strømmen-Bakhtiar, A. (2017). *Effekt av Airbnb på det generelle utleiemarkedet og bomiljøet i Norge*. Bodø: Nordlandsforskning.

Virkkala, S. and Mariussen, Å. (2019a). Emergence of new business areas in regional economies through entrepreneurial discovery processes. In Mariussen, Å., Virkkala, S., Finne, H. and Aasen, T.M. (eds) *The entrepreneurial discovery process and regional development: New knowledge emergence, conversion and exploitation*. Abingdon: Routledge.

Virkkala, S. and Mariussen, Å. (2019b). Self-discovery enabling entrepreneurial discovery processes. In Mariussen, Å., Virkkala, S., Finne, H. and Aasen, T.M. (eds) *The entrepreneurial discovery process and regional development: New knowledge emergence, conversion and exploitation*. Abingdon: Routledge.

14 Historical examples of entrepreneurial discovery

Revisiting the manufacturing history of Raufoss evolving between exploration and exploitation

Asbjørn Karlsen

14.1 Introduction

Smart specialisation has been introduced as the basis for a policy framework for the EU's Innovation Policy and Cohesion Policy in 2011. Integral to this move, strategies for inducing smart specialisation have given public agents a key role. Entrepreneurial discovery processes are central in designing and implementing smart specialisation strategies (Foray, 2017). With regard to industrial change and agency, the concepts of smart specialisation and entrepreneurial discovery have much in common with the concept of 'path creation' (Garud and Karnøe, 2003; Simmie, 2012). The former concept is about discovery of new domains and transforming regional industries, while the latter concept focuses on 'development of new technologies and industries'. Both conceptualisations deal with collective entrepreneurial efforts for structural change in industry.

This chapter is inspired by the concepts of exploration and exploitation found in the study of organisation learning by March (1991). It aims to analyse local industrial development through phases of exploration and exploitation. How could the history of a Norwegian manufacturing town be explained by concepts such as smart specialisation and path creation? A case study will shed light on these concepts and their relevance for analysing regional development and renewal.

Empirically the chapter will tell a story of entrepreneurial discovery from a particular regional context: a local cluster originating from a company town. In the academic literature (see e.g. Steen and Karlsen, 2014), such a point of departure is regarded as a poor seedbed for entrepreneurial discoveries (Foray, 2017). This chapter, however, recognises capabilities for diversifying arms production into a wide range of civilian manufacturing activities. Through demerger of a state-owned company, spinoff processes and inward investments, a quite high-tech manufacturing cluster emerged. The local industry is followed through four distinct phases of exploration or exploitation. The study recognises institutional tension between strategies of exploration leading to path creation on the one hand and strategies of exploitation implying path extension on the other hand. The story of industrial development confirms that entrepreneurial discovery may be driven by unique historical events in line with suggestions from the literature on path creation.

14.2 Discussing the concepts of 'smart specialisation' and 'path creation'

For decades, scholars from various social sciences have discussed how to explain continuity and change in local and regional economies. Some of them have even made a distinction between radical change and continuous improvements and the role of learning in this regard. As a starting point for a historical study on industrial development, it is tempting to apply the two kinds of organisational learning introduced by March: 'exploration of new possibilities or exploitation of old certainties' (March, 1991: 72). The first is about searching, discovering, experimenting and finding new solutions, while the latter is about refinement and efficiency in resource utilisation and work organisation. The allocation of search resources has implications for the consecutive adaptive processes. Exploitation relates to a shorter time horizon than exploration, which relates to a longer time horizon.

The conceptualisation above was developed for studies at an organisational level. For the study of industrial agglomeration on a local or regional level, we have to draw on further conceptualisations appropriate for these levels of investigation. In his study of the Danish wind power industry, Simmie (2012) applies the concepts of path dependence and path creation, which corresponds to the concepts of exploitation and exploration respectively. March (1991) finds that the choices between two contrasting ways of allocating resources for searching are made strategically at an organisational level. At a regional level, the strategy of exploration is reflected in the more recent policies of smart specialisation (Foray, 2014).

Foray (2015) gives historical examples of smart specialisation that emerge spontaneously. In today's world, where path dependence appears very strong in regions that would benefit the most from creating new industrial paths, a strategy led by public authorities seems to be required. This includes a process of identifying and realising new opportunities by integrating dispersed knowledge from many sources. Foray (2015) argues that the prioritisation should be based on knowledge integrated from the economic actors and knowledge institutions themselves. Smart specialisation strategy is a process of self-discovery which ends up in priorities of new domains within a smart specialisation policy. It appears as a staged process where the initial phase is expected to precede, go in parallel or even include processes of innovation. The strategy is not a process of self-discovery by itself, but it may support and even instigate or result in such a process.

I will argue that smart specialisation appears as a new policy strategy, but corresponding phenomena to entrepreneurial discovery processes are recognised and discussed elsewhere in the academic literature. There are some remarkable commonalities across the strands of literature on smart specialisation on the one hand and that of path creation on the other hand. Both strands of literature elaborate core processes of entrepreneurial discovery over time. As we will elaborate further below, they seem to focus on different stages of the change processes and may as such complement each other. As smart specialisation policy is assigning certain change agents strategic roles, based on analyses of the local context, it attempts to influence the processes of path creation as conceptualised on the basis of numerous empirical studies.

The literature on smart specialisation and that on path creation both explain structural change in the economy. Foray (2015) argues that entrepreneurial discovery allows the system to reorient and renew itself. Strategies of smart specialisation are, however, about deliberately developing new domains of opportunities or new specialisation in order to diversify the structure of a regional economy. Strategies of smart specialisation precede the innovation stage: application of general purpose technology has the potential to transform processes in a traditional sector and even generate many innovations. Relevant knowledge is found in science, but entrepreneurial and economic knowledge is just as relevant. As such, Foray goes beyond theories of technological development to also include regional institutions and scientists, in other words, the collective entrepreneur of the triple helix. The path-creation literature focuses more explicitly on the development of new technologies and new industries. Garud and Karnøe (2003) elaborate on the emergence of new technology paths, as they highlight deviations from existing trajectories. In the end, both strands of literature deal with diversification of the economy, which means some sort of exploration at a regional level.

In the literature of smart specialisation and that of path creation, reflexive actors take an entrepreneurial role. Both approaches emphasise the collaborative efforts of such actors across further domains. Strategies of smart specialisation should primarily be place-based. Smart specialisation strategy assigns policy-makers a role to help different stakeholders to discover a new and promising domain to develop. In order to build knowledge platforms in a region, it is necessary to exploit knowledge also from extra-regional sources such as universities and demanding customers. Garud and Karnøe (2001) argue that novel paths emerge as knowledgeable actors purposefully deviate from existing trajectories. These knowledgeable agents deliberately pursue certain courses of action. Key entrepreneurial firms discover and create new opportunities, whereas other actors, such as R&D institutions and other public bodies, interact with the firms and support them with complementary assets required to develop a new path. Not just producers, but regulators, designers, users and evaluators co-create new industrial paths (Garud and Karnøe, 2003). The path-creation approach values the interaction with users of the technology. Agency has a distributed nature in both strands of literature emphasising the efforts of the many.

Path creation takes place as an accumulation of inputs (tools, artefacts, rules, practices and knowledge) that creates a momentum. An emerging path begins to enable and constrain the activities of the actors involved, who become embedded in the path they strive to form in real time. In a study of the emergence of wind turbines, Garud and Karnøe (2003) recognise a strategy of 'breakthrough' in the US industry as research-based attempts to create radical changes in technology. This strategy is contrasted with a more successful strategy of bricolage employed by Danish actors. The term bricolage explains how actors improvise and draw on many resources of relevance. Bricolage is the co-shaping of an emerging technological path in order to obtain modest but steady gains. These actors mobilise specific sets of events from the past in their endeavour to take new initiatives. Path creation is not a linear process. It is rather contingent on learning processes, where actors reflect explicitly upon past events and how they could be significant for entrepreneurial discovery. Both strands of literature emphasise learning processes, dialogues and local experimentation.

Different from the path-creation approach, the smart specialisation approach explicitly discusses the regional context. Foray (2017) finds that less advanced and transition regions have a special need for support of microsystems of innovation, as there are holes in their industrial ecosystem. Companies and specialised service and research institutions have to be mobilised to address the whole set of capabilities to develop novel domains. From the literature on industrial development of old industrial regions, we learn that such regions are inclined to different types of lock-in that restrain change and radical innovations (Grabher, 1992; Hassink, 2005). We find corresponding regional contexts in single-industry areas (Chapman, 2005) and company towns (Dale, 2002; Karlsen, 1999). The latter economies are typically dominated by one large firm surrounded by a limited number of smaller firms. As the smaller firms are more or less relying on transactions with the large one, the whole economy becomes dependent on a very limited number of external markets and external actors. Consequently, the local economy appears quite vulnerable. Even if these regions may prosper for long periods of time, such organisationally thin regions are considered to lack the heterogeneous composition of firms and institutions, and the innovative capacity, needed to initiate and develop new domains of activities (Isaksen and Trippl, 2017). Thin regions are typically trapped in path extension, characterised by incremental product innovations within existing industries and incremental process innovations along prevailing technological paths (Isaksen, 2015).

Simmie (2012) explains, however, how reflexive agents create new paths within the context of path-dependent development influenced by the economic environment, technological paradigms, institutions and technological regimes. The basic idea of path creation is that new paths are latent in old paths, spin out from existing ones or even draw on further related industries as they combine existing resources in new ways (Martin, 2010). From this perspective, the legacies of the past are significant, not as constraints, but rather as resources that entrepreneurs and businesses may draw upon (Karlsen, 2011; Steen and Karlsen, 2014).

In light of the discussion above, it is reasonable to suggest that explorative strategies lead to path creation, while exploitative strategies imply path extension.

The following case study will investigate phases of exploration and phases of exploitation in the industrial history of Raufoss. It will form a basis for a further discussion of the concept 'smart specialisation' and the concept 'path creation', and their relevance for approaching regional development.

14.3 The story of Raufoss manufacturing industry through four phases

The following empirical section takes a historical approach. The story does not follow the traditional distinction into phases given by the changes in formal organisation and ownership (demerger and privatisation). Each phase in this story is rather recognised by wider institutional capabilities in the region that underpin explorative strategies and exploitative strategies, respectively. The empirical section follows the regional industry through four distinct phases: (1) from an industrial district to a company town; (2) entrepreneurial discovery within the company; (3) cluster turning into path extension; and (4) facing a new technology landscape.

(1) From an industrial district to a company town (1850–1950)

In the middle of the nineteenth century a sociologist characterised the Toten region, including the town of Raufoss (120 kilometres north of Oslo), as the most industrialised rural district of Norway (Sundt, 1867). He recognised craft-based industries specialised in wall clocks and sheath knifes having customers all over the country. The craftsmen and traders brought other products and knowledge home as input to innovation and the upgrading of existing industry in the district. A relatively advanced mechanical production emerged – an industry characterised by adaptability (Johnstad and Utter, 2015).

In the second half of the nineteenth century the Toten region turned, however, into a manufacturing region dominated by the Raufoss Ammunition Factory (RA), established in the town of Raufoss in 1896 (Wang, 1996). The central government established the state-owned company RA to strengthen domestic defence in a period of nation-building. The ammunition factory was located west of Lake Mjøsa for strategic reasons in a situation marked by tension between the two nations constituting the Swedish–Norwegian union. Modern industry and technology displaced the traditional ones. After the Second World War this defence industry was integrated into the strategies of NATO. RA experienced more or less continual growth, reaching the peak of 2,600 employees in 1980.

The state was not just an owner of the company, but also had responsibilities for the local community and the local economy. Production for the civilian market, as an additional activity to ammunition manufacturing, was put on the agenda of a commission in 1918. Additional production should work as a buffer and balance fluctuating demand from military activity over shifting periods of war and peace around the world. Therefore, central authorities and local management strove to keep the entire workforce employed. This endeavour was one example of the paternalism that characterised the RA organisation. The local factory and machinery were prepared for entrepreneurial discovery. The first example of additional production for the civilian market was the manufacturing of ball bearings in the 1920s. For the decades to come, the company tried to diversify into further activities within the company, particularly into civilian production. Initiatives to move into car fabrication were taken in 1923 and again in 1931, but these intiatives soon stalled (Wang, 1996). These initiatives may be considered as a sort of 'smart specialisation strategy' that was initiated by the central state rather than regional or local public actors, which recent literature proposes.

After the Second World War, RA became a state-owned but independent company that produced military-related articles. The Minister of Defence facilitated and coordinated industrial development in the region in close collaboration with local management (Wang, 1996). The working life relations were characterised by short distance of communication between managers and the shop floor, inclusiveness and democratic values. As such, social relations at Raufoss were the prototype of the Nordic model of close collaboration between social partners supported by a proactive state. This consent between employers and employees, the unions included, paved the way for growth in production of ammunition by rationalisation and enhanced efficiency. In this way, these social relations supported exploitation strategies.

(2) Entrepreneurial discovery within the company (1950–2000)

From 1950 RA was given the role as a major supplier of ammunition to NATO. From 1960 RA prepared the production of rocket motors as an additional activity. As we will soon learn, this advanced manufacturing, still a core activity at Raufoss, spawned further projects and spinoffs directed towards the civilian market. In the 1950s the idea emerged to convert knowledge on material technology (particularly aluminium) into civilian production, an entrepreneurial discovery that had major implications for the industrial development to come. The idea materialised for the first time in the 1960s, when RA started producing articles for the construction industry, particularly extruded frames for doors and windows and façade sheets, for domestic office buildings and hotels. RA collaborated with national and international institutes in the construction industry. They were also into aluminium components for the oil and gas exploitation industry, such as heli-decks and pipe joints. Later and to a much greater extent, the idea of converting this knowledge of material technology to other uses was realised in manufacturing components for the automotive industry. In summary, many initiatives of entrepreneurial discovery took place and some failed. Other initiatives for developing a new domain showed success in the long run, but were typically realised decades after the first initiatives.

Conversion of knowledge for use in civilian production was evidently more successful when it came to the idea of producing aluminium profiles from the company's extruding press and rolling of aluminium sheets. The Swedish car company Volvo requested Norwegian firms to become suppliers to its automotive production, and in 1955 RA was mentioned as a relevant subsupplier of car components. The company units enjoyed some autonomy and capability for developing new products demanded by the market, an activity that was encouraged by the top management. RA had allocated more resources to R&D activities, which were aligned to develop prototypes based on competence in material technology. In 1974 a new tool factory was ready, and the next year a new project department was created (Johnstad and Utter, 2015). The central authorities put pressure on companies in the domestic aluminium industry to connect thus far disconnected companies, in order to integrate a domestic value chain within aluminium. Soon the major metal producer (ÅSV) entered into formal collaboration with further processors of aluminium, such as the units at Raufoss, in order to prepare further downstream activities. In 1965 RA signed an agreement with Volvo to supply 500,000 bumpers in aluminium for their cars.

This contract was a milestone in the industrial history of the manufacturing town, as a first successful step in the direction of diversifying the local economy. First, manufacturing of car components turned out to become a fast-growing activity until the turn of the century. Second, the entrance into the automotive value chain implied a change in manufacturing culture. RA faced a demanding customer with regard to product dimensions and tolerance. The company strove to comply with quality and safety standards and requirements for cost-efficient, flexible and responsive production. The production demanded further competence building in material technology, but also new knowledge about up-to-date production processes. The car component division, in collaboration with research institute SINTEF, was also able to introduce new products, such as wheel suspension arms and steering wheel systems (columns). In the late 1970s, another Swedish car manufacturer, SAAB, became a customer of RA. In the 1980s the local manufacturers supplied various car components for a wider European market, and later also for a North American and an Asian market (Wang, 1996).

The company explored and implemented modern production processes and made investments in new machines and factories. RA relied on core competences in metallurgy, construction and tool making. The combination of competences in compression moulding and mass production of heat compression products provided capabilities for production of light metal components for the civilian market. The company prepared various products based on metal sheets, rods and profiles made at the works.

There are three examples of converting core competencies from arms production into new civilian products: (1) the manufacturing of cartridge shells in aluminium starting in the 1950s was the first step in developing various aluminium products. This production provided basic competence in alloys and processing for later production for the civilian market, first as bumpers (owned by German company Benteler since 2009), some decades later also as the wheel suspension arms for the automotive industry (owned by the Austrian company Neumann Aluminium since 2004). (2) Lessons learned from using brass in small arms ammunition were crucial for the development of break pipe fittings for utility vehicles. The unique fittings were easy to handle and ensured tight joints. In the hands of Kongsberg Automotive since 2004, brass material was increasingly substituted by composite materials, but far from completely. (3) As space rocket motors were partly made of composite materials, the activity provided material competence for LPG containers made of corresponding materials since 2000, in the hands of Hexagon Ragasco (Johnstad and Utter, 2015). These are examples of diversifications based on the entrepreneurial discovery made in-house at RA decades earlier. As diversification was at least partly directed towards the automotive sector, we could talk about a spontaneous smart specialisation.

From 1997–1999 the new CEO relied on external consultants and made risky acquisitions internationally. RA turned into quite an international company, with half of its activities abroad. The governing idea of the CEO was to turn the traditional manufacturer of car components into a provider of systems for the automotive industry. His strategies lacked local rooting. This was a break with the tradition of inclusive management and he entered into conflict with the employees and their union. In the wake of these actions, an economic crisis emerged. The local industrial activity was saved by the state and restructured. The return to locally recruited leadership appeared as a kind of a re-embedding and represented a continuation of the traditional industry culture at Raufoss. Lessons were learned by trial and error.

In the same period RA's division of forming technology, together with GM (Saab and Opel), had developed the aforementioned wheel suspension arms. Raufoss Technology was to establish a new factory in Norway serving the European market and another factory in Canada serving the US market. In contrast to the former top manager, who wanted to sell this business out, the new CEO went all out for keeping this activity in-house. This turned out as a risky business and the investments failed as productions at GM halted. After a troublesome period searching for a new owner for Raufoss Technology, the company was acquired by the Austrian company Neumann Aluminium in 2004.

To cope with an economic crisis at the start of the century, the RA company was split into 11 manufacturing firms, and soon Raufoss Industrial Park consisting of 45 firms emerged. The paternalistic state ensured the new firms an economic foundation and handed the ownership over to companies with long-term interest in the respective industrial branches. The owners, typically German, Austrian and Swedish, allowed the local units a certain degree of autonomy as they recognised the local manufacturing culture and competencies. This entrepreneurial discovery with regard to new business ideas on industrial organisation was a further step into new path creation. More precisely, the new firms and ownerships represented some sort of layering by adding new structures to the existing ones characterised by the defence company.

The diversification took place by bricolage – local actors drew on events from the past and improvised by combining many resources. Government bodies, local industrial actors and R&D units have been co-shaping the emerging technological path based on some core competences, which have been refined in the following. The core competence of the R&D unit was material technology, which was cutting-edge, particularly with regard to stretch bending and forging of aluminium profiles. The competence included knowing who the key suppliers of various qualities of materials were. Tool production and process technology for automation made production efficient and provided the customers with functional solutions.

The local R&D unit, demerged as Raufoss Technology & Industrial Management (RTIM) in 2002, was as good as bankrupt in 2003–2004. This crisis was solved by the support of the Arena cluster initiative,[1] project funding from the county council, and a patient bank. Soon RTIM was in the hands of various local and national stakeholders. SINTEF gradually increased their share of ownership, before the research unit became a subsidiary of SINTEF, renamed SINTEF Raufoss Manufacturing (SRM), and was subsequently further integrated in a national innovation system. In general, the R&D unit supported efficient serial production, particularly of high-quality car components. These innovation capabilities were stimulated by demanding customers, such as NATO, Volvo and GM, and the collaboration with research institutions at a national level, such as the Norwegian Defence Research Establishment (FFI), SINTEF and the Norwegian University of Science and Technology (NTNU).

(3) Cluster turning into path extension (2000–2015)

As the attention of the demerged firms turned inwards, concentrating on their own core business, the regional industry appeared more fragmented than before (Johnstad and Utter, 2015). This industrial structure consequently faced a risk of losing projects diverging from ordinary activities. In this situation, the challenge was to develop cooperation across the regional firms in order to enhance innovation and competitive capabilities. Cluster creation strategies soon appeared as a turning point for local collaboration and for embedding the industry regionally. Based on experiences from the Arena project, the Raufoss manufacturing industry became a National Centre of Expertise (NCE)[2] in 2006. The success of the Raufoss manufacturing industry in obtaining status in succeeding cluster programmes rests on the efforts of key actors in local industry who have been proactive through stages of application and operation of the programmes. NCE Raufoss has launched a portfolio of research projects that involve the manufacturing industry as well as R&D institutions in order to support the innovative activities in regional industry.

Toten Aluminium Group (TotAl) was another network constellation of small firms that partly were spinoffs from RA (Karlsen, 2011). This group of SMEs outside the industrial park was particularly involved in processing of aluminium and other lightweight materials. The cluster programme Arena revitalised this network. The SMEs are partly suppliers to larger firms in the industrial park. The TotAl Group was an initiative to build a bridge to the industrial park and collaborate in upgrading the SMEs as suppliers. In 2016 the industrial cluster at and around Raufoss embraces more than 40 companies and more than 5,000 employees. In 2004 the industry re-established contact with the university college in the neighbouring town of Gjøvik. In 2016 this unit merged with NTNU in Trondheim. The merger appeared as a formal integration of a regional and a national innovation system.

SRM became the hub of the cluster network. As a key actor offering relevant competences for regional firms, SRM compensates for the shortages in R&D capabilities of the individual manufacturing firms at Raufoss. The R&D unit works as a common knowledge infrastructure for these firms. It maintains and develops material and manufacturing technology competence. The unit has test plants and workshops for prototypes and pilot production and offers competence on business management. The combination of research-based competence and experience-based competence provides a basis for a form of combined and complex innovation (Isaksen and Karlsen, 2012). The network constellations mentioned above imply further collaboration and integration in regional manufacturing industry. To put it simply, the glue was reinvented around 2005.

Evidently, the strategies of regional industry had turned from exploration to exploitation after the crisis in RA and the following restructuring at the turn of the century. The exploitation strategies were to a large degree based on previous discoveries and explorations. Core firms' attention and activities were directed towards the demands of customers in an international market characterised by tough competition. The production of car components appears as extensions of the assembly lines in Germany, Sweden and France. Customers demanded high-quality products and continuous cost reductions as well as reliable and responsive suppliers. As customers, a limited number of automotive companies had a captive relation to their suppliers. This kind of relation does not apply to the ammunition manufacturer, Nammo (the only core company that has its headquarters at Raufoss), operating with larger margins in the defence sector, but rather for manufacturers of car components operating with smaller margins in the automotive sector. We could thus talk about a layering process resulting in the co-existence of two contrasting types of relations between local suppliers and their foreign customers.

How do the cluster formation and innovation system, both regionally and nationally, work with regard to strategies of exploration or strategies of exploitation? The industry leaders find that their businesses have an advantage from their location in a local manufacturing cluster. By tradition, cluster firms share equipment and labs and they exchange knowledge, also enabled through mobility of personnel. They particularly appreciate participation in research projects initiated by the local R&D unit, SRM. Cluster dynamics have been enhanced through participation in lasting R&D programmes. By the help of programmes and centres such as the Norwegian Centre of Expertise, SRM has launched several projects for enhancing competence in local manufacturing firms. At the turn of the century, 'lean production' received much attention. The manufacturer of bumpers trained operators as well as managers to improve both product quality and flow of materials and components (eliminating waste) and productivity in general. Since 2005 further companies took part in corresponding activities. Such incremental improvements appear in line with the exploitation type of strategy.

In the former RA there was both space and autonomy for developing new ideas. After restructuring, this space was lost within the slim organisations that demerged from RA. As such, they may have lost their capability to diversify. The R&D shortage of individual firms was partly compensated for by a common infrastructure found in the demerged R&D unit (now SRM) and related collaboration through cluster initiatives and other research programmes. The collaboration had more success in ensuring increased productivity among existing firms, and less success in new firm formation and creating spinoffs. Manufacturing firms report that they need to have high focus on daily operations. Their activities are directed towards improving the production process or incremental product innovations (interviews in manufacturing firms, 2017). The strategies of existing companies seem to underpin path extension. Cluster organisations have taken initiatives to facilitate entrepreneurship in the form of start-ups, but recognise shortages in new business formation and spinoffs in later years (interview with cluster organisations, 2018).

We could conclude that during recent decades few local actors have been exploring new domains that would potentially lead to new path creation. Programmes such as NCE seem rather to underpin path extension, which has been successful with regards to maintaining economic activity and employment in a demanding automotive sector characterised by intensive international competition.

(4) Facing a new technology landscape – exploitation or exploration from 2015 onwards?

Core companies at Raufoss have been involved in two centres of research-based innovation (SFI) succeeding each other. Four larger companies in Raufoss Industrial Park took part in SFI Norman (2007–2014) in order to improve the competitive strength of the industry through long-term research and innovation in collaboration with SINTEF and NTNU. SFI Normann was consecutively followed by SFI Manufacturing (2015–2022) involving the same four manufacturing companies, university (NTNU) and R&D institution (SINTEF), and headed by the latter's subsidiary SRM. SFI Manufacturing is a multidisciplinary centre for research-based innovation (SFI) for competitive high-value manufacturing in Norway. It aims at providing sustainable innovations for automated manufacturing of multi-material products. Its vision is to demonstrate that sustainable and advanced manufacturing is possible in a high-cost country. SFI Manufacturing is organised in three research areas: (1) multi-material products and manufacturing processes; (2) robust and flexible automation; and (3) sustainable and innovative organisations. The focus on how to develop and manufacture multi-material products is particularly relevant for the producers of components for the automotive industry. This market requires the combination of strong and lightweight components (typically substituting steel components) in order to make cars more environmentally friendly.

Many of the activities within SFI manufacturing are, however, about introducing new general purpose technologies related to Industry 4.0. Core firms are adapting to a 'fourth industrial revolution', partly stimulated through their foreign ownership. Industry 4.0 is explained as a convergence between four increasingly powerful technological capabilities: robotics, 3D printing, artificial intelligence, and autonomous vehicles (Schwab, 2015). According to Kagermann et al. (2013), the future will see companies establishing global networks incorporating machinery, warehousing and production facilities in the shape of cyber-physical systems (CPS). Even if these scholars describe Industry 4.0 as a revolution that introduces disruptive technologies, the Raufoss companies have already approached and adapted to these new technologies, quite incrementally (interviews with management of local manufacturing firms, research institute and cluster organisations, 2017). As such, the new technologies have so far been used in exploitation strategies.

Basically, these general purpose technologies may be used for exploitation as well as for exploration. Both firms and knowledge institutions are preparing for these new technologies, introducing robots and additive manufacturing, etc. The vocational school, the vocational colleges, and the university are adjusting their curriculums in order to prepare their students for digitalisation and related new technologies in the industry of tomorrow. On behalf of the NCE, SRM applied for funding for a Norwegian Catapult Centre at Raufoss in 2017. The centre is, in 2018, ready to develop and demonstrate innovative production processes and general purpose technologies in mini factories, in collaboration with industry, research and educational institutions. This represents entrepreneurial discovery. The investments and efforts have potential for further exploration in the years ahead.

14.4 Discussions

The approach of 'smart specialisation' and approach of 'path creation' are both emphasising collective efforts for industrial renewal. Smart specialisation is a place-based strategy where policy-makers have a key role. It includes a procedure for selecting adequate activities for developing the most promising domain. The path-creation approach recognises the selection process rather as an outcome of learning processes and mindful deviations taking place through time.

The industrial story of Raufoss through four phases shows that local and central actors over decades strove to diversify a local activity. Step by step, local industry was able to convert knowledge on material technology from ammunition production into knowledge on lightweight products for the civilian market and lastly for car components. On the way, the industry was involved in aluminium products for the construction industry for a short period, but this turned out to be a dead end. Diversification was a process of trial and error and tension over defining the most promising domain for local manufacturing activity. Together the local entrepreneurs drew on historical events, experiences and knowledge accumulated over decades, in various kinds of bricolage. The industrial trajectory has been contingent on the distributed agency and learning processes, which could not have been predicted. This open trajectory seems in line with scholars' explanation of path creation (Garud and Karnøe, 2003).

Cases of collaboration between the many actors in central government, local industry and R&D institutions both regionally and nationally on entrepreneurial discovery are partly in line with the ideas of smart specialisation policy (Foray, 2017). Through the industrial history of Raufoss, central policy-makers have led on as facilitators of local industrial development, but local industrial leaders have increasingly taken the initiative. These entrepreneurial discoveries were a precondition for the formation of an agglomeration of firms that soon developed into a dynamic cluster. They relied on a legacy of experiences in material technology and tool-making. The fact that three core companies started serving the automotive industry by serial production of components did not happen by accident. The specialisation of industry had been deepened particularly through decades of perfections of operations, collaboration and more generally through the co-evolution of industry, suppliers and knowledge institutions (Sæther et al., 2011). We can recognise some sort of continuity in expertise in material technology, across periods of crises and restructuring. In retrospect, the latter discontinuities typically receive too much attention as the major milestones in the industrial history of Raufoss.

At the turn of the century, the second phase characterised by exploration was followed by a third phase of path extension – the strengthening of the exploitative dimension. Exploration is something beyond purely economic considerations, rather drawing on knowledge about developments in society and new technologies. It requires organisational capabilities that may have been lost due to restructuring of local industry. An institutional layering of an exploitative trajectory is due to integration in international value chains, foreign ownership, and responsive streamlining and refining of local activities. Capacity and capabilities for such exploration is hard to find within organisations tuned for daily operations. Industrial actors focused on exploitative strategies were thus not able to handle explorative strategies in addition. This exploitative strategy is contingent on the character of the particular industrial sector the suppliers are integrated into through the value chain. Suppliers' relation to a limited number of clients direct the attention towards enhancing quality of products and processes, and cutting costs. The domain of the industry is more or less taken for granted. This development appears as a successful path extension, at least in the short run.

In the fourth phase, local industry and knowledge institutions are facing technologies that scholars regard as disruptive. So far, the economic actors have had an incremental approach to the new technologies. The new technologies may substitute labour. This means less employment at least on the level of the single firm. Implementation of new technologies is necessary for firms to stay competitive. At the outset of the fourth phase it is hard to say whether the new technologies only will ensure successful path extension or even become a departure for developing a new domain. Only time will tell if the adoption of the technologies in educational and research programmes and a new catapult (Manufacturing Technology Centre) will result in new promising domains.

14.5 Conclusions

Theoretical and policy lessons from this study are threefold:

1 According to the academic literature, the economies of organisationally thin regions are hard to diversify. This study shows, however, that entrepreneurial discoveries may take place even in a company town. Furthermore, a cornerstone company could have the capability for initiating entrepreneurial discoveries. The realisation of new domains is supported through industry's collaboration with research units, both at the local and the national level, and involvement in R&D programmes. The state evidently has a supportive role in diversifying the local economy.
2 Successive entrepreneurial discoveries taking place in a local manufacturing industry are not independent of each other. Rather, successive entrepreneurial discoveries take place as the latter ones draw on the former ones. In line with the path-creation approach, mindful deviations are based on learning processes taking place through time. Experiences from the past and knowledge accumulated over time appear as a vital heritage in developing a promising domain for an industrial future.
3 The study shows that strategies of exploration and strategies of exploitation are hard to combine at the same time. This is in line with studies of ambidexterity, that is, the ability of firms to maintain both their exploitative and their explorative capabilities at the same time (Tushman and O'Reilly, 1996; see also Nguyen and Mariussen, 2019, Chapter 10 in this volume). In this study, the two types of strategies follow each other sequentially, creating alternate periods of path creation and path extension. If new technologies primarily are applied for substituting labour, job loss in the local labour market should be addressed by new entrepreneurial discoveries. A robust and dynamic industrial cluster should develop capabilities, allocate resources and ensure organisational autonomy also for explorative strategies. Existing organisations should also work as incubators for spinoff processes. Awareness of smart ambidexterity strategies, balancing exploration and exploitation, across the various types of regional actors, is a challenging, but still a reasonable piece of advice for ensuring vital manufacturing industry in the short as well as the long run. The Raufoss case shows that alternatives to simultaneous strategies for exploration and exploitation in individual firms can be instituted by building a regional capacity for flexibly supporting

both strategies over time. A project-oriented R&D organisation with high legitimacy and strong relations to strategic management in the local firms appears as a vital instrument in this regard. Whether this solution will be sufficiently responsive in a situation where the major firms have their strongest allegiances to their foreign owners remains to be seen.

Notes

1 Arena is funded by Innovation Norway, SIVA and the Research Council of Norway, aiming to stimulate innovation and collaboration between firms, R&D and eductional milieus and public actors.

2 The NCE programme is directed towards dynamic industry clusters that have established systematic collaboration and have potential for growth in national and international markets. Within their respective sectors and technology areas, the clusters are to have a national position.

References

Chapman, K. (2005). From 'growth centre' to 'cluster': Restructuring, regional development, and the Teesside chemical industry. *Environment and Planning A: Economy and Space*, 37 (4), pp. 597–615.

Dale, B. (2002). An institutionalist approach to local restructuring: The case of four Norwegian mining towns. *European Urban and Regional Studies*, 9 (1), pp. 5–20.

Foray, D. (2015). From smart specialisation to smart specialisation policy. *European Journal of Innovation Management*, 17 (4), pp. 492–507.

Foray, D. (2017). The concept of the 'entrepreneurial discovery process'. In Kyriakou, D., Martínez, M.P., Periáñez-Forte, I. and Rainoldi, A. (eds) *Governing smart specialisation*, pp. 5–19. London: Routledge.

Garud, R. and Karnøe, P. (2001). Path creation as a process of mindful deviation. In Garud, R. and Karnøe, P. (eds) *Path dependence and creation*, pp. 1–40. Mahwah, NJ: Lawrence Erlbaum.

Garud, R. and Karnøe, P. (2003). Bricolage versus breakthrough: Distributed and embedded agency in technology entrepreneurship. *Research Policy*, 32 (2), pp. 277–300.

Grabher, G. (1992). The weakness of strong ties: The lock-in of regional development in the Ruhr area. In Grabher, G. (ed.) *The embedded firm: On the socioeconomics of industrial networks*, pp. 255–277. London and New York: Routledge.

Hassink, R. (2005). How to unlock regional economies from path dependency? From learning region to learning cluster. *European Planning Studies*, 13 (4), pp. 521–535.

Isaksen, A. (2015). Industrial development in thin regions: Trapped in path extension? *Journal of Economic Geography*, 15 (3), pp. 585–600.

Isaksen, A. and Karlsen, J. (2012). Combined and complex mode of innovation in regional cluster development: Analysis of the light-weight material cluster in Raufoss, Norway. In Asheim, B.T. and Parrilli, M.D. (eds) *Interactive learning for innovation: A key driver within clusters and innovation systems*, pp. 116–136. Basingstoke: Palgrave Macmillan.

Isaksen, A. and Trippl, M. (2017). Exogenously led and policy-supported new path development in peripheral regions: Analytical and synthetic routes. *Economic Geography*, 93 (5), pp. 436–457.

Johnstad, T. and Utter, H. (2015). *Fra konsern til klynge: Transformasjon og innovasjon på Raufoss*. Oslo: Universitetsforlaget.

Kagermann, H., Wahlster, W. and Helbig, J. (2013). *Securing the future of German manufacturing industry: Recommendations for implementing the strategic initiative INDUSTRIE 4.0*. Final report of the Industrie 4.0 Working Group. Occasional report. München: Forschungsunion and Acatech.

Karlsen, A. (1999). *Institusjonelle perspektiver på næringsomstilling*. Trondheim: Norges teknisk-naturvitenskapelige universitet, Fakultet for samfunnsvitenskap og teknologiledelse, Geografisk institutt.

Karlsen, A. (2011). 'Cluster' creation by reconfiguring communities of practice. *European Planning Studies*, 19 (5), pp. 753–773.

March, J.G. (1991). Exploration and exploitation in organizational learning. *Organization Science*, 2 (1), pp. 71–87.

Martin, R. (2010). Roepke lecture in economic geography: Rethinking regional path dependence: Beyond lock-in to evolution. *Economic Geography*, 86 (1), pp. 1–27.

Nguyen, N. and Mariussen, Å. (2019). Moving beyond related variety, creating firm-level ambidexterity for economic growth via the entrepreneurial discovery process. In Mariussen, Å., Virkkala, S., Finne, H. and Aasen, T.M. (eds) *The entrepreneurial discovery process and regional development: New knowledge emergence, conversion and exploitation*. Abingdon: Routledge.

Schwab, K. (2015). The fourth industrial revolution. *Foreign Affairs*.

Simmie, J. (2012). Path dependence and new technological path creation in the Danish wind power industry. *European Planning Studies*, 20 (5), pp. 753–772.

Steen, M. and Karlsen, A. (2014). Path creation in a single-industry town: The case of Verdal and Windcluster Mid-Norway. *Norsk Geografisk Tidsskrift – Norwegian Journal of Geography*, 68 (2), pp. 133–143.

Sundt, E. (1867). *Om husfliden i Norge: til arbeidets ære og arbeidsomhedens pris : første beretning*. Christiania: J. Chr. Abelsted Bogtrykkeri.

Sæther, B., Isaksen, A. and Karlsen, A. (2011). Innovation by co-evolution in natural resource industries: The Norwegian experience. *Geoforum*, 42 (3), pp. 373–381.

Tushman, M.L. and O'Reilly, C.A. (1996). Ambidextrous organizations: Managing evolutionary and revolutionary change. *California Management Review*, 38, pp. 8–30.

Wang, T. (1996). *RA i skuddlinja. Industriutvikling og strategiske veivalg gjennom 100 år*. Raufoss: T Wang.

Part V

Summary and conclusions

15 Summary and conclusions

Åge Mariussen and Håkon Finne

15.1 What is and what is not EDP?

Entrepreneurial discovery processes (EDPs) start with exploration for new business areas, based on existing strengths, generating knowledge that is used for exploitation. This opens the mystery of discovery, that is, first, how relevant knowledge is created, converted and shared at the micro level in the process of discovery, and second, how these micro-level discoveries influence the macro level. In short, how is the change in emphasis from exploitation to exploration supposed to take place, and what are the implications for actors, processes and knowledge?

We can now summarise the answers and recommendations.

But first, let us briefly compare EDP with the two related policy models that were there before: systems of innovation and clusters. Here, the focus on exploration is not equally clear.

The definition of the entrepreneurial discovery process of smart specialisation strategies has become quite an issue. Even some of its most ardent proponents admit that:

> capturing its essence in implementation-friendly terms is so notoriously difficult that a famous dictum, and ultimate easy way out, comes to mind (. . .): 'I cannot define it, but I know it when I see it.'
>
> (Kyriakou et al., 2017)

As pointed out repeatedly in this book, EDP is an explorative, experimental approach.

The Foray definition of EDP became hegemonic on the backdrop of shortcomings of these two partly competing and partly complementary approaches. On one hand there was the national innovation system approach, where the state was supposed to invest in R&D (in universities or institutes) in ways which supported innovation in the private economy. Here, 'flows' of knowledge between universities and firms were taken for granted. There was a particular focus on certain 'high tech' sectors, such as ICT and biotechnology. Barriers between knowledge spaces and helices were allowed to grow wider and deeper.

R&D investments, measured through the GERD indicator (R&D investments as percentage of GDP), seemed to rely on the wisdom of the government, and the importance of high-tech sectors in the economy. Critics say that the result was a fragmentation of the European systems of innovation, where each country was supposed to create their own micro clusters of high-tech sectors.

On the other hand, there is the cluster policy approach. Clusters ride on the strong wings of cumulative, self-reinforcing processes of growth, studied by geographers. According to cluster policy, some regions are growing, and their growth must be supported and continued. Knowledge is spatially embedded in the regional clusters. Cluster organisations must be connected to, possibly owned by, existing core companies and stakeholders.

The EDP strategy builds on components of both these traditions. Yes, policies are crucial, but entrepreneurial policy institutions should be balanced by equally entrepreneurial providers of science-based knowledge and entrepreneurs with in-depth knowledge of market trends, the triple helix. Knowledge is embedded in regions. Regions, accordingly, should make place-based strategies. EDP is a somewhat hybrid creature. Depending on which angle you look at it from, there are components that make it look like cluster and systems of innovation policies.

Figure 15.1, discussed extensively in Chapter 9 (Virkkala and Mariussen, 2019), shows one of several possible ways of looking at EDP as the first phase in the formation of a new cluster. More generally, it may be seen as a story of how some micro-level actors are sometimes able to have an impact on economic structures. These impacts might not always be as spectacular as in the cluster literature. It does not have to become a fully fledged cluster; it might be something more modest. It might not be just one discovery; it could be several, building on or correcting each other in a process of experimentation. Outcomes might be something more modest than growth, may be sustainability through renewal. Nevertheless, it should be something new, one or several discoveries, providing sustainability and/or growth. This focus on discovery provides a unique micro-level point of departure. We are, after all, talking about entrepreneurs, exploring actors involved in processes of learning through new combinations of different forms of knowledge, conversion of knowledge, new knowledge recombinations, or similar. EDP is different from cluster and innovation system analysis because it explicitly starts at the micro level.

Entrepreneurial discoveries (micro level)

In this stylised story of a journey of exploration creating a cluster, the three first phases are micro-level events:

1 First, there is the organisation of the S3 strategy, or creation of the collective actor. Here, self-discovery takes place, where stakeholders with knowledge and technologies that are crucial in the regional domain find each other and make a common place-based strategy of smart specialisation.

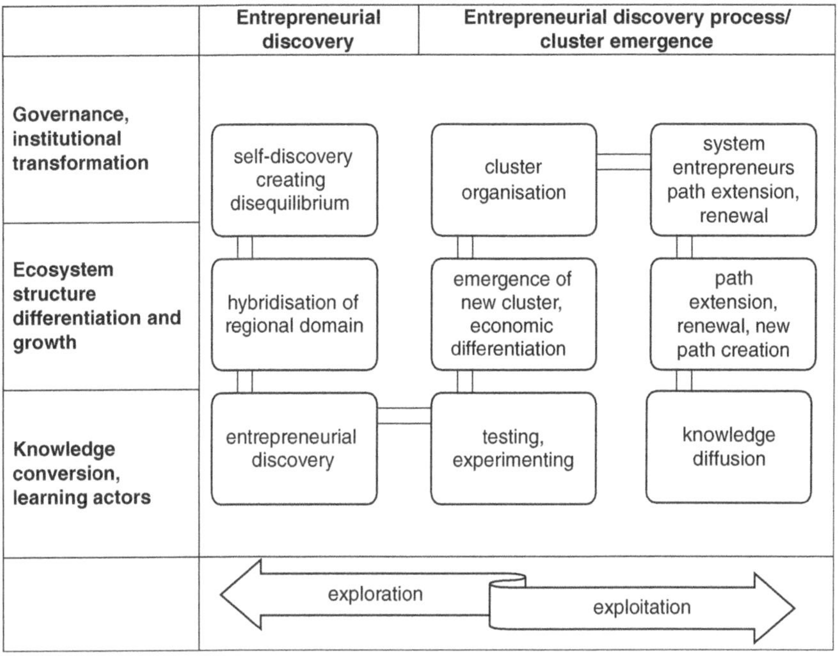

Figure 15.1 Entrepreneurial discovery processes and cluster emergence

2 Creation of hybrid knowledge. As a part of this strategy, different bits and pieces of knowledge and competencies, or knowledge spaces, open up for each other and mix in new ways. Hybridisation opens new business opportunities.
3 This results in entrepreneurial discoveries of new business opportunities, which is the first phase in a successful EDP. These three steps take place as micro-level events. So far, they go below the radar of regional economy statistics.

From micro to macro, cluster formation

Then comes the first phase of growth, extensively discussed in Chapter 8. Here, the successful discovery is copied by others. A new agglomeration is emerging. The initial entrepreneurial discovery leads to one of several possible new discoveries. The embryo of the cluster is planted, and the cluster emergence process starts. This is where the emerging cluster may be discovered by geographers and planners, and supported by cluster policies. Whereas EDP puts the focus on exploration, as the cluster starts to grow, it moves in the direction of exploitation of knowledge. In Chapter 9, Virkkala and Mariussen (2019) explain emergence of clusters through growth and institutional transformation in the following way:

1 The initial success is likely to reinforce the patterns and the knowledge configurations of the innovation networks, which created it. The cluster grows its value chain, and its suppliers. It connects to supporting institutions, like universities.
2 At some point, successful solutions are copied by others. This is referred to as a mechanism of downward causation through knowledge spillovers. It leads to entry of new firms into the expanding new industry.
3 A self-reinforcing mechanism drives the growth of what has now become an agglomeration.
4 Once established as an agglomeration, the new cluster is likely to evolve mechanisms of learning through selection and memory, including formal institutions, cluster organisations, as well as its own storytellers, remembering what happened and pointing the way forward. The cluster is now an institution.

Innovation-leading regions are leaders because, in the past, their regional systems of innovation hosted entrepreneurs who made entrepreneurial discoveries, set up cluster organisations and discovered new practices, shaped routines, and built institutions. The cluster institution may become an important stakeholder in the region. This kind of spontaneous cluster growth does not start anywhere. They prosper in certain well-known cities and regions, where conditions are optimal, with, say the right mix of industries, universities and other institutions.

As pointed out in Chapter 2 by Isaksen et al. (2019), specialised regions have a few strong clusters, organisationally thick regions have several clusters, and organisationally thin regions have weakly developed or no clusters. These types of region have different expectations. Organisationally thick regions have system entrepreneurs, actors who take care of and discuss the clusters and the region.

Organisationally thick regions are innovation leaders. Their system-level entrepreneurs have learned to build clusters. They have done it before, they have seen clusters emerge and grow, they discuss the evolution of the cluster, and they know how to exploit the opportunities they offer. Here, it is sometimes also possible to move from a situation with exploitation of mature clusters into exploration. Cluster policies, one might say, have the advantage of riding on the back of processes of collective learning based on initial discoveries, which feeds cumulative loops of causation, structural transformations, growth and institutionalisation of methods which favour further growth.

These cumulative causation loops are likely to drive increasing polarisation, as innovation leaders pull ahead. The situation is not the same in organisationally thin regions. This is where the barriers of change from exploitation of existing knowledge to exploration for new opportunities become visible.

15.2 Challenges

A shift towards exploration and entrepreneurial discoveries means that existing knowledge barriers must be overcome. But crossing barriers between knowledge spaces requires knowledge conversions and translations. Knowledge conversion (or translation) is a micro-level phenomenon involving actors, including the creation of hybrid knowledge spaces, where different types of knowledge interact. The complexity of this requirement was not properly reflected. According to Blažek and Morgan (2019) (see Chapter 3):

> Moreover, within all levels of the public administration in Central East European (CEE) countries, there is a deeply embedded 'play it safe' mentality, which severely limits the scope for manoeuvre and flexibility in decision-making (Blažek and Morgan, 2016). (. . .) Consequently, the cooperation among business, researchers and the public sector has to start literally from scratch, underlining the fact that the triple helix model of regional development is a triumph of rhetoric over reality in the vast majority of LDRs (Marques and Morgan, 2018).

In looking inside public administration in organisationally thin regions, we soon discover that regional planners appear to be caught between impossible dilemmas. Whatever a regional leader or planner may do, something wrong is going to happen. According to Mäenpää and Lundström (2019) (in Chapter 4), regional planning may reach a state of paralysis:

> Wicked problems were originally introduced by Rittel and Webber (. . .) the crisis, which planning faced, was not about the planners' lack of knowledge or intelligence. Instead, they challenged the very nature of the problems. The main idea of Rittel and Webber was to divide problems into two different categories: tame and wicked.

There are three major factors making regional planning into a wicked problem. First, it is not completely clear what the right solutions are. Second, there are different stakeholders with different interests. Regional planning has to satisfy many different considerations, such as schools for children, provision of health services, care for old people, environmental protection, planning of housing areas, and so on. Even within industrial development, there are different sectors with different interests and potentially powerful stakeholder organisations protecting vested interests. Third, these problems are defined and understood in different ways by different stakeholders. This presents a difficult problem to public sector planners. Whatever they do, something will go wrong.

15.3 Solutions

Under these difficult wicked conditions, the appropriate strategy is learning by doing. Instead of starting with abstract, long-term priorities, a point of departure may be to start with a concrete, short-term experiment: a project with a start, an end date, and an expected outcome. In this way, a regional strategy that gets stuck may be restarted through a surprisingly simple solution. There is likely to be at least some entrepreneurial actors around. Invite them and ask them for solutions. In the context of an organisationally thin region, they may be few. They might not influence political decision-making or command lots of economic power. But they are likely to have some local legitimacy. In the wicked problem-solving process, they are invited into dialogues where the problem is presented, and there they may find simple, concrete and tangible solutions to planning problems, holding the region back, such as a pilot project with verifiable outcomes. A small project which succeeds may set an example to build on. It is a process of learning by doing.

Blažek and Morgan are on to such a bottom–up experimental approach in growing institutions for innovation:

> In practical terms, we argued that the following steps could help to fashion a more authentic entrepreneurial discovery process in less developed regions: (1) identify the key bottlenecks for business and innovation activity (i.e. identification of horizontal priorities) and agree the method for their elimination by assigning responsibility for accomplishing these tasks; (2) search for the comparative advantages of the region; (3) launch the entrepreneurial discovery process so as to identify new market opportunities offering high value-added products and services.

Most regions have universities within them or nearby. Despite their shared traits, they vary immensely in their readiness, and in their acceptance, as triple helix partners.

Universities driving brokering, bridging and bonding

In Chapter 6, Finne and Aasen (2019) explain how NTNU (the leading sci-tech university in Norway) developed arrangements to build a bridging capacity towards small (and larger) industry firms by establishing in 1950 its first spinoff, the independent research institute SINTEF. Bridging worked best when university professors were in charge and developed personal bonds to industry. As the activities grew, the institute became a popular first stop for engineering graduates from the university, where they could learn to master state-of-the-art technology in projects together with firms that became their future industry employers. This arrangement was a cost-effective method of knowledge transfer and construction of an absorptive capacity in industry, but too costly for the institute because of the high personnel turnover. In the late 1980s, they also instituted dedicated knowledge brokers to link smaller firms without sufficient absorptive capacity to appropriate researchers in universities or institutes.

These bridges, brokers and bonders were supported by their academic employers, NTNU and SINTEF, to follow careers that were different from ordinary academic careers. The university and later the institute established these arrangements in response to new threats and opportunities in their environment. In order for these to work under other conditions, it is imperative to have some trusted university–industry relations to start with and find niches of expansion that serve actors on both sides well.

These organisational innovations resulted in a new breed of academics, with hybrid knowledge. Professors who knew industry and its needs very well, and who were able to combine industrial and scientific knowledge:

> What is quite clear in our case study is that the professors, researchers and brokers we have studied in this chapter all combined an intimate knowledge of subject matter and context of use on both sides of the bonds and bridges they went into, knowledge and relations they started acquiring simultaneously once they were introduced to a firm and its challenges and technology, and that the institutional bridge that the university established as a defensive business measure in 1950 has served well as a space for developing these exact knowledge-conversion skills and their concomitant trust relations. This at least looks like a requisite condition for success in our case study, even as industry has built its absorptive capacity by taking over many of the bridge travellers.
>
> Closer relations between a relatively narrow range of highly specialised researchers and industrial firms as assumed by smart specialisation in the strict sense may work well as long as the relationship-building starts early; otherwise the cognitive distance may become too long to easily bridge. And, remember, we have not said much about the limits to bridging, either. Without relations to the context of future use the new expertise may end up in the ivory tower again.

In more general terms, what we are looking at in SINTEF and NTNU and their relations to local industries in Norway is hybridisation of knowledge spaces.

Hybridisation of knowledge spaces

According to Alice Lam (2019) in Chapter 5, hybrid knowledge spaces may evolve within different types of networks, systems and ecologies of innovation. Hybridisation is a result of mobility of people between academia and industry, and across sectors.

> (. . .) the 'third space of hybridity' (. . .) denote(s) the agency space where career actors construct hybrid role identities and undertake knowledge-brokering. (. . .)
>
> It highlights the agentic and creative potential of actors situated at the intersection of social domains, and the newness that emerges from dialogical encounters between heterogeneous social groups.

People who embody hybrid knowledge are likely to become scientist-entrepreneurs:

> Although their main employment affiliation is academia, these scientist-entrepreneurs are active participants in the industrial world. They are aware of the industrial contexts of their scientific work and play an active role in bridging the interface between science and business. (. . .) They are 'strategic' knowledge brokers who actively negotiate boundaries and reconcile differences in cognitive frames, research goals and interests between science and business. (. . .) one in computer science described 'entrepreneurial engagement' as part of 'the repertoire, base skills' that he should retain as a professional scientist. Another pointed out in the interview that knowledge transfer in his case was his 'academic self' talking to his 'industrial self': 'It all happens together . . . that's the heart of how it works, no barriers right. You can do the same thing at once. . .'. This 'talking to himself perspective' reflects the fusion of two different role identities into a hybrid, two-faced one.

A complementary approach to hybridisation is discussions across knowledge borders. Brokers, bridges and bonders talk with lots of people, because they can cross borders between different forms of knowledge. Talk is an important part of exploration. It may come before discoveries, and open the way for them.

Talk jobs

In a micro-level perspective, a discovery is experienced as a series of *dialogues* between people, a big talk job. In Chapter 7, Tone Merethe Aasen (2019) summarises these processes in this way:

> The entrepreneurial discovery phase involves speculation, imagination and fantasy on the part of numerous people in various roles, inspired among other things by regional knowledge resources, local characteristics and current trends. Gradually, recognisable patterns of 'discoveries' may emerge as the consequence of recurring themes and negotiations of the meaning of such themes. If accepted by sufficiently many, or supported by somebody who has the power to authorise the use of resources, openly or covertly, the recurrent themes, perceived as opportunities, may be attempted to be realised through experiments and development activities.

Talk creates knowledge and leads to discoveries:

> Perceiving entrepreneurial discovery as learning processes means that new ideas are formed as existing and new knowledge is shared, developed and changed in various ways. (. . .) One element is individual knowledge, which can be brought together with others' knowledge so that the knowledge 'expands'. The other element is the alternating nature of knowledge, internalised as tacit experiences, or articulated as explicit themes. New explicit and tacit knowledge is created as knowledge is shared. Knowledge conversion can be understood as a key concept, core to entrepreneurial

> discovery as well as to the subsequent events leading to the perceived existence of an opportunity for profit on the part of many people.

Talk is also crucial in other forms of exploration.

Evidence from cases: whales and salmon

In Chapter 13 by Løvland and Finne (2019), the impacts of such a talk job on the development of tourism in an organisationally thin region, the Lofoten islands, is analysed. The discovery was here the transition from tourism seen as hotels and restaurants in a short summer season to the creation of a wide variety of experiences all year round. Here, entrepreneurs, planners and researchers from a nearby university cooperated:

> The initial changes and the initial entrepreneurial discovery mainly came about through the role of private entrepreneurs of the tourism industry in Lofoten, but this effort was highly related to and dependent on the actions of public sector actors, especially at the regional level in Nordland. (. . .) Gradually more second-order effects through downward causation can be observed in the next stage, from 2007 onwards, when the process was increasingly supported by research and the development of applied methods and knowledge. In this stage this also led to the inclusion of the experience economy approach in regional planning and strategies.

Other evidence is presented by Aasen et al. (2019) in Chapter 12, with the story of salmon production in Norway. What started as an entrepreneurial discovery made among coastal fishermen became a high-tech, large-scale industry. In this context, the salmon was the border object, attracting attention from a wide range of scientists and sectors (medicine, breeding, fodder, maritime technologies, ICT), public policy institutions, entrepreneurs, and, in the more mature phase, large-scale investors. When it came to salmon, one might say, maritime coastal skills came first, then came science, and turned the cluster into a high-tech success story.

Today, science-based knowledge becomes more and more crucial in the front end of exploration.

Moving beyond related variety

The salmon and experience economy cases illustrate a fairly general phenomenon throughout the twentieth century. Entrepreneurial discoveries are made by industrial entrepreneurs, often through new combinations of technologies. Research-based knowledge comes later.

Knowledge conversion was predominantly seen as taking place through related variety, new knowledge recombinations (whale watching with tourists) literally growing out of existing strengths (whale hunting).

As pointed out in Chapter 10 (Nguyen and Mariussen, 2019), in some of the industrial policy-based theories backing up the smart specialisation strategy, emphasis is put on theories of innovation through related variety. One version of this approach seems to suggest that economies may start to diversify and create new emerging sectors based on recombinations of their existing industrial skills. In other words, science is not really needed.

The relevance of this strategy of innovating through related variety is measured by the model of the *Atlas of Economic Complexity* (Hausmann and Pritchett, 2018) and its growth forecasts. Growth expectancy is based on distances to new products from the current export basket of 122 countries. Short distance means that it is easy to take the jump to the next product. Among these 122, the majority are 'emerging' economies. These countries have a high potential for growth precisely through related variety and other strategies of diversification. They have lots of easy targets, or new products that are closely related to already existing products in the export basket. The complexity model of Hausmann referred to in Chapter 10 (Nguyen and Mariussen, 2019) also shows how the growth potential of advanced economies would have looked without science to back up innovation. For example, Germany is a developed country where the easy strategy of innovation through related variety/self-discovery *without a science and innovation component* is exhausted.

Therefore, if Germany had depended only on increasing country complexity without investing in R&D, their expected growth is low. This is consistent with the idea that the dynamics analysed by the complexity model of growth on its own, without the assistance of science and innovation, is driving convergence in the global economy. In emerging economies, such as Mexico and Turkey, innovation and growth through related variety may go on without R&D policies. But for advanced economies, this model of growth does not fit anymore. Based on OECD data, the chapter argues that for advanced countries, product diversification and growth goes hand in hand with firm investments in R&D. The chapter argues that this combination of innovation based on existing industrial knowledge and R&D works best if the innovators, i.e. firms, have the capability to carry out research-based exploration activities in new domains while still running normal business based on their core competence. The ambidextrous capability, simultaneously explore and exploit, is crucial for the innovators to survive the technological changes and for the economy to grow. Accordingly, S3 strategies should move beyond the related variety approach and facilitate ambidexterity – both exploration and exploitation in firms.

Based on the assessments of the achievements of smart specialisation during the first phase of implementation, the European Commission has, as documented in Chapter 11 (Mariussen et al., 2019), come to a somewhat similar conclusion. They promote key enabling technologies in regional strategies. This is a move beyond place-based development.

Interregional learning via transnational thematic partnerships

Through a series of initiatives taken in 2016 and 2017, the Commission is arguing for a closer contact between industrial policies promoting key enabling technologies (KETs) and regional S3 strategies. This is not a 'back to the nineties' strategy where all regions are supposed to grow similar small-scale applications of high-tech clusters. Instead, it is a question of developing new applications of KETs inside already existing regional domains, in cooperation with innovation leaders and clusters with core KET technologies. The challenge is to combine regional partnerships, organised to mobilise for place-based strategies, and transnational thematic partnerships. This strategy relies on potential synergies between leading regions and their institutions providing access to KET technologies, and other regions interested in applying these technologies within their domains. This is now tested across a wide range of sectors. Chapter 11 (Mariussen et al., 2019) documents how this is done, and it presents a conceptual framework for how these challenges may be understood, as hybrid combinations of regional (spatially embedded) and relational knowledge spaces.

This experiment illustrates an important synergy between regional strategies and clusters. Regional strategies might help to nurture emerging clusters, but they may also be reinforced and supported by clusters. In this way, leading European institutions and clusters are expected to contribute to innovation in other European regions. The transnational knowledge spaces created in this way are based on shared communities of expertise, with an institutional framework providing legitimacy, guidance, support and continuity, as well as facilitation of meeting places, where experts meet, discuss ideas and monitor progress. They are strengthened by experimental investments in pilots. As documented in Chapter 11, one of the cases, photonics, has created a common institutionalised framework for co-management of a knowledge commons.

15.4 Closing comment of structuration theory

Systems are elements with sustained interdependence that are kept in place by institutions. Systems have structures (rules and resources) that impose constraints on actors, but also support their activity. Actors are skilled; they are able to understand situations and norms. Sometimes, these forms of understanding change and actors start to redefine rules and use resources in new ways. These new forms of understanding may sometimes have the power to change routines and rules for allocating resources, in other words, institutions. If they go deep and far enough, these institutional changes can transform structures, for instance regional economic structures. This dynamic perspective on structures is called structuration. Structuration is thus, according to Anthony Giddens, to, 'involve an interplay of meaning, norms and power' (Giddens 1977: 161).

Distinguishing between institutions, actors and structures illuminates how micro-level actors operating in different roles can become partially independent of structural constraints. They may change institutions in ways that open a potential for the transformation of structures.

In the geographical tradition, it is common to classify regions in ways that can be seen to favour 'structural' geographic factors, such as self-reinforcing causal loops, reinforcing strong regions. The strong becomes stronger and the weak continue to be marginalised.

From the point of departure of structuration theory, we can now start to understand how micro-level actions might create new, institutionalised practices that sometimes have the power to transform structures. These transitions may be enabled by actors capable of knowledge conversion across gaps between helices (policy-makers, entrepreneurs, and scientists) and boundaries between knowledge spaces in different territories.

15.5 Recommendations

So how is the change in emphasis from exploitation to exploration following EDP supposed to take place, and what are the implications for actors, processes and knowledge?

We can now summarise our findings in eight recommendations.

1 *Discover new solutions by asking citizens and other stakeholders for guidance.* Regional planning is full of difficulties. Powerful stakeholders may have widely different objectives and interests. They may not relate to each other and they might not even want to discuss common challenges. However, there will always be at least some citizens, firms, entrepreneurs, institutions and other stakeholders who are open for dialogues and new approaches. By presenting analyses to them, and listening to their suggestions and advice, it might be possible to discover concrete experimental solutions, small projects with local stakeholders in key positions, which point in the right direction. Below, we also include other regions and transnational thematic partnerships in this effort to build a regional partnership.

2 *'Tame' wicked problems, learn by doing successful experiments.* By enabling local stakeholders to start small-scale projects and pilots which work and deliver, you may start a process of 'learning by doing'. A small project may become a step in a much wider process of learning how to grow and become sustainable. This logic of learning may shortcut more general objections and start a process that evolves in the direction of something more substantial.

3 *Take care of and learn from emerging success stories.* Once small-scale projects start, there may be many stumbling blocks. If you want to build a hybrid knowledge space, where actors from different places, sectors and helices cooperate and do things together, it is crucial to follow and nurture some of the best projects in the direction of success. Successes should

be made visible, appreciated, talked about, and used as building blocks in new, more advanced projects. They could be the beginning of new, institutionalised ways of cooperation which becomes routine, and generate self-reinforcing loops. This is illustrated by the whale watching case in Chapter 13.

4 *Talk, talk, talk.* It is crucial to set up fora for discussions and dialogues, where people involved in the process from different positions regularly meet, exchange experiences, and discuss new, possible approaches. They can be organised in widely different ways, but it is crucial to give them a common platform, the analysis as input, and share information, knowledge, analysis and evaluations on a regular basis. This is the phase before a new discovery, it is a breeding ground for learning from experiments, and a continuation of the search process.

5 *Promote mobility across helices and sectors.* Entrepreneurs are able to cross barriers between sectors, helices and different forms of knowledge. They may do that because they have careers where they have learned different things in different places. They may be valuable partners and translators. They should be listened to and involved. It is equally important to promote mobility of clever people between helices and sectors.

6 *Encourage universities to do brokering and bridging.* Academic careers are usually structured by institutions that are actively discouraging cross-disciplinary, industry-related research, and careers where professors become industrial leaders or entrepreneurs. The book documents a case (NTNU/SINTEF) where this was done differently. An organisational innovation aimed at maintaining the university's attractiveness for students and professors resulted in a culture and institutional arrangements for academics to act as brokers and bridges between university research and innovation processes in the economy.

7 *Develop ambidexterity: perform R&D inside firms.* Whereas emerging economies like India may still grow through related variety-inspired innovations combining skills from different sectors without R&D input, innovation networks in advanced countries increasingly need science-based knowledge. What is more, advanced economies need to integrate key enabling technologies across most sectors. This increasingly demands more in-house R&D in firms. In-house R&D also helps firms to combine exploration with exploitation of their existing domain, through strategies of ambidexterity, and it drives growth.

8 *Connect place-based knowledge with transnational networks.* The need for absorption of key enabling technologies also makes it necessary for regions to develop transnational European networks with advanced regions and institutions. This strategy has a potential to strengthen the regional partnership, and extend the scope of innovation from place-based to transnational. The ambition is to create synergies between strong European clusters and lagging regions.

References

Aasen, T.M. (2019). Approaching entrepreneurial discovery and knowledge conversion from a complexity perspective. In Mariussen, Å., Virkkala, S., Finne, H. and Aasen, T.M. (eds) *The entrepreneurial discovery process and regional development: New knowledge emergence, conversion and exploitation*. Abingdon: Routledge.

Aasen, T.M., Ullern, E.F. and Mariussen, Å. (2019). Science/practice knowledge interaction in the Norwegian fish farming industry. In Mariussen, Å., Virkkala, S., Finne, H. and Aasen, T.M. (eds) *The entrepreneurial discovery process and regional development: New knowledge emergence, conversion and exploitation*. Abingdon: Routledge.

Blažek, J. and Morgan, K. (2016). *Launching entrepreneurial discovery process in regions with less developed research and innovation systems*. SMARTSPEC Policy Brief. Cardiff: Cardiff University.

Blažek, J. and Morgan, K. (2019). The institutional worlds of entrepreneurial discovery: Finding a place for less developed regions. In Mariussen, Å., Virkkala, S., Finne, H. and Aasen, T.M. (eds) *The entrepreneurial discovery process and regional development: New knowledge emergence, conversion and exploitation*. Abingdon: Routledge.

Finne, H. and Aasen, T.M. (2019). The bond, the bridge and the broker: Knowledge conversion in the university-industry nexus. In Mariussen, Å., Virkkala, S., Finne, H. and Aasen, T.M. (eds) *The entrepreneurial discovery process and regional development: New knowledge emergence, conversion and exploitation*. Abingdon: Routledge.

Giddens, A. (1977). *Studies in social and political theory*. London: Hutchinson.

Hausmann, R. and Pritchett, L. (2018). *The atlas of economic complexity [database]*. [Cambridge, MA]: Harvard's Center for International Development (CID)'s Growth Lab. Available: http://atlas.cid.harvard.edu/.

Isaksen, A., Kyllingstad, N., Rypestøl, J.O. and Schulze-Krogh, A. C. (2019). Entrepreneurial discovery processes in different regional contexts. A conceptual discussion. In Mariussen, Å., Virkkala, S., Finne, H. and Aasen, T.M. (eds) *The entrepreneurial discovery process and regional development: New knowledge emergence, conversion and exploitation*. Abingdon: Routledge.

Kyriakou, D., Martínez, M.P., Periáñez-Forte, I. and Rainoldi, A. (2017). Introduction. In Kyriakou, D., Martínez, M.P., Periáñez-Forte, I. and Rainoldi, A. (eds) *Governing smart specialisation*, pp. 1–4. London: Routledge.

Lam, A. (2019). Career mobility, hybridity and knowledge combination: A 'third space' perspective. In Mariussen, Å., Virkkala, S., Finne, H. and Aasen, T.M. (eds) *The entrepreneurial discovery process and regional development: New knowledge emergence, conversion and exploitation*. Abingdon: Routledge.

Løvland, J. and Finne, H. (2019). The transformation of Lofoten islands into a year-round experience destination. In Mariussen, Å., Virkkala, S., Finne, H. and Aasen, T.M. (eds) *The entrepreneurial discovery process and regional development: New knowledge emergence, conversion and exploitation*. Abingdon: Routledge.

Mariussen, Å., Hegyi, F.B. and Rakhmatullin, R. (2019). Smart specialisation: Interregional learning via thematic partnerships. In Mariussen, Å., Virkkala, S., Finne, H. and Aasen, T.M. (eds) *The entrepreneurial discovery process and regional development: New knowledge emergence, conversion and exploitation*. Abingdon: Routledge.

Marques, P. and Morgan, K. (2018). The heroic assumptions of smart specialisation: A sympathetic critique of regional innovation policy. In Isaksen, A., Martin, R. and Trippl, M. (eds) *New avenues for regional innovation systems: Theoretical advances, empirical cases and policy lessons*, pp. 275–293. Cham: Springer International Publishing.

Mäenpää, A. and Lundström, N. (2019). Entrepreneurial discovery processes through a wicked game approach: Civil society engagement as a possibility for exploration. In Mariussen, Å., Virkkala, S., Finne, H. and Aasen, T.M. (eds) *The entrepreneurial discovery process and regional development: New knowledge emergence, conversion and exploitation*. Abingdon: Routledge.

Nguyen, N. and Mariussen, Å. (2019). Moving beyond related variety, creating firm-level ambidexterity for economic growth via the entrepreneurial discovery process. In Mariussen, Å., Virkkala, S., Finne, H. and Aasen, T.M. (eds) *The entrepreneurial discovery process and regional development: New knowledge emergence, conversion and exploitation*. Abingdon: Routledge.

Virkkala, S. and Mariussen (2019). Emergence of new business areas in regional economies through entrepreneurial discovery processes. In Mariussen, Å., Virkkala, S., Finne, H. and Aasen, T.M. (eds) *The entrepreneurial discovery process and regional development: New knowledge emergence, conversion and exploitation*. Abingdon: Routledge.

Index

Page numbers in **bold** and *italics* refer to tables and figures, respectively.

For Product Safety Concerns and Information please contact our EU representative GPSR@taylorandfrancis.com Taylor & Francis Verlag GmbH, Kaufingerstraße 24, 80331 München, Germany